Knowledge Management

The Catalyst for Electronic Government

Knowledge Management

The Catalyst for Electronic Government

Edited by

Ramon C. Barquin, PhD
Alex Bennet
Shereen G. Remez, PhD

MANAGEMENTCONCEPTS

Vienna, Virginia

MANAGEMENTCONCEPTS

8230 Leesburg Pike, Suite 800
Vienna, Virginia 22182
Phone: (703) 790-9595
Fax: (703) 790-1371
Web: www.managementconcepts.com

Printed in the United States of America

Library of Congress Cataloging-in-Publication Data

Knowledge management: the catalyst for electronic government/
edited by Ramon C. Barquin, Alex Bennet, Shereen G. Remez.
p. cm.
Includes bibliographical references.
ISBN 1-56726-129-9 (hc.)
1. Knowledge management. 2. Technical innovations—Management. 3. Organizational effectiveness. 4. Administrative agencies—Technological innovations—Management. I. Barquin, Ramon C., 1942– II. Bennet, Alex, 1947– III. Remez, Shereen G., 1948–

HD30.2 K638 2001
352.3'8—dc21

2001030067

Table of Contents

Preface .... **ix**

Acknowledgments .... **xi**

Part I: A Framework for Knowledge Management **1**

Chapter 1. *What Is Knowledge Management?* 3
Ramon C. Barquin, PhD

Chapter 2. *The Rise of the Knowledge Organization* 25
David Bennet and Alex Bennet

Chapter 3. *Creating Business Value from Knowledge Management: The Fusion of Knowledge and Technology* 49
Tom Beckman

Part II: Setting the Stage for Electronic Government **97**

Chapter 4. *Setting the Stage for Electronic Government* 101
Joseph Leo, Michael Alexander, and Stuart Kieffer

Chapter 5. *Organizational Readiness for Knowledge Management* 127
Moonja P. Kim, PhD

Chapter 6. *Information Technology and Knowledge Management: The Medium and the Message* 155
Shereen G. Remez, PhD, and Jon M. Desenberg

Chapter 7. *HR Knowledge Crafting: The FAA NetFusion Model* 179
Robert G. Turner

Chapter 8. *KM and E-Gov: Can We Have One without the Other?* 207
Shereen G. Remez, PhD

Chapter 9. *Knowledge Management and Document Management in the Public Sector* 225
Elias Safdie

Chapter 10. *A Systems Approach to Engineering a Knowledge Management System* 263
Michael Stankosky, ScD, and Carolyn Baldanza

Part III: Leading Knowledge Management 283

Chapter 11. *Who Will Lead the Knowledge Revolution? An Examination of the Differing Roles of CIO and CKO* 285
Shereen G. Remez, PhD

Chapter 12. *Leadership and Knowledge Management—Perspectives* 301
Joseph Williamson, PhD

Chapter 13. *Knowledge Management and the Role of the CKO* 317
Robert E. Neilson, PhD

Chapter 14. *Managing Change in a Knowledge Environment* 335
Alex Bennet

Chapter 15. *Knowledge Management: The Business Proposition for Government Organizations* 361
Kelvin K. Womack

Chapter 16. *Creating Knowledge-Based Communities of Practice: Lessons Learned from KM Initiatives at AMS* 393
Cathy Hirsh, Mark Youman, and Susan Hanley

Chapter 17. *Harnessing Customer Knowledge: Merging Customer Relationship Management with Knowledge Management* 415
Timothy L. Cannon, PhD

Part IV: Case Studies in Knowledge Management 451

Chapter 18. *The GSA Story: Swimming with the Dolphins* 453
Shereen G. Remez, PhD

Chapter 19. *Knowledge Sharing at the World Bank* 469
Stephen Denning

Conclusion 503

Glossary 507

Editors and Contributing Authors 533

Index 541

Preface

Knowledge is transforming government—the way government transacts business, the relationships among government organizations and citizens, and the value placed on intellectual capital. This new world of "e-Gov" brings with it the excitement of creating a government that operates at Internet speed while meeting the challenge of protecting the security of information and the privacy of citizens.

The first annual "e-Gov Knowledge Management Conference" was held in April 2000 with more than 600 leaders from federal, state, and local governments in attendance, as well as international and industry participation. The theme of the conference was "Knowledge Management: The Foundation for Electronic Government." The four-day conference focused on the fundamentals of knowledge management (KM) and their application for the public sector; the evaluation of tools, technology, and professional support services available for implementation; the sharing of perspectives from public and private sector KM leaders; and the lessons learned and best practices from early adopters of KM in the federal government.

Knowledge management is exploding. Today more than 80 percent of all Fortune 500 companies have significant knowledge management initiatives underway, and more than 30 percent have appointed chief knowledge officers. The government is not far behind, with chief knowledge officers and knowledge managers emerging at every level.

The time and place are right. With the advent of the Internet, everyone has access to everything, and that everything is increasing almost exponentially. That means we are living in a world where good information and knowledge become the value proposition of government.

We face two challenges. The first is to enhance the government-citizen relationship and support the move toward self-service and self-governance. An example is the recent launching of the "Firstgov Portal," which provides citizens one-stop shopping for government information. The second challenge is to transform the inner workings of government to enable the horizontal sharing of information and knowledge across agencies, which translates into faster and more effective service to citizens. Knowledge management provides the foundation for meeting these challenges.

The incredible enthusiasm and explosion of new ideas sparked by the first e-Gov KM event compelled us to attempt to capture the essence of the rich intellectual exchange during this conference. We would like to believe that we have done that in this book. But the reality is that while providing the foundation, we must leave it to the reader to create the knowledge and ignite the spirit. We invite you to explore KM through these pages and begin the journey toward translating knowledge into action.

Ramon C. Barquin, PhD
Alex Bennet
Shereen G. Remez, PhD
April 2001

Acknowledgments

In the tradition of knowledge management, this project was a true collaborative effort involving many people sharing information and ideas. Of critical importance are the sponsors of the first e-Gov Knowledge Management Conference, specifically Israel Feldman, Chuck Lockart, Don Arnold, Martha McGrath, and Suzanne Young.

We also appreciate the important role played by the Knowledge Management Conference Program Advisory Board. It includes Stowe Boyd, Miriam F. Browning, Paul Brubaker, Steve Denning, Israel Feldman, Jane G. Fishkin, Belkis Leong-Hong, C. Lawrence Meador, Alvin M. Pesachowitz, Bob Turner, Ed Vitalos, Douglas Weidner, and Michael Yoemans. Many of them are also authors of chapters in this book, and are true pioneers in the field.

A significant number of this book's contributors presented at the conference. They took the months following this event to further develop these ideas as chapters for this book. Other authors took on the challenge of building new material that introduces state-of-the-art thinking and tools for implementing knowledge management and explaining how it interacts and underpins electronic government.

No effort of this size and scope occurs without considerable help from both work and home environments. Wendy Stoner and Rachael Sedeen organized numerous meetings and worked directly with authors to coordinate their input. Lynda Pierce and Jack Hawxhurst tirelessly read manuscripts. Lee Johnson, David Bennet, and Jean Barquin provided support and encouragement to the authors.

Likewise we are grateful to our publishers, Management Concepts, Inc., and specifically to Beverly Copland, Cathy Kreyche, and Jack Knowles, for believing in the importance of this book and making the decision to publish it.

Finally, we extend our appreciation to the U.S. General Services Administration, the U.S. Department of the Navy, and Barquin and Associates, Inc. for their support of this effort. The profits from the government editors will go to support the Children's Inn of the National Institutes of Health and the Navy Relief Society.

PART I

A Framework for Knowledge Management

Knowledge management encompasses a broad range of topics and perspectives. To help guide the reader to an understanding of and appreciation for the many facets of knowledge management, the editors have arranged the chapters of this book into four major sections:

1. A Framework for Knowledge Management
2. Setting the Stage for Electronic Government
3. Leading Knowledge Management
4. Case Studies in Knowledge Management.

This first section, *A Framework for Knowledge Management,* is intended to position the reader for entering the world of knowledge management by providing historical context and basic definitions. It opens with "What Is Knowledge Management?" by Ramon Barquin, a leading authority in the field and a co-editor of this book, who presents an overview of the overall topic and provides a framework for understanding this volume's layout.

"The Rise of the Knowledge Organization," by David Bennet and Alex Bennet, follows. The former is CEO of Dynamic Systems, Inc., and the latter, another of this book's co-editors, is

Deputy Chief Information Officer of the U.S. Department of the Navy; she is in charge of knowledge management for the Navy and the Marine Corps. The chapter provides the backdrop for understanding the interaction between knowledge and social evolution as a central theme throughout history.

Last, in "Creating Business Value from Knowledge Management: The Fusion of Knowledge and Technology," Tom Beckman, from Amplifi, offers a unified framework for knowledge management by presenting a review of the literature and culling from existing work.

CHAPTER 1

What Is Knowledge Management?

Ramon C. Barquin, PhD

It has been said that an enterprise *is* what it knows. That being true, this knowledge has to be at the core of any attempt to improve the enterprise's performance. Hence, managing knowledge is the quintessential function of any organization.

In effect, knowledge management (KM) has been sweeping through the corridors of enterprises over the last few years. It is part of a trend that shows little sign of abatement because it is central to moving any organization to a stronger competitive stance. It rides the disciplines of the moment—electronic commerce, data warehousing and mining, document management, enterprise information portals (EIP), the Internet, collaborative technologies, customer relationship management, supply chain management—and is tightly coupled with them to facilitate their exploitation by the organization.

ENTER THE CHIEF KNOWLEDGE OFFICER

Another key indicator of this KM movement is the appearance of chief knowledge officers, or CKOs. They have started to emerge throughout industry as stewards of an enterprise's knowledge, with a wide range of roles and responsibilities. Today, AMOCO, AMS, SAIC, KPMG, Monsanto, Accenture, Pricewaterhouse-Coopers, and many other companies have CKOs. Furthermore, the federal government named its first CKO in the summer of 2000 at the General Services Administration (GSA). Now, several other agencies and departments, including the Navy, the Coast Guard, and the Department of State, have named CKOs.[1]

Facing strong commercial and competitive pressures, many private enterprises have already launched substantial KM initiatives. Public agencies, facing the challenges of smaller budgets and privatization trends, are also deciding how to do more with less and, hence, perform in a more focused and intelligent mode.

WHAT IS KNOWLEDGE?

An in-depth discussion of knowledge itself is not within the scope of this chapter.[2] However, it is difficult to explain KM without using knowledge at least as the starting point.

It is said that technology is what one has to know in order to do, and science is what one has to do in order to know. The Oxford Dictionary simplifies it with its definition: *Knowledge is understanding gained through experience, observation, or study.*

Knowledge exists primarily in an individual's head. We can sometimes capture that knowledge in an explicit manner (explicit knowledge), or it may stay trapped inside a human brain (tacit knowledge) either because it has never been actually made explicit or because of the difficulties inherent in describing the specific knowledge, such as attempting to explain how one rides a bicycle. Again, this is an attempt to simplify reality. In effect, Beckman speaks of four types of knowledge, focusing on our availability to access it—explicit, implicit, tacit, and unknown.[3] And Firestone offers some interesting arguments and counterarguments relative to the role of "knowledge-based cultural artifacts" and of the social interactions that occur in the process of refining knowledge.[4] Much depends on whether you take a strong or a weak anthropic point of view relative to knowledge.

WHAT IS KNOWLEDGE MANAGEMENT?

What exactly is KM? As with any emerging discipline, there are many definitions (see Table 1). Practically every scholar, author, and organization offers his or her own definition. But at its core, KM is *the process through which an enterprise uses its collective intelligence to accomplish its strategic objectives*. Focusing on this definition can provide some insights.

Table 1. Definitions of Knowledge Management

Author/Source	*Definition*
Yogesh Malhotra (@brint.com)	KM caters to the critical issues of organizational adaptation, survival, and competence in face of increasingly discontinuous environmental change. Essentially, it embodies organizational processes that seek synergistic combination of data and information-processing capacity of information technologies, and the creative and innovative capacity of human beings.
Joseph Firestone, Executive Information Systems, Inc.	KM is human activity that is part of the knowledge management process (KMP) of an agent or collective. KMP, in turn, is an ongoing, persistent, purposeful interaction among human-based agents through which the participating agents aim at managing (handling, directing, governing, controlling, coordinating, planning, organizing) other agents, components, and activities participating in the basic knowledge processes (knowledge production and knowledge integration) into a planned, directed, unified whole, producing, maintaining, enhancing, acquiring, and transmitting the enterprise's knowledge base.
Thomas M. Koulopoulos, The Delphi Group	KM is the leveraging of collective wisdom to increase responsiveness and innovation.

continues

Author/Source	*Definition*
Public Service Commission of Canada	KM refers to the processes of creating, capturing, transferring, and using knowledge to enhance organizational performance.
Joseph Williamson, EDS	KM is an integrated, systematic approach for identifying, managing, and sharing all of an enterprise's information assets, including databases, documents, policies, and procedures, as well as previously unarticulated expertise and experience resident in individual workers.
Douglas Weidner, Litton/PRC	KM is handling, directing, governing, or controlling natural knowledge processes (producing, acquiring, integrating knowledge) within an organization to better achieve the goals and objectives of the organization
Ramon Barquin, Barquin and Associates, Inc.	KM is the process through which an enterprise uses its collective intelligence to accomplish its strategic objectives.

First, KM is a *process*, and thus it has phases and components, is rule-governed, and is embedded in time. As such, the process involves more than one approach and different structures and architectures.

Second, *uses* implies that this intelligence must lead to action. This means that expected outcomes and performance are measured.

Third, *collective intelligence* must be interpreted. *Collective* means that a community of participants is involved, and, hence, there is a need to identify ownership and source of the knowledge, as well as to provide mechanisms and incentives for sharing their knowledge. *Intelligence* necessitates specifying what it is and how one obtains it. We may take it to mean both "capacity to learn" and the informational constructs that do not yet qualify as knowledge. Think of intelligence here in a military sense, where one gathers as much "intelligence" as possible to understand a specific situation better. This leads inevitably back into separating the tacit from the explicit, and extracting, storing, and processing bits and bytes to obtain data, information, and intelligence—and then knowledge—from it.

Lastly, *to accomplish its strategic objectives* means that KM is strongly tied to strategy. It has to fit into, and enable, an enterprise's broad plan to achieve its long-term goals.

When Professors Ikujiro Nonaka and Hirotaka Takeuchi pioneered some basic KM concepts in Japan in the early 1990s, their principal concern was understanding how Japanese companies were managing their intellectual capital—what they knew or had the yet unrealized potential to know—for competitive advantage, especially for the purpose of bringing better products to market more quickly. Nonaka and Takeuchi's work contains precious little mention of information technology. Computers do not play a prominent role in their analysis, nor do they address object-oriented data warehouses, the Internet, document management systems, data mining techniques, or enterprise information portals. Of course, the work was written just prior to the emergence of these disciplines; nevertheless, their main concern was with understanding some very basic things. Who owns an enterprise's knowledge? Where does it reside? How is it transferred from an individual or group of individuals to others? What are the incentives for sharing? What is the impact of resistance to change? These were the types of questions at the heart of Nonaka and Takeuchi's research.

WHO OWNS KNOWLEDGE MANAGEMENT?

KM is a multidisciplinary field claimed by many of its constituent disciplines. Certainly, it is difficult to argue with the *philosophers,* for whom knowledge is a principal pursuit. Or with the *educators,* who have been responsible for the creation of knowledge since the earliest of times. Or with the *librarians* or *informa-*

tion scientists, who have been classifying and organizing knowledge for millennia. Or with the *cognitive psychologists,* who have been trying to understand how we acquire, store, and manipulate knowledge through the human brain. Or with the *management scientists,* who have been looking at how the enterprise deals with this most valuable organizational asset. Or with the *computer scientists,* who are directly concerned with the design and implementation of real systems that produce and deliver knowledge from the bits and bytes stored in their data warehouses.

So while acceptance is growing that the management of knowledge, including its delivery, is one of the most compelling requirements of the enterprise, there is little common ground regarding which community of professionals has the responsibility for its pursuit. And yet, it seems quite obvious that KM is essentially a multidisciplinary endeavor because we are all in this together.

THE KNOWLEDGE ORGANIZATION

At least a brief look back in history is essential in any attempt to provide an overview of KM. The history of mankind is coupled very tightly to knowledge. Our very name as a species—homo sapiens, or "knowing man"—points to the central relationship between man and knowledge. The ascent of man, if you will, is nothing but our ability as a species to engage successfully in the very practice of KM.

Man wanders and explores looking for food, shelter, and warmth, following basic instincts and guided by his senses. Over time, what ultimately made us develop distinctly was our capacity to start collecting observations and then draw information, intelligence, and knowledge from them; and finally, most importantly, to communicate those insights and observations to others. Using our expanding knowledge base, we started to compete ever more effectively in the evolutionary scheme.

By the time man emerges in recorded history, we have ample proof that mankind is simply a species that excelled at KM. We had developed many tools and techniques to assist in capturing, representing, disseminating, sharing, and managing knowledge. Among these are speech, writing, counting, drawing, measuring, and then establishing stores for our explicit knowledge, eventually known as libraries.

Over history, society moved through the agrarian, industrial, and service stages. We entered the information age, and now we are quickly moving into the knowledge age. But throughout, the historical role of knowledge, and of the knowledge organization, is central in understanding the development of the KM discipline.[5]

KNOWLEDGE MANAGEMENT AND INFORMATION TECHNOLOGY

Today, KM has been overwhelmed by information technology (IT). Many of the IT disciplines and the tools that they have enabled have undoubtedly transformed the face of KM for the better. Yet most of the truly difficult barriers to successful KM environments do not lie in the problem domains that IT can address but in those initially identified by Nonaka and Takeuchi.

Today, we can say that while IT may be the cornerstone of an enterprise's KM architecture, one cannot be successful at KM with IT alone. Too many other components outside the IT domain must play an active role to ensure success.

COMPONENTS AND PROCESSES OF KNOWLEDGE MANAGEMENT

KM is riding the "disciplines of the moment," including electronic commerce, data warehousing and mining, document management, EIP, the Internet, collaborative technologies, customer relationship management, and supply chain management. Yet KM is not necessarily about technology. Nonetheless, it takes a fair amount of technology, especially IT, a number of soft disciplines, and a significant measure of leadership to make KM take within an organization. Knowledge that is in people's heads must be captured and made explicit, communities of practice have to be identified, and, within them, "best practices" must emerge. Resistance to change must be overcome in most cases, and the enterprise must be willing to learn continuously from its experiences. All this must be underpinned and supported by a robust business intelligence platform and a very solid IT infrastructure. Business intelligence primarily means data warehousing and data mining. An enterprise's knowledge is delivered mainly though an EIP. Currently, the Web is the prime vehicle for all communications and sharing.

Many other methods or techniques, however, must be addressed as part of the KM discipline. Some would appear to be anathema to IT practitioners because they are "soft" by most IT standards. Yet they are certainly very important and need to be considered. For example, the role of critical success factors, communities of practice, and change management techniques must be understood. We must be able to identify and use, as necessary, leadership techniques, best practices, and storytelling. The role of the CKO and his/her relationship with the chief information officer (CIO) must be defined.

Looking at it from another angle, here's what the process looks like: Information must be acquired, new knowledge must be invented, and then it must be incorporated into the universal knowledge stores in order to be shared. This implies that it must be organized, stored, transferred, shared, and taught.

Because knowledge ultimately resides in someone's head, all knowledge must be looked at first from the human perspective. It is the individual who starts out to learn (acquire information) through browsing, exploration, observation, and research, often structured through channels like formal education. In today's environment, learning is assisted by a number of tools and techniques. Some are ancient, such as verbal communication and physical observation. Others are somewhat more recent, like reading and writing. Still others are very new, such as browsing the Internet to research some special area of interest.

As man acquired knowledge, repositories of this knowledge started to emerge outside the brain. Clearly, collections of anything have the effect of being an available resource for observation or analysis. As documents emerged (e.g., books), they were stored in places and ways that made retrieval easy and convenient. Hence, physical libraries were born to house books and other documents. Physical libraries are now yielding to virtual libraries as the repositories of all content, in electronic format. They are essential cogs in the knowledge acquisition process.

But individuals, using different levels of cognition, such as recall, comprehension, application, analysis, synthesis, and evaluation, are able to build incrementally from the existing base and invent and create new knowledge. This, in turn, must be named, organized, stored, transferred, taught, and shared.

Kamran Parsaye and Mark Chignell speak of five basic properties of knowledge that can be used to define and represent objects, properties, and interactions: naming, describing, organizing, relating, and constraining.[6]

TAXONOMIES AND METADATA

Taxonomy is the science that classifies all organisms. Taxonomies usually embed naming conventions. A taxonomy is also needed to classify and organize knowledge. As a matter of fact, it is a very important part of KM. How can you transfer, store, retrieve, and share knowledge if you do not have a clear way of identifying and referring to it?

When dealing with bases of explicit knowledge stored in electronic format, any taxonomy used is tightly coupled with the body of metadata used to define, identify, point, describe, and characterize the contents of the knowledge base.

Technology has now also wrought data warehouses, which have become the principal stores of structured content to be mined for knowledge. In effect, today's data warehouses are slowly but surely morphing into knowledge warehouses as we continue to add value to the bits and bytes along the Barabba-Haeckel Framework,[7] which starts with data and advances all the way to wisdom. Like a continuum, it goes through stages: data, information, intelligence, knowledge, and eventually wisdom.

KNOWLEDGE LIFE-CYCLE MODEL AND KM PROCESSES

The key to understanding the mechanics of KM lies in moving into the nuts and bolts of it. Focusing on an organization's life cycle of knowledge is a good starting point. Edward Swanstrom, Joseph M. Firestone, Mark McElroy, Douglas Weidner, and Steve Cavaleri at the Knowledge Management Consortium International (KMCI) jointly initiated this in a paper called "The Age of the Metaprise." It has now been further refined, but it provides a solid point of departure.[8]

The knowledge life cycle provides the platform for looking at the KM process itself. In fact, Firestone defines KM only in terms of the knowledge management process (KMP), which is "an ongoing, persistent, purposeful interaction among human-based agents through which the participating agents aim at managing (handling, directing, governing, controlling, coordinating, planning, organizing) other agents, components, and activities participating in the basic knowledge processes (knowledge production and knowledge integration) into a planned, directed, unified whole, producing, maintaining, enhancing, acquiring, and transmitting the enterprise's knowledge base."

If the basic knowledge processes are knowledge production and integration, Firestone, following a conceptual framework of Henry Mintzberg's, then breaks the KMP down into "three task clusters: interpersonal behavior, knowledge processing behavior, and decision-making behavior." In effect, these processes are embedded in the enterprise in multiple organizational processes and at a number of different levels. Activities make up tasks, which, in turn, migrate to task patterns and to task pattern clusters on the way to integrating the business process level.

However, knowledge must first be acquired. Douglas Weidner of Litton/PRC, who delves into the KM process in substantial detail, reminds us of this. He inserts knowledge acquisition as part of the KMP and also makes the link to the critical issue of people—people with a commonality of interests, or communities of practice.[9]

COMMUNITIES OF PRACTICE

The term "communities of practice" can conjure up any number of interesting images. In the main, it refers to a group of individuals engaged in certain common endeavors. At its core, it has to do with identifying best practices and sharing knowledge. It is essential for the right hand to know what the left hand is doing in any organization.

The traditional "water cooler" model, around which people gather to discuss common interests, works well in small organizations; however, when the modern enterprise starts growing, this approach becomes untenable. Communities of practice have to be discovered, structured, and nurtured. Some of the most interesting work in this area is described by Cathy Hirsh, et al., based on the knowledge initiative at AMS.[10] From a very successful program over several years, AMS has learned five important lessons:

1. Individual achievement must be recognized.
2. Group identity must be built.
3. Motivation and reward are tools that must be utilized.
4. Successes have to be celebrated.
5. Value has to be delivered.

Without people—without communities of practice—both knowledge processing and KM would be somewhat meaningless.

THE KNOWLEDGE MANAGEMENT TOOLKIT

The KM "toolkit" includes data warehousing and data mining, enterprise knowledge portals, document management, and storytelling.

Data Warehousing and Data Mining

A key tool in the KM toolkit is data warehousing.

The advances leading to mainstream data warehousing represent the seminal point from which contemporary analytical processing developed. Data warehousing served as the first thrust for the rigorous and methodical production of knowledge from our data.

More technically speaking, Herb Edelstein defines data warehousing as "the consolidation of data from multiple sources into a query database." This process of integration for purposes of analysis is the hallmark of data warehousing.

The process of building data warehousing environments involves working with data marts. These are simpler data structures or databases that support a single workgroup, department, business process, or application in an organization.

Data mining, according to Joan Conover, SAIC, is "the nontrivial discovery of meaningful new correlation, patterns, and trends and the extraction of implicit, previously unknown, and potentially useful information from large amounts of data. It uses pattern recognition technologies in conjunction with machine learning, statistical, and visualization techniques to discover and present knowledge in a form that is easily comprehensible to humans."[11]

The ascent from bits and bytes to data, information, intelligence, and knowledge starts with the manipulation of an enterprise's data through these decision-support and database management tools. All sound KM environments are richly supported through data warehouses and data marts that are mined to produce important insights for the different communities of practice.

Furthermore, the emergence of IT and computer systems has led to substantial inroads in knowledge production and integration. The resulting insights tie very directly to the concept of data warehousing—not so much in terms of the tool, the data warehouse, but rather the process. In addition, data warehousing is the continuation of the age-old process of obtaining meaning from a collection of data points or observations. Daniel Boorstin, former Librarian of Congress, offers some fascinating insights into these data points and operations in his essay "The Age of Negative Discovery," included in his book *Cleopatra's Nose*. Boorstin points out that "for most of Western history interpretation has far outrun data." He also says, "The modern tendency is quite the contrary, as we see data outrun meaning." He attributes this "outrun" to the advent of "mechanized observers" or machines that generate vast numbers of observations, or data points, and make navigating through these oceans of facts essential.

The essential insight in all this has to do with the importance of negative discovery. In other words, we need to discover that which is not and, hence, through analysis, be able to discard all data patterns that do not contribute to a better understanding of reality. The implication for knowledge management is that in order to "use our collective intelligence" we must increasingly utilize tools and techniques that enable us to interpret large amounts of data as we strive to achieve understanding.

Enterprise Knowledge Portals

The principal delivery mechanism for an enterprise's knowledge is the portal. Portals have become omnipresent in corporate parlance and planning, and they are the main switchboards for extracting value from the Internet. They seem to be part of e-everything. For purposes of this discussion, both the enterprise information portal (EIP) and the enterprise knowledge portal (EKP) are referred to simply as enterprise portals.

Ed Vitalos of PWC Global System Support Center defines the EIP as: (1) "an information system integration framework," (2) "an access and management mechanism to information and services," and (3) "an environment providing integrated, role-focused views."[12] EIPs sit as a semantic layer over infrastructure, repositories, and applications, and have an architecture composed of a network, server, and browser.

Joseph Firestone of Executive Information Systems, Inc., while asserting that an EKP is also an EIP, defines the EKP as "an enhanced EIP, which: (1) is goal-directed toward knowledge production, knowledge integration, and KM; (2) focuses on, provides, produces, and manages information about the validity of the information it supplies; (3) provides information about your business and meta-information about the reliability of that information; (4) distinguishes knowledge from mere information; (5) provides a facility for producing knowledge from information; and (6) orients one toward producing and integrating knowledge rather than information."[13]

Knowledge management is fundamentally about accomplishing useful things for an organization. The portal, whether an EIP or a true EKP, moves us substantially in that direction as it becomes the principal vehicle for the dissemination and sharing of common knowledge.

Document Management

A document is a record of some event or observation that captures data, information, intelligence, or even knowledge. As technology has revolutionized the media used to produce and store documents, document management has become a more important part of any KM environment. The classification of documents for fast and easy retrieval and support of the knowledge and KM processes is an essential aspect of good KM. Document management is basically moving toward becoming almost paperless.

Elias Safdie of Cordis Group, Inc., states that the U.S. Department of Defense (DoD) is set on some clearly established goals, even though some have not yet been met. "By January 1, 2000, all aspects of contract processes were to have been paper free; DoD will expand use of electronic catalogs and electronic shopping malls to put buying decisions into the hands of the people who need the product. On July 1, 1998, DoD discontinued volume printing of all DoD-wide regulations and instructions and made them available via the Internet and CD ROM."[14]

The move of more and more organizations toward electronic media for their documents should result in more effective and efficient knowledge management environments.

Storytelling

And then there is the telling of stories.

"Once upon a time, in a land far, far away. . . ." So start so many fairy tales. What does this have to do with KM? It has long been known that a good story focuses our attention, and children's stories have for millennia served the purpose of transmitting lessons, values, and other cultural tenets from generation to generation. In effect, stories are excellent tools for knowledge sharing.

In KM, storytelling has become a well-accepted and used technique. Steve Denning, Program Director, Knowledge Management, for the World Bank, might well make his case by saying, "Let me tell you what happened in Madagascar in November of 1998." He gives us an example of a story that is currently making the rounds at the World Bank:

In November 1998, the World Bank was conducting a public expenditure review in Madagascar with the government, the IMF, and other development partners. The program included a simplification of the tax system, including the introduction of a Value Added Tax (VAT). A controversy emerged as to whether the VAT should be applied to medicines. Some participants in the review argued strongly for exempting medicines so as to avoid a negative poverty impact. Others argued that once exemptions were allowed, implementation became so complicated that many of the intended benefits were lost. The mission was inclined to allow no exemptions but contacted the thematic group on tax administration and asked for help within 72 hours. Within that timeframe, the mission received advice from Indonesia, Moscow, the Middle East, North Africa, the research complex of the World Bank, a retired staff member in Canada, and an external partner at the University of Toronto. The mission concluded that the sounder course of action was to exempt medicines from the VAT, and advised the Government and its partners accordingly. As a result, medicines were exempted from the VAT that was implemented in Madagascar.[15]

With the advances in technology, storytelling has been substantially transformed. Most cultures no longer rely on the oral tradition, nor is it necessary to rely on the written word. Today, with the advent of digital video cameras and their integration into the Internet, corporate storytelling can be implemented as a critical part of an enterprise's knowledge management environment.[16]

We defined knowledge management as *the process through which an enterprise uses its collective intelligence to accomplish its strategic objectives.* In this context, storytelling becomes a powerful tool for knowledge sharing, which is the essential component for harnessing collective intelligence to achieve objectives.

CONCLUSION

Peter Drucker has said that the single greatest challenge facing managers for the next several decades "is to raise the productivity of the knowledge [...] workers. . . ."[17]

Who is the knowledge worker? What does a knowledge worker do? In the context of the workplace, the knowledge worker is the professional who must command and constantly update a body of relevant knowledge to do his or her job.

A few months ago, the annual report of a leading bank provoked some thought. In this document, attempts were made to articulate the bank's business model in terms of a value proposition: "*Value* is that combination of *product, service, and price* that customers find attractive and our company finds profitable."

However, it is clear that *value,* in the context of that statement, depends almost completely on the ability to produce, deliver, and manage knowledge about customer behavior, customer satisfaction, and product and account profitability. Furthermore, for decisions to be made in a business-like and timely manner, it is essential that specific *knowledge* be delivered to the knowledge worker at the time when it is needed. In a sense, the retail equation needs to be resolved in this new context to deliver the right knowledge product, at the right place, at the right price, and of course, at the right time.

If this seems to be a challenge, it is. It is difficult, and we still do not known how to do it very well. Today, we are seeing the emergence of some of the early KM systems. Yet to understand whether we are on the right track, we have to go back to basics.

Ultimately, knowledge is needed to make decisions. In this context, it is well to remember the words of Admiral A. W. Radnor: "A decision is the action an executive must take when he has information so incomplete that the answer does not suggest itself."

This is our challenge in KM: to minimize the decision domain for knowledge workers and to provide the tools they need to do their jobs.

NOTES

1. See Remez, Shereen G. "Who Will Lead the Knowledge Revolution? An Examination of the Differing Roles of CIO and CKO"; and Neilson, Robert E., "Knowledge Management and the Role of the CKO." See chapters 11 and 13 of this book.
2. See Beckman, Tom. "Creating Business Value from Knowledge Management: The Fusion of Knowledge and Technology." See chapter 3 of this book.
3. See note 2.
4. In a personal communication to the author, Joe Firestone makes the following important observations:

   The implication is that tacit knowledge is ultimately all the knowledge that exists, since explicit knowledge is not inside an individual's head. If you deny this by saying that explicit knowledge is tacit knowledge that has been made explicit, I say in response that we cannot know this because (a) there is an "epistemic gap" between tacit and explicit knowledge in that we have no way of putting them side-by-side with each other to compare them, and (b) the evidence we have from scientific investigation is while explicit knowledge is linguistic in form, knowledge in the brain is in the form of neural structures associated with predispositions to express what we believe. So, again we can't compare the semantic networks in our brain with the semantic networks in explicit knowledge-related expressions. We can only infer the latter from behavior resulting from the interaction of our environments with our wetware.

   Next, I think the idea that ultimately knowledge exists only in an individual's head is clearly opposed to the idea of knowledge-based cultural artifacts, including scientific knowledge. It devalues the idea of objective culture as providing the environment in which all individuals interact. When we refer to "scientific knowledge," we are not generally referring to what is in the heads of scientists. We refer instead to artifacts such as Einstein's theory of relativity, or quantum theory, which are instances of explicit knowledge. To say that these instances are "ultimately" the expressions of tacit knowledge is not something that can be easily proven or even made sense of.

   Yes, the theory of relativity was originally the expression of the neural structures and functioning of a single mind. The theory has been enhanced and enriched since by the work of the scientific community. Relativity as it exists today is not Einstein's knowledge captured in docu-

ments. Instead, it is a cultural product that is the result of all of the social interaction that has occurred around the theory since its first expression.

This interaction is motivated by the minds of all of the individuals who have contributed to it, by the documents containing explicit knowledge about relativity that have been produced, and by the social processes that are producing new tacit and explicit knowledge about relativity all of the time. So the theory of relativity, as it exists today, is not "ultimately" in someone's head, or even in multiple heads. Instead, it is ultimately distributed. It is shared throughout the community of scientists working on it and trying to comprehend and develop it. It is tacit and explicit at the same time. It is in many heads, in many documents, and is continuously undergoing change as people interact over what it says."

5. See Bennet, David and Alex Bennet. "The Rise of the Knowledge Organization." See chapter 2 of this book.

6. See note 2, above.

7. See Barquin, Ramon. "From Bits and Bytes to Wisdom: A Framework for Understanding." See *Building Knowledge Management Environments for Electronic Government,* forthcoming from Management Concepts, Inc.

8. See Firestone, Joseph. "Enterprise Knowledge Portals, Knowledge Processing, and Knowledge Management." See *Building Knowledge Management Environments for Electronic Government,* forthcoming from Management Concepts, Inc.

9. See Weidner, Douglas. "The KM Endgame: "Connect and Collect." See *Building Knowledge Management Environments for Electronic Government,* forthcoming from Management Concepts, Inc.

10. See Hirsh, Cathy, et al. "Creating Knowledge-Based Communities of Practice: Lessons Learned from KM Initiatives at AMS." See chapter 16 of this book.

11. See Conover, Joan. "Data Warehousing, Data Mining, and Digital Libraries." See *Building Knowledge Management Environments for Electronic Government,* forthcoming from Management Concepts, Inc.

12. See Vitalos, Ed. "Enterprise Information Portals: The Vehicle for Knowledge Delivery." See *Building Knowledge Management Environments for Electronic Government,* forthcoming from Management Concepts, Inc.

13. See note 8, above.
14. See Safdie, Elias. "Knowledge Management and Document Management in the Public Sector." See chapter 9 of this book.
15. See Denning, Stephen. "Storytelling As a Knowledge Management Technique." See *Building Knowledge Management Environments for Electronic Government,* forthcoming from Management Concepts, Inc.
16. See Kull, Michael. "Corporate Storytelling and the New Media: Bringing Hollywood Inside the Enterprise." See *Building Knowledge Management Environments for Electronic Government,* forthcoming from Management Concepts, Inc.
17. Quoted by Mark Towers in speech at GSA Event, St. Louis, Missouri, April 10, 1998.

SUGGESTED ADDITIONAL READINGS

Davenport, Thomas H. and Laurence Prusak. *Working Knowledge: How Organizations Manage What They Know.* Harvard Business School Press, 1998.

de Hoog, Robert, et. al. "Investigating a Theoretical Framework for Knowledge Management: A Gaming Approach." *Knowledge Management Handbook.* Jay Liebowitz, ed. CRS Press, 1999.

Denning, Stephen. *The Springboard: How Storytelling Ignites Action in Knowledge Era-Organizations.* Butterworth Heinemann, October 2000.

Earl, Michael J. and Ian Scott. "What Is a Chief Knowledge Officer?" *Sloan Management Review.* 40(2), 1999.

Koulopoulos, Thomas M., Spinello, Richard A., and Wayne Toms. *Corporate Instinct: Building a Knowing Enterprise for the 21st Century.* Van Nostrand Reinhold, 1997.

Leonard-Barton, Dorothy. *Wellsprings of Knowledge: Building and Sustaining the Sources of Innovation.* Harvard Business School Press, 1995.

Liebowitz, J. and T. Beckman. *Knowledge Organizations: What Every Manager Should Know.* St. Lucie Press, 1998.

O'Dell, Carla S. and C. Jackson Grayson, with Nilly Essaides. *If Only We Knew What We Know: The Transfer of Internal Knowledge and Best Practice.* New York: Free Press, 1998.

Nonaka, Ikujiro and Hirotaka Takeuchi. *The Knowledge-Creating Company*. Oxford University Press, 1995.

Nonaka, I. "The Dynamic Theory of Organizational Knowledge Creation." *Organization Science*. 5(1), 1994.

Stewart, Thomas A. *Intellectual Capital: The New Wealth of Organizations*. Currency/Doubleday, 1997.

Quinn, J.B. *Intelligent Enterprise: A Knowledge and Service Based Paradigm for Industry*. New York: Free Press, 1992.

Senge, P.M. *The Fifth Discipline: The Art and Practice of the Learning Organization*. New York: Doubleday, 1990.

Wenger, E. *Communities of Practice: Learning, Meaning, and Identity*. Cambridge University Press, 1999.

Wiig, K. *Knowledge Management Foundation*. Schema Press, 1993.

CHAPTER 2

The Rise of the Knowledge Organization

David Bennet
Alex Bennet

The progress of humanity over the past 30,000 years has been predominantly due to the effectiveness of the organizations used to achieve human goals. For example, religious goals have been achieved through organizational structures developed by the world's major religions. Economic progress throughout history has been driven by commerce and business organizations. Political organizations have both provided stability and been the catalyst for change.

Organizational systems have internal structures that mediate roles and relationships among people who work toward some identifiable objective. These internal structures, together with cultural, leadership, and management characteristics, provide the ability to interact effectively with their environment and achieve desired goals.

Organizations have a much longer history than is usually understood. While a study of evolution demonstrates the ubiquitous role of interactions and relationships among all life, the beginnings of structure, function, and dedicated efforts to meet objectives through intention, planned action, and individual roles had to wait until *homo sapiens* reached the hunter gatherer/ agriculture transition.

Since the early hunter gatherer, circa 35,000 B.C., the success of small bands of humans gathering berries, leaves, and grubs and occasionally hunting larger animals is clear from the world-wide distribution of archeological sites where human colonies lived. Environmental forces demanded specific actions for survival, leading to the development of culture via the need and propensity to cooperate. Thus began the first attempts at structure and organization, driven by the same forces that drive organizations 37,000 years later: threats and opportunities in the environment and a strong desire to survive and achieve goals.

As demonstrated in this early grounding, organizations usually existed through a successful balance between the forces in their environment and their own creativity and adaptivity. The boundary between the organization and its environment is almost always porous, flexible, and foggy. This frequently unpredictable external environment is driven by physical, political, sociological, economic, natural, and technological forces.

Organizations, a product of *homo sapiens'* superb cognitive and linguistic capabilities, have always made use of knowledge and one of its offspring, technology, to survive during their hour on the stage of history. An early example of this occurs during the eighteenth through twentieth Egyptian dynasties (1550 to 1069 B.C.). The Overseer of All the King's Works—a man of science, an architect, and the authority figure—directed the massive labor force required to build a pyramid. "His palette and papyrus scrolls were the symbols of the authority of knowledge, and bureaucratic lists and registers were the tools of political and economic power."[1] Knowledge, demonstrated by writing, provided the authority, and the use of technology (in the form of pulleys, levers, and wheels) provided the means.

The success of the Taizong dynasty (626–49 A.D.) was a direct result of Taizong's strong leadership and management approaches built on a solid cultural and military base. While building and stocking the latest instruments of war, he used literature to spread manners and guide customs. He instituted a system of state schools and colleges (one reserved for children of the Imperial family) and gave the highest positions in the government to those who passed literary exams. Thus, he not only recognized the value of learning and knowledge but also used it to expand the Imperial family's influence throughout the empire.

Throughout history, the environment has become increasingly complex, dynamic, and technologically sophisticated. In response, organizations have become more complex, more flexible, and more ègalitarian, with success very much dependent on making optimum use of all available information, experience, and insight.

The technology revolution of the late 1700s began with the invention of the steam engine and ultimately brought about factories and mass production. With the emergence of the tycoons of oil, railroads, steel, and automobiles came the rise of the modern bureaucracy and the great test of its precepts of specialists and rigid rules. While economically successful, it took a large toll on human freedom. Specialization, limited learning and initiative, and assembly lines made mechanical robots out of workers. As new technology was developed, it was frequently misunderstood or misapplied and ended up restricting employees rather than liberating their potential.

THE BUREAUCRATIC ORGANIZATION

Max Weber (1864–1920) developed the formal theory recognized today as the bureaucratic model. Weber, a lawyer familiar with power politics, economics, and religion, migrated to sociology through his attempt to understand how capitalism came into existence. His world of ideas was multidimensional.

The bureaucratic framework created by Max Weber in the late 1800s called for a hierarchical structure, clear division of labor, rule and process orientation, impersonal administration, rewards based on merit, decisions and rules in writing, and management separated from ownership. The bureaucratic model was built on management power over workers in what Weber called "imperative control." The key success factors of Weber's bureaucracy rested on authority and its acceptance by workers and on the design and management of processes, rigid rules, and procedures.

Weber linked knowledge with power. He believed that "every bureaucracy seeks to increase the superiority of the professionally informed by keeping their knowledge and intentions secret."[2] Because the pure interest of the bureaucracy is power, secrecy would grow with the increase of bureaucracy. We still live with the legacy of this intent.

With the rise of large corporations in the early 20th century came a strong interest in research in fields such as leadership, management, organizational theory, and capitalism. Frederick Taylor, Henri Fayol, Mary Parker Follet, Chester Bernard, Adam Smith, Herbert Simon, and Abraham Maslow (the list goes on and on) all contributed to the foundational research and set of organizational concepts of the early 20th century. This era created the formal foundation of management and organizational theory. Although the origins lay in Weber's bureaucracy, church and state autocracy, and military leadership, these were all modified by the social, political, and capitalistic drives in the free world after World War II. The new theories and concepts such as Theory X, Theory Y, Theory Z, Charismatic and Transformational Leadership, General Systems Theory, and Organizational Linking Pins, became popular, and a noticeable shift occurred from bureaucracy toward a more benign and malleable organizational structure. Tools such as Management by Exception, Span of Control, Kurt Lewin's Force Field Analysis, and Taichi Ohno's Toyota Production Line techniques helped both managers and workers implement change throughout their organizations.

While some changes occurred, most organizations continued to be hierarchical. Knowledge and information were held close by supervisors and managers and protected as they represented their personal power and authority. Economic progress was relatively steady and, until the 1970s, fairly predictable. During this post-bureaucratic era, the key factors were a combination of Tayloristic time and motion management and participative management, slowly bringing some of the workforce into the arena of worker responsibility and empowerment.

As the affluence, mobility, and expectations of the workforce in developed countries continued to rise, coupled with the explosive growth of information and communication technologies and the creation of knowledge, organizations found themselves in situations of restructure or collapse. The old mechanical metaphor would no longer serve in the nonlinear, dynamic, complex global Web of the mid 1990s. Many organizations failed, some were acquired, and the best set about seeking the popular vision of the "world-class" corporation. The stage was now set for the rise of information and knowledge organizations, with the information organizations taking the lead via computers and communications technology in the early 1980s and 1990s and the knowledge organizations, currently in their embryonic form, focusing on networking and knowledge creation, sharing, and application.

Because we will use three terms extensively in describing the current and future organization, it is important to communicate what we mean by data, information, and knowledge. Data are discrete, objective facts about events, including numbers, letters, and images without context. Information is data with some level of meaning. It is usually presented to describe a situation or condition and, therefore, has added value over data. Knowledge is built on data and information and created within the individual. Knowledge, of course, has many levels and is usually related to a given domain of interest. In its strongest form, knowledge represents understanding of the context, insights into the relationships within a system, and the ability to identify leverage points and weaknesses and to understand future implications of actions taken to resolve problems. Thus, knowledge represents a richer and more meaningful awareness and understanding that resonates with how the "knower" views the world. Knowledge is frequently considered actionable.

ORGANIZATIONS OF THE YEAR 2000

Time accelerates. Distance shrinks. Networks expand. Interdependencies grow geometrically. Uncertainty dominates. Complexity overwhelms. Such is the environment and the context within which current organizations must survive and thrive.

This situation is a result of many years of evolution driven by a number of major factors. Of significance is the increasing economic affluence of workers in the developed countries, coupled with their increased education level. This has resulted in a strong demand by workers to be recognized, respected, and allowed to participate and have determination in their work. Economics and technology provide both the means and pressures for mobility, thereby giving workers the freedom to leave their jobs for other, more challenging positions. While the last 50 years have seen many ups and downs in terms of employment, productivity, interest rates, and investments, the recent decades have provided increasing wealth and economic success.

Consistent with this history, every organization lives at the pleasure of its environment—economic, sociological, political, and legislative. For example, state charters legitimize corporations, the Occupational Safety and Health Administration (OSHA) and the Department of Labor mandate tight restrictions on both safety and personnel regulations, the Environmental Protection Agency (EPA) regulates organizational behavior relative to environmental impact, and the business media heavily influence corporate stock values depending on local and temporal events. Technology plays a dominant role in determining both the landscape of competition and the cultural and educational needs of the workforce. It is arguably true that technology has played the strongest role in creating the present environment within which organizations must adapt and learn how to excel compared to their competitors. For example, tremendous increases in processing speed, communication bandwidth, miniaturization of technology (nanotechnology), and the development of complex algorithms and application programs have spawned the rapidly changing pace of society and the increasing need and capability for communication, collaboration, and networking, both virtual and real. The phenomenal rise of the Internet, coupled with the spin-offs of intranets, extranets, etc., has created a networking potential that drives all of society and corporations in terms of speed, interdependencies, global markets, and the creation and spread of memes instantaneously throughout the world. Memes are ideas that become a part of the culture. Those organizations that have found ways to compete successfully within this nonlinear, complex, and dynamic environment may dominate their competitors by as much as 25 percent in growth rate and profitability relative to the average in their industry.

Specific characteristics of these "world-class" organizations are key to their success. Consider the distribution of all organizations within the United States versus their normalized performance (i.e., the number of organizations having a specific level of performance plotted along the vertical axis and performance along the horizontal axis). This graph would likely be represented by the commonly known bell curve, with the high-performing organizations represented at the far right of that bell curve. While most of today's organizations are far from this world-class region, many are working hard to improve their performance—that is, their efficiency, effectiveness, and sustained competitive advantage—in an effort to improve their competitive status and in some cases prevent being acquired or going bankrupt.

Often the tools, methods, structures, and principles that the best organizations have found to drive high performance are neither new nor, in many cases, unique. For example, many of the ideas that Toyota developed in the late 1940s and early 1950s relative to lean manufacturing in the automobile industry (although refined and improved) are still considered world class, and, in fact, Toyota is considered by many to be the leader throughout the world in automobile manufacturing.[3] Taichi Ohno created the Toyota production system just after World War II as a response to potential bankruptcy and changing consumer demands.[4] The system eventually included just-in-time supply parts delivery, floor workers in the factory taking responsibility for product quality and having authority to stop the production line, and teams of workers solving problems on the factory floor and learning cross-functional jobs to ensure continuous production line flows. Recognize that it took Toyota more than 20 years to create its present system, and it is still improving it. Approximately 50 years later many of these early ideas are still considered best practices and are used by manufacturing organizations worldwide. Significantly, these ideas represent a significant departure from the bureaucratic hierarchical chain of command and minimum freedom of the worker.

In *Built to Last,* Collins and Porras did a six-year study of 18 companies that had outstanding performance over time periods between 50 and 200 years. Reviewing their results, together with other research on long-lived world-class companies, we offer the following factors as representative of long-term, highly successful organizations:

- Continuous striving to improve themselves and doing better tomorrow than what they did today, always remaining sensitive to their customers and their environment.

- Not focusing on profitability alone, but balancing their efforts to include employee quality of life, community relations, environmental concerns, customer satisfaction, and stakeholder return.

- A willingness to take risks with an insistence that they be prudent, and an overall balanced risk portfolio. In general, they were financially conservative.

- A strong feeling about their core ideology, changing it seldom, if ever. Their core values form a solid foundation and, while each company's individual values were unique, once created they were not allowed to drift with the fashions of the day. This core value molded their culture and created a strong sense of identity.

- Relative to their employees, these companies demanded a strong "fit" with their culture and their standards. Thus,

> employees either felt the organization was a great place to work and flourished or they were likely short-term. At the same time, they were tolerant of individuals on the margins who experimented and tested for possibilities.

Many current top organizations have made significant changes in the way they do business in the past decade and have been able to create performance through change management and deliberately develop the fundamental characteristics needed for success. These characteristics must provide those responses necessary to excel in today's environment. For example, time-to-market and the ability to quickly develop new products are key factors in many industries because of the decreased production time created through technology, concurrent engineering, and agile manufacturing techniques. Simulation, integrated product teams, and world-wide subject matter experts operating virtually have been instrumental in bringing new knowledge and ideas together to rapidly produce products desired by a sophisticated and demanding market. (Examples of this capability are: (1) mass customization where economic order quantities of one are being pursued and (2) agility, the ability of an organization to move rapidly in response to changing and unique customer needs.) Creativity and innovation have come to the forefront as key success factors, with organizations striving to develop and unleash these capacities throughout their workforce, using a combination of management, workers, customers, and the ability to pull collaborative teams together as a situation or problem dictates.

Employee involvement has now been accepted and understood by world-class organizations and many "hope to be's." Examples are Wal-Mart, Hewlett-Packard, IBM, Texas Instruments, Motorola, and the Chaparral Steel Company. These world-class organizational structures have moved significantly away from bureaucratic decision-making and have modified their hierarchies to include team-based organizations and horizontal structures with minimum "white space." These firms encourage cross-communication by all employees, supported by technology such as e-mail and groupware,[5] and reward employees who play a strong role in influencing organizational direction and decision-making.

These same organizations, working predominantly in the fast-moving world of information and knowledge application, recognize the value of decisions made at the lowest qualified level and the payoff from smart workers who know their jobs. However, for employees at all levels to use their knowledge to make effective decisions, they must understand the context within which those decisions are made. This context is provided through shared vision, clear values, and strong organizational direction and purpose, combined with open communication. As described by Peter Senge in the *Fifth Discipline*, smart companies put significant effort into transferring their vision, purpose, and goals to all employees. Good employee decision-making stems from understanding their work in terms of its impact on adjacent areas of the organization, as well as its direct impact on the customer. The first of these requires effective empowerment and systems thinking and the second comes from customer orientation and focus.[6] Note how far we have departed from Weber's description of bureaucracy and its relative impotency in the current world context.

Nurtured by Total Quality Management (TQM) and Total Quality Leadership, the transfer of better business practices has recently become a hallmark of high-performing organizations. Many tools are continuing to be developed to help organizations create environments that make maximum use of employee knowledge and creativity. These practices include benchmarking, business process reengineering, lean production, value chain analysis, agility, integrated product teams, balanced scorecard, and, most recently, knowledge management.

The birth of knowledge management (KM), occurring in the early 1990s, grew from a recognition of the difficulty of dealing with complexity and with ever-increasing competition spurred by technology and the demands of sophisticated customers. First came an awareness of the importance of information and knowledge, followed by a constant search for ways to create, store, integrate, tailor, share, and make available the right knowledge to the right people at the right time. Although still in its infancy, as indicated by the large number of meanings and uses of the words "knowledge" and "KM," the field has pushed many organizations far from the classical Weberian bureaucracy. For example:

- The knowledge organization's focus is on flexibility and customer response compared to bureaucracy's focus on organizational stability and the accuracy and repetitiveness of internal processes.

- Current practices emphasize using the ideas and capabilities of employees to improve decision-making and organizational effectiveness. Bureaucracies use autocratic decision making by senior leadership with unquestioned execution by the workforce.

- Current efforts bring technology into the organization to support and liberate employee involvement and effectiveness. Classical bureaucracies use technology to improve efficiency and expect employees to adapt.

- Current actions eliminate waste and unnecessary processes while maximizing value added. Bureaucracy seeks to establish fixed processes to ensure precision and stability with little concern for value.

- Current organizational emphasis is on the use of teams to achieve better and more balanced decision-making and to share knowledge and learning. The axiom is, "knowledge shared is power." Bureaucracies minimize the use of teams to maintain strong control and ensure knowledge is kept at the managerial and senior levels. The axiom is, "personal knowledge is power."

As valuable as these ideas are, their implementation continues to be a challenge to all organizations. Although many of these tools were originally touted as silver bullets, after they become popular, and as companies try them without fully understanding the difficulties of their implementation, they frequently achieve less-than-anticipated results. Michael Hammer, one of the co-creators of business process reengineering (BPR), has defined BPR as "the fundamental rethinking and radical redesign of business processes to achieve dramatic improvements in critical contemporary measures of performance."[7]

We find that ten years later, BPR is just now being understood well enough to provide a good chance of success, if applied to the right situation by experienced professionals. The unproven perception was that as many as 70 percent of BPR implementations failed to meet expectations. Many feel TQM has suffered the same difficulties. As time progresses and more organizations learn how to implement these tools successfully, they are becoming more and more useful and contributing significantly to organizational improvement.

From the authors' personal experience, major reasons for the difficulty in applying these tools comes more from the lack of infrastructure support and the inability to change culture than it does from the individual workforce and leadership. Research has indicated that the resistance arising from cultural inertia causes great difficulty in transferring the knowledge to effectively implement better business practices.[8] Thus, we expect the road to a highly effective and efficient knowledge organization to be filled with bumps and potholes. Every change in the basic beliefs of the workforce, or of "the way the work gets done" is slow, erratic, and painful. The move to a knowledge organization is no exception. But the move is occurring and will continue. There appears to be no other viable alternative.

For any new ideas to provide long-term value, they must be better understood and continuously improved through a process of ongoing learning. As our environment changes, our organizations must be molded and sometimes even reinvented into something that better fulfils an important need. Thus we see that in today's environment, no solutions can be independent of either time or context. This also applies to organizational structures. To the extent that this is true, there is not—and likely may never be—any single form of organizational structure that provides maximum overall effectiveness or that can even be offered as a model for reference. However, they all must be able to move quickly and make knowledgeable decisions coupled with effective follow-through.

A significant challenge still facing the modern knowledge organization is how to harness the benefits of information technology. While the rapid growth and widespread influence of information technology has resulted in huge investments by many corporations, there has been some disillusionment with its hoped-for increase in productivity. However, those companies that have recognized the close relationship between information technology and culture, using the technology to support people in achieving corporate objectives, have found information technology highly effective in creating a competitive advantage. To achieve this not only requires selecting and adapting the technology to the individual organization's needs, but also a carefully designed process that brings the technology into the culture in a manner that the workforce finds acceptable and motivates workers to make the necessary cultural changes to imbed workflow adaptations successfully.

In addition to these difficulties in applying information technology and the requisite culture change, "to-be" knowledge organizations face a number of fundamental barriers as they attempt to become world class and to develop and maintain continuous competitive advantage. It is widely known that change management is a broad and challenging field that offers many theories and processes to consider, but no guaranteed solutions. Fundamentally, the process of change is highly situational and dependent not only on the environment, goals, and objectives of the organization, but also on its specific history, culture, and leadership. Each year finds a number of new books and journal articles offering the latest and greatest solutions to implementing change. To the authors' knowledge, there is no "solution" to implementing change because each situation offers its own set of unique challenges, pitfalls, and potentially successful tactics.

A major source of opposition to creating a knowledge organization is likely to come from middle management's unwillingness to give up its prerogatives of decision-making and authority. Because most of the workforce gets their direct information from, and usually develops trust in, their immediate supervisors, they are heavily influenced by the attitudes and actions of these middle managers. This barrier has occasionally been overcome when senior management has circumvented the mid-level and worked directly with the workforce.[9]

Although communication is essential in stable times, it becomes critical and extremely important during times of change and uncertainty. Rumors, informal networks, official organizational policies, and rules, as well as personalities and fear of job loss or power changes, all heavily influence the accuracy, noise level, and usefulness of communication. The classic solution seems to be to communicate as much as possible, as accurately as possible, and as often as possible, keeping all of the workforce informed on events and changes in the organization. Although theoretically sound and occasionally successful, this practice may be difficult under conditions where major changes are needed, but the rationale for these changes is difficult for employees to understand and accept. Thus, building a knowledge organization under conditions less than life threatening is challenging at best.

Before the workforce will accept new practices, workers must be willing to recognize and admit that their current efforts are inadequate. This usually requires a paradigm shift and a willingness to adapt new assumptions in terms of how the business works and what must be done. The resistance to this paradigm shift is usually high and often unrecognized by management. The historic paradigm that produced past success is so ingrained in the belief systems of most middle and upper managers, and the risk of adapting totally new assumptions about the business is so large, that the "double loop" learning required—as discovered and explained so eloquently by Argyris and Schon[10] in their book *Organizational Learning: A Theory of Action Perspective*—is a major challenge.

Still another challenge faced by leadership is the willingness to give up some of its own authority and decision-making and to empower the workforce (including teams) to make decisions based on local circumstances. This diffusion of information and knowledge from upper and middle management throughout the workforce means that they give up authority while maintaining responsibility—something very few people want to do. Yet, to successfully release the worker's knowledge and experience for organizational improvement, the context, direction, and authority to make local decisions must be made available to all personnel, and those same personnel must be qualified to accept the challenge of empowerment.

A knowledge organization must, of necessity, become a learning organization so that the entire firm will learn while it works and be able to adapt quickly to market changes and other environmental perturbations. Except for a few professional firms, most workers are not in the habit of continuous learning as part of their job. Unfortunately, many supervisors and managers believe that learning on the job is not appropriate. It is no surprise then that individuals who have worked for years without learning or even the expectation of having to learn on the job find it highly challenging and difficult to "learn how to learn" and to continuously keep updated in their area of expertise. Creating the emergent characteristic represented by a learning organization will take much more effort than simply offering courses and training to the workforce.

Another challenging final barrier particularly relevant to those firms seeking to become knowledge organizations is that of creating a culture in which knowledge and knowledge sharing are valued and encouraged. As discussed earlier, many workers consider knowledge as power and job security and are frequently unwilling to share ideas and experience with their colleagues. The solution to this barrier is an area of current research, and ideas are being offered and tested. As always, they are situation-dependent and represent another step toward complexity.

The evolution of organizations has passed from cooperative hunting bands to farming groups to city/towns to bureaucracies. These changes took almost 10,000 years, or about 500 generations.[11] Yet during the past fifty years (two generations), they have moved from enlightened bureaucracies to employee-centered, team-based, networked, information, and knowledge-intense structures struggling to keep pace with change. Recall that we are speaking primarily of those firms at the right side of our bell curve. In one sense, we are moving back to small bands of people working together to solve their common and immediate problems. In another, everyone lives, works, and relates in a totally new and strange world.

At the forefront of organizational performance are the knowledge-based organizations that have successfully adopted several or many of the practices discussed above while concomitantly taking advantage of the new technological advances such as knowledge portals, intelligent search engines and agents, and knowledge repositories. These organizations have achieved high levels of efficiency and effectiveness, sustained competitive advantage, and, above all, an effective balance that satisfies stakeholders, customers, the workforce, the environment, and local community needs. While there is still much experimentation with organizational design and trial and error is on the daily menu, general patterns of success seem to be emerging. These patterns are creating new metaphors for organizations, such as agile production systems, living organisms, complex adaptive systems, self-organizing systems, virtual organizations, the spiritual workplace, and, of course, the knowledge organization. Which of these metaphors—or new ones to be generated in the future—will become the successes of the year 15 to 20 years ahead cannot be predicted. In all likelihood, the future organization will contain parts of all of them. One can certainly be confident that information, knowledge, and their intelligent application will be essential factors in future success. However, speculation may be useful in describing potential/probable visions of what the future knowledge-based organizations will look like. A lighthouse in the darkness serves a mariner well, even if his course is not directly in line with it.

THE KNOWLEDGE ORGANIZATION

As in all forecasting, we must first identify our approach and our assumptions. Our approach will be to consider the most probable world-class organization circa 2020 A.D. Recognizing the distinction between probable, preferable, and possible, we concentrate on the most likely characteristics of the leading organizations (i.e., what we believe to be the most probable). Even to do this, however, requires a number of assumptions relative to the environment and external forces. For example, we assume relative stability and peace, historically represented by about 25 percent of all nations in conflict at any one time, throughout the world,[12] and that information technology continues to advance at its current "Moore's Law" rate, i.e., doubling in processing power and speed about every 18 months, while reducing size at the same rate. However, we recognize that bioengineering and the rapid improvement of nanotechnology may well accelerate processing ability and the impact of technology on organizations much faster than Moore's Law.

While artificial intelligence will greatly improve the application of logic and processing to narrow, well-bounded problems, it will not compete with human cognition and consciousness in understanding, situational awareness, and learning. Thus, we believe that deep knowledge, broad scope of interests, and high adaptability are unique to *homo sapiens.*

While the Internet represents a network that may potentially shrink the world, it may well take another track, with the Internet becoming saturated and chaotic. Thus, while the best organizations will almost certainly have become porous systems with multiple connections beyond their immediate organizational boundaries, they may do so through private networks versus the Internet, but they will do so!

The Information Age is intensifying interactions among processes previously isolated from each other in time or space. "Information can be understood as a mediator of interaction. Decreasing the costs of its propagation and storage inherently increases possibilities for interaction effects. An Information Revolution is therefore likely to beget a complexity revolution.[13]"

The metaphor we choose to use for the future knowledge-based organization is best given as an intelligent complex adaptive system (ICAS). By complex we mean an organization that can take on a very large number of states. A complex system is made of a "large number of individual, intelligent agents," each with its own ability to make decisions and strive for certain goals. These agents (workers) have multiple relationships within the system and externally through its boundaries, and these relationships can become highly complex and dynamic. Groups of these agents may work together to form typically what are considered components of the system, and these components together may form the whole system or organization under consideration. The word "adaptive" implies that the entire system is capable of studying and analyzing its environment and taking actions that adapt itself to forces in the environment in fulfilling its overall (organization) goals. Intelligent, complex adaptive systems may be highly unpredictable or superbly self-organized, depending on their precise internal structure and relation to their environment. They will exhibit a unity of purpose and a coherence of action, while being highly selective in their sensitivity to external threats and opportunities. They will be able to bring diverse knowledge located anywhere in the organization (or beyond) together to solve problems and take advantage of opportunities. They will possess a number of emergent characteristics that permit them to survive and successfully compete in the future world.

Our view of the world-class organization of 2020 would encompass an intelligent complex adaptive system consisting of a combination of hierarchical management and individual, quasi–self-organizing agents who can be cross-coupled to each other as needed. The balance achieved between these two components of the system will depend on the specific environment, mission, and leadership of the organization. This organization may operate reasonably close to what is known as the "edge of chaos."[14] The advantages of operating near this edge are that the opportunity for creativity and innovation are maximized through the motivation and freedom of individual agents or components. Unfortunately, this edge is narrow, and there is always a danger that the organization may become chaotic with its agents and components going in locally divergent directions, yielding little overall benefit to the organization, and perhaps exacting a heavy cost. Innovation and creativity are essential to provide the large number of potential actions and ideas necessary to adapt to an environment that is most likely much more uncertain, dynamic, and dangerous than that encountered today. This "edge of chaos" will be obtained by much more emphasis on individual worker competency and freedom in terms of learning, making decisions, and taking actions in their area of responsibility coupled with multiple and effective networks that provide sources of knowledge, experience, and insights from others.

These dynamic networks will represent the main infrastructure of the new knowledge-based organization. Made available by increased bandwidth and processing power of both silicon and biotechnology, they offer the opportunity for a virtual information and knowledge support system that will connect data, information, knowledge, and people through virtual communities, knowledge repositories, and knowledge portals. The foundation and grounding of these future firms will be strengthened through a common set of strong, stable values held by all employees. Such values not only provide guidance that enhances empowerment but also motivate and strengthen the self-confidence of the workforce, thereby magnifying the effectiveness of the self-organized teams within the intelligent complex adaptive system.

Learning and knowledge will have become two of the three most important emergent characteristics of the future world-class organization. Learning will be continuous and widespread (using mentoring, classroom, and distance learning), and will likely be self-managed with strong infrastructure support. The creation, storage, transfer, and application of knowledge (and perhaps wisdom) will have been refined and developed such that it becomes a major resource of the organization as it satisfies customers and adapts to environmental competitive forces and opportunities. The last ten years have been called the decade of the brain, one in which neuroscience research has made large gains in our understanding of the mind-brain problem and, in particular, the role of consciousness in how we learn, perceive, and sense our environment.

The third characteristic of knowledge-based organizations will be that of organizational intelligence. Karl Wiig, in his seminal book, *Knowledge Management Methods,* describes intelligent behavior as: "Be well prepared, provide excellent outcome-oriented thinking, choose appropriate postures, and make outstanding decisions."[15]

"Be well prepared" includes acquiring knowledge continuously from all available resources and building it into an integrated picture, bringing together seemingly unrelated information to create new and unusual perspectives and to understand the surrounding world.

"Provide excellent outcome-oriented thinking" is to be continuously innovative and creative and use all relevant knowledge. It also includes reframing problems and using different perspectives for their solutions, understanding situations beyond their appearances, and discriminating and characterizing as an aid to problem solving.

"Choose appropriate postures" includes adopting suitable behavior in a given situation and anticipating future changes, expending effort in proportion to the situation's importance, and coordinating all relevant parties to build consensus.

"Make outstanding decisions" consists of identifying objectives, considering alternatives and consequences, setting priorities, and selecting the best alternative.

Intelligent behavior of subsystems within a knowledge-based organization can best be seen in the effective use of teams. Bennet has identified four fundamental processes that high-performance teams have mastered that lead to successful outcomes: innovation, problem solving, decision-making, and implementing team decision. Guidelines are provided for maximizing the effectiveness of each process, thereby creating intelligent behaviors. For example, under decision quality, nine factors are considered necessary for a good decision: shared vision, efficiency, risk, timing, balance, impact on product value, political consequences, decision scope, and worst-case scenario.[14]

For an organization to behave intelligently as a complex adaptive system, it must achieve continuous, interdependent collaboration and interplay among all levels of the system. This means balancing the knowledge and actions of its agents to achieve both the lowest-level tasks and highest-level vision of the organization, creating a distributed intelligence throughout all levels of the system. This is done by using teams and communities to amplify local intelligence levels, accelerate quality decision-making, and foster innovation and creativity. However, this "future world-class" organization will have overall direction and goals and have developed measures of performance that serve to cull out inadequate ideas, decisions, and actions. Selection of the best ideas and actions is as difficult as implementation of that selection. Evolution has taught us that complex organizations evolve through a process of the random generation of ideas and individuals, which are then modified by chance encounters and eliminated by others more fit to survive.

The ICAS is a knowledge-based organization that learns from evolution by building in the equivalent characteristics that include: survival of the fittest (a threshold of performance); trial and error by mutations and genetics (brainstorming, innovation, analysis, and problem solving); and recombining by sexual reproduction and combination (systems thinking, collaborative decision-making, and implementation). These three will be replicated in future organizations by teams combining new ideas, employees coming in to offer new and different ideas and actions, and the system as a whole creating performance thresholds, which filter out the bad ideas and decisions.

This capability highlights the importance of both internal and external networks as they heavily influence the relationships and amplify knowledge diffusion among agents, components, and external systems. As these networks increase, the organization becomes more complex, harder to manage, and potentially capable of handling more complexity in its environment.

An effective ICAS will have a permeable boundary and optimize its results through partnering, alliances, and close relationships with customers and all stakeholders. Thus, where in a bureaucracy policy, rules, and power are dominant, learning, knowledge, networking, and relationships will be dominant in the knowledge-based organization of the future.

The knowledge-based organization of the future (what we propose as ICAS) clearly breaks away from the bureaucratic model described by Weber. The future world where knowledge shared becomes power and the entire organization behaves as an intelligent, self-selecting, self-adapting system, continually integrating and processing incoming data and information to determine its actions, is clearly idealistic—but not beyond the possible. The present recognition and popularity of the importance of knowledge to organizational success is merely the beginning of creation of the truly intelligent organization.

As we move into the 21st century, the goal of an organization has rightfully moved away from the oppressive working conditions of the early 20th century. The ultimate challenge of the future is to liberate and amplify the knowledge and creativity of all organizational members. For in them alone lives the source and power of intelligence and wisdom.

NOTES

1. Silverman, D.P. (ed). *Ancient Egypt.* New York: Oxford University Press, 1997.
2. Gerth, H.H. and C.W. Mills, C.W. (ed. and trans.). From *Max Weber: Essays in Sociology.* New York: Oxford University Press, 1946.
3. Womack, J.P., D.T. Jones, and D. Roos. *Machine That Changed The World.* New York: McMillan Publishing Co., 1990.
4. Shingo, S. *A Study of the Toyota Production System.* Cambridge: Productivity Press, 1989.
5. Coleman, D. *Groupware: Collaborative Strategies for Corporate LANs and Intranets.* New Jersey: Prentice Hall, 1997.
6. Senge, P.M. *The Fifth Discipline: The Art & Practice of The Learning Organization.* New York: Doubleday, 1990.
7. Hammer, M. and J. Champy. *Reengineering the Corporation.* New York: HarperCollins Publishers, 1993.
8. Brown, J.S. "Conversation." *Knowledge Directions: The Journal of the Institute for Knowledge Management,* Volume 1, Spring, 1999.

9. Carlzon, J. *Moments of Truth.* Cambridge: Ballinger Publishing Co., 1987.
10. Argyris, C. and D.A. Schon, *Organizational Learning: A Theory of Action Perspective.* Philippines: Addison-Wesley Publishing Co., 1978.
11. Berger, L. *In the Footsteps of Eve: The Mystery of Human Origins.* Washington, D.C.: National Geographic, 2000.
12. Durant, W.A. *The Lessons of History.* New York: Simon and Schuster, 1968.
13. Axelrod, R. *The Complexity of Cooperation.* Princeton: Princeton University Press, 1997.
14. Bennet, D. *IPT Learning Campus: Gaining Acquisition Results through IPTs.* Alexandria: Bellwether Learning Center, 1997.
15. Wiig, K.M. *Knowledge Management Foundations.* Arlington, TX: Schema Press, 1993.

BIBLIOGRAPHY

Collins, R. *Four sociological traditions.* New York: Oxford University Press, 1994.

Cummings, T.G. and E.F. Huse. *Organization Development and Change* (4th ed.). New York: West Publishing Company, 1989.

Daft, R.L. and R.M. Steers. *Organizations: A Micro/Macro Approach.* New York: Harper Collins Publishers, 1986.

Ebrey, P.B. (ed.). *Chinese Civilization: A Sourcebook.* New York: The Free Press, 1993.

Edelman, G. *A Universe of Consciousness: How Matter Becomes Imagination.* New York: Perseus Books Group, 2000.

Handy, C. *Understanding Organizations.* New York: Oxford University Press, 1993.

McKelvey. B. *Organizational Systematics.* Berkeley: University of California Press, 1982.

Outhwaite, W. and T. Bottomore (eds.). *The Blackwell Dictionary of Twentieth-Century Social Thought.* Malden, MA: Blackwell Publishers, Inc., 1994.

Roberts, J.A.G. *A Concise History of China.* Cambridge: Harvard University Press, 1999.

Skyrme, D.J. *Knowledge Networking: Creating the Collaborative Enterprise.* Boston: Butterworth Heinemann, 1999.

Wren, D.A. *The Evolution of Management Thought.* New York: Ronald, 1972.

CHAPTER 3

Creating Business Value from Knowledge Management

The Fusion of Knowledge and Technology

Tom Beckman

Knowledge management (KM) is a broad-scoped methodology and framework for managing enterprise knowledge to better realize and increase its potential value. KM enables organizations to capture, formalize, organize, store, access, apply, and share knowledge, experience, and expertise to enable superior performance, create new capabilities, encourage innovation, and enhance customer value. Additional benefits from managing knowledge include better business solutions and decisions, better collaboration and knowledge sharing, and improved workforce proficiency and knowledge.

Business value is created by understanding and applying the precepts of knowledge architecture and innovative information technology (IT). A basic tenet expounded in this chapter is that accessible explicit knowledge, especially in electronic form, creates much more value than the same knowledge in tacit form, such as that contained in the minds of the workforce. A second core belief is that structuring and organizing such explicit knowledge also significantly increases its value. A third key principle is that innovative IT embodied in artificial intelligence (AI) disciplines, such as expert systems, machine learning, and natural language, can and should be applied to capture and increase the body and value of organizational knowledge, experience, and expertise. A final tenet is that significant value is realized by transforming knowledge from lower to higher forms in a knowledge hierarchy.

Too much has been written about the benefits of KM and too little about the nature, structure, and characteristics of knowledge and expertise and the concepts, methods, and technologies needed to achieve the promised benefits. KM consists of several dimensions: conceptual/methodology, business practice, and technology. Without a conceptual framework, the practice of KM and the application of technologies will be disorganized and ineffectual. Without sound KM business practices, the potential value of knowledge will not be realized. Without innovative IT, the efficiency and effectiveness of knowledge accessibility and sharing will be greatly diminished.

Many KM practitioners believe that it is most important to develop communities of practice[1] to share knowledge and expertise among its members about a subject. Other approaches focus on valuing and managing a firm's intellectual capital,[2] training and developing the workforce,[3] and organizational learning and changing management to deliver business value.

This chapter examines another approach that emphasizes business value created by fusing explicit knowledge with innovative IT. The importance of explicit symbolic knowledge, knowledge architecture, expert systems,[4] and object methods[5] in creating electronic knowledge repositories, integrated performance support, and Web applications systems[6,7,8] is discussed.

The KM umbrella embraces disciplines as diverse as intellectual capital, organizational learning, archiving, business intelligence, and customer relationship management. KM also encompasses technologies, including:

- Web technologies: extensible markup language (XML), metadata, intelligent search, e-commerce, and content management

- Document and record management, archiving, and backup

- Collaboration, groupware, and directed creativity technologies
- Training: e-learning, distance training, multimedia, and intelligent tutoring systems
- Case management, workflow management, and performance support systems
- AI: expert systems, machine learning, text generation, and natural language
- Knowledge discovery: data mining, text mining, and visual knowledge exploration.

Many applications have been developed to meet specific KM needs of various user communities. However, no integrated toolkits or technology frameworks have been developed and implemented in practice, although I have proposed a conceptual model.[9,10] Recently, software tools have been developed to support a variety of business needs, including corporate memory, fraud detection, measurement systems reporting and analysis, Web portals, content analysis and organization, communities of practice, performance support systems, distance learning, automated help desks, e-mail analysis, and intelligent search.

KM is an emerging discipline that has its origins in many sources:

- Information and records management
- Data warehousing and data mining
- AI, expert systems, natural language, cognitive science, and knowledge elicitation
- Library science and archiving
- Organizational learning and distance learning

- Collaboration, document management, and groupware technologies
- Web technologies and IT infrastructure.

As yet, no paradigm exists to explain the characteristics and nature of knowledge, how and under what circumstances knowledge increases in value, and the implications for managing knowledge. This lack of consensus regarding fundamental concepts in KM has provoked disagreement and controversy among theoreticians and practitioners. KM consultants have found that discussions about these issues with clients seem to provoke confusion and disagreement, while adding little value. So unfortunately, these issues have often been neglected or ignored.

First, there is no consensus on the definition and characteristics of knowledge. A related problem involves distinguishing among data, information, and knowledge. Second, most KM consultants believe that IT is a minor contributing factor. They also believe that there is no way to make the vast amount of tacit and implicit knowledge explicit, accessible, and usable, despite the large number of successful expert systems in diverse fields. Finally, the potential value from formalizing, categorizing, and organizing knowledge and understanding user needs and goals is unrecognized by most practitioners. Only when these issues are better understood and addressed can the great potential value be realized from collecting, creating, refining, using, and sharing knowledge.

There are many dimensions around which knowledge can be characterized. Essential are definitions of knowledge, forms in which knowledge resides, and accessibility of knowledge. Next, representing knowledge in symbolic form is discussed, and an explicit knowledge hierarchy is proposed. Finally, expert knowledge and its representation in humans and computers as symbols, structures, and processes are explored.

Understanding the nature and characteristics of knowledge, expertise, and experience are crucial to the discipline of KM. Such expertise and the means to transform tacit knowledge into electronic expertise using expert systems are discussed. A knowledge repository is then proposed that is an electronic storehouse and resource for all types of knowledge in a variety of levels, forms, and formats. A number of services can be provided from the knowledge repository that culminate with the development of integrated performance support systems. The chapter concludes with a discussion of technologies that support and enable the KM business practice areas.

DEFINITION OF KNOWLEDGE

Philosophers, AI researchers, cognitive scientists, and KM practitioners have proposed a variety of definitions for knowledge, ranging from the practical through the conceptual to the philosophical, and from narrow to broad in scope. The following definitions of knowledge are relevant:

- Knowledge is organized information applicable to problem solving.[11]

- Knowledge is information that has been organized and analyzed to make it understandable and applicable to problem solving or decision making.[12]

- Knowledge encompasses the implicit and explicit restrictions placed upon objects (entities), operations, and relationships, along with general and specific heuristics and inference procedures involved in the situation being modeled.[13]

- Knowledge consists of truths and beliefs, perspectives and concepts, judgments and expectations, methodologies, and know-how.[14]

- Knowledge is the whole set of insights, experiences, and procedures that are considered correct and true and, therefore, guide the thoughts, behaviors, and communications of people.[15]

- Knowledge consists of symbolic descriptions of definitions, symbolic descriptions of relationships, and procedures to manipulate both types of descriptions.[16]

- Knowledge is reasoning about information and data to enable performance, problem solving, decision making, and learning.[17]

Taken together, these definitions give an overview of knowledge. Some of the distinctions that separate it from information and data are discussed later.

KNOWLEDGE ARCHITECTURE

A knowledge architecture is proposed that provides a unifying framework for knowledge, as well as a blueprint for organizing and designing Website content—the primary knowledge delivery vehicle. This framework examines the nature, structure, characteristics, taxonomy, and representation of knowledge. The knowledge architecture describes varied schema needed to represent knowledge, experience, and expertise. A knowledge hierarchy is also created that explains the relationship between data, information, reasoning, and expertise. Understanding knowledge, expertise, and experience is crucial to the discipline of KM. The nature of human knowledge, expertise, and experience are explored, and the means to transform tacit knowledge into electronic expertise are discussed.

Constructing a knowledge architecture is the key concept in integrating knowledge and IT. At the highest level, core competencies are partitioned into selected knowledge domains. For each domain, knowledge can exist in four media: document, electronic, human, and organization. The document and electronic forms constitute explicit knowledge, the focus of this chapter. Human knowledge can be either implicit or tacit. Humans can readily supply implicit knowledge by responding directly to queries or by pointing to known, trusted knowledge sources.

For each KM project, a knowledge architecture blueprint should be created by knowledge engineers to define the knowledge needs and flows, ensure alignment with business strategies, and foster understanding among the development partners. The knowledge architecture consists of five model views, each containing several criteria for each KM project:

- **Business model view**

  —Business strategy

  —Business intelligence

  —Industry practices

  —Organization-specific practices

  —Customer profile

  —Product/service

  —Business processes

  —Improvement methods.

- **Meta-knowledge model view**

  —Knowledge media

  —Knowledge accessibility

  —Knowledge types

  —Knowledge hierarchy

  —Knowledge representation

  —Teaching methods.

- **Intellectual capital model view**
  —Core competencies
  —Knowledge domains, disciplines
  —Development
  —Management
  —Relationship
  —Organization.
- **User model view**
  —Purpose
  —Proficiency
  —User history
  —Learning style
  —Interface and presentation preferences.
- **Technology model view**
  —Web based
  —Directories
  —Collaboration
  —Advice systems
  —Workflow management
  —E-training

—Knowledge repository

—Performance support system.

SELECTING KNOWLEDGE DOMAINS

The first step in designing value-added Websites is the selection of critical core competencies required to accomplish present operational and future strategic needs. Although not all Websites meet the needs of all individual users, they must meet broader business and customer/user needs to create sustainable value.

I propose the following content domain selection procedure:

1. Determine the business purposes for the Website.
2. Identify the present and future core competencies and key capabilities needed to accomplish the purposes.
3. Partition the key capabilities into knowledge domains.
4. Identify potential users and knowledge sources.
5. Assess the domain proficiency levels, needs, and preferences of likely users.
6. Determine the size of any domain deficiencies or gaps.
7. Determine where the explicit, implicit, and tacit knowledge reside, and what levels of knowledge from the knowledge hierarchy will best suit user needs.
8. Prioritize the resulting domains by importance and proficiency gaps.
9. Determine organizational readiness and development capabilities and develop sourcing strategy.

A knowledge inventory should be conducted to determine the proficiency and number of workers needed with regard to existing core competencies, skills, knowledge, education, training, experience, and performance. In addition, explicit stores of data and information must be documented. Further, the assessment must look at existing organizational culture, values, and reward system regarding knowledge and expertise. Finally, user domain proficiency and AI/IT proficiency must be examined to determine what knowledge to make explicit and in what sequence. The knowledge hierarchy and domain characteristics must be examined for clues.

Another approach to domain selection comes from business reengineering.[18,19] This involves determining critical domains by business system components: customer, product, service, employee, competencies, process, resources, management, IT, culture, and environment. In my experience, selecting customer, employee, product, and service as domains is always succesful.

The domain characteristics often determine the selection of knowledge levels from the explicit knowledge hierarchy, as well as the choice of expert system type:

- Maturity: How well they are understood, have theories, hypotheses, models, and bodies of practice
- Complexity:

  —Number of variables and attributes

  —Number and type of relationships

  —Type, depth, and breadth of inferencing.
- Dynamic, static, or stochastic domain.

- Coupling

  —Structure—static

  —Reasoning—dynamic.

Nielsen[20] conducted Web usability studies that concluded that complex tasks often end in failure due to difficulties in site navigation and form design. These ultimately result from poor content and site design.

KNOWLEDGE MEDIA

A basic knowledge characteristic is concerned with the forms that knowledge can take. Knowledge resides in four media or forms:

- **Electronic:** Captures and organizes information, knowledge, experience, and expertise explicitly into actionable forms, such as knowledge repositories, performance support systems, simulations, smart templates, and electronic documents to supplant, support, and enable human work.

- **Document:** Describes and organizes information, knowledge, experience, and expertise to support human work.

- **Human:** Applies personal mental knowledge to perform and manage tasks. Improve skills, capabilities, and knowledge by study, experience, and experimentation.

- **Organization:**

  —Structural knowledge is captured in formal and informal reporting relationships, authority, roles, and responsibilities.

  —Social knowledge is imparted through communities of practice, formal and informal teams, and project/task forces.

—Cultural knowledge is inculcated through values, beliefs, assumptions, and stories about what and who are important in the organization and what behaviors are rewarded and acceptable.

Both storage and processing of knowledge should be considered. Document-based knowledge ranges from free text to well-structured charts and tables. Although knowledge can be stored in document form, it is the only form that cannot be directly processed. Electronic knowledge can be in digitized documents and images, tables, and expert systems. In contrast, knowledge that resides in the human mind can be difficult to access and capture explicitly. Finally, organizational knowledge is found in diffuse and distributed form. Business value is created when knowledge is captured and converted into electronic form. Media vary in their characteristics and ability to represent, store, process, and communicate knowledge, expertise, and experience (see Table 1).

Table 1. Media Characteristics

	Capability	*Storage*	*Processing*	*Distribution*
Media Type	**Electronic**	Strong	Strong	Strong
	Paper	Strong		Strong
	Human Mind	Strong	Strong	Weak
	Organization	Strong	Weak	Weak

KNOWLEDGE ACCESSIBILITY

Next, there is the dimension of knowledge availability or accessibility. Nonaka and Takeuchi[21] have divided availability into two categories: tacit and explicit. I believe there may be three[22] or possibly four levels of availability:

- **Explicit knowledge:** Formally represented in documents or electronically, usually structured and organized, and able to be readily distributed.

- **Implicit knowledge:** Readily available by asking or observing workers or organizations.
- **Tacit knowledge:** Resides in the human mind or organization. Inaccessible to others, but often can be extracted using knowledge elicitation techniques.[23]
- **Unknown knowledge:** Unavailable until discovered or created.

Knowledge gains in business value and power as it becomes explicit and more accessible across media:

- **Explicit** (document, computer): Readily accessible, documented into formal knowledge sources that are often well organized.
- **Implicit** (human mind, organization): Accessible through querying and discussion, but informal knowledge must be located and then communicated.
- **Tacit** (human mind, organization): Accessible indirectly only with difficulty through knowledge elicitation techniques and observation of behavior.[24]
- **Unknown** (human mind, organization): Created or discovered during action, reflection, insight, discussion, research, and experimentation.

Harry Collins[25] also relates knowledge types to their accessibility:

- Symbol-type knowledge (explicit)
- Embodied knowledge (implicit)
- Embrained knowledge (implicit/tacit)
- Encultured knowledge (tacit).

Knowledge becomes of greater value to an organization when it is made explicit and put in electronic form. Knowledge can be made explicit through four methods:

- Collect existing available explicit knowledge
- Querying humans for implicit knowledge and observing behaviors, relationships, and events
- Eliciting tacit knowledge from domain experts using special techniques[26]
- Discovering and creating new knowledge.

KNOWLEDGE TYPES

Three general types of knowledge are:

- **Symbolic:** Consisting of symbols that represent objects, entities, and concepts, as well as facts, assertions, data, and information. These are compact symbols that have common meanings and can be organized into a knowledge structure consisting of nodes and links. Symbolic knowledge is the most abstract, efficient, and powerful form of knowledge.
- **Language:** A vital communication mechanism, but not as powerful as symbols. Text in the form of documents, books, periodicals, and papers usually exists in semi-organized state to be useful. It can often be converted into symbolic form.
- **Sensory:** Consisting of raw images, video, speech, sounds, and signals. This is the least efficient form of knowledge. Sometimes it is interpreted and converted into text and symbolic forms.

How knowledge can be explicitly represented and processed as symbols is a very critical and complex topic for AI, as well as KM. Bit for bit, symbols are a more abstract and efficient means of representing knowledge than text, images, or signals. The reason behind this power is the ability to organize, manipulate, and process symbols by means of structures and algorithms to achieve reasoning.

Humans internalize explicit symbols corresponding to actual objects, entities, and concepts in the external world, and they also construct images, values, and beliefs in the mental world. In humans, emotions and motivations are also linked to symbols to attach relative importance and value, as well as additional context and meaning.[27] Minsky[28] believes that the richness of the meaning and understanding of symbols is a result of the number and quality of connections to other perspectives (agents), such as function, structure, and appearance.

Kamran Parsaye and Mark Chignell[29] describe five elementary properties of knowledge that can be used to define and represent objects, properties, and interactions:

- Naming (proper nouns)
- Describing (adjectives)
- Organizing (categorization and possession)
- Relating (transitive verbs and relationship nouns)
- Constraining (conditions).

These elementary properties are somewhat similar to a simplified object methods approach[30] that uses language grammar to describe some of the levels and transformation processes in the explicit knowledge hierarchy.

KNOWLEDGE REPRESENTATION FRAMEWORK

Knowledge representation is the structuring, organizing, and processing of knowledge in symbolic form. Knowledge representations consist of two parts:

- **Knowledge structures:** Static objects
- **Reasoning mechanisms:** Dynamic behaviors.

Knowledge structures consist of symbols that explicitly define, describe, organize, and link knowledge elements together. All knowledge structures have two basic parts:

- **Nodes:** Symbols
- **Links:** Relationships between symbols.

Nodes are symbols that can be conceptual primitives that represent the basic building blocks of knowledge:

- **Objects:** Physical, non-living things with properties
- **Entities:** Living, dynamic things with properties and behaviors (e.g., humans, organizations, e-agents)
- **Concepts:** Non-physical, abstract, and mental things.

Links are knowledge relationships that connect nodes. They are defined initially or generated during reasoning. There are many types of links or knowledge relations, including:

- **Definitional:** Symbol naming and describing
- **Taxonomic:** Class hierarchy and membership
- **Structural:** Composition and parts
- **Functional:** Behavior and preconditions

- **Procedural:** Process
- **Causal:** Logic and models
- **Empirical:** Events and associations
- **Chronological:** Temporal sequencing and planning
- **Spatial:** Physical nearness
- **List:** Collection or aggregation of related nodes.

Nearly all objects have links to sets of attributes that describe their nature in terms of properties and behaviors, and each attribute has related links to values that in turn describe the character of the attributes. Many representations, including object methods and most expert systems, use the same basic knowledge structure format:

<object attribute value> Ex.: <bird color green>

Relational tables contain many records (cases) organized implicitly around an entity with explicit attributes and values. Knowledge structures of considerable complexity and richness can be built from these two simple elements. Some of the most common structures are:

- **Relational tables:** Attributes and values for an entity
- **Cases:** Situation attributes, values, result, and outcome
- **Rules:** If these conditions hold, then assert this
- **Networks:** Propagate values through these relations with dynamic weightings
- **Models:** Objects, properties, and behaviors simulate situations according to algorithms and guidelines.

Reasoning mechanisms are the algorithms and control strategies to process and manage knowledge structures. Mechanisms are designed for application to matching knowledge structures to create new assertions, inferences, and relations. More importantly, reasoners usually require defined initial and goal states and monitor progress toward such goals. In addition, they also provide facilities for measuring uncertainty and importance, and explaining and justifying reasoning and outcomes. Table 2 shows common pairs of structures and reasoners, along with their results.

Table 2. Common Knowledge Representations

Structure	*Mechanism*	*Results*
Table →	relational operators →	query results
Case →	similarity engine →	closest cases
Rule →	inference engine →	advice
Network →	constraint satisfaction, Bayesian, semantic →	solutions
Model →	object methods, systems dynamics →	behaviors, assertions, advice

The object methods approach[31] extends the power of symbols by creating taxonomies and frameworks for structuring and reasoning about objects, entities, and concepts that include classification, inheritance, class typing, and default reasoning. In object modeling, domain objects, entities, and concepts are identified and organized into a concept hierarchy. The features and attributes of objects are then assigned, as well as their range of values. Next, use cases consisting of relationships, behaviors, and interactions among objects needed to reach the task goals are developed. Finally, the whole model is optimized using uncertainty and importance measures.

EXPLICIT KNOWLEDGE HIERARCHY

Consider the premise that knowledge can be organized into a knowledge hierarchy and that value can be added by transforming knowledge from a lower to a higher level in the hierarchy. Many authors, including Alter,[32] Ackoff,[33] and Allee[34] draw distinctions among data, information, and knowledge, and some of these authors also distinguish wisdom/expertise. However, other models do not distinguish between explicit and tacit knowledge, nor do they focus only on explicit knowledge.

The author has developed a six-level knowledge hierarchy that defines the forms of explicit knowledge that can exist in humans, computers, documents, and organizations. The hierarchy includes:

1. **Experience:** Tacit, nonsymbolic, nondigital, external, and internal stimuli and memories of individuals, groups, and organizations

   - **External:** Sensing objects, entities, events, behaviors, images, speech, and sounds

   - **Internal:** Senses, emotions, motivations, beliefs, biases, thoughts, and memories.

2. **Data:**

   - **Non-symbolic:** Stimuli that are recorded in explicit forms and are primarily digital

   - **Symbolic:** Stimuli and memories recorded as text, symbols, concepts, assertions, codes, and variables.

3. **Information**: Knowledge structures consisting of nodes and links. Data are converted to information by categorizing/organizing, structuring, creating static relationships, interpreting, and summarizing.

4. **Reasoning:** Processing of and inferencing on information structures toward goals according to an algorithm or method.

5. **Expertise:** Superior performance in a domain or discipline. Fast and accurate results, explanation and justification of results and reasoning, certainty and importance measures, abstraction into guidelines and principles, learning, innovation, and creativity.

6. **Capability:** Enterprise-level core competencies, organizational expertise, memory, learning, and human intellectual capital development.

Knowledge can often be converted or transformed from a lower level to a higher level, often greatly increasing its value. The actions in parentheses specify the activities that transform knowledge from one level to the next.

1. **Experience:**
   (+ select + record =)

2. **Data:**

   - **Non-symbolic:**
     (+ assign symbol + define + interpret =)

   - **Symbolic:**
     (+ select relevance + categorize/organize + structure + create relationships + summarize + interpret =)

3. **Information:**
   (+ apply inference mechanism + set goals + apply experience + format + present =)

4. **Reasoning:**
   (+ refine + explain + justify + abstract + generalize + learn =)

5. **Expertise:**
   (+ collaborate + integrate + research + teach =)

6. **Capability.**

The items in angle brackets specify the general format of symbolic knowledge at that level, and the items in curly brackets specify the forms that the knowledge can take.

1. **Experience**:

   {senses, emotions, motivations, beliefs, biases, thoughts, memories}

2. **Data**:

   - **Non-symbolic:** <digital> {image} {video} {audio} {signal} {speech} {digital}

   - **Symbolic:** <attribute value> {symbols}

3. **Information**: <relation object attribute value>

   {document} {index} {list} {sequence} {hierarchy} {table} {case} {rule} {network} {model} {process}

4. **Reasoning**: <process relation object attribute value>

   {relational operators, similarity and inference engines, propagation, inheritance and default reasoning}

5. **Expertise**: <process relation object attribute value certainty importance>

   {judgment} {advice} {forecast} {solution} {discipline}

6. **Capability**: <many varied formats>

   {knowledge repository} {integrated performance support system} {intelligent tutoring systems}

Knowledge is transformed as it moves up the knowledge hierarchy. Content complexity, abstraction, and value increase, and breadth and scope of knowledge and entities widen. A key argument is that both human and electronic intelligence/knowledge can be created and increased in value by applying the activities to convert knowledge from one level to the next.

HUMAN EXPERTISE

Expertise is a primary source of significant business value and sustainable competitive advantage. Our understanding of expertise comes primarily from observing the performance of domain experts and understanding how they perform. Choose any world-class expert, from Peter Lynch (stock picker) to Gary Kasparov (chess player). How good are they? What makes them so much better than everyone else? If we have no measures of performance, how can we know whether someone is an expert? The answer is, we really can't. We can compare Peter Lynch's performance at the Magellan stock mutual fund to the Standard and Poors (S&P) 500, as well as other mutual fund managers over differing periods of time. In chess, Kasparov and every other serious chess player has a statistically based rating that, in Gary's case, indicates that he is the strongest player who ever lived. However, if we try to compare most organizational managers' performance in the absence of standard measures, we are reduced to opinions, politics, authority, and guessing.

Expertise is superior performance in reasoning—using knowledge to perform and manage tasks, solve problems, make decisions, and learn new knowledge. Expertise is knowing what information and knowledge are most important in the situation—how best to apply and reason with them. The power of explicit knowledge and expertise comes from the abstraction of countless experiences, successes, and failures into condensed, organized symbolic forms. Expertise is also being able to explain one's reasoning and justify results. The highest form of understanding is the ability to teach another person. However, in teaching a discipline, additional methods and knowledge are required about how humans learn, what typical misconceptions are, how to repair them, and how best to communicate the subject.

For most cognitive tasks, knowledge workers with some background knowledge can perform at relatively high levels simply by understanding and applying the procedures, process, guidance, concepts, and principles found in the explicit knowledge from a discipline, practice, or industry. In most cases, knowledge workers do not have to experience numerous varied situations to succeed—rather, they can gain experience efficiently and vicariously through guidelines, best practices, and lessons learned. For physical tasks, however, development, apprenticeship, and experience are necessary. For example, reading how to drive a car is not the same as doing it. But, with proper manuals and tools, novices can perform many auto repairs.

Eventually, routine cases are remembered and generalized in experts' unconscious in the form of cases, rules, networks, and models. An example is grandmaster chess players who play blitz chess almost as well as at regular slow time controls. Another example is doctors making quick diagnoses and treatment decisions in hospital emergency rooms.Unique, unusual cases require something different, however: application of first principles and guidelines, sometimes including analogies from other domains and creative thinking.

There is a strong link between a domain expert's expertise and the knowledge hierarchy. The characteristics of an expert include fast and accurate performance, explanation and justification of advice and reasoning, active learning, and formulation and application of first principles. First, principles and guidelines are used in unique and unfamiliar situations to guide the expert to a successful resolution. Ultimately, world-class domain experts develop comprehensive frameworks that include phenomena, theory, practice, and model comparisons.

Many cognitive frameworks have been suggested consisting of varying typologies and architectures[35,36,37] that may often share common reasoning schema:

- **Semantic:** Knowledge of basic concepts, their definition, attributes, values, and relationships

- **Classification:** Creating domain taxonomies, categorizing new data, and measuring similarities
- **Episodic:** Reasoning from experience, events, cases, and stereotypical events or scripts
- **Declarative:** Structural knowledge and relationships, heuristics, productions, and rules
- **Procedural:** Functional and behavioral knowledge, processes, and mental models
- **Meta/control:** Managing reasoning through failure/impasse detection, selection, attention, and activation.

In the next section, the power derived from the ability to represent tacit human cognitive frameworks and knowledge as explicit e-expertise in expert systems and knowledge repositories will become apparent.

ELECTRONIC EXPERTISE

Computer intelligence can be accomplished through several very different approaches:

- **Brute force search:** Examine all possibilities by generating and evaluating alternative futures
- **Connectionism:** Wet-ware brain functioning, neural networks, and distributed parallel processing
- **Expert systems:** Modeling human symbolic reasoning through cases, rules, networks, scripts, processes, and models
- **Knowledge repository:** Diverse knowledge sources and schema, with a blackboard architecture for control over reasoning—the society of mind[38] model.

The first approach, brute force search, was the original AI reasoning method. In this approach, a search space is defined in terms of a goal state, initial state, and rules of state transformation. Then, following domain rules of inference (e.g., logic for deduction or rules of chess), all possible alternatives are generated from the current state and evaluated in the allotted computing time. Raw computing power is used to examine millions of possibilities and alternatives to find the best outcome. Searches can start from either the initial or goal state and work forward or backward, respectively.

Deep Blue is the best known and most successful example of this approach. This chess program examines several million positions per second, can easily look at 16 half-moves in several minutes, and is flawless tactically—no wonder Gary Kasparov was worried. At present, human experts must first specify which features/parameters and relationships are important and how they interact before they are encoded into a program.

The second approach to cognition is connectionism, or neural networks. This is how our brains work at the lower levels of operation. In this approach, weights on links and nodes in the neural network are modified to learn the relative importance of features and relationships and to adapt to changing circumstances. Even here, human experts often specify which features should examined. The connectionist approach is not symbolic, but rather subsymbolic, because the relevant knowledge is contained in the relative weights of the nodes and their links and is distributed across regions of the network.

In the third approach, symbol-based expert systems model human expertise that is organized into narrow domains—disciplines, specialties, subjects, and competencies. Narrow domains are used because expertise often requires considerable commonsense reasoning and general world knowledge that are difficult for expert systems.

Expert systems have their own schema hierarchy within the larger explicit knowledge hierarchy:

Case → Rule → Network → Model

Expert system types are synonymous with the knowledge structure or memory schema, and their characteristics are summarized in Table 3.

Table 3. Expert System Characteristics

Type	*Inputs*	*Process*	*Outputs*
Case	Situation features	Finds and orders similar cases	Similar cases
Rule	Goal, situation features	Fires rules to draw assertions	Advice, solution
Network	Situation features	Activates best path through network	Advice, solution
Model	Goal, situation features	Applies logical or mathematical algorithm	Prediction, advice, solution

- **Case-based reasoning** is similar in structure to a relational table but also includes a case output (advice, conclusions) and outcome results. Also, case features can be weighted, and performance gracefully degrades when given incomplete inputs and conflicting results. Worked examples or cases are often used when less is known about a discipline or topic.

- **Rule-based systems** consist of many rules, each with the structure: If (all conditions are true) → Then (assert conclusions). Rules represent generalizations taken from countless cases that represent inference fragments or heuristics. A rule is fired when all its conditions are met.

- **Networks** have a spider web–type of structure with many links between nodes. Types of networks include semantic nets, symbolic neural nets, constraint reasoning, fuzzy logic, and Bayesian belief networks. Networks are more condensed and tightly coupled than rules.

- **Models** have tightly coupled structures and reasoning methods that are often unique to that domain. They may use mathematical, statistical, and logical reasoning methods such as system dynamics, formulas, processes, algorithms, and qualitative reasoning. Models are used when the domain is highly understood, structured, and regular or predictable. Models are often used for monitoring, simulation, and forecasting tasks.

To create an expert system, knowledge engineers determine which knowledge representation schema—cases, rules, networks, or models—are used by experts in their domain. Then explicit knowledge is collected, and implicit/tacit knowledge is elicited and organized through special interview and observation techniques, such as object modeling[39] and protocol analysis.[40] A mapping is made between the expert's internal knowledge representation and the symbols, variables, and relationships; measures of uncertainty and importance; and reasoning methods found in expert system schema. There are many examples of successful expert systems across many disciplines, industries, and generic tasks. In general, expert systems learn by external means of adding or modifying cases, rules, networks, or objects, or adjusting the uncertainty and importance measures.

Table 4 presents a rough correspondence between human cognitive schema and types of expert systems.

Table 4. Correspondence between Human and Computer Reasoning

Cognitive Schema	*Expert System Type*
Semantic	Networks: semantic, decision
Classification	Object, neural network, case-based reasoning (CBR)
Episodic	CBR, scripts
Declarative	Rule-based systems
Procedural	Model-based systems
Meta/control	Object, blackboard architecture

A discussion of the fourth approach, knowledge repository, is presented in a later section of this chapter. Knowledge repositories and related integrated performance support systems are the critical software artifacts that fuse knowledge and technology to apply expertise, knowledge, and experience in practical contexts that support and enable user tasks and goals.

INTEGRATING EXPERTISE

It is important to understand the strengths of computers and humans and how they can be complementary. There are great synergies to be gained from integrating human and electronic knowledge. Fortunately, computer strengths often can offset human weaknesses; the reverse is also true. In fact, the most effective KM strategy integrates complementary strengths from human and electronic reasoning to create a valuable synergy. An organization can start with existing explicit knowledge and determine what knowledge should be automated next.

Human Strengths:

- Goal setting
- Valuing attribute importance
- Context setting
- Commonsense reasoning
- General world knowledge
- Reasoning by analogy
- Learning
- Creativity and synthesis
- Generalizing
- Naming and categorizing.

Computer Strengths:

- Speed of computing and communication
- Accuracy of computing and communication
- Consistency of computing and communication
- Parallel processing
- Explicit knowledge representation
- Explicit algorithms for reasoning
- Distributing knowledge to subscribers
- Storing and retrieving knowledge
- Communicating between computers
- Accessibility of computing and communication
- Searching large lists (Websites) and databases.

The Cyc AI project[41] attempted to make reasonable inferences that a normal human could make by using only the knowledge found in a one-volume encyclopedia. They found that more than 20 different knowledge structures and algorithms are involved in commonsense reasoning and that humans know thousands of general facts and heuristics.

USER CHARACTERISTICS

User characteristics and preferences are considered after the content domain has been selected and structured.[42]

- **Purpose of request:**
  —Request types: information, browsing/research, analysis, learning, and certification

—Ask user

—Induce from request and user history.

- **User history/profile:**

—Keep record by domain, topic, and request type

—Retain transaction log of frequently visited topics

—Date log

—Help predict future user needs.

- **User proficiency—level of domain knowledge:**

—Ask user

—Induce from employee profile

—Induce from user history.

- **Organizational knowledge and task context:**

—Who is the final customer for the request?

—Organizational culture, values and beliefs, behaviors

—Organizational practices and policies.

- **Domain content:**

—Amount of knowledge required: is it one fact, one topic, or an entire domain for skill development?

—Navigation through system

—Knowledge source types desired/required.

- **Presentation preferences:**

  —Simple or complex

  —Amount of information on screen

  —Display of available options

- **User feedback:**

  —Solicit user satisfaction and feedback through a survey

  —System can modify its behavior for each user based on complaints and suggestions

  —Improve content selection and selectivity.

MAPPING USER NEEDS AND ABILITIES TO AVAILABLE KNOWLEDGE SOURCES

Using the knowledge architecture as a framework, existing organizational and personal knowledge and skills, as well as all explicit knowledge, can be mapped. Next, similar mappings for present and future needs are constructed. Any knowledge gaps that are uncovered can be remedied as follows:

- Provide targeted training and practice in deficiencies
- Encourage, recognize, and reward desired behaviors, learning, and improvement by the workforce
- Reorganize existing staff around needed skill sets
- Hire new employees with needed expertise
- Contract vendor to provide needed expertise and transfer knowledge and skills to organization

- Develop knowledge repositories, integrated performance support systems (IPSS), and intelligent tutoring systems to support and enable the workforce.

KM TECHNOLOGIES

KM also encompasses a wide range of technologies that include:

- **Web technologies:** including enterprise portals, XML/metadata tagging, intelligent search, e-commerce, content management, record management, archiving, and backup
- **Training:** including e-learning, distance training, multimedia, and intelligent tutoring systems
- **Communication:** including document management, collaboration, groupware, and directed creativity technologies
- **Systems:** case management, workflow management, and integrated performance support
- **AI:** including expert systems, machine learning, text generation, and natural language
- **Advice:** including FAQ and auto-help desk
- **Knowledge repository**
- **Knowledge discovery:** including data warehousing, data mining, text mining, and knowledge visualization.

To date, many applications have been developed to meet specific KM needs of various user communities. However, no integrated toolkits or technology frameworks have been developed and implemented in practice, although several conceptual models have been proposed. Recently software tools have been developed to support a variety of business needs, including corporate memory, fraud detection, measurement systems reporting and analysis, knowledge access, content analysis and organization, communities of practice, performance support systems, distance learning, automated help desks, e-mail analysis, and intelligent search.

WEB TECHNOLOGIES

Web technologies are the essential core component to nearly all KM efforts. Enterprise Web portal sites provide a universal gateway to explicit knowledge, an organizing focal point for knowledge, navigation and research tools, and links to Internet resources. Web portals provide easy access to the underlying knowledge repositories. Portal benefits also include providing knowledge resources that are well organized and structured and providing users with corporate and application server pages, e-business, and document services. Enterprise Web portals should include some or all of the following functions:

- **Website:** including portal, navigation, search engine, site taxonomy, and hypertext links
- **Directories:** including expertise, resources, interest/subscription, and colleagues/communities of practice
- **Information and knowledge:** including policies, procedures, articles, databases, and Web links
- **Training:** including online courses and course administration
- **Interaction:** including discussion forums, course alumni, and communities of practice and interest
- **Advice:** including help desks, FAQ, performance support system, process simulation, and communities of practice
- **Current events:** including conferences, forums, course announcements, news, and hot topics

- **User response:** including evaluation, feedback, contribution, and surveys

- **Project management:** including program framework and progress monitoring.

XML provides superior description and handling of metadata tagging—document structure, semantics, and style—in typing objects and creating taxonomies for Web pages. XML also supports e-commerce by providing business-to-business (B2B) information exchange and content management by structuring and typing content and by delivering dynamic content.

Advanced search engines, such as google.com, can greatly improve navigation and search relevancy through techniques such as linguistic inference, conceptual hierarchies, user profiling, and user feedback. Finally, content management software provides functions for authoring and loading content and structure, workflow management, version and configuration management, auditing, managing links, publishing, and personalization that support e-business.

INTRANET WEBSITE FUNCTIONS

An enterprise portal to an intranet Website can have the following components and functions:

- **Website:** including portal, navigation, search engine, site taxonomy, and hypertext links

- **Directories:** including expertise, resources, interest and subscription, colleagues, and communities of practice

- **Content:** including policies, procedures, articles, databases, and web links

- **Training:** including on-line courses and course administration

- **Interaction:** including discussion forums and communities of practice
- **Advice:** including help desks, FAQ, performance support system, process simulation, and communities of practice
- **Current events:** including conferences, forums, course announcements, news, hot topics, and events
- **User response:** including evaluation, feedback, contribution, and surveys
- **Project management:** including program framework, collaboration, and progress monitoring.

COLLABORATION TECHNOLOGIES

A number of collaboration technologies add value through knowledge creation and sharing. These include:

- Document review and management
- Discussion forums
- Directories of expertise and interest
- Communities of practice
- Groupware and directed creativity
- Virtual project team.

The results of the interactions and collaborations are edited, summarized, and then added to the knowledge repository in forms such as worked cases and threaded discussions.

E-LEARNING

KM training software focuses on e-learning, also called distance learning or distance training. E-learning includes components for subject matter expert (SME) authoring, course and module content, teaching methods, discussion groups, and learning management systems. E-learning converts knowledge into learning modules by:

- Archiving synchronous class sessions
- Creating virtual team rooms
- Mentoring or coaching facilities
- Selecting and editing the best of discussion forums
- Applying learning methods.

Ideally, course authors would like to be able to take existing knowledge chunks from a knowledge repository and impart the knowledge by applying selected teaching methods. One might imagine an instructor deciding on several of the following methods based on criteria such as conceptual-concrete continuum, user learning styles, and the type of knowledge to be taught:

- Concepts and definitions
- Theoretical framework
- Literature review
- Examples
- Case studies
- Exercises and practice
- Simulations

- Tests, including pretests, quizzes, and post-tests
- Class contributions and discussions
- Research projects.

The Instructional Management System Global Learning Consortium defines course modules as learning objects that allow authors to mix and match pieces to assemble new courses, easily customize existing courses, reuse course modules, post their instructional content, and receive royalties for their use.

INTELLIGENT TUTORING SYSTEMS

Intelligent tutoring systems (ITSs) are interactive teaching and learning tools that use expert systems to teach subjects on a cognitive level. ITSs provide customized instruction through monitoring user responses and feedback and dynamically adjusting content and teaching methods. ITSs are advanced e-learning systems that consist of the following modules:[43]

- **Domain expertise**, which is accessed from the knowledge repository
- **Student model**, which tracks progress and diagnoses errors and misconceptions
- **Teaching expertise**, which includes methods of teaching, learning, correcting errors, and testing
- **Interface**, which presents material in varying formats depending on student preferences and proficiency.

Examples of ITS capabilities include but are not limited to:

- Teach domain concepts and relationships (models)
- Demonstrate execution of procedures or making decisions (rules)

- Explain and justify method and results (rules or decision trees, and text generation)
- Select worked examples and practice exercises (cases)
- Simulate processes and forecast outcomes (models)
- Test and certify workforce levels of proficiency (all).

KNOWLEDGE REPOSITORY

A knowledge repository[44] organizes and stores data, information, knowledge, expertise, and experience for one domain. The repository is an electronic memory and expert that has access to a number of knowledge sources in a variety of representations. It uses a blackboard architecture to query, manage, summarize, and integrate results from available knowledge sources. Repositories support and enable IPSS, intelligent tutoring systems, and knowledge discovery. Technologies and schema included are:

- **Object framework**, including a hierarchy of objects, entities, concepts possessing attributes, values, and links
- **Non-symbolic**, including images, video, speech, and signals
- **Text**, including raw, hypertext, organized by topic, and document type
- **Data**, including raw facts, facts in context, and form templates
- **Databases**, including object, relational, network, hierarchical, and flat
- **Expert systems**, including cases, rules, networks (semantic, causal, constraint), processes, scripts, and models
- **Attribute link**, including importance and uncertainty weights

- **Machine learning**, including induction, genetic algorithms, neural nets, explanation-based learning, statistical methods, case-based reasoning, as well as text and data mining
- **Intelligent tutoring systems,** IPSS, and knowledge discovery.

When a blackboard architecture is used as a meta-controller, a knowledge repository[45,46] can represent knowledge of various schema organized using object methods.

INTEGRATED PERFORMANCE SUPPORT SYSTEMS

IPSS access knowledge and expertise from the knowledge repository in support of user tasks. IPSS consider the totality of user needs by providing extensive services that can include (after Winslow and Bramer[47]):

- Infrastructure
- Controller
- Navigation
- Presentation
- Acquisition
- Advisory
- Instruction
- Learning
- Evaluation
- Reference.

Table 5 lists technologies often employed by IPSS.[48]

Table 5. Technologies Employed by IPSS

Service	*Activity Description*
Advice	• Problem solving, decision making, coaching, reminders, alerts
Tools	• Job aid, smart forms, help • Messaging
Reference and research	• Policies, procedures, process maps • Expert/expertise directories, Internet
Tutoring and training	• Intelligent tutoring • Theory (principles, methods, and guidelines) • Practice (case studies, exercises, simulations)
Testing and certification	• Dynamic pre-tests and post-tests • Knowledge and proficiency testing • Levels of expertise certification
Workforce profile	• Work responsibilities, interests • Career goals, expertise, training • Certifications
Workload management	• Workforce availability, performance, interest, developmental assignments, work classification, scheduling, assignment
Process management	• Modeling, monitoring, measurement, assessment, feedback, improvement
Systems control	• Interface, navigation, presentation • Customization, coordination services

SYSTEM-GENERATED ACTIONS

The knowledge repository in concert with the IPSS can proactively generate a number of user actions:

User Action Confirmations and Suggestions:

- Knowledge subscriptions:
  - —Users may sign up to receive information and knowledge on selected topics.

—Information and knowledge will be mailed directly to subscribers based on interest and expertise.

—Users can specify which knowledge sources/media are desired (e.g., no video clips).

—The system must keep track of what knowledge items have been sent to avoid duplication.

- Proactive intervention:

  —The system may actively intervene if it believes that the user is making or is about to make an error.

  —The system may also intervene with suggestions.

  —The system would intervene in tutorial mode.

  —Levels of proactive intervention would vary depending on user expertise (e.g., novices might experience many more interventions).

  —The system may induce the likelihood of error from request, expertise, and user history.

  —For tutorials, it may induce the likelihood of error, based on student, and suggest repair.

  —User can disable or customize proactive intervention.

Usage/Activity Reports:

- Maintain domain and topic site counts.
- Analyze users and relevant sites for activity: what knowledge is considered valuable?
- Query users about failure to use the repository.

Smart Search:

- User purpose and context
- Domain conceptual hierarchy
- Format <task object>
- What to do if too few hits
- What to do if too many hits.

KNOWLEDGE DISCOVERY

Knowledge discovery (KD) is the process of identifying valid, novel, potentially useful, and ultimately understandable patterns in data and text. KD involves a new generation of techniques and tools to assist humans intelligently and interactively in analyzing mountains of data and text for nuggets of useful knowledge. To analyze data and text, there must be underlying sources of knowledge such as data warehouses, document text bases, and knowledge repositories. The KD process entails five steps:[49]

1. Selection
2. Preprocessing
3. Transformation
4. Data mining
5. Interpretation/evaluation.

Data mining involves the application of algorithms for extracting patterns from data without further processing or human intervention. Text mining involves using conceptual hierarchies to extract semantically relevant information from document repositories. Visual knowledge exploration involves building graphical representations of the structure, process, and organization of available knowledge so users can explore content to satisfy their needs and preferences. Visual exploration is applied during the selection, preprocessing, and interpretation steps.

Promising business applications for knowledge discovery include:

- Business intelligence
- Marketing and sales
- Enforcement, including fraud detection and collection target identification
- Automated dynamic workload assignment and management
- Dynamic skill-based call routing and management
- Customer profiling and segmenting
- Trend detection in MIS measurement systems
- Process improvement.

Once significant patterns are detected, the results should be added into the knowledge repository and related decision support systems.

EVOLUTIONARY PATH FOR KM APPLICATIONS

Given the breadth of potentially useful technologies, some advice is in order regarding prioritizing potential KM applications. A suggested evolutionary path is presented in Table 6. Creating a Website or adding content to an existing site can be an efficient platform for storing and sharing knowledge.

Table 6. An Evolutionary Path for KM Applications

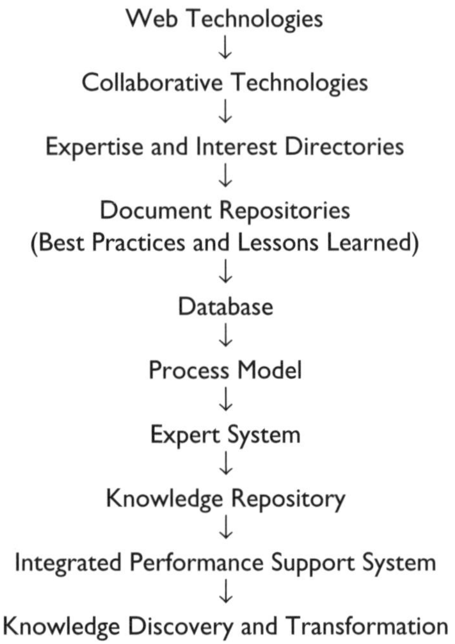

Web Technologies
↓
Collaborative Technologies
↓
Expertise and Interest Directories
↓
Document Repositories
(Best Practices and Lessons Learned)
↓
Database
↓
Process Model
↓
Expert System
↓
Knowledge Repository
↓
Integrated Performance Support System
↓
Knowledge Discovery and Transformation

CONCLUSIONS

I believe that the case has been made for gaining significant potential business value by fusing explicit knowledge and innovative IT. Existing knowledge, in the form of directories, tables, charts, documents, manuals, procedures, forms, journals, and texts, is collected, refined, and organized into coherent domains and knowledge repositories. Implicit knowledge is made explicit in forms such as those listed above through querying practitioners, reflection, and observation of organizational structures, processes, social interactions, and culture. Specialized elicitation and observation techniques, such as conceptual hierarchy classification and verbal protocols,[50] convert tacit knowledge found in the minds of experts and senior practitioners into explicit, formal knowledge. New knowledge is discovered through communities of practice discussions, lessons learned, best practices research, environmental scanning, and state-of-the-art conferences and seminars. New knowledge is created through basic research, experimentation, analysis, data and text mining, reflection, and directed creativity.

The value of existing knowledge can be greatly increased in several ways. First, make as much knowledge as possible explicit and place it in electronic form on a Web portal. Second, organize and structure knowledge around coherent content domains. Third, transform knowledge from a lower to a higher level in the knowledge hierarchy—for example, by organizing and structuring data into information. Another example would be to transform cases into a rule-based or network-based system through machine learning induction. Finally, organize all types of knowledge about a domain into a knowledge repository.

I am not naïve enough to believe that simply demonstrating the benefits of this explicit knowledge approach will make it happen. In fact, the most difficult obstacles to implementing, using, and realizing business value are not technical ones, but rather cultural and social ones. However, I do believe that developing easily accessible sources of explicit knowledge can help break down the bureaucratic and functional barriers that restrict the sharing and free flow of knowledge in an organization.

NOTES

1. Wenger, E. *Communities of Practice: Learning, Meaning, and Identity.* Cambridge: Cambridge University Press, 1999.

2. Stewart, T. *Intellectual Capital: The New Wealth of Organizations.* New York: Bantam Books, 1998.

3. Schreiber, D. and Z. Berge (eds.). *Distance Training: How Innovative Organizations Are Using Technology to Maximize Learning and Meet Business Objectives.* San Francisco: Jossey-Bass, 1998.

4. Beckman, T. "Meta-Knowledge and Other Knowledge Dimensions: A Unified Framework for Explicit Knowledge." In *Proceedings from the 3rd AI and Soft Computing Conference.* Calgary, Canada: IASTED, 2000.

5. Graham, I. *Object Oriented Methods.* New York: Addison-Wesley, 1991.

6. Refer to note 4.

7. Liebowitz, J. and T. Beckman. *Knowledge Organizations: What Every Manager Should Know.* Boca Raton: St. Lucie Press, 1998.

8. Beckman, T. "Applying AI and KM Concepts in Designing Web Sites." *Proceedings from the 3rd AI and Soft Computing Conference.* Calgary, Canada: IASTED, 2000.

9. Refer to note 7.

10. Refer to Note 8.

11. Woolf, H. (ed.). *Webster's New World Dictionary of the American Language.* Springfield, MA: G. and C. Merriam, 1990.

12. Turban, E. *Expert Systems and Applied Artificial Intelligence.* New York: Macmillan, 1992.

13. Sowa, J. *Conceptual Structures.* New York: Addison-Wesley, 1984.

14. Wiig, K. *Knowledge Management Foundation.* Arlington, TX: Schema Press, 1993.

15. van der Spek, R. and A. Spijkervet. "KM: Dealing Intelligently with Knowledge." *Knowledge Management and Its Integrative Elements.* Page 36. Liebowitz & Wilcox (ed.). Boca Raton: CRC Press, 1997.

16. Hayes-Roth, F., D. Waterman, and D. Lenat. *Building Expert Systems.* New York: Addison Wesley, 1983.

17. Refer to note 4.

18. Refer to note 3.

19. Beckman, T. *Applying AI to Business Reengineering.* Seoul, Korea: Third World Congress on Expert Systems, 1996.

20. Nielsen, J. *Designing Web Usability: The Practice of Simplicity.* Indianapolis: New Riders Publishing, 2000.

21. Nonaka, I. and H. Takeuchi. *The Knowledge-Creating Company: How Japanese Companies Create the Dynamics of Innovation.* New York: Oxford University Press, 1995.

22. Refer to note 7.

23. McGraw, K. and K. Harbison-Briggs. *Knowledge Acquisition: Principles and Guidelines.* New York: Prentice Hall, 1989.

24. Refer to note 23.

25. Collins, H. "Human, Machines, and the Structure of Knowledge." Ruggles, R. (ed.). *Knowledge Management Tools*. Boston: Butterworth-Heinemann, 1997.

26. Refer to note 23.

27. Beckman, T. *The Role of Attention, Motivation, and Emotion in Cognition*. MIT Masters Thesis, 1986.

28. Minsky, M. *Society of Mind*. New York: Simon and Schuster, 1986.

29. Parsaye, K. and M. Chignell. *Expert Systems for Experts*. New York: John Wiley and Sons, 1988.

30. Refer to note 4.

31. Refer to note 5.

32. Alter, S. *Information Systems: A Management Perspective, 2nd ed.* Menlo Park: Benjamin/Cummings Publishing, 1996.

33. Ackoff, R. *The Democratic Corporation*. 1994.

34. Allee, V. *The Knowledge Evolution: Expanding Organizational Intelligence*. San Francisco: Butterworth-Heinemann, 1997.

35. Refer to note 27.

36. Refer to note 28.

37. Refer to note 8.

38. Refer to note 28.

39. Refer to note 5.

40. Refer to note 23.

41. Lenat, D. and R. Guha. *Building Large-Scale Knowledge-Based Systems: Representation and Inference in the Cyc Project*. New York: Addison-Wesley, 1990.

42. Refer to note 8.

43. Burns, H., J. Parlett, and C. Redfield (eds.). *Intelligent Tutoring Systems: Evolutions in Design*. Hillsdale NJ: Lawrence Erlbaum Associates, 1991.

44. Refer to note 7.

45. Refer to note 7.

46. Beckman, T. *Knowledge Management Seminar.* Monterrey, Mexico: ITESM. 1998.

47. Winslow, C. and W. Bramer. *Future Work: Putting Knowledge to Work in the Knowledge Economy.* New York: Free Press, 1994.

48. Refer to note 46.

49. Fayyad, U. et al. (ed.). *Advances in Knowledge Discovery and Data Mining.* Cambridge MA: AAAI/MIT Press, 1996.

50. Refer to note 23.

PART II

Setting the Stage for Electronic Government

In Part I, we provided an introductory framework for knowledge management, including a positioning and a historical perspective. In this section the intent is to address the management and policy aspects of knowledge management that are preludes or foundations for electronic government. Some of these topics deal with issues such as: managing change in the knowledge world, organizational readiness for knowledge management, and the people aspects of knowledge management.

This book advances the proposition that knowledge management is the catalyst for electronic government. Hence, it is important to introduce electronic government, a topic that is still far from clear in most people's minds. Leo, Alexander, and Kieffer provide some direction and clarity in "Setting the Stage for Electronic Government." Joe Leo is the CIO of the U.S. Department of Agriculture and a long-time actor and observer of the e-gov phenomenon; Mike Alexander and Stu Kieffer are colleagues in USDA's Office of the CIO.

Not all organizations are automatically ready to implement and take advantage of knowledge management environments. Moonja Kim, from the U.S. Army Engineer Research and Development Center, leads us in analyzing some of the important questions surrounding readiness in her chapter, "Organizational Readiness for Knowledge Management."

The interaction between IT and KM is a much-discussed topic. There are many issues surrounding the assignment of responsibilities between these two major functions and their leadership. Should the CKO report to the CIO? Should the CIO report to the CKO? Who should handle what responsibilities? These are the questions jumping out of the current debate. Shereen Remez, former CKO of the U.S. General Services Administration, and the third of our book's co-editors, takes aim at some of these issues, together with Jon Desenberg, Knowledge Manager, GSA, in their chapter, "Information Technology and Knowledge Management: The Medium and the Message."

Given that knowledge resides primarily in some person's brain, knowledge management must be inexorably tied to human beings. In this context, "HR Knowledge Crafting: The FAA Net Fusion Model," by Bob Turner, Director, FAA Team Technology Center, does a good job of linking the two together.

Then Shereen Remez, the first CKO in the federal government, takes her turn at arranging the stepping stones between knowledge management and electronic government in her chapter, "KM and E-Gov: Can We Have One without the Other?"

We are reminded by Elias Safdie, President of Cordis, that it's quite probable that the "laws of planetary motion were known to the ancient Greeks, but that the followers of Pythagoras, for religious reasons, suppressed that knowledge and prevented its codification and dissemination. As a result, that knowledge was lost to humanity for several thousand years." This is an interesting way to engage the reader in what is clearly going to be one of the most significant aspects of e-government—managing knowledge embedded in our documents; he addresses this in "Knowledge Management and Document Management in the Public Sector."

The last chapter in this section is by Michael Stankosky and Carolyn Baldanza, from George Washington University's Cyberspace Policy Institute. They attempt to show, in "A Systems

Approach to Engineering a Knowledge Management System," how systems thinking, a systems perspective, and proven systems engineering best practices ensure successful design and implementation of a knowledge management system.

CHAPTER 4

Setting the Stage for Electronic Government

Joseph Leo
Michael Alexander
Stuart Kieffer

Electronic government, or e-government, follows on the heels of the reinventing government movement as the latest moniker for revolutionizing the delivery of public services. In large part spawned by the explosion in information technology, the Internet, and the resulting new "digital economy," many observers believe e-government will ultimately produce change far beyond the magnitude of that generated by earlier transformations. Some governments, such as Singapore and Australia, are early adapters. In the United States, however, many federal, state, and local leaders are still struggling to understand the basic implications of e-government and even to come up with a definition that adequately describes its numerous possibilities.

Policy makers, managers, and officials at all levels face the challenge of surveying the e-government landscape, defining what it means, analyzing what is taking place, and using that information to make decisions that are in the best interests of the citizens that they serve.

This chapter focuses on what the vision of e-government means, explains why e-government is a rising item on many government leaders' agendas, and attempts to synthesize the numerous and often conflicting challenges government leaders face in developing a framework for creating and executing an e-government strategy.

We view the challenge of e-government from four distinct, yet highly interrelated, perspectives: programmatic, organizational, technical, and funding/resources. Within each of these four arenas, barriers as well as opportunities for success abound. We touch on common knowledge management (KM) strategies, such as thinking "horizontally" across organizations to search for "natural complexes" where similar services are now delivered by disparate agents.[1] Our primary experience and, therefore, bias is federal. Yet, we believe these ideas extend to all government levels.

A FUZZY VISION OF "CITIZEN-CENTRIC" ELECTRONIC GOVERNMENT

E-government encompasses online government-to-citizen information sharing and transactions, as well as government-to-business, government-to-government, and government-to-employee transactions. While e-government also includes online voting and similar "digital democracy"–related initiatives that will one day revolutionize public participation in politics and governance, such topics are beyond the scope of this chapter. In this discussion, e-government is about using enabling technology to share information and knowledge so that government may deliver reengineered services that are content-rich, convenient, and efficient, thereby reducing the burden (paper, time, travel, training, costs, etc.) on customers, suppliers, and employees.

As popularly envisioned, e-government is citizen-centric: Information and services that are now delivered by autonomous departments, agencies, and even smaller units of government are realigned so that government customers need not be overly concerned with which agency is the provider nor which level of government (i.e., federal, state, or local) is furnishing that information or service. Our future envisions citizens interacting with government through integrated electronic interfaces—or portals—and any coordination or information sharing between agencies necessary to complete transactions will occur behind the scenes, made possible by interoperable information systems. For the citizen, government becomes a virtual "one-stop shop."

Today, governments require citizens to navigate through a complex and often bewildering maze of separate departments, agencies, and offices to receive services. In the future, citizens will no longer need to provide the same information to more than one agency or to go from agency to agency across various levels of government to complete paper-based processes related to the same service (e.g., to fill out and file the numerous applications required to open and operate a business).

Citizens encountering e-government will eventually access programs and services organized primarily along the lines of what might best be described as "natural complexes." For example, citizens concerned about food safety will be able to access all the information they need, and businesses will be able to conduct all their related transactions from one online location, even though there are currently some twelve federal agencies and every state—all part of a "natural complex"—involved in ensuring the safety of our food supply. Already, citizens interested in recreational opportunities on federal lands can visit one site (www.recreation.gov) to inspect resources and make reservations on parks managed by at least eight federal agencies.

One day, state and local recreational opportunities will be available via this "one-stop-shop" as well. Citizens interested in government grants can visit fedcommons.gov and, eventually, will be able to apply online for any grant at any agency.

The portal FirstGov.gov, announced in June 2000 by the Administration, is clearly the most ambitious effort yet to create a one-stop online shop for the entire federal government (see Figure 1). The site enables citizens to search the full text of every government web page currently on the Internet—estimated to be between 50 and 100 million pages at the time of the announcement. The site aggregates access to sites, such as recreation.gov, fedcommons.gov, and others, including all federal procurement opportunities above $25,000.

When the site is fully operational, information critical to farmers from, for example, the Commerce Department, the National

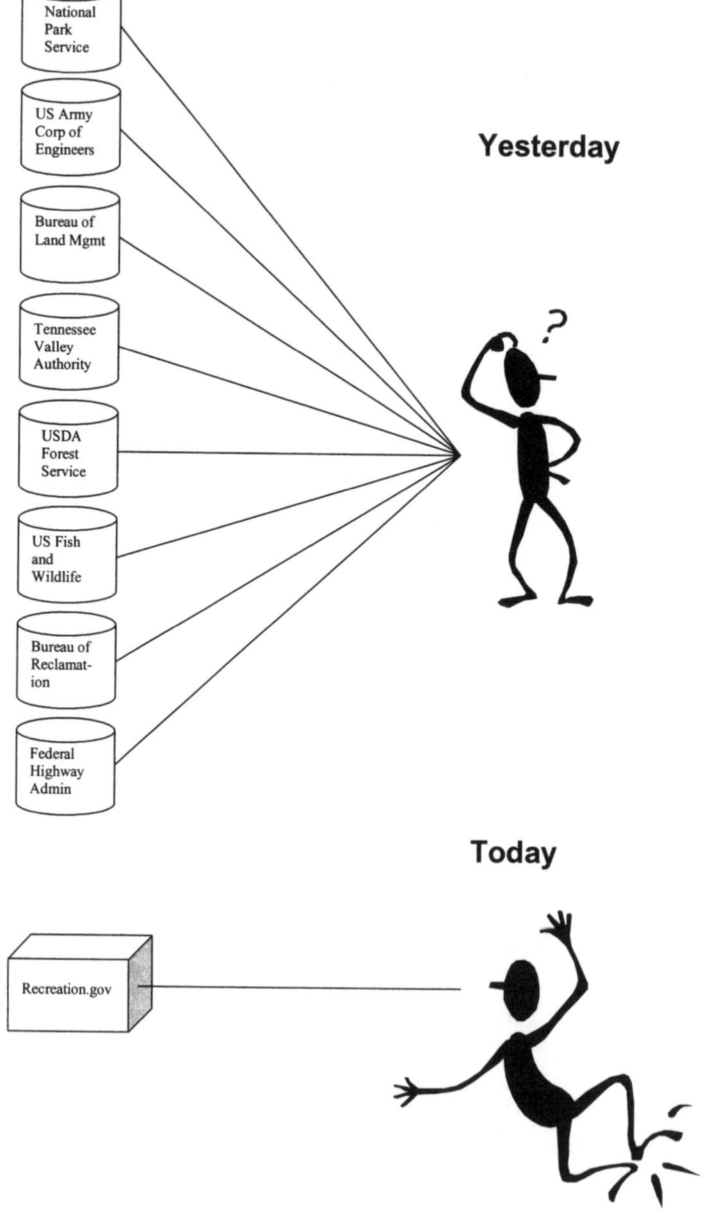

Figure 1. One-Stop Online Shop for the Federal Government

Weather Service, the Labor Department, and of course, the Department of Agriculture, will also be easily accessible through a single online location—an important step toward organizing government by services rather than by agencies. Another administration initiative (pay.gov), developed by the Treasury's Financial Management Service Electronic Money Program Office, will allow citizens, businesses, and federal agencies to process some two trillion dollars in annual transactions, such as government collections of fees, fines, sales, leases, loans, and certain taxes, on the Internet.

In the distant future, e-government will enable citizens to serve themselves via secure electronic transactions with the government 24 hours a day, seven days a week, 365 days a year, with instantaneous response times. This will be a profound change from traditional government service models, which are based mostly on personal interaction between customers and government employees, 9 a.m. to 5 p.m., five days a week, often with response times of weeks, if not months. However, developing the kind of "expert systems" required for *complete* online self-service will be difficult to achieve. For that reason, governments will still require extensive human interaction, or human-ware, to support citizens as they enter the new world of cyber-services. In any event, those citizens conducting business with governments at all levels will spend more time online, and much less time, if any, waiting in line.

For some time to come, many citizens will continue to conduct business using traditional means, especially those who are on the wrong side of the "digital divide"—the gulf between citizens and even businesses who have access to and know how to use the Internet and other information technology and those who do not. All governments will be challenged with maintaining legacy systems, and they will be forced to operate parallel processes online and off for many services.

As the title of this book suggests, the vision of e-government is closely related to and directly depends on knowledge management (KM). Broadly defined, KM is about managing information resources, including intellectual assets, so that citizens, businesses, policy makers, researchers, government employees, and other government stakeholders can readily access the specific information they need, when they need it, and where they need it, irrespective of which agency owns the information. Access to information is no longer restricted or limited by which department, agency, individual, or other entity captures it; rather, information is managed from the perspective of the user. KM is the basic foundation of e-government. As leaders think about how to transform their agencies' delivery systems, they must first assess who needs what information, determine which entities possess it, and integrate their information systems and processes as necessary to deliver the services. This must be accomplished while ensuring confidentiality of information, protecting citizens' privacy, and securing information systems from hackers and other online predators.

WHY E-GOVERNMENT? WHY NOW?

The trend toward e-government, similar to e-commerce and e-business in the private sector, is being driven in large part by the rapid pace of technological change and resulting enhancements in corporate productivity, especially efficiencies generated by use of the Internet to link computer networks across the globe. According to *Nua Internet Surveys*, Internet access is growing significantly in all regions of the world, rising from 171 million people in March 1999 to approximately 333 million in June 2000, an increase of 95 percent (see Table 1). For the United States and Canada it has grown from 97 to 147.5 million people during the same time period, an increase of 52 percent. The Commerce Department notes that while Canada and the United States still account for a large proportion of worldwide users, the rest of the world is catching up fast. While Internet access in the United States and Canada grew by more than 40 percent in the last year, Internet access in the rest of the world more than doubled during the same time period.[2]

Table 1. World Internet Access—June 2000

World Total	332.73 million
Africa	2.77 million
Asia/Pacific	75.5 million
Europe	91.82 million
Middle East	1.90 million
Canada and USA	147.48 million
Latin America	13.19 million

Source: Nua Internet Surveys

According to the industry standard, forecasts for the dollar value of "business to business" (B2B) transactions in 2003 range from $634 billion to $2.8 trillion. The Commerce Department notes that all market researchers predict that B2B e-commerce will continue to experience strong growth as companies streamline business processes and increase efficiencies, with the goal of cutting costs.[3]

Federal Reserve Board Chairman Alan Greenspan has attributed much of today's unprecedented economic growth to the impact of information technology (IT) on enhanced productivity. Well-documented increases in efficiency and cost savings due to the Internet and other IT are placing tremendous pressure on all organizations to respond or risk being swept aside by competitors who can deliver more timely, convenient, higher-quality services at dramatically less cost. One consulting firm estimates that conducting certain transactions online that now take place in person or over the phone could save governments as much as 70 percent in paper and labor costs *for each transaction.* Clearly, governments, often with mandates to do more with fewer resources, cannot afford to forgo the improved services and long-term savings to be had from becoming e-governments.

Many private sector companies face stark realities: either adapt to the Internet or risk falling behind to competitors who do. Governments typically operate without the same competitive pressures as the private sector. However, at the state level, e-government is already emerging as a competitive advantage in attracting and keeping business. How long can it be before corporate decisions at the national and international level are based in part on their capacity to conduct business electronically with e-governments?

Leaders of e-government must transform their business processes; however, they must also ensure that communities, local businesses, schools, hospitals, and other constituents have access to the broadband technologies on which so much of the future increasingly will depend. Broadband (or high-speed) Internet access, still in short supply in homes and especially in many rural areas, has become a necessity for localities to attract and retain companies and technology-savvy workers. Communities, like citizens, who are on the wrong side of the digital divide face crippling isolation from a global marketplace that is increasingly being fueled by the flow of large amounts of all kinds of data at ever-increasing rates of speed. Governments, businesses, and individual citizens alike have much to lose; without high-speed Internet access, companies cannot participate in "electronic marketplaces," which are emerging in industry after industry. For example, customers will not order products from local businesses if they have to wait more than two seconds for web pages to download. Students will not be able to easily access online lectures by leading professors from any university in the world. Without broadband access, communities simply will not be competitive.

While federal, state, and local governments' responses to the Internet and the IT revolution are mixed, the political signals are clear. Farsighted federal, state, and local e-government leaders are already touting the benefits to the electorate, as did major party candidates in the 2000 presidential election who included e-government as part of their agendas. Politicians in states such as Virginia, Georgia, Washington, and Arizona are already claiming credit for saving tax dollars while providing citizens and businesses far more efficient and convenient services over the Internet. The sense of urgency has increased for others to do the same.

One of many examples of the cost savings to be had by Web-enabling processes is provided by the state of Arizona, where a Website designed to process motor vehicle registrations has reduced processing costs from $6.60 to $1.60. This has saved the state some $1.7 million per year, with only 15 percent of renewals processed electronically. The state is using the extra resources to improve offline processes.[4]

In the private sector, networking giants Cisco Systems, Oracle, Dell, and many other businesses have documented millions of dollars in savings from Web-enabling their extensive internal and external processes, customer relations, and supply chains. Having invested up front in the necessary technology and totally revised their business processes, these companies have claimed as much as 20 percent annual savings by putting their supply chains on the Web—an amount that would equal some $110 billion per year if applied to government services across the United States.[5] With those kinds of possibilities, the imperative for e-government becomes clear.

As the Internet is fast becoming a mainstream way for citizens to conduct business with the private sector, pressure is increasing on public sector organizations to provide the same quality of service. Citizens' confidence in governments will surely erode where government continues to lag badly behind the private sector in delivering services through the Internet. Indeed, across the country literally a thousand flowers (or e-government applications)—and some weeds—are now blooming. Yet they are mostly at the level of individual agencies or units within agencies, uncoordinated by theme, technology, approach, or purpose. In many cases, agencies have simply Web-enabled existing ways of doing business; the process of actually using the Internet to reengineer programs and services, and fundamentally change the way the business of government is conducted, has barely begun.

LEGISLATIVE AND EXECUTIVE MANDATES, LEGAL HURDLES

At the federal level, Congress is starting to pay attention. In 1998 Congress passed and the President signed the Government Paperwork Elimination Act (GPEA), which by October 1, 2003, requires all federal agencies to provide individuals or entities that deal with agencies the option to submit information or transact business with the agency electronically and to maintain records electronically, when practicable. GPEA (Public Law 105-277) also provides that electronic records and their related signatures are not to be denied legal effect, validity, or enforceability merely because they are in electronic form. It also encourages agencies to use a range of electronic signature alternatives.

The Government Paperwork Elimination Act

Agencies must provide:
- E-Forms as ***Alternatives*** to paper,
- E-Signatures to ***Authenticate*** sender, and
- E-Receipts to ***Acknowledge*** successful submission.

Guidance also requires:
- Evaluation of customer/user needs,
- Risk assessment of proposed technology, and
- Implementation by **October 1, 2003.**

Source: GSA Office of Governmentwide Policy

Guidance issued in August 2000 by the Office of Management and Budget (OMB) requires that agencies' plans for GPEA address transactions that collect information under the Paperwork Reduction Act (PRA), non-PRA covered transactions, interagency reporting requirements, and information products that agencies disseminate to the public, as well as other transactions. The guidance also requires agencies to report on how they are updating their business processes, including automating those transactions that serve common customers, whether within an agency or across several agencies.

Federal agencies also face some requirements as a result of the Electronic Signatures in National and Global Commerce Act (Public Law 106-229) or "E-Sign," which was signed on June 30, 2000. The law, which provides a legal basis for the use of technology to sign contracts and perform other electronic legal transactions, is primarily focused on legalizing and enabling electronic transactions in the private sector. However, under the Act, federal agencies will still have to update their regulations to indicate that private parties must retain records electronically. In addition, agencies such as Commerce, Treasury, and Justice conduct transactions covered by E-Sign. OMB has issued guidance to agencies providing a general overview and explanation of how E-Sign relates to federal agencies, suggesting steps for agencies to implement the law, and ensuring that agencies are in compliance with its requirements.

In addition to broad government-wide legislation like GPEA and E-Sign, Congress has also begun legislating specific e-government initiatives by function as well as by agency. For example, the Federal Financial Assistance Management Improvement Act of 1999 (Public Law 106-107) directs all federal agencies to enable "applicants to electronically apply for, and report on the use of funds from the federal financial assistance program(s) administered by the agency." The Freedom to E-File Act (S 777, H.R. 852) requires four U.S. Department of Agriculture (USDA) agencies to enable agricultural producers to access and file all forms and selected records and also to have electronic access to USDA farm-related information now available to the public in paper form.[6] Although these congressional mandates have undoubtedly pushed the process of e-government forward, Congress has yet to grapple with critical systemic issues that pose significant barriers to the kind of fundamental change that e-government makes possible.

Significant legal issues also must be addressed. In May 2000, the Department of Justice issued to agencies extensive guidance describing two broad legal issues that they must be sure to address as they move from paper-based to electronic transactions. First, should agencies decide to convert each type of transaction to an electronic-based process? Second, how should they design the process to protect the agency's legal rights and minimize legal risks that may compromise the agency's mission?

Answering the first question will require agencies to consider issues such as accessibility (i.e., whether or not information regarding the transaction will be needed years later). They must also consider legal sufficiency issues addressed by GPEA and E-sign. A third category of issues involves reliability—whether or not electronic records will be persuasive in courts. And, finally, the issue of legality—agencies must be certain that their methods of obtaining, sending, disclosing, and storing electronic information comply with laws governing privacy, confidentiality, and accessibility to persons with disabilities and others.

Primary Federal e-Legislation

- The Government Paperwork Elimination Act
- Electronic Signatures in National and Global Commerce Act
- Federal Financial Assistance Management Improvement Act of 1999

Justice also recommended steps that agencies should incorporate into their decision-making processes to mitigate legal risks of conducting processes online; noted the types of information that must be gathered, retained, and made available on demand; and made particular recommendations on issues such as contracting, regulatory programs, benefit programs, and other programs that require reporting of information.

NOT JUST A TECHNOLOGY ISSUE

While IT undoubtedly plays a vital role in achieving e-government, the most significant challenges involve fundamentally transforming the way agencies interact with customers, employees, business partners, and each other. Such overwhelming cultural change involves critical managerial, program, policy, budget, and legal issues that can only be addressed by an agency's senior political and career program officials—not just the Chief Information Officer (CIO) and the IT staff. These include:

- Preparing the leadership to "lead" the transformation
- Allocating sufficient program resources for agency-specific and, in many cases, cross-agency initiatives
- Prioritizing which programs and transactions to place online and in what order
- Effectively involving the public and key stakeholders, including labor, in the change process
- Identifying and changing business processes to respond to customers' needs
- Ensuring adequate integration between similar and dependent processes by looking horizontally across agencies, departments, and different levels of government
- Establishing appropriate policies and legal processes (e.g., to protect citizens' privacy)
- Retraining workers to perform new value-added functions as more and more paper-based transactions are conducted online
- Educating current and potential customers to access government services electronically
- Ensuring that electronic accessibility extends to the disabled, as required under Section 508 of the Rehabilitation Act (Public Law 105-220)
- Continuing to reach and serve customers who do not have or want access to the Internet or other means of electronic access

- Ensuring that e-business contributes to closing rather than widening the digital divide.

These issues require leadership from senior political and career programmatic officials at all government levels. As noted earlier, at the state and local level, some governors and other officials are already out front. But for the most part, many of the leaders who must make key decisions about e-government lack sufficient understanding of just exactly what is taking place or how it will fundamentally change the nature of government. Others, with vested interests in government as it is currently organized, will not easily embrace efforts designed to move towards citizen-centric, rather than agency-centric, models of government, as the National Performance Review's reinventing government initiative has demonstrated. Moreover, resistance to change will be evident when e-government is perceived as threatening to traditional lines of authority. One solution is for those leaders who do understand to work hard to educate those who currently do not. The other far more difficult approach, especially in government, is to find ways to hold leaders accountable and nudge aside those who refuse to move forward.

E-government leaders will need a basic understanding of how information technology is changing the way we live and work; they must be able to envision a government as different from today's as the information age is different from the industrial era; and perhaps most importantly, they must be highly skilled at managing complexity, as well as cultural change. To succeed, they will also need extraordinary fortitude; no one should underestimate the amount of effort and perseverance that will be required to reengineer government based on the best interests of citizens, whom government is supposed to serve.

AFTER THE STRUGGLE, SAY GOODBYE TO SILOS

Many programmatic issues involved in e-government stem directly from how government is organized. The many departments, agencies, bureaus, and other units of government typically operate with as much autonomy as they can muster. They are most often the result of legislative bodies that divide power and create programs based on political considerations, not necessarily organizational efficiency. However, creating an e-government based on natural complexes, as described earlier, requires a degree of interagency cooperation that is difficult to achieve within one department, much less between different departments or across different levels of government. The *Economist* points out that:

> One basic reason for public-sector inefficiency—"bureaucracy"—is that, whereas departments are vertically organized, many of the services that they have to deliver require complex collaboration between employees across departments. The British government has for several years been preaching the need for "joined-up government," but has found that the underlying structures of government conspire against it.[7]

Needless to say, the experience in the United States has been no different from that in Great Britain. For example, for well over a decade the Agriculture Department—with limited success—has been trying to create essentially "one-stop-shops" for farmers, who now must interact with at least four separate USDA agencies for various programs and services.

USDA is finally succeeding at putting in place a common technical infrastructure for its "county-based agencies." However, as in Britain, "underlying structures, sometimes in the form of congressional overseers, agriculture interest groups, and bureaucracies, have consistently stymied the department's efforts to reengineer actual programs and services across existing organizational silos."

E-government requires that information flow across organizations that have historically been designed to operate mostly as separate entities and where turf protection is a natural part of organizational culture. Indeed, the Gartner Group points out that one major barrier to KM, and consequently e-government, is the notion that knowledge is power: Individuals competing for economic gain are reluctant to share knowledge (or information) across organizational boundaries. The key to implementing KM successfully, Gartner notes, is the shift to an attitude that *knowledge sharing* is power.[8]

Along with enlightened and motivated leadership at the top, successfully overcoming organizational barriers and transitioning to e-government will require that incentives for managers and employees at all levels of government be aligned with the vision. Agencies must change their performance measures and rewards program so that individuals are recognized for team, as opposed to simply individual, performance. Within the federal government, program managers, as well as individual employees, must be rewarded for helping increase efficiencies; creating more convenient, customer-centric services; and reducing costs *across organizational boundaries*, as well as within their own. Otherwise, most can be counted on to resist fundamental changes that will radically alter the status quo, and, as they perceive it, could even threaten their job security and power bases.

Overcoming organizational barriers will also require that agencies shed any reluctance to transfer and implement best practices from other agencies. The concept of "speed to market" drives private-sector organizations to adapt quickly to new technologies before they are adapted and used by competitors. Government must act with the same sense of urgency: Solutions should be readily shared across boundaries so that every agency does not waste time and precious resources reinventing the same wheel.

BUILDING THE E-INFRASTRUCTURE

Thus, e-government is far more than just an IT issue and cannot be managed as another IT project. That said, transitioning to e-government obviously involves significant technology issues that will tax governments' IT resources, both physical infrastructure and staffs. Key challenges include:

- Developing and implementing IT standards to ensure that agency computer systems can communicate with one another and other agencies and that customers are presented with common interfaces to programs

- Building the Web-enabling IT infrastructure (hardware and software) necessary to conduct secure transactions online

- Installing and managing telecommunications equipment and capacity to meet growing demands as the Internet increasingly becomes a mainstream way for the vast majority of citizens to conduct business

- Identifying problems where enterprise-wide or even multilevel, vs. individual agency, solutions are preferable (such as verifying the identities of online customers) and implementing common solutions

- Protecting customer privacy and the confidentiality of information provided to the government and stored electronically

- Operating this new and constantly changing infrastructure while also maintaining existing legacy systems

- Securing the Web against the constant and growing challenges posed by hackers

- Recruiting and retaining an IT workforce with the skills to build and operate in the new e-environment.

CIOs, telecommunications, security, hardware, software, privacy, and electronic records management experts and others must work collaboratively as government builds the necessary infrastructure to conduct secure, reliable, online transactions while efficiently utilizing its IT resources. E-government will be open 24/7/365. System outages, like the highly publicized hacking events that have frustrated leading private sector e-businesses, cannot be tolerated. The e-government infrastructure must be scalable to account for fluctuating and increasing demand; sufficient bandwidth must be a given.

This requires skill sets that are in short supply in the private sector, much less in government. E-government will require expertise in a wide range of technology components. These include servers, networking, storage, performance management, cybersecurity, web application development, and more. Many IT organizations simply will not have the level of expertise required to build and manage the scope and complexity of this kind of infrastructure, especially in large, complex enterprises.

Operating effectively in this new e-environment will require that government has enough highly skilled IT professionals to run the ship: Human-ware will be just as important, if not more so, than hardware and software. Moving quickly to solve government's well-publicized deficit in skilled IT talent is paramount. The Office of Personnel Management's current efforts at reviewing job titles and testing a new compensation plan that will tie the salaries of IT employees to their abilities, rather than longevity, is a welcome development. However, without stock options to offer, government must use every incentive it can muster, including education, flexible work schedules, bonuses, and prime attention to quality of work/life issues to compete.

Building and maintaining e-infrastructure and solving these technical problems also will require governments at all levels to partner successfully with other agencies, other levels of government, and with the private and nonprofit sectors. With resources in short supply, agencies will need to share their expertise and manage their assets wisely by taking advantage of economies of scale.

In addition, partnering with private-sector companies that have proven track records is a must. Virtually all technologies necessary for e-government are already being deployed in the private sector. These include applications for KM, customer-relationship management, supply-chain management, business intelligence and data-mining, Web-based procurement systems, and security systems. Acquiring and deploying these technologies so that they work together smoothly, while deciding what should be maintained in-house and what should be turned over to the private sector, and even other government partners, will present extremely difficult challenges. Some argue that government is not in the IT business and that it should rely totally on the private sector to build and maintain its e-infrastructure. However, government has already invested billions of dollars in its own infrastructure that can be leveraged; in most cases, it cannot afford to simply start over. Also, government must be sure to keep certain strategic IT skills in-house. Where unions are involved, government must seek partnering arrangements to uphold bargaining agreements and foster a positive, win-win relationship with its employees.

In any event, technology solutions need to be fully aligned with programmatic objectives and be determined largely from the perspective of customers rather than individual governmental entities. Web-enabling existing processes and ways of conducting business will not create an e-government; they will merely transfer existing inefficiencies into cyberspace, much to the dismay of citizens who are fast coming to expect better.

SHOW ME THE MONEY

The investment in physical and human infrastructure and fundamental reengineering of the business processes required for e-government will be substantial. E-government cannot be implemented "on the cheap." Yet in most cases, federal agencies are expected to use existing resources to implement congressional and executive e-government mandates. The memorandum on electronic government issued by the president in December 1999 directed that the top 500 government services be online by December 2000. No funding was provided. GPEA requires that by 2003 all information and services, to the extent practicable, be available electronically. Again, no new funding has been provided.

Unless the federal government solves its funding problems, e-government will be very, very slow to develop. In most cases federal agencies are being forced to use all of their current IT resources to maintain existing—or legacy—systems. Legacy applications will have to be continued well into the foreseeable future because programs and services must still be delivered in the "old way," even as agencies migrate to new Web-based applications and processes. Further, some citizens may never feel comfortable using the Internet to conduct transactions nor have access to the technology for some time to come. Government will still be responsible for providing them services. The need to "manage the bubble" between existing and new business models will strain government resources at all levels.

The resource problem is also acute because, as the experience of the private sector shows, organizations must invest heavily in new IT before realizing savings. Initially, overall costs for IT are likely to increase before agencies realize the benefits of increased efficiency, and, also as in the private sector, some initiatives can be counted on to fail. Success might well hinge on agencies' ability to convince skeptical policy makers that savings will surely come, if only they support up-front investments. Even then, agencies face strong disincentives to demonstrate significant savings because that typically results in reductions in next year's appropriation. Pressure from constituents might be the only way to convince lawmakers that e-government investments will result in better government and more satisfied taxpayers.

Clearly, more creative funding mechanisms also must be found to finance e-government. At the local level, the private sector is already stepping in to Web-enable government processes in exchange for transaction fees. Companies such as GovConnect, Ezgov.com, govWorks.com, IBM, and others are supplying e-government infrastructure for state and local governments, which in turn charge citizens transaction fees.

Taxpayers in Dekalb County, Georgia, who choose to pay via electronic checks pay a $3 transaction fee that goes to Ezgov.com. IBM, which developed the motor vehicle registration program for the state of Arizona, receives a $1 fee per transaction, along with a percentage of revenues.[9] GovConnect.com claims to have processed 97 million electronic transactions while collecting $20 billion in revenues for 34 states.[10]

In the future, Ezgov.com plans to make additional revenue by generating advanced reports using online data targeted primarily at real estate attorneys, mortgage brokers, and other businesses for additional fees. These transaction-based arrangements for licenses, vehicle registrations, etc., appear to be quite beneficial for local and state officials, who can move to online transactions with minimal up-front expenditures, as long as citizens do not mind paying transaction fees in exchange for the convenience of conducting business online. At the federal level, fee-based transactions are possible but limited in supply because most taxpayers rightfully believe that they have *already* paid for the service.

Aside from Congress providing funds for individual agency initiatives, e-government will also require that funds be made available for cross-agency initiatives. Few mechanisms exist to fund these initiatives directly. Proposals to address this issue at the federal level include establishing a federal CIO, who would be appropriated funds for cross-agency initiatives, as well as codifying and funding the federal CIO council. However, neither Congress nor the administration has yet to really consider how e-government's requirement for funding mechanisms that transcend the traditional boundaries established by its thirteen appropriations committees will be met.

A major shift is also necessary in how many in Congress (as well as the executive branch) perceive IT investments. In the existing paradigm, IT investments, like other "administrative expenses," are considered to be "overhead"—a cost of doing business that should be cut as much and as often as possible, or at least minimized. Congress typically makes major changes or adds program responsibilities to agencies without any resources to ensure that IT is modernized sufficiently to support the increased service delivery. Unchanged, this paradigm will cripple e-government. IT investments are critical to program delivery. In fact, in the digital age, programs and the IT used to deliver them become virtually indistinguishable.

THE FUTURE IS ALREADY HERE

Overcoming these challenges will require progressive and determined leadership from all levels of government—the legislative as well as executive branches. E-government, if properly implemented, offers unlimited potential to reinvent government in the image of the citizens it is supposed to serve. For those same reasons, it poses serious threats to existing governmental arrangements that will be difficult to change. In the near term, government will move toward change deliberately. Most e-government projects will still predominantly involve individual programs or applications (e.g., to Web-enable procurement) in individual agencies. Multi-level program delivery or cross-agency and cross-department projects will continue to be difficult to achieve.

Still, the future is becoming increasingly clear, even if the path to it is uncertain. Governments, like their most successful private sector counterparts, must learn the value of sharing information and knowledge across all boundaries, while at the same time protecting citizens' privacy and securing their information assets from unauthorized users. Providing service to customers based on their interests, rather than along individual agency or bureau lines, requires that KM become a key part of the way the business of government is conducted. Lifting the burden governments impose on their citizens will depend on how quickly they become customer-centric, knowledge-centered organizations.

Countries such as Singapore are already leading by example, creating virtual e-societies where citizens habitually interact with government via one-stop-shop portals on almost every issue imaginable. For example, Singapore's adult males, who must perform some military duty into their fifties, now interact with the defense ministry via a Website where they can claim training pay, get it sent to the right bank account, send information about trips and update it from anywhere in the world, book fitness tests and training courses, take classes at an online military academy, and even provide feedback to the ministry. Access to medical data and other confidential information is by PIN number, and family members can use the site to check on the status and location of recruits. Some sessions are already accessible by wireless devices such as mobile phones.

Closer to home, local, state, and federal agencies are independently deploying Web-based applications to provide citizens easy access to information and innovative services, with noticeable results. For example, landlords, restaurants, and others who violate health codes are being forced into compliance with local regulations after inspection results are published on easily accessible Websites. Enforcing local regulations through this kind of adverse publicity is proving to be far more effective than levying fines. Similar applications provide parents with performance information about local schools, as well as doctors, dentists, and other licensed health care professionals. States are also realizing impressive savings from Web-enabling license renewals, permits, registrations, tax filing, and other transactions that previously occupied reams of paper, not to mention employees' and citizens' time. Web-based procurement is resulting in increased numbers of bids, more competition, and far better prices for governments.

At the federal level, the Internal Revenue Service (IRS) has been out front by enabling citizens to file tax returns online. In 1999, approximately 25 million federal taxpayers filed their returns electronically. The IRS has set a goal of having 80 percent of all tax returns filed electronically by 2007.

The Social Security Administration, another early leader in creative e-government applications, now allows citizens to start planning for retirement by estimating their Social Security benefits online. Citizens can also obtain information on acquiring a Social Security number, and the agency's Website provides information for employers on reporting earnings.

One of the earliest and most successful e-government applications to date—accomplished through extensive collaboration between the federal and state governments—is the transformation of the USDA's $16 billion food stamp program, with 18.2 million recipients in fiscal year 1999, from a paper-based to an electronic delivery system. The electronics benefit transfer (EBT) system allows food stamp recipients to use a card like an automatic transaction machine (ATM) card to authorize transfer of their government benefits from a federal account to a retailer account to pay for food. About 47 percent of food stamp benefits are currently being issued by EBT, with plans for all states to be on board by the end of 2002. Elsewhere, the federal government transfers some $500 billion annually in benefits to citizens covering various nutrition, medical, education, housing, job, and other programs, with hundreds of millions of dollars in potential operational savings waiting to be claimed by federal and state agencies when these transactions are fully digitized.

The U.S. Department of Defense (DoD), the U.S. Postal Service, and other agencies are among the first to utilize online "reverse auctions," which allow sellers to bid down the price. The Navy has already reported savings in the million of dollars. GSA is promoting the idea and has established a Website (Buyers.gov) that offers agencies opportunities to conduct private buyer auctions and reverse auctions and serves as an online shop for information technology.

Most early e-government applications basically aggregate and publish useful information for citizens. Yet they are also having tremendous impact. The USDA's Natural Resources Conservation Service's PLANTs Website is a single source of standardized information, including photographs, on thousands of plant species—all available free for scientific and educational use.

These applications are fast changing the way citizens and businesses routinely interact with their government. However, as already discussed, changes that will radically alter the fundamental nature of government are also on the horizon. For example, the state of Washington, recognized as one of the leaders in e-government, has plans to create a Web application that will enable citizens who move into the state to request license plates for their automobiles, register to vote, enroll their children in school, send change of address forms to their old post office, and even order tags for the family dog. Citizens would enter their personal information once, and it would automatically be shared with the appropriate agencies' computer systems. Similar to the model in Singapore, "Moving to Washington" would be one of several services for citizens organized based on "life events."

It seems likely that many other governments will also opt to provide electronic services to their citizens with organizational schemes based on "life events." Although the challenges are significant, the magnitude of the potential benefits to citizens will drive government, step by step, through the transformation process. In the final analysis, those political leaders and governmental officials at all levels who ultimately are accountable to the public will be compelled to act. As in the private sector marketplace, those officials who fail to respect the imperatives of the growing e-government marketplace will surely find themselves challenged and increasingly at risk of being replaced by others who do.

NOTES

1. In his work *Metaphysics of Natural Complexes* (New York: Columbia University Press, 1966), philosopher Justus Buchler describes a metaphysics in which the "natural complex" is the fundamental unit. Buchler defines natural complexes as "whatever is discriminated in any degree." All natural complexes share certain characteristics. Each complex is itself both an order of complexes and part of an indefinite number of other complexes.
2. According to Nua Internet Surveys, the art of estimating how many people are online throughout the world is an inexact one at best. Nua notes that numerous surveys exist and that they use varying methodologies and parameters. These estimates are derived from observing many of the surveys published over the last two years and represent an "educated guess" as to the number online as of June 2000.
3. The Department of Commerce's report *Digital Economy 2000* notes that the wide disparity in estimations of the dollar value of business-to-business (B2B) transactions is due to a combination of methodological and definitional differences. One key difference is

the degree to which non-Internet network transaction systems, including electronic data interchange, or EDI, are included.

4. Symonds, Matthew. "After e-commerce, get ready for e-government." An *Economist* Survey. *The Economist,* June 24–30, 2000.

5. See note 4 above.

6. The "Freedom to E-file Act" was signed into law on June 20, 2000. It requires that not later than 180 after enactment, the Secretary of Agriculture shall "to the maximum extent practicable" establish an Internet-based system that enables agricultural producers to access all forms for the three county-based agencies (Farm Service Agency, Natural Resources Conservation Service, and Rural Development) and Risk Management Agency (RMA). The legislation further requires that no later than two years after enactment, the system be expanded to enable producers to access and file all forms and selected records, and also to have electronic access to USDA farm-related information already available to the public in paper form. The legislation requires the secretary to reserve not more than $3 million for FY 2001 and $2 million for each subsequent year from existing appropriations of the specified agencies to establish and expand the system.

7. See note 4 above.

8. Gartner Group's Research Note, January 23, 1998, "Obstacles to Knowledge Management" observes that addressing the problem of knowledge sharing must start with the recognition that it is a cultural change management issue to which business process reengineering techniques can (and should) be applied.

9. Wasserman, Elizabeth. "The County Clerk Moves to the Web." *The Industry Standard,* September 20, 1999.

10. www.GovConnect.gov

CHAPTER 5

Organizational Readiness for Knowledge Management

Moonja P. Kim, PhD

Today, knowledge is the most important product in most organizations. Consequently, organizations are seeking to create systematic ways to identify and convert individual expertise, skills, and experiences into organizational knowledge. London-based analyst firm Ovum has predicted the worldwide growth of the market for knowledge management systems, fueled by wider use of existing intranets, at $12.3 billion by 2004! In its report *Knowledge Management: Building the Collaborative Enterprise,*[1] Ovum found that the knowledge management (KM) market is growing rapidly and will continue to evolve and expand over the next five years as KM becomes a core element of corporate information technology (IT) strategies. The Foundation for Malcolm Baldrige Award's survey of the nation's leading chief executive officers (CEOs) reported that 88 percent indicated that their second top priority is improving KM. Gartner Group projects that by 2001 enterprises that lack ongoing KM infrastructure will lag behind KM-enabled competitors by 30–40 percent in speed of deployment for new competitive programs and products.

There are many different definitions of KM. Dow Chemical defines KM as ". . .providing the right information to the right decision-maker at the right time, thus creating the right conditions for new knowledge to be created." American Productivity & Quality Center (APQC) defines KM as "the conscious business strategy of putting both tacit and explicit knowledge into action by creating context, infrastructure, and learning cycles that enable people to find and use the collective knowledge of the enterprise." Tacit knowledge includes experience, know-how, skills, and intuition and is most often embedded in the individual; explicit knowledge is available information put into words or pictures or that is easy to articulate and communicate. Both are essential to an organization and must be captured and shared for others to benefit. The Department of the Navy (DON) defines KM as "a process for optimizing the effective application of intellectual capital to achieve organizational objectives."

While most large enterprises are still in the early stages of implementing a KM strategy, these organizations recognize that harnessing and sharing corporate knowledge can provide a competitive advantage. Many organizations want to move forward aggressively but are concerned about cultural disruption. Managers are not used to sharing information; the enterprise is characterized by jealously guarded information silos. They face uncertainty regarding which aspects of KM should be dealt with today, which can wait until tomorrow, and how the organization must change to deal with various KM issues. Organizations attempting to initiate a KM project need to know whether their organizations are ready to adopt KM as a strategy and identify specific areas for improvement before starting any new KM initiatives. Organizations wishing to move toward becoming a knowledge-centric organization (KCO) must assess their readiness for adopting KM.

A KCO is one that organizes virtually around its critical knowledge needs and then builds useful and relevant information to fill those needs. This virtual organization is an overlay to the existing organizational structure; personnel integrate knowledge sharing into their everyday lives. By providing access to the breadth of organizational knowledge, people have the ability to draw quickly and accurately upon critical lessons learned to make work time more efficient. The bottom line is that knowledge workers will be up and running faster and more effectively than ever before. To assess the KM readiness of an organization, an understanding of what stages or phases organizations go through to become effective KCOs is needed. The characteristics or key components of each stage of the journey toward the KCO need to be identified. This chapter will review several models that portray the stages of KM implementation/adoption, as well as key components of KM. From this review, a model for the stages of KM implementation and critical components can be selected for developing a KM readiness index. The objective is to develop an index to measure an organization's readiness for moving forward with KM initiatives and to suggest what actions an organization can take, depending on its level of readiness.

MODELS FOR THE JOURNEY TOWARD BECOMING A KNOWLEDGE-CENTRIC ORGANIZATION

One model that identifies the stages of KM implementation/adoption appears in *The State of the Knowledge Industry—Progress Report 1999* by Boyd and Kull.[2] This model depicts five stages to help organizations understand where they stand on their KM initiatives and how to move toward becoming KCOs. Another five-stage model has been presented by American Productivity and Quality Center (APQC).[3, 4] Microsoft has created another model with eight stages, the Information Technology (IT) Landscape Model. Information regarding this model can be found at http://www.microsoft.com/enterprise/building/advisor/KM/index.asp. DON has also developed a five-stage KCO journey.[5] Table 1 provides a comparison of these four models.

Boyd and Kull Model for KM Adoption Stages[6]

The five stages of KM adoption developed by Boyd and Kull (1999) include: (1) awareness, (2) experimentation, (3) production, (4) scaling, and (5) enterprise. The characteristics and key features of each stage are:

- **Stage 1: Awareness**—Leadership recognizes the value of KM, but current KM projects are ad hoc, fragmented, or in the early research phase. The organization makes small investments, but KM is largely unsupported by critical resources.

Table 1. Stages of KM Adoption

Boyd & Kull Model	*APQC Model*	*Navy's KCO Model*	*Microsoft IT Landscape Model*
Awareness	Enter & Advocate	Awarenesss	Unaware
Experimentation	Explore & Experiment	Prepare Organization	Random initiation
Production	Discover & Conduct Pilots	Build KCO	Acceptance
Scaling	Expand & Support	Sustain KCO	Building Efficiency
Enterprise	Institutionalize	Connect Communities	Controlled Experimentation
			Adopting Effectiveness
			Focused Growth
			Leadership

At this stage, KM success depends on individual heroics. Little or no technology is applied to enable KM, knowledge is hoarded and unarticulated, and knowledge leaves the organization through employee attrition. The attitude of the organization toward KM is mixed or judgment is reserved. It is critical at this stage that KM advocates display a willingness to take action and test the theory in practice.

- **Stage 2: Experimentation**—KM has basic project support, and pilot projects are initiated to demonstrate feasibility. Initial cultural and technology shifts are designed and planned. Best practices are studied and incorporated into the business case for KM. Some effects of KM are emerging, recurring problems are recognized and captured, project histories are documented and stored, and content from past projects can be acquired and reused. Technology is rudimentary, but it supports KM activities. At this stage, people initiating KM projects begin to show the early positive results of their work.

- **Stage 3: Production**—KM practices and tools are becoming integrated and documented based on the successes or failures of earlier KM initiatives. KM technology has spread, and cultural changes are taking hold. Members of the organization are involved and given incentives to contribute knowledge and navigate the KM environment. Databases and applications support the creation and sharing of knowledge, and the roles of managers and leaders with regard to KM are understood and accepted. Communities of practice are being linked together, and organizational learning is becoming a cultural norm. At this stage, the focus shifts from looking at early results to managing the process of the work itself and getting adequate resources to the people who need them.

- **Stage 4: Scaling**—KM systems are being rolled out across the enterprise, and the organization is systematically working to implement change. Measures of KM are established to gauge effectiveness and appropriateness for different divisions or work groups. New initiatives are weighted against aggregated project histories and given a prediction of success. KM implementation problems are generally anticipated, and the solutions that emerge are on target. At this stage, the change initiatives in process can be measured, streamlined, and used to make sure other parts of the organization are in compliance. The organization tailors its efforts to build cohesion and efficiency.

- **Stage 5: Enterprise**—KM systems and practices have been deployed across the organization, and the enterprise now focuses on continuous innovation. KM processes for evolving organizational culture are fluid and intelligent, and ideas flow freely among communities of practice. New technologies are aggressively pursued and strategically deployed. Knowledge creation cycles are rapid, and data are used to accelerate innovation. Strong teamwork exists, and everyone is involved in organizational learning. At this final stage, the organization as a whole has instituted a KM environment. The challenge is to continually add, remove, and refine tools and practices as the organization strategically adapts to its external environment.

APQC Model for KM Implementation[7]

The five stages of the APQC model are very similar to the stages of the Boyd and Kull model. The Boyd and Kull model includes leadership's recognition of KM value at the first stage, while the APQC model recognizes the importance of a KM champion at this stage, not necessarily at the leadership level. A more detailed description of the APQC model follows:

- **Stage 1: Enter and Advocate**—The fire to manage knowledge starts with the spark of inspiration. A new source of energy or interest must cause KM to arise within the organization. Someone becomes inspired with the vision of what it would be like if the organization could effectively support human knowledge capture, transfer, and use. Energized by his or her vision, this champion (advocate or "evangelist") begins to search for opportunities to share the vision with others and to find opportunities to demonstrate the value of KM to the organization. This was previously the most difficult stage for the early adopters, but this stage proceeds more quickly at many organizations now that more is known about KM. The central task for the evangelist at this stage is to create a vision that inspires others to join in the exploration of how managing knowledge might contribute value to the enterprise and its people. IT functionality is not critical at this stage, but the IT organization is often the catalyst to support KM efforts. The nature of the business case is qualitative and based on the advocate's belief in the value of knowledge and its ability to enhance effectiveness. At this stage, there is seldom any formal budget for KM.

- **Stage 2: Explore and Experiment** —This stage is the turning point from individual interest in KM to an organizational experiment. It is characterized by the decision to explore "how KM might work here" and an evolution to the need for a senior executive sponsor. The central task at this stage is to formulate the first iteration of the KM strategy, how it fits with the business, pilots to test the concept, and the initial steps for moving forward. A small group is usually formed to undertake this on behalf of the organization.

- **Stage 3: Discover and Conduct**—This stage signals the formal implementation of KM initiatives. The goal is to provide evidence of KM's business value by conducting pilots and capturing lessons learned. An oversight steering committee is formed that identifies resources to fund KM pilots. It is important to measure results and understand what makes the pilots work or not work. There will be mixed funding from a central resource, as well as the donation of time, people, and money from the pilot units.

- **Stage 4: Expand and Support**—When an organization reaches Stage 4, KM has proven to be valuable enough to be officially expanded to become part of the organization's funded activities. Demand for KM assistance by other parts of the organization tends to be high, providing additional evidence of its value. Pilot results are an added benefit. High visibility and the authority to expand are a mixed blessing. The added visibility of costs and resources devoted to KM will require more formal business evaluation and rates of investment (ROI) justification. KM is on its way to being considered a strategic and necessary competency.

- **Stage 5: Institutionalize**—Stage 5 is a continuation of Stage 4; full enterprise-wide deployment of KM is underway. This stage differs from Stage 4 in three fundamental ways:

  - It does not happen unless KM is embedded in the business model.

  - The organizational structure must realign.

  - Evidence of KM competency becomes part of the formal performance evaluation.

Sharing and using knowledge become part of the organization's way of doing business, as well as an expected management competency. Leadership articulates knowledge-sharing strategies, and their priority is signaled by budget allocation. Communities of practice will be included in the budget. CEO, Chief

Knowledge Officer (CKO), Chief Operations Officer (COO), and business unit leaders get involved with KM. There are IT specialists, content specialists, and increased dependence on operations staff for KM. Information tools are built around communities, and knowledge flows. KM is identified with increased productivity and cost savings. Examples of organizations that have reached this stage are World Bank, Xerox, Siemen's ICN Company, Buckman Laboratories, and HP consulting.

Knowledge-Centric Organization Journey Developed by DON

DON's model also has five stages:

- **Stage 1: Build Awareness**—At this stage, people learn how KM can help prepare for the upcoming knowledge-centric organization (KCO) deployment. Every deployment is different, yet most share a common language and understanding of operating procedures. People explore and develop an understanding of KM fundamentals. Comparisons are encouraged and supported. Commitment from the top is demonstrated. Incentives for KM are embedded in the formal organizational structure (i.e., strategic plan).

- **Stage 2: Prepare Organization**—This stage represents the *unknown* as an organization begins the journey to becoming a KCO. People explore, gather salient features, and develop an important understanding of what it takes to prepare the organization to become knowledge-centric and how this fits into their organization's business plan. This stage requires an understanding of how to change culture and the importance of leadership, relationships, and communications. Relationships are built to implement a KCO, identifying or creating the various communities that currently exist within and beyond the organization and defining the way that knowledge flows through informal and formal channels.

- **Stage 3: Build KCO**—At this stage, people explore their organizations, create processes, motivate personnel, and design a knowledge-centric system that strategizes and develops performance measures and incentives. The focus is to identify the knowledge, skills, and information required to support people in performing critical actions and begin the process of sorting these requirements into content centers so that they might be addressed. As a starting point in creating KCOs, it is important that each organization identify the components of its core strategic process. At this stage, performance measurement systems should be designed to allow for the collection of baseline data, so that improvement can be accurately traced and any weaknesses corrected. It is critical to develop incentives and rewards for knowledge sharing, where appropriate, and to establish a plan to communicate the relevant measures and rewards to all personnel. Roles and responsibilities for all levels of personnel should be developed and communicated to launch the KCO.

- **Stage 4: Sustain KCO**—At this stage, people develop processes and capabilities to operate the KCO long term, continuously evaluating its performance and remaining adaptable as the organization restrategizes to meet changing needs over time. As knowledge-centric capabilities are developed, it is important to ensure a strong basis for long-term survival and growth. The focus is on the building of processes by which the knowledge manager can successfully operate and maintain the KM system. The KM system's performance should be evaluated based on outcome, output, and systems performance measures, and an assessment of the stickiness of the system, with a reevaluation of incentives and reward schemes. It is important to identify components of the core strategic process, key individuals, and essential information, and to create knowledge-sharing communities that are integral to the success of the organization's mission. Feedback should be collected and quarterly reports should be produced showing aggregated measures of system performance indicators.

- **Stage 5: Connect to Communities**—At this stage, people connect to communities of practice (CoP) within the organization and across other organizations within the enterprise.

CoPs enable organizations to become successful enterprises that create, share, apply, and value knowledge. To build the foundations for successful KCOs and expand to reach other communities, it is important to understand why CoPs are important, learn what is involved in building strong ones, and maximize their effectiveness within an organization and at the enterprise level. The first step of this stage is to mobilize the CoPs by increasing awareness, interest, and participation in CoPs within the enterprise. CoPs are beneficial to the organization as a whole because individuals directly benefit from the knowledge they gain through participation. Hence, quality of work and efficiency of labor are increased, and the organization becomes more successful. Individuals will not participate in CoPs unless the benefits of participation are evidenced or participation rewarded (directly or indirectly), or their participation stems from a desire to learn about a particular area of interest. Without individuals, CoPs cannot exist.

An organization can promote CoPs by addressing the needs of individuals and organizations in a manner that triggers interest. CoPs are often by nature self-organizing. Encouraging and nurturing them does not require much in terms of hiring new personnel to orchestrate the formation of CoPs or constructing an elaborate infrastructure; however, CoPs require places to congregate, opportunities to travel, time to be together as a community, and the ability to contribute. CoPs should be motivated by learning and doing, not by command or delegation of work. Every CoP requires a champion (i.e., someone who will be responsible for ensuring the objectives of the community are met). This champion also focuses on ensuring the infrastructure is in place to meet the knowledge objectives of the CoP.

Microsoft's IT Landscape Model for KM

Microsoft's model is based on a conceptual framework called IT Landscape Model and focuses on the IT aspects of KM. It includes eight stages: (1) unaware, (2) random initiation, (3) acceptance, (4) building efficiency, (5) controlled experimentation, (6) adopting for effectiveness, (7) focus on growth, and (8) leadership. A short description of each stage follows.

- **Stage 1: Unaware**—Organizations at the "unaware" stage are frozen in the past, supporting centralized, largely host-based computing infrastructures that are stable but inflexible. These organizations are not ready to respond to rapid business change and take advantage of new technology.
- **Stage 2: Random Initiation**—Organizations at this stage are about to fall into the IT abyss. They seem to be getting a healthy return on their investment, but complexity in their IT environment, driven by poor management processes, can build up liability.
- **Stage 3: Acceptance**—Organizations are in the IT abyss, and their complex systems mandate more spending to operate but yield little business value in return.
- **Stage 4: Building Efficiency**—Organizations avoid the IT abyss and have maintained good management processes in the face of rapid business and technology change.
- **Stage 5: Controlled Experimentation**—Organizations are climbing out of the abyss and have identified and corrected their management shortcomings but require time before their systems and IT performance reflect the improvements.
- **Stage 6: Adopting for Effectiveness**—Organizations are competitive and have established excellent systems and an excellent IT organization.
- **Stage 7: Focused on Growth**—Organizations are moving ahead and choose to establish IT as a source of competitive advantage. These organizations have put in place not only excellent systems and people but also excellent processes for identifying and pursuing competitive opportunities through IT.
- **Stage 8: Leadership**—Organizations are on the leading edge and have established true competitive advantages from IT.

They are excellent on all dimensions and achieve very high value from their IT investments.

This IT Landscape Model is useful only for the technology aspect of KM. It does not consider any other areas of KM, such as culture, leadership, or processes; therefore, this model is limited as an assessment tool for evaluating an organization's readiness for KM. Excluding this IT model, review of the other three models shows more similarities than differences. Although terms used to describe the stages are different, the concept of the five stages is the same for all three models. For example, the first stage was named "awareness" by Boyd and Kull model, "enter and advocate" by APQC model, and "building awareness" by DON's KCO Journey model; however, all three models include the important role of individual champions as evangelists or heroics. Top-level leadership and a passionate champion, who is inspired with the vision to transform the organization and has effective knowledge capture, transfer, and reuse, are important. All three models claim that IT functionality is not critical at the first stage. Because the models are very similar, the DON's KCO Journey model has been chosen for developing the KM readiness measures discussed later in this chapter. KM readiness measures at various stages can be used for the three models.

CRITICAL COMPONENTS FOR KM READINESS

An organization's KM readiness for each stage should include various factors or components, such as the organization's cultural readiness, IT infrastructure readiness, and leadership readiness. What are the critical factors for KM readiness? What are the critical elements that make the organization reach the highest stage of knowledge management adoption? Is cultural readiness more important than IT infrastructure readiness? If cultural readiness is present in the organization, then the knowledge sharing is tightly linked to the organizational culture. It could include factors such as whether the style of each knowledge-sharing approach closely matches the style of the organization as a whole and whether there is strong management and peer pressure for people to help each other, collaborate, and share their knowledge. Arthur Andersen identified five critical factors for KM in its Knowledge Management Assessment Tool (KMAT): leadership, technology, culture, measurement, and KM process. These critical elements are reviewed and evaluated for use in developing a KM readiness index for various stages of KM implementation.

Arthur Andersen's KMAT[8]

The KMAT was developed to help make an initial high-level assessment of how well an organization manages knowledge. It can direct the organization toward areas that require more attention as well as identify KM practices in which the organization excels. Five enablers were selected that can foster the development of organizational knowledge: (1) leadership, (2) culture, (3) technology, (4) measurement, and (5) KM process. These are the key components of creating KCOs, and they are present in all of the stages/phases of the KM journey. Keeping these enablers in mind throughout each stage of KM will allow the implementation of a holistic, effective, and balanced system and ensure the creation of the most optimal KCO. Indicators of the appropriate level for each of five components are described below.

Leadership

Leadership commitment is a critical component for successful KM implementation at all stages. Indications of leadership commitment can be found in the organization's business strategy that includes KM as a critical competitive advantage and in the creation of a KM position with authority and resources to facilitate KM relating to the core competencies of the organization. Another indication is the performance evaluation system for senior executives on how well they manage organizational knowledge. Individual employees at every level are also rewarded for their contribution to the organizational knowledge base and for sharing knowledge with others. Leadership believes that sharing knowledge will broaden the organizational knowledge base and bring enormous value to the organization. Leadership commitment also includes cultivating open-minded listening to KM champions (evangelists) who are passionate about KM initiatives. Multiple approaches are encouraged and strong team players promoted.

Culture

Organizational culture is one of the most important key components for KM adoption and implementation. Employees at all levels share ideas and technology as the way they do work every day because they get the information they need from the right person, and connecting with right person makes their jobs easy. Management encourages and promotes knowledge sharing but discourages information hoarding. Management and employees believe that "knowledge-sharing is power" rather than "knowledge is power." Employees take proactive roles in professional groups, keep up with external changes, and obtain different viewpoints from outside the organization. Openness and trust are the norm for the organization. Boundaries that prevent employees from having the right information are eliminated, and employees are empowered to respond quickly to customer needs.

Management rewards employees who share solutions they have provided to customers with others, encourages risk-taking and experimentation, and tolerates uncertainty and ambiguity. The organization considers failure as an opportunity for learning, and employees are given the time and resources to pursue new ideas and accomplish their learning goals. Employees are responsible for their own learning. Mentors and advisors are promoted to help employees customize their own learning plans. Employees decide what they want and need to know, and how and when they want to learn it. Creativity and innovations are passionately celebrated, and creativity-boosting techniques, brainstorming sessions, and scenario planning help discover unexpected solutions.

Technology

The pervasive use of groupware and Internet/intranet/extranet technologies has had a profound effect on people's ability to share knowledge and practices effectively. Technology is necessary, but not sufficient, to make knowledge transfer happen. It helps minimize barriers of geography and time and links all employees within the organization and to appropriate external organizations, including suppliers, customers, and academic institutions that provide knowledge on emerging technology. Top managers personally use new technology and set examples. All employees have access to technology and are well trained in how to use it. Institutional memory is captured formally and accessible to the entire organization through the use of appropriate technology. Lessons learned or knowledge repository systems prevent employees from "reinventing the wheel." All employees contribute to the content of the knowledge repository system across functional lines and have access to and view the rest of the organization's activities.

Information technology is developed with a clear vision of the business problems it is meant to solve, with emphasis on human interface. User-friendly systems are a priority and are based on how people in the organization actually acquire, share, and use information. Collaboration technology is in use throughout the organization and is continually upgraded and replaced with new hardware and software. Resident specialists, who understand both technology options and the organization's business needs, select technology that will be rapidly and easily adopted. Information systems provide relevant information to decision makers in a timely fashion so they can contribute to business decisions.

Measurement

To understand what is working, what is not, and what the payoffs are, KM activities and results are tracked and measured. The organization develops methods to evaluate the value of KM related to the organization's financial results. For example, management measures the value of intellectual capital, including human, social, and corporate capital, by tracking the incremental revenues generated when employees or teams modify existing products and services. The organization calculates a return on its knowledge investment by tracking the cost of getting information into its processes and products. The set of measures includes hard and soft indicators as well as financial and nonfinancial indicators. Soft measures, such as success or "war stories," are systematically collected and used as evidence of knowledge development. The organization estimates how a lack of investment in organizational knowledge will erode or retard growth through lost revenues to competitors, and this estimate is used to convince nonbelievers of the usefulness of KM.

KM Process

Business processes for KM must be developed for successful KM implementation. For example, to move forward to becoming a KCO, the organization must identify core strategic processes, critical actions, critical action personnel, and knowledge requirements, and then aggregate knowledge requirements into content centers and develop communication strategies to build awareness of KM program goals. Customers and employees are surveyed frequently to identify knowledge gaps. The organization creates and updates a knowledge map, indicating where information is located and how to access it. Knowledge directories exist that list employees' skills, knowledge, location, and how to reach them. The organization excels at scanning the environment for information on industry trends, customers, suppliers, and competitors and has a mechanism to share this information with employees across the enterprise. Legal and financial interests in intellectual property are well protected. Benchmarking is regularly conducted to look for best practices. Conferences, industry roundtables, and visits to other facilities are used as sources of creative inspiration.

The process of transferring best practices is formalized, including documentation and lessons learned. The organization has mapped its business processes. Success stories involving new tools or new approaches are widely communicated in the organization. Knowledge is rapidly diffused through the organization, making it easy to transfer best practices. "Tacit" knowledge is valued and transferred across the organization. Past know-how is made explicit, making it easy to access, understand, and apply. Employees are receptive to new ideas, and there is much learning by doing. A large percentage of employee knowledge remains within the organization when employees leave.

KMAT is an excellent tool for assessing how well an organization manages knowledge in terms of five key components. KMAT uses four or five questions to measure the level of each component, each asking if an employee agrees with a statement regarding his or her organization. The statement for each question describes some indications of an effective KCO. Completion of a total of 24 questions will produce the analysis of individual answers with a graphical depiction showing which key components are strong and which are weak.

For example, KMAT analysis of a particular organization by an employee may show that the culture component received a low rating and the technology component received a high rating. This result implies that, according to the employee's perception, the organization needs to work on improving cultural areas, but the technology area is ready for KM. At the individual level, KMAT can be used as an awareness-building tool. When many employees at various levels of the organization take KMAT, the results can be combined to indicate the level of each component for that organization. If the combined results still show a low rating of culture-related questions, then it is desirable to take some action to improve the culture to move the organization toward the KCO.

DEVELOPMENT OF KM READINESS INDEX

KMAT provides measures for key components of KM implementation, but it does not consider an organization's stage of KM implementation. It shows weak areas and strong areas, but it does not help identify which area is more important at an organization's current stage. Because most KM best-practices organizations undergo several stages of KM adoption/implementation, the necessary conditions for each stage need identification. Which key components are important for each stage, and what is the necessary level of readiness? This question can be answered by developing a KM readiness index that includes measures of all key components.

For example, an organization may be at Stage 1 (building awareness), the leadership component measurement may be low, and the technology component measurement may be high. A comparison of the organization's current and necessary levels of readiness will indicate which component area is not quite ready for KM adoption/implementation. The organization needs to perform additional work on the deficient key component area. A KM readiness index level necessary for each component for each stage can be developed using the template shown in Table 2.

Each component may cover several issues related to the component. For example, the leadership component may include questions regarding senior leadership recognizing KM value, supporting KM with reasonable resource allocation and commitment, and the existence of a strong champion regardless of management position. For the development of the KM readiness index, the five stages of the DON's KCO were selected: build awareness, prepare organization, build KCO, sustain KCO, and connect to communities. Of the six key components selected for successful KM implementation, five were adopted from KMAT. Resource allocation is so critical for successful KM implementa-

Table 2. Template for KM Readiness Index

	Leadership	*Culture*	*Measurement*	*Resource Allocation*	*Business Processes*	*Technology*
Build Awareness						
Build KCO						
Sustain KCO						
Connect Communities						

tion that it has been added as a sixth component. The KM readiness index for each component ranged from zero to five, with the numbers representing the following for each component:

- **Leadership**—Five represents the highest level of the leadership component and indicates that senior management recognizes the value of KM and supports KM initiatives with reasonable resources of people and funding. Zero represents the lowest level of the leadership component and indicates that senior management does not pay any attention to KM.

- **Culture**—Five represents the highest level of the KM culture component and indicates that people are open to new ideas and share information with appropriate people; informal discussions occur at the water cooler or cafeteria. Many innovative ideas are generated from these informal discussions. People are encouraged to take risks and try new ideas. They frequently volunteer to help each other, even if they are in different functional areas. Problems and errors are openly discussed, and solutions are shared. Successful innovations are enthusiastically celebrated. Management provides employees with the time and resources necessary to achieve learning goals. Zero represents the lowest level of KM culture index and indicates that people do not share information and hoard knowledge based on the idea that "knowledge is power." People who take risks get punished and reprimanded.

- **Measurement**—Five represents the highest level of the measurement component and indicates that strong measurement systems exist within the organization. These measures are connected to business strategy, such as increased productivity, cost savings, and high customer satisfaction level. The organization monitors the value of human capital by tracking the incremental value generated when employees modify existing products or services. Zero represents the lowest level of the measurement component and indicates that there is no measurement system in place within the organization that can be used to measure the results of KM.

- **Resource Allocation**—Five represents the highest level of the resource allocation component and indicates that an appropriate amount of funding and skilled personnel are allocated for KM. Zero represents the lowest level of the resource allocation component and indicates that there is no funding allocated for KM, with no potential for future funding.

- **KM Business Processes**—Five represents the highest level of the business processes component and indicates that the organization benchmarks regularly to look for best practices. Conferences, industry roundtables, and visits to other facilities are used as sources of creative innovation, and everyone spends some time visiting and listening to customers. The organization has formalized the process of transferring best practices, and success stories involving new tools, technologies, or approaches are widely communicated throughout the organization. "Tacit" knowledge is valued and transferred across the organization. Past know-how is made explicit, making it easy to access, understand, and apply. A large percentage of employees' knowledge remains within the organization when they leave. Zero represents the lowest level of the business processes component and indicates that there is no plan to transfer best practices or tacit knowledge within the organization.

- **Technology**—Five represents the highest level of the technology component and indicates that the maximum amount of emerging information technology is available within the organization for KM projects. Technology is seen as a means of enhancing collaborative efforts among members of the enterprise and is used to minimize barriers of geography and time. Technology brings the organization closer to its customers; customer information is shared across the organization, ensuring that customers' perspectives are incorporated into all services. Zero represents the lowest level of the technology component and indicates that the organization is not paying any attention to emerging information technology that would be useful for KM implementation.

Using the scale of zero to five described above, numeric values were assigned to the six components for all five stages to represent the necessary level for successful KM implementation. The author developed the numeric assignment, utilizing the findings of the APQC benchmarking study *Successfully Implementing Knowledge Management.* The following paragraphs explain the reasoning for the numeric assignment to indicate the necessary levels for all 30 cells, as shown in Table 3. This table represents the recommendation for the necessary levels of readiness for each component for each stage of the KM journey.

At the first stage (build awareness), leadership commitment for KM is critical; however, in reality, it is very difficult to garner leadership support at this early stage. Most organizations that have implemented KM successfully did not have strong leadership commitment from the first stage. Having buy-in of senior-level leadership at the first stage will be a bonus for promoting KM initiatives.

At this stage, a champion for KM is also critical. This person is convinced of the value of KM to the organization, or to what he or she does, and is also convinced of the value of emerging technology that could help KM. He or she has probably heard about successful examples from external sources. This champion, with

Table 3. Necessary Level of KM Readiness for Each Component for Each Stage

	Leadership	*Culture*	*Measurement*	*Resource Allocation*	*Business Processes*	*Technology*
Build Awareness	3	3	3	2	3	1
Build KCO	4	4	4	3	4	2
Sustain KCO	5	5	5	5	5	5
Connect Communities	5	5	5	5	5	5

strong interest and enthusiasm, usually enlists others to support KM and brings the concept of KM into the organization; thus, the champion almost acts as an evangelist. If the KM champion at the early stage happens to be at the senior leadership level, KM efforts will be more likely to succeed, as evidenced at the World Bank.[9]

At this stage, a high level of leadership readiness, including KM champions, is needed (=3). The openness of the organization's culture is important for this stage because the champion's KM idea will be stifled by the culture if people are not willing to listen to new ideas (=3). KM efforts can move faster if the culture allows people to talk freely about new ideas and try new things by taking risks. If the organization has lots of water cooler conversations, or informal chats, the KM stage will develop faster. Some kind of measurement is desirable from the beginning so that there will be shared expectation (=3). There is no formal resource allocation at this stage, but some redirection of existing resources may occur to support this champion (=2). The KM business process must be flexible enough to allow for change as new technology is introduced or as best practices are imported from other organizations (=3). Information technology is not critical at this stage (=1); however, the IT organization is often the catalyst to support KM efforts.

At the second stage (prepare organization), a high level of leadership support and a strong champion are required to be successful (=4). Organizational culture is also critical at this stage to encourage employees to generate innovative new ideas (=4). In preparing the organization, a good measurement system must be developed to assess the results of KM effectively (=4). At this stage, some pilot opportunities with limited funding may be selected (=3). KM business processes need to be established to promote knowledge sharing across the organization (=4). The importance of technology will increase as the organization progresses from Stage 1 to Stage 2, and the IT organization may become a key player on a KM task force (=2).

At the third stage (build KCO), the readiness level for each component is the same as the second stage, except a higher level of technology is needed (=3). Resource allocation could still be lower (=3), as long as other components are at the high level (=4) for leadership, culture, and KM business processes. At the fourth and fifth stages (sustain KCO and connect to communities), readiness levels for all components should be at their highest (=5). Without a high level of balanced components, it is difficult to sustain the KCO.

The necessary readiness level is also depicted in a spider diagram, shown in Figure 1. The spokes represent the six key components, and the readiness level is indicated as the distance from the center. Therefore, the closer to the center the point is located on the spoke, the lower the readiness level is for that component. The shaded area created by connecting the points for each spoke (component) represents the desired readiness level for that stage.

The necessary readiness level can be compared with any organization's actual readiness to find which component area needs improvement. For example, the actual readiness index (light area) for the organization "ABC Co" at Stage 1 is shown in

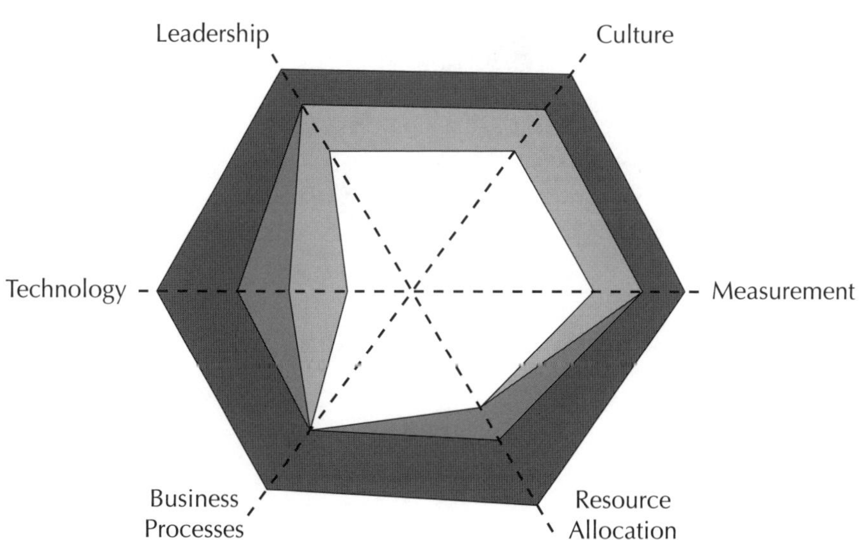

Figure 1. KM Readiness for Various Stages

Figure 2; the dark area shows the necessary level for that stage. This example shows that the organization's leadership, culture, and measurement are at lower than necessary levels, while technology and business processes are at higher levels than needed. This situation may indicate that someone in this organization sold the idea of implementing new emerging technology to senior leadership and made some investment in new technology, but people are not using it much, and the benefit of technology to the organization may not be clear.

As organization "ABC Co" moves toward the KCO, its KM readiness can be measured for each stage and compared with the desired level for that stage. After measurement of readiness for Stage 1, the organization could improve leadership and culture components to be ready for the later stages. The changes in KM readiness can be measured at each stage and kept for comparison as the organization moves through the stages of its KCO journey.

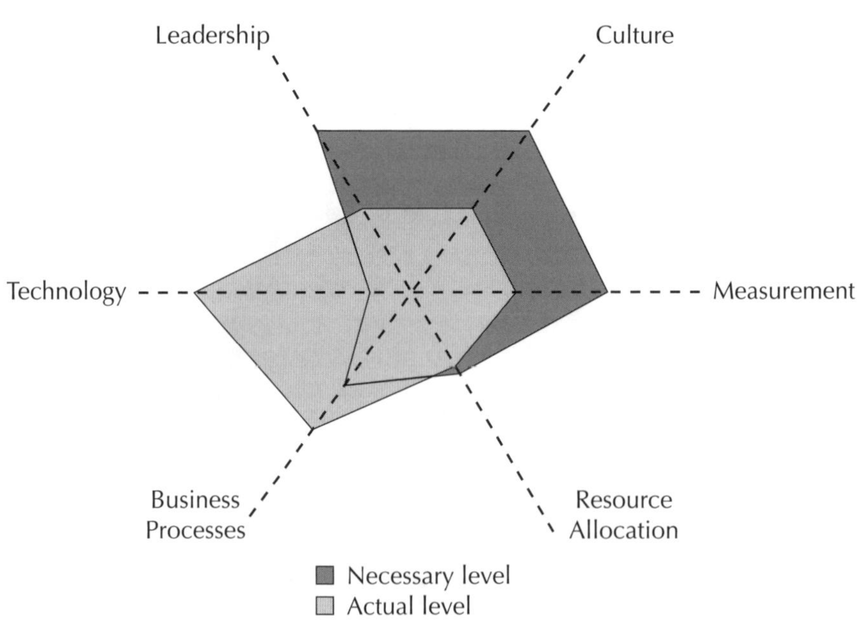

Figure 2. KM Readiness for Stage 1

Examples of different readiness levels from Stage 2 to Stage 5 are shown in Figure 3. This example shows that the organization's KM readiness for leadership and culture improves as it moves to higher stages. It also identifies which key components need improvement at each stage.

The index for each component can be measured using the KMAT questions, with equal weights for each question. The list of questions for each component can be found in the KCO toolkit CD developed by DON. KMAT provides 24 questions for five components: leadership, culture, technology, measurement, and KM business processes. These 24 statements have been tested and validated by Arthur Andersen. The following statements can be added for the additional component—resource allocation:

- Formal budget in the business unit is allocated for KM function.
- Specific budget is allocated for activities for communities of practice.
- There is reasonable headquarters (HQ) funding and people resources to provide assistance to KM activities across the enterprise.
- Local funding is available for pilot KM projects.

STEPS TO IMPROVE READINESS FOR EACH COMPONENT

How to measure the organization's readiness for KM and the necessary level of key components for successful KM adoption and implementation for different stages has been discussed. Now what can be done to improve each component area when it does not meet the necessary level? For instance, the example organization "ABC" does not have the high level of KM readiness for the leadership and culture components necessary for Stages 1 and 2. What should be done to improve these two areas if the organization is at Stage 1 or 2? The culture component is critical for any

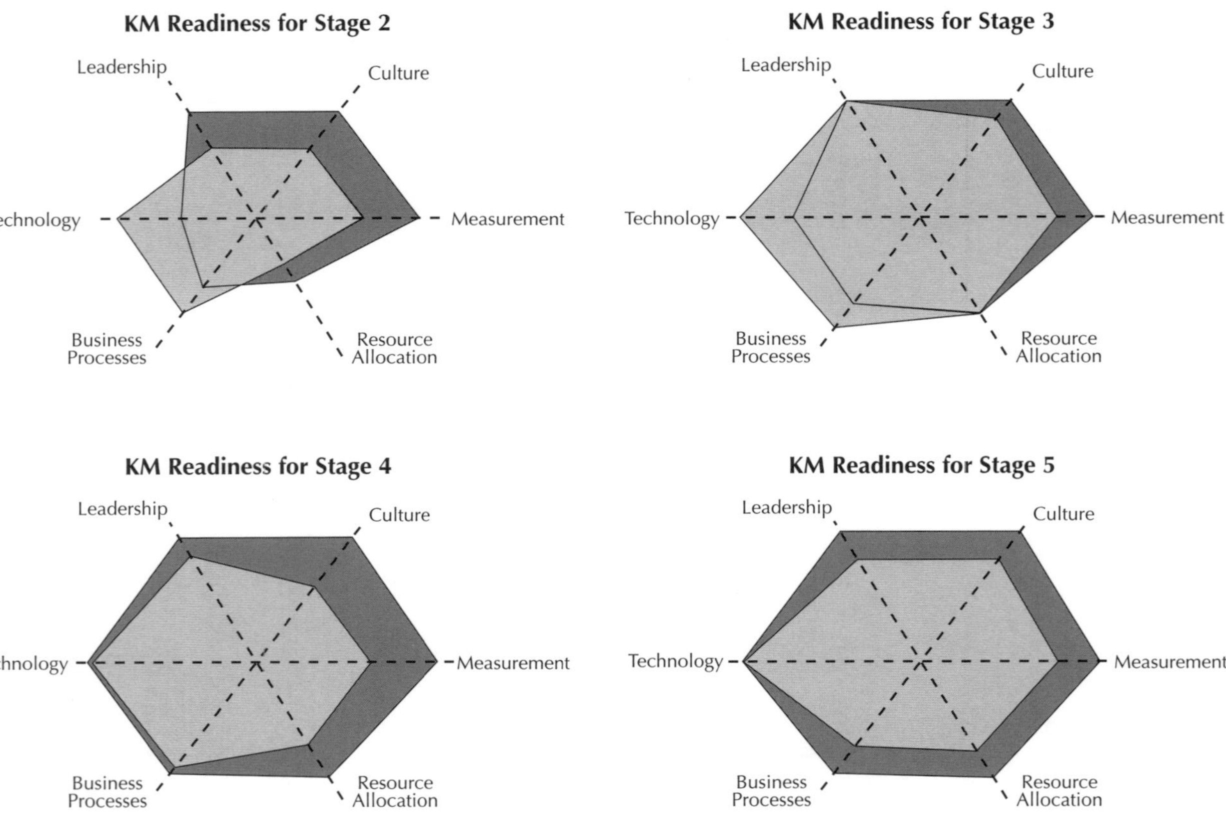

Figure 3. KM Readiness for Five Stages

organization to initiate a KM effort. If not listening to new ideas and not sharing knowledge characterize the culture of the organization, the first thing to do is educate senior leadership on the importance of the organization's culture in order to be competitive in this fast-changing environment. If the organization does not change the culture into a more sharing culture with trust, it will be very difficult to add much value to the organization from KM efforts.

One way to improve readiness for both the leadership and culture components is for senior leadership to have several offsite meetings facilitated by KM gurus to learn about what KM will do for the organization in the next five to ten years. Senior leadership needs to recognize that the organization can be left behind and will not be competitive if KM is ignored. Because most successful organizations are rapidly adopting KM, it will take much longer to catch up. It is an urgent matter to investigate the possibilities of what KM can do for the organization. Once senior leadership recognizes the value of KM and the necessary culture to support it, they will start to consider providing more opportunities to employees to share knowledge and have more informal meetings to encourage innovation.

Considering each organization's actual readiness level and desired level at various stages, different steps will be needed to improve and narrow the gap between the actual level and desired level. Depending on the stage and gap for each key component, different steps will be needed. Due to space limitations, steps needed for all possible 30 situations (five stages with six components) are not included in this discussion.

SUMMARY

This chapter provides an overview of KM implementation stages and tools to measure KM readiness for these stages. Based on DON's five stages of a KCO Journey and Arthur Andersen's KMAT, necessary readiness levels were identified for each component at each stage. Resource allocation was added as a key component. Some steps that can be taken to improve KM readiness are discussed in terms of an example case in which leadership and culture components were not ready to start the KCO journey. The approach recommended is beneficial to anyone who is starting KM initiatives or planning a KM program. It is critical that investments in KM be made where benefits are most likely to result. Anyone implementing KM should consider whether investments are being made at the right stage of the KCO journey.

NOTES

1. Ovum Market Research Report. *Knowledge Management: Building the Collaborative Enterprise*. December 1999.
2. Boyd, S. and M. Kull. *The State of the Knowledge Industry Progress Report '99, Summary Report.* Lighthouse Consulting Group, 1999.
3. APQC. *Successfully Implementing Knowledge Management, Final Report.* 2000.
4. APQC. *Knowledge Management—A Guide for Your Journey to Best-Practice Processes.* 2000.
5. U.S. Department of the Navy. *Knowledge-Centric Organization Toolkit.* 2000.
6. Permission granted by Michael Kull through personal communication to use description of the model.
7. Permission granted by APQC (Farida Hasanali) through personal communication to use description of the model. Farida Hasanali was the project leader of Benchmark Consortium Learning Forum on "Successfully Implementing Knowledge Management."
8. KMAT tool was included in the Navy's "Knowledge-Centric Organization Toolkit."
9. Denning S. *The World Bank and Knowledge Management: The Case of the Urban Service Thematic Group.* Harvard Business School Case (draft), February 2000.

CHAPTER 6

Information Technology and Knowledge Management

The Medium and the Message

Shereen G. Remez, PhD
Jon M. Desenberg

Knowledge has always existed. The emergence of the Internet, e-mail, and other "connecting" technologies was necessary to create what we now call knowledge management. Without these new tools, sharing, creating, and growing new knowledge in large organizations would have been extremely difficult, if not impossible. At the same time, it has become more important to ensure that technology does not become the medium that overtakes the important message of a knowledge culture.

Sometimes the best technology to implement knowledge management is nothing more than hamburgers and french fries. To symbolize the value he placed on his employees' knowledge, a new vice president at Interbrew Corporation, Andrew Brennan, brought in fast food to encourage a frank and casual conversation with his junior managers. He spent only a few dollars, but no executive had ever invested even that much in listening and learning from this group before. For these employees it was enough evidence to show a real cultural change and to demonstrate that their experiences were really valued by someone in charge.

Interbrew is the second largest beer brewer in the world and owns familiar brands like Bass, Rolling Rock, and Labatt's. As the company grew and acquired brands in Europe, North America, and Asia, some of the results were disappointing. Interbrew owns extensive corporate databases, electronic mail systems, and more information on efficiently producing beer than almost any other organization in the world. Still, in some divisions the company was having trouble both passing along its experience and learning from its new employees; management agreed that more expensive technology was not the solution.

For Andrew Brennan, the new vice president, not even the best data repository or collaborative software application was going to help him gain knowledge from employees who were so disconnected that he recalled, "I didn't even know what their job was."

Technology, especially the Internet, has brought us together, just as it connects information and data. Connecting people and their experiences is a primary goal of knowledge management, especially in large and dispersed organizations like the federal government. But when employees, like those in many large organizations, don't feel that their corporate culture values or encourages their input or ideas, technology alone cannot add their intellectual capital to the organization's total assets.

In a forum with the MIT Learning Organization, Interbrew discussed its decision to simplify through hamburger lunches or something as simple as a magic marker and a whiteboard. In another effort to spread knowledge among new employees, a quiet marketing manager was handed a marker and asked to run the rest of a staff meeting. She panicked, but with her boss' encouragement she relaxed and answered questions from the rest of the staff. "I felt very important," she said. "I felt like I achieved something."[1] Typing data into a knowledge warehouse probably would not have had the same effect. By the end of 1999, Interbrew's Asian operations had improved and were turning a profit.

YING AND YANG: THE TECHNOLOGY AND KNOWLEDGE CONTINUUM

Technology is necessary for the large-scale knowledge transfer that large organizations need today. Without it, the worldwide operations we take for granted would be impossible. For this reason, technology and knowledge management operate on a continuum—they are inseparable and interconnected. However, while technology is simply the enabler and driver of knowledge transfer, it is ultimately only a means to an end.

Technology and knowledge management have been wrapped together and confused with each other for so long that their separate paths are almost indistinguishable. Guttenberg invented the printing press, but was his ultimate gift knowledge sharing? Marconi's box would have been a tangle of wires and circuits without the value of its content.

Gartner Group, the technology research and consulting firm, estimates that more than $5 billion was spent on KM projects in 2000. Of that amount, more than 75% is being used for the software, hardware, and infrastructure upgrades most businesses feel are the core of knowledge management. The future will require an equal emphasis on content, culture, and human behavior.

Many executives in both public and private enterprises have a higher comfort level buying an expensive piece of collaborative software than spending less to facilitate face-to-face discussions, lunches, or regular conferences with their employees, suppliers, and customers.

The results from early government KM projects at the Navy and the U.S. General Services Administration, as well as private organizations such as Texas Instruments, revealed that portals, online forums, and other technologically enabled knowledge-sharing applications worked best when they were presaged by low-tech meetings and casual networking. Why would anyone pay attention to a question or comment from someone they had never met and never would meet? Frequently, they wouldn't. Yet the results were much more encouraging after initial time spent together.

At the U.S. General Services Administration, a KM project with the Census Bureau featured an innovative real-time tracking system of all 1,027 census offices around the country. Census and GSA employees were given passwords and used the system to stay informed and in communication around the clock. When asked why the knowledge sharing worked so well on the project, however, both Census and GSA employees mentioned the team-building sessions that went on in low-tech conference rooms throughout the country.

Why does paying for burgers and french fries seem slightly irreverent, but paying for new routers, switches, and applications passes by almost unnoticed? The safety of a large technology purchase is as much about corporate conformity as it is about return on investment.

In reality, according to Larry Prusak, the Executive Director of the IBM Institute for Knowledge Management, the same three measurements can be used for gauging the return on investments in technology and any other resource area.

1. **Effectiveness:** Frequently, large investment decisions are brought before financial boards or others seeking to measure dollars saved. However, effectiveness or business improvements are just as important and simply need to be measured. Whether that measurement is increased customer satisfaction, timeliness, or time to market, effectiveness can often be the single leading indicator for return on any KM technology investment.

2. **Innovation:** In today's economy, innovation is not a bonus. It is required for continued business survival in a growing number of businesses. Knowledge management technology can often be linked to new innovation and ideas and must be measured to capture investment value.

3. **Efficiency:** Dollar savings are often the most impressive, but perhaps this is an overused statistic in today's government environment. Technology has traditionally been used to increase efficiency and save or defer spending. While this indicator is still important, it is not the sole indicator of success.

Although many IT projects fail, it is a rare boardroom meeting today that questions the general wisdom of moving forward with new technology. The U.S. Department of Commerce reports that high-tech investment soared at a 31% annualized pace in the first half of 2000. In contrast, total business investment has been increasing by a solid but more modest rate of 10% per year in recent years (see Figure 1).

On the other hand, changing corporate culture to encourage a new level of employee interchange and exchange of knowledge and ideas is rarely even considered. Investing in the kind of cul-

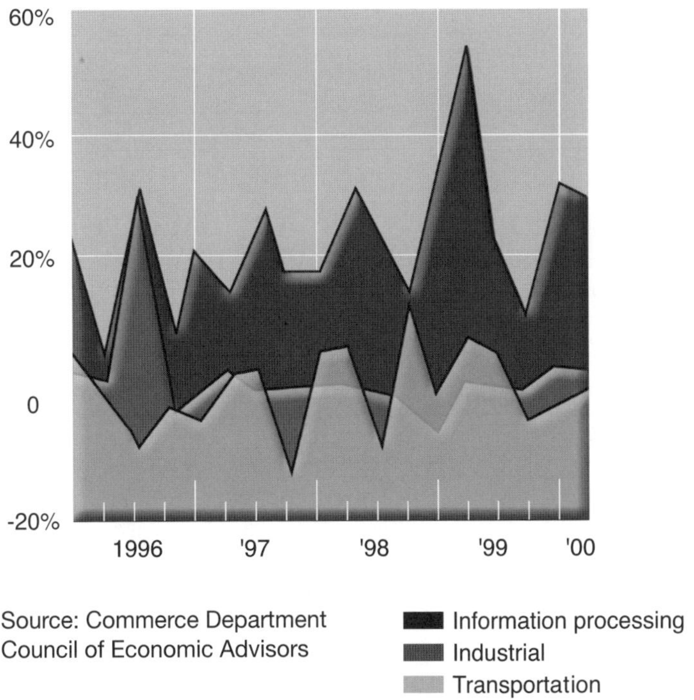

Figure 1. Proportion of GDP Growth from Investment in Various Equipment Sectors

tural change that truly enables KM can be hard to justify in dollars and cents, especially when it may take time away from the organization's "real work." With no firm projected return on cultural investment, many KM projects turn to technology first, sometimes inviting disappointment.

The best portals, communities of practice, and e-mail systems create open feedback loops among groups and individuals, creating a culture of learning. They also allow users, through human interaction, to make sense of a situation much more quickly than would ever be possible by studying reams of information from a corporate databank.

Too often we have seen technology breed isolation, but today's most successful KM technologies concentrate on the three "Cs":

- Context
- Collaboration
- Communication.

Three large organizations, Microsoft, British Petroleum, and Kimberly-Clark, have successfully looked for context, collaboration, and communication in their KM technology investments.

Microsoft's Talent Market

At Microsoft, a changing marketplace has de-emphasized the PC operating system and brought the Web, mobile devices, and corresponding new applications into the spotlight. While there have been attempts to purchase some companies and their internal knowledge, a need is growing to bring current managers and staff together. Employees and team leaders need to exchange knowledge and learn about the new organizational focus, skill sets, and opportunities that are becoming available.

The company uses a combination of technologies to profile its employees' knowledge before connecting them to their peers and projects, where they can have the most impact. The Corporate Executive Board study on the project found that to react quickly in a dynamic environment, the firm established a corporate taxonomy to identify all employees' competencies with standard terminology. Software is the prototypical knowledge business, and this internal "talent market" puts the organization's biggest asset, employee know-how, exactly where it's needed the most. In addition, the system analyzes each employee's current profile against needed competencies and then provides access to customized training resources and Web seminars. While most organizations are not yet ready to leverage their knowledge in quite this manner, the larger lessons of sharing, expanding, and fully using every employee's expertise and knowledge can produce value in any organization.

BP's Virtual Teamwork Project

While the majority of Microsoft's knowledge can be found somewhere on its sprawling Redmond, Washington, headquarters, other companies are highly decentralized. British Petroleum (BP) employs more than 55,000 workers in 70 countries and, after a recent merger, became the world's second largest oil company. BP's Virtual Teamwork project brought high-speed teamwork "stations" to PCs around the world, even using satellite links for the most remote drilling and refining locations.

By combining collaborative and communication technologies into one integrated suite, the organization was able to integrate knowledge management into the daily work environment, even in the middle of the North Sea. Net meeting, electronic whiteboard, virtual meeting places, expert locating, and other systems are all part of the teamwork stations and saved BP $30 million in just the first year of operations. Kent Greenes, the head of BP's knowledge management team, talked to Andersen Consulting's Thomas Davenport about KM technology's enduring business value: "If you have been really successful, people not only want to use the knowledge asset, but they want to support it further because they think it is going to continue to make a difference in their work."[2] When an equipment failure in the North

Sea was diagnosed and fixed remotely from an office in Scotland, the company was able to keep up and running a $150,000 a day project instead of returning to port.

Much of the credit for successful technology implementations, including BP's, can be traced to the use of "coaches," who help project teams utilize the new systems to meet their business goals. Far from frivolous, coaches or technology liaisons bridge the gap between what a system *can* do and what it *will* do for employees and project teams.

Kimberly-Clark and Costco: Intercorporate Knowledge Sharing

While most organizations use KM technology to find, share, and use knowledge internally, a growing number have realized that the knowledge they need lies elsewhere. New KM technology looks to bring knowledge across corporate boundaries. Indeed, big companies' increasing focus on applying technology to leverage specialized knowledge is one reason that U.S. prices for general merchandise—goods from laundry detergent to wool sweaters—fell 1.5% in 1998 and again in 1999, according to Richard Berner, chief U.S. economist at Morgan Stanley Dean Witter.[3]

The Costco chain of warehouse stores and Kimberley-Clark Corporation, for example, have discovered how to share knowledge and expertise. When a Kleenex shortage looms in a Costco store in Philadelphia, long before the store would ever notice it, a Kimberly-Clark data analyst is already working at a computer hundreds of miles away in Neenah, Wisconsin.

"When they were doing their own ordering, they didn't have as good a grasp" of inventory, Kimberly-Clark's data analyst, Michael Fafnis, told *The Wall Street Journal*.[4] Now, a special computer link with Costco allows him to use his knowledge and make snap decisions about where to ship more Kleenex and other products. The knowledge-sharing technology means that he has even more access to sales and inventory details than many Costco executives.

Companies, like individuals, have been taught to hoard knowledge. However, today's businesses, even in old-line areas like paper products, have realized that sharing the right knowledge can be a win-win proposition. Even tissue paper has become a knowledge business. Costco shares customer knowledge and buying trend information with Kimberly-Clark in exchange for the paper company's expertise in inventory, promotion, and other areas. As a knowledge exchange, the two companies do not pay each other, and both agree that the new KM technology is responsible for recent sales increases.

They are also looking at the next stage in intercorporate knowledge technology: collaborating and sharing systems for forecasting, not just analyzing, trends. "This is what the information age has brought to this industry," said Kimberly-Clark. CEO Wayne Sanders. "It gives us a competitive advantage."[5]

THE TECHNOLOGY OF TALK

Companies in knowledge-centric businesses like consulting, software, and pharmaceuticals have had success adjusting their systems to ensure both the speed and convenience of remote access without sacrificing the implicit value and trust employees give each other's ideas through personal contact. Dai-Ichi Pharmaceuticals, for example, established "talk rooms" for the R&D staff to share their concepts and work. The talk room's technology is as simple as a pot of tea and a conference table—formal agendas are purposefully excluded.[6] Promoting casual KM is not limited to a few innovative companies. According to Ann Boyle of Sodhexo Marriott, more than 90% of West Coast high-tech companies offer free coffee rooms as a place to share ideas, stay on-site, and network.

Determining a return on investment from something as "soft" as this informal networking clashes with many accounting departments. But does the barrier in measuring such activities justify not investing in an organization's human capital? Technology is a huge item on any large organization's balance sheet, and 70% of those costs are in maintenance, according to the Gartner Group.[7] While technology upkeep has skyrocketed, maintaining intellectual capital trails woefully behind. Some leading companies are changing that formula by investing in and listening to their employees. Amazon's Jeff Bezos hires for intellectual capital, sometimes without a specific opening in mind. As Steve Jobs said about his management style at Apple Computers at the 1999 annual meeting, "It doesn't make sense to hire smart people and tell them what to do; we hired smart people so they could tell us what to do."[8]

Doing this takes a mixture of old and new technology, but whether it's shared in physical or virtual space, the knowledge itself must be valued, trusted, and felt to be important by the entire community.

THREE MYTHS OF KM TECHNOLOGY

With knowledge management so closely related to technology, many now equate one with the other. Three prevalent myths have helped create the confusion between technology and creating an effective knowledge environment.

Myth: Personal knowledge can be transferred into databases and IT systems.

Fact: Groupware and data warehouses store data, not knowledge. The difference? Laurence Prusak, Executive Director of IBM's Institute for Knowledge Management, explains that "knowledge becomes data when it's written down."[9] When it enters a database, information often loses the context and meaning that made it knowledge. One large company had entered over two million "objects" into its data warehouse when it realized the organization was drowning in data but starving for useful knowledge. Systems make good tools and are often the first step in an organization's KM strategy, but no organization can put bits into a database and assume that somebody else can get back the experience of the first person.

Myth: Technology puts knowledge to work.

Fact: Even the most robust portal or e-mail distribution system cannot ensure that people will see or use the information. Most of our knowledge management technology concentrates on efficiency and logical formulas, but this can rule out the odd piece of knowledge delivered in a face-to-face setting that spurs a dramatic new idea or innovation. Effective knowledge management happens when new knowledge creates action and new ways of working. Simply delivering additional federal real estate information to a professional already overwhelmed with books, journals, and Websites may not deliver the desired impact or return on investment.

Myth: The right technologies can deliver the right information to the right person at the right time.

Fact: As the economy shifts in ever-faster cycles, executives can no longer foresee change by examining the past. In a more stable economy, CEOs and CIOs could look forward and extrapolate their business model into the future before settling on an application or IT system to move information where it was needed. Today, however, it is much more difficult to plan beyond the near term. Thus, it's impossible to build a system that predicts who the right person at the right time even is, let alone what constitutes the right information.

MAKING CONNECTIONS

Knowledge management systems are gaining in popularity even as other forms of communication technology proliferate. Pitney-Bowes Inc., the postage-meter company, annually looks at how the world's workforce is communicating, and its 2000 report reveals that the world is awash in electronic messages. The report also highlights that "knowledge work" is growing in the United States and other industrialized countries. For the first time, the survey showed that e-mail tops the telephone for U.S. workers. According to Pitney Bowes, American employees send and receive more e-mails—50 a day—than phone calls (48 each day). However, they also have 21 voice mails and six cell-phone calls, showing that voice still predominates (see Figure 2).

Americans' voice-mail use is about double that in the other countries. One effect of all this is that American workers say they are less likely to be frequently interrupted at work. About 38% of Americans are interrupted six times or more an hour, compared with 50% in Germany and 43% in France and the United Kingdom. But Americans hold more meetings, both face-to-face and by teleconference, averaging 9.7 a week compared with 5.7 in the U.K., 4.1 in Germany, and 3.3 in France.

Despite the abundance of knowledge and the technology that has allowed it to grow and travel, the gap between knowledge, technology, and results is still large, and the payoff on KM technology has had different outcomes for different organizational cultures. As the technology behind knowledge management has developed, it has mirrored the earlier development of physical management practices.

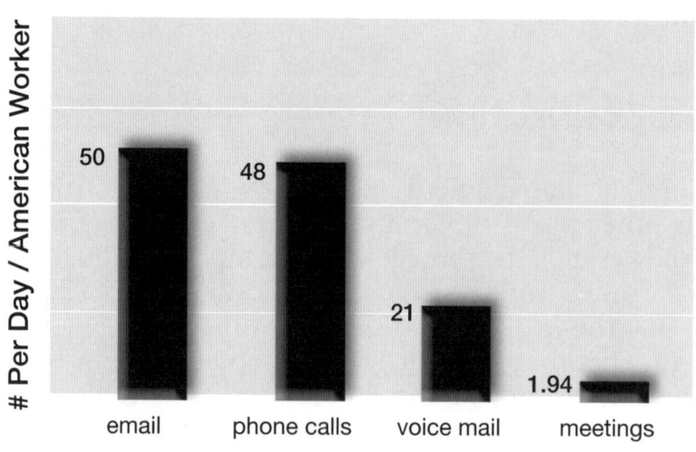

Source: 2000 Pitney-Bowes Workforce Communication Report

Figure 2. Forms of Communication

The parallels are especially striking in the data warehouse area. In the 1980s, America's large manufacturers scaled back the expensive practice of warehousing large supplies of parts and components for later use. "Just in time" delivery enabled factories to save space and resources storing and sorting through components. Jack Welch, General Electric's well-known CEO, toured a GE subsidiary factory in the Czech Republic in 1991, and his Czech hosts could not understand his disapproval of their immense warehouses, capable of storing more than 60 days' worth of inventory. Five years from now data warehouses, with their emphasis on storage and size, may face similar disapproval. Just as industry applied new supply-chain and just-in-time theories to bring what they needed to the right place at the right time, knowledge management may have to rethink the huge and often underused data inventories that have been amassed during the last five years.

THE FUZZY LOGIC OF TACIT KNOWLEDGE

The science of bringing information together in a meaningful way and acting upon it is still in its early stages. Today's knowledge-centric organizations are only beginning to capture more than just raw data. Knowledge, specifically tacit knowledge, is difficult for even today's smartest computer systems to capture and utilize. Tacit knowledge includes all the imprecise information that allows individuals and organizations to form judgments and make decisions. Values and insights—the unwritten skills that make any employee valuable—form the essence of an effective knowledge management program. The ability to store and sort data has formed a solid foundation, but now many organizations are overwhelmed in their abundance. As Wayne Janzen of Lotus Development Corporation's Knowledge Management division says, the next step "is being driven largely by the fact that people are needing to find ways to structure the amount of data they have available to them. New KM tools and techniques are a way to do that."[10]

For technology to address tacit knowledge, it must respond to workplace cultural norms like the "50-foot rule." Michael Kull,

Associate Professor of Knowledge Management at George Washington University, has found that employees are not as likely to collaborate on projects with co-workers who sit more than 50 feet away. Despite our worldwide connections, most work environments still value face-to-face interaction with trusted peers. Ironically, this trend is seen even in supposed technology meccas, such as Silicon Valley, where top dot-coms and others have long been disinclined to telecommuters. Allen Barrales of the Joint Venture Silicon Valley Network says the mentality there still leans toward "face time."

THE KNOWLEDGE EXCHANGE

To test KM technology, it is important to find those who simply can't get face time in their organization. For this reason management consultants, who often work alone with their clients, have served as an ideal proving ground for evaluating new tacit knowledge technology. Andersen Consulting operates around the world, with employees unable to collaborate unless they use Andersen's "Knowledge Exchange" system. The system operates on the company's e-mail servers but replicates itself onto its employees' desktops every day. With more than a dozen categories in areas such as "People," "Industry Knowledge," "Special Topics," "Cost Information," and "Metrics," a consultant can find information on any Andersen project through a variety of different methods. The information can be so valuable that the company is considering the future possibility of selling the knowledge from the system directly to clients. While consultants rely on the Exchange to find knowledge on projects similar to their own, they still face the daily challenge of entering information on their own projects at the end of already busy days. Andersen culture encourages every employee to enter data on a regular basis; but without a more automated method, this task can be onerous and the results sometimes unstructured.

As Lotus's Janzen understands about KM systems, "It has to be automatic in the sense that it's not invasive, allowing people to go about their daily work routine with having to do a lot of additional work."[11] Some promising new technologies take advantage of the computerized work environment already so prevalent in today's organizations, without adding any new layers of complexity or drudgery.

In many organizations, the most accepted and integrated piece of software is e-mail. E-mail itself was the first step in KM for many organizations, as it got people to communicate on a more frequent basis. Ubiquitous and now used more often than any other form of office communication, e-mail is cited as the primary force behind the Internet's rapid growth in users. As the 1999 MIT *Technology Review* study showed, the Web reached 50 million users faster than radio, telephone, television, or cable. Interestingly, the telephone's growth rate from 1940–1945 came closest to approach that of the Web, indicating that two-way communication or knowledge transfer is a major incentive in adopting a new technology (see Figure 3).

E-mail's Knowledge Potential

In large-scale enterprises with hundreds or thousands of employees, e-mail has become the most used and most up-to-date knowledge repository. Even face-to-face conversations are often followed up with an electronic paper trail. It's no wonder, then, that new technologies use e-mail to begin capturing tacit knowledge. By finding key concepts that are repeated in individuals' outgoing e-mail and their attachments, knowledge management technology is now beginning to understand what individuals really do know, as opposed to what they're willing to say they know or what they think they know.

Some systems allow users to change their profiles by adding documents to their individual profile or manually editing their keywords. Once the system establishes profiles, a government manager, for example, can simply type, "Who knows about new courthouse construction in Boston?" The system would quickly produce a list of the best possible contacts. Other systems contact the "experts" first, letting them know that others are interested in

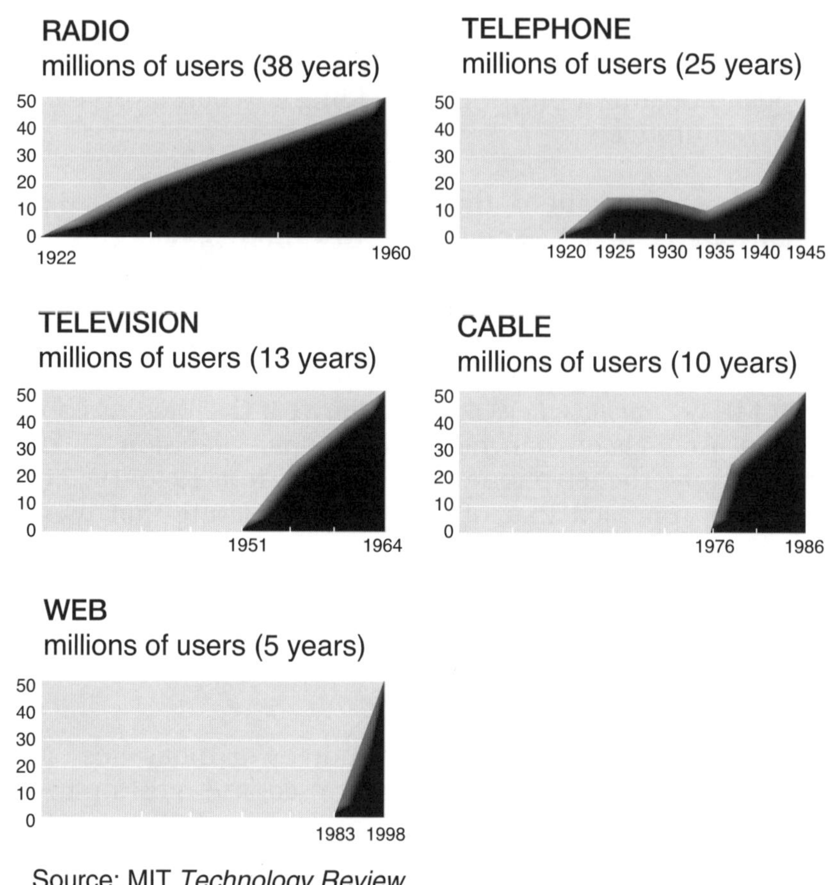

Figure 3. Moving Faster to 50 Million Users

talking and giving them a polite way to evaluate the importance of the requests anonymously and avoid being interrupted in their own work.

While data warehouses and document management systems have understood the importance of formal statistics and other final reports, the knowledge management concept has only recently grown to grasp the importance of tacit knowledge and the unstructured, everyday communications where it can be found.

Certainly, there are important privacy concerns in e-mail-based systems. But in today's workplace, few people question that e-mail ownership and its contents belong to the organization, not the employee.

A final and important difference in these newer KM systems is that they encourage, not discourage, face-to-face and real-time communication. As Laurence Prusak has said, "If people are sitting hunched over your computer all day, the organization is not practicing knowledge management."[12] The best technologies, including these systems, encourage people to meet, share ideas, and perhaps, for a change, actually walk away from their computers. Communities of practice and affinity groups also bring people together, but these latest e-mail–based systems create a direct peer-to-peer contact. These one-on-one relationships are, as anyone who has had the benefit of a private tutor or mentor knows, the best model for learning and knowledge transfer.

Portals: Personalizing Knowledge

While knowledge retrieval systems are wonderful tools to reach out actively for specific information, a more ideal tool might send the right person the right knowledge at the right time before they even know they need it. While no computer can tell exactly what any employee will need in the future, portal technology is beginning to come very close. Portal software sifts through information overload and offers a customized knowledge view for every group or individual.

While mass-market portals such as "My Yahoo" (http://my.yahoo.com) let anyone build a home page from a list of possible news and content components, the more functional internal portals are driving knowledge management inside organizations. These portals, available in various degrees of scalability, are now available from more than a dozen companies. Almost all of them allow users to combine customized information from the Internet, such as weather and news, with windows to corporate applications. From the moment employees come into the portal at the beginning of the day, most of the information they need is available with a single sign-on and password.

Government agencies are already using these systems to bring geographic and industry-specific news to the appropriate employees through crawler and spider technology (which use automated methods to comb through the Internet for specific key phrases) while simplifying the myriad in-house processes that seem to multiply by the month. Portals also offer the ability to develop communities of practice and direct communication links to knowledge keepers for every area and process.

The key to portals is their customization—no two users have to see the same information, and the view can change based on an employee's evolving knowledge profile. The portal industry is now distinguishing customization from personalization. Cormac Foster, an analyst at the research firm Jupiter Communications, says the difference involves explicit versus implicit knowledge. "Customization is giving users what they've told you they want," he says, "and personalization is anticipating what they want."[13]

In this way the technology prevents information overload and increases efficiency. It must be noted that no profile is ever perfect, and many great ideas were launched through a piece of knowledge that would not have made it through a highly filtered user profile. By automatically personalizing and pushing knowledge to employees, however, knowledge management becomes far more seamless and integrated into every employee's daily work routine. The concept is striking a chord with large firms; according to the Delphi Group more than half of the country's 300 largest organizations were planning portal projects in 2000–2001.

Peer-to-Peer: Communities of the Future

KM technology mirrors larger technology trends. Customized and personalized information was developed, for example, as ways for businesses like Amazon.com to maximize their marketing efforts. Today one of the largest new trends is peer-to-peer networking, popularized by Gnutella and others using file-sharing system that do not rely on central computers.

The Internet was originally developed by the Department of Defense as a decentralized system that could withstand a military-style attack on any one component. Only as the Web developed commercially did corporations popularize the server-to-client Web pages, in part to sell advertising and create large audiences based on the model of television and radio. Inside organizations, the Web model was adopted through intranets and departmental Web pages.

Today, peer-to-peer networking looks to take the Internet model "back to the future" by de-emphasizing large, centralized sites and putting individuals directly in touch with each other. To many corporate CKOs, peer-to-peer networking appears tailor-made for knowledge management applications. In fact, limiting such a powerful tool to sharing knowledge only within an organization appears shortsighted to some. Ray Ozzie, the creator of Lotus Notes and the CEO of Groove Networks Inc., feels that peer-to-peer networking will create new ways of facilitating knowledge management within and between organizations through spontaneous, secure interaction on specific issues. "Partners in different companies will be able to work together very closely and define what they want each other to see."[14]

This technology is already being used by Boeing, Hess Oil, and Intel, who have all been able to reduce spending on servers and mainframes while increasing computing power and lessening bandwidth requirements. While security is an issue, one firm, Applied MetaComputing, is offering a turnkey system that includes software that authenticates peers on the network and lets managers create policies, fault-tolerance mechanisms, and file-sharing protocols. Bill Burnham, managing director at Softbank, says the peer-to-peers impact on knowledge management is "a question of when, not if. This is going to have a huge impact across industry."[15]

KM technology and especially peer-to peer knowledge sharing have let many organizations see an entirely new way of working.

With knowledge as a product, a new style of knowledge-based employment is taking advantage of technology breakthroughs. One Silicon Valley executive recruited a group of PhDs in discrete mathematics and graph theory from Minsk, Belarus, to design semiconductors. Using KM systems, the team passed its work from time zone to time zone around the clock, beating a tight deadline. These teams began on Web job sites such as Nationjob.com, Wetfeet.com, and NetTemps.com. Now portals and communities of practice are creating high-powered labor forces without borders. More traditional organizations have also tapped into KM technology for two central reasons:

- Knowledge transfer is a key source for value creation, and organizations now see these investments as keys to a competitive advantage (see Figure 4).

- Leveraging intellectual assets is behind today's major corporate investment in KM systems and technologies (see Figure 5).

David Gelernter, a professor of computer science at Yale, is a leading figure in the third generation of artificial intelligence scientists and is one of the seminal thinkers in the field known as parallel, or distributed, computing. As Gelernter explored using new technology to enhance knowledge management, he discovered its value and its limitations in bringing minds and people together. "A community is not a community of disembodied spoken statements, in part because the most important aspect of the communication that people have is emotional, and one often communicates emotion not in terms of the text but as a subtext. The emotional subtext of human communication is crucial to human thought."[16] It is for this reason that Gelernter and others see the real power of KM technology in capturing the human subtext that has too often been stripped by more primitive data and document management technology.

John Sealy Brown, the Chief Scientist and noted KM leader at Xerox, sees technology in a similar vein. For Brown, the model KM space is an architectural studio, where all the work underway is publicly displayed to peers and supervisors. When one archi-

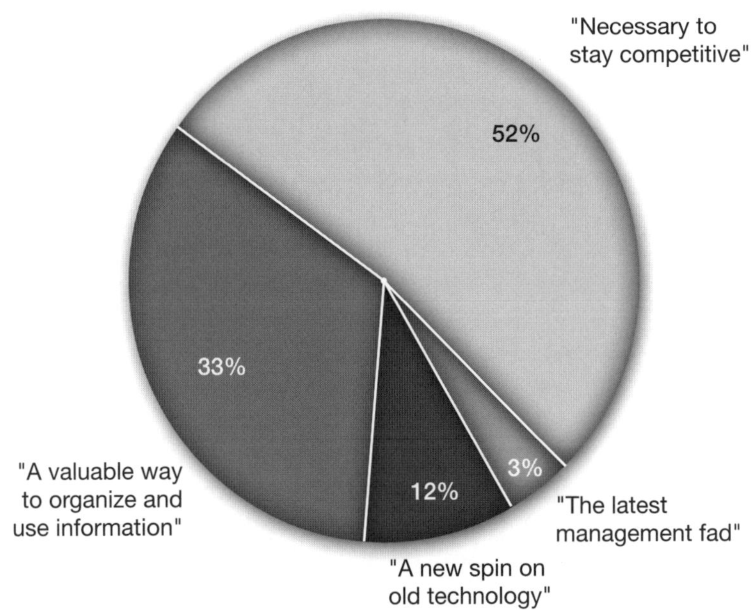

Source: Corporate Executive Board Study, 1998.

Figure 4. The Value of KM Technology Investment

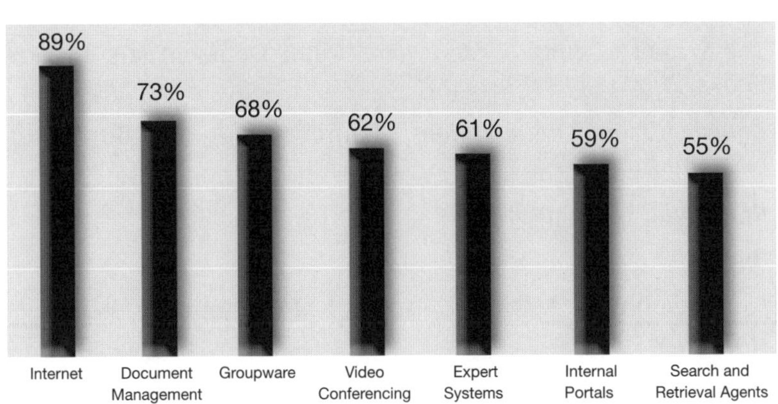

Source: Corporate Executive Board Study, 1998.

Figure 5. Technologies Implemented in Large Organizations

tect critiques another, everyone overhears the dialogue and is influenced in some respect. If the physical space of an architectural studio can be virtually recreated using peer-to-peer or other new technologies, a much greater cross-pollination of ideas can begin. It is appropriate that the most advanced new technologies can only hope to build on the oldest and still most effective method ever devised—the exchange of knowledge from one person to another.

NOTES

1. MIT Learning Organization Forum Report, July 2000
2. *Working Knowledge: How Organizations Manage What They Know,* by Thomas H. Davenport and Laurence Prusak. 1998 Harvard Business School Press.
3. Morgan Stanley Witter Research Report, S&P Earnings Outlook, June 2000.
4. *Wall Street Journal,* September 9 2000.
5. Ibid.
6. Gartner Group Research Note, May 1999.
7. Gartner Group Research Note, April 2000.
8. *The Second Coming of Steve Jobs,* Allan Deutschman, Broadway Books, 2000.
9. *Knowledge in Organizations,* Laurence Prusak, Butterworth-Heinemann, 1997.
10. *KM World,* February 2000.
11. Ibid.
12. Laurence Prusak, Speech to Federal KM Community, Washington D.C., July 2000.
13. *The Personalization Chain: Demystifying Targeted Delivery.* Jupiter Communications Research Note, July 11, 2000
14. "Will Knowledge Management Succumb to Peer Pressure?" IDC Consulting's *IT Forecaster,* September 2000

15. "The Evolution of An Enterprise Data Warehouse," *Information Management Forum Report*, October 2000.

16. *The Muse in the Machine: Computerizing the Poetry of Human Thought*, David H. Gelernter, Macmillan Press, 1994.

ADDITIONAL BIBLIOGRAPHY

Brown, John Seely and Duguid Paul. *The Social Life of Information.* Harvard Business School Press, 2000.

Buckholtz, Thomas J. *Information Proficiency, Your Key to the Information Age.* International Thompson Publishing, 1995.

Davenport, Tom and Laurence Prusak. *Information Ecology: Mastering the Information and Knowledge Environment.* New York: Oxford University Press, 1997.

Edmondson. *Organizational Learning and Competitive Advantage.* London: Sage Publications, 1996.

IBM Consulting Group and the Economist Intelligence Unit. *The Learning Organization: Managing Knowledge for Business Success,* 1996.

Myers, Paul S. ed. *Knowledge Management and Organizational Design.* Boston: Butterworth-Heinemann, 1996.

Robinson, Alan G. and Sam Stern. *Corporate Creativity: How Innovation and Improvement Actually Happen.* San Francisco: Berrett-Koehler Publshers, 1997.

http://sol-ne.org (MIT Learning Organization Network)

http://web.mit.edu/roi (Sloan Research publications)

http://world.std.com/~lo/ (Learning organization discussion pages)

http://www.brint.com (A comprehensive list of links to knowledge management)

CHAPTER 7

HR Knowledge Crafting
The FAA NetFusion Model

Robert G. Turner

This chapter addresses knowledge management from a human resource (HR) perspective. It also presents early thinking about a work in progress at the Federal Aviation Administration (FAA) entitled The FAA NetFusion Model. The model is a coalescing of principles, practices, and concepts that have been evolving at the FAA Team Technology Center over the past decade regarding the role of knowledge workers in the 21st century federal government. FAA NetFusion is offered here as a human resource approach to knowledge management. This new model has been developed and is being explored by an FAA HR research and development team known as the @work Futures Group. While this chapter tends to focus on the cutting edge of HR thinking, it also discusses new e-government technology options that appear to make it feasible to create workspace for knowledge crafters.

> *Nora Watson may have said it most succinctly. 'I think most of us are looking for a calling, not a job. Most of us, like the assembly line worker, have jobs that are too small for our spirit. Jobs are not big enough for people.*
>
> From *Working* by Studs Terkel[1]

Ageless notions of craftsmanship convey images of quality work accomplished by skilled workers in enriching ways. During certain periods in history, the innovative and productive capacities of communities of craftsmen created such unprecedented technological advancements that the future of their civilization was at their door. Sometimes the door opened, sometimes it did not. For example, China came imminently close to industrializing in the 14th century. Then they lost half of a millennium waiting at a door that did not open. There are other all-too-vivid examples of great nations doing this in the last millennium.[2] As we begin the 21st century, we are at such a juncture. Knowledge crafting, as knowledge management is affectionately referred to in this chapter, is a key to the door of our future. This chapter addresses the significance of the new interest in creating and sharing knowledge with the help of advanced technologies and peeks through the keyhole to see what lies just beyond the door.

This chapter weaves together principles, models, and technologies to provide a glimpse of a new tapestry of human resources. This may help provide a vision for future directions for human resources and knowledge crafting in this new era. It is hoped that what is provided here and in the other chapters of this book will catch the attention of human resource leaders and managers, as well as other federal government leaders, and resonate with them. Our federal government agencies' human resource activities reside here together in the nation's capital in one of the leading centers of the global knowledge revolution. More important, these human resource activities serve the most knowledgeable organization of civil servants that has ever existed in any nation at any time.

Civil servants at the FAA are seriously concerned about preparing for the future. At the agency, one finds great pride in helping provide the most amazing transportation system on the planet. Nevertheless, as demand for air transportation increases, it becomes a struggle to create the future. FAA modernization represents the most extensive technology infrastructure renewal project in the country for an organization of its size. Program management of new technology development and acquisition and the integration of new technologies are unusually complex challenges because of the uniqueness and scale of the undertakings. Related organizational and investment issues at the FAA are also challenging.

In the aggregate, modernization at the FAA is hardwired to the innovative capacities of its leaders, managers, unions, and employees. Knowledge crafting provides the opportunity for expanding these capacities. One of the powerful value propositions of knowledge crafting is that it unleashes human capital for being creative and innovative with expandable human processes and scalable technologies. This chapter discusses human resource research and development activities at the FAA in the Human Resource Office that are aimed at discovering and implementing knowledge crafting in a systemic manner using the FAA NetFusion Model. The following sections provide background and description of these endeavors:

1. From Knowledge Worker to Knowledge Crafter
2. The Future of HR and Knowledge-based Work
3. The FAA NetFusion Model
4. People Networks
5. Learning Networks
6. Knowledge Networks
7. Technology Networks
8. mynetwork.gov: From Workplace to WorkSpace

1. FROM KNOWLEDGE WORKER TO KNOWLEDGE CRAFTER

> *A genuine craftsman will not adulterate his product. The reason isn't because duty says he shouldn't, but because passion says he couldn't.*
>
> Walter Lippmann

Over the last four decades, the principal connotation of *knowledge worker* has been an individual that performed work significantly oriented to data, information, and knowledge. It usually meant that the individual's principal resource was knowledge and that he or she created products or services that were substantially knowledge-based. In the work of the @work Futures Group the use of the term *knowledge crafter* refers to an individual who skillfully draws upon her or his knowledge while using knowledge networks and tools to create products and services. The idea of craftsmanship implies not merely working with knowledge, but also managing the knowledge creating processes. A knowledge crafter optimizes the *knowledge flow* between his or her knowledge, the knowledge available through networks, and the knowledge elements of their offering. The knowledge crafter seeks a clear knowledge flow and strives for his or her products and services to embody the best knowledge possible.

Little interest was stirred when Peter Drucker coined the term *knowledge worker* in 1959[3]. Later, as other analysts described the economic shift to a post-industrial society, the knowledge worker label became increasingly popular. By the mid-1980s, it was at the core of discussions about the nature of the emerging economy. The following quote from an article by Peter Drucker entitled "Managing Knowledge Means Managing Oneself," provides a sense of how far the thinking about knowledge management has evolved:

> *In a few hundred years, when the history of our time will be written from a long-term perspective, it is likely that the most important event historians will see is not technology, not the Internet, not e-commerce. It is an unprecedented change in the human condition. For the first time—literally—substantial and rapidly growing numbers of people have choices. For the first time, they will have to manage themselves. And society is totally unprepared for it.*[4]
>
> Peter F. Drucker

Drucker's emphasis on the role of the individual has been consistent over time. While he is considered the father of business management, it is not because of the incapacities of employees that he advocates the need for management. It is interesting to consider that Drucker said of "MBO" that he never capitalized the letters in the concept *management by objectives* and that he always used it as follows: *management by objectives* **and** *self control*. This is quite a different perspective than popularized by the business school programs of the sixties and seventies. From the beginning of his work, Drucker saw the true value of the individual in the workplace.

At the heart of the knowledge crafter concept is the operating principle that the knowledge crafter is self-managing. This concept is not intended to diminish the larger environment and immediate context to which the knowledge crafter is accountable. What it focuses on is the growing complexity of work and the increasing need for judgment and decision making in the performance of work. Over the past two decades, writers have increasingly described the concentration of decision making in organizations as moving to the periphery. Hence, the question increasingly becomes, *What conditions does an employee require to be in an optimal decision making position?* This question could be taken as either a question for management or a question for the employee. Preferably it is a question for both. In terms of the knowledge crafter concept, the employee increasingly has the responsibility to create the conditions for effective decision making. Ideally employees find themselves in a position that is knowledge rich and deeply collaborative.

2. THE FUTURE OF HR AND KNOWLEDGE-BASED WORK

HR needs to be a harbinger and leader of knowledge crafting in every agency and throughout the federal government. Although other activities in organizations may have more resources, such as technology expertise or infrastructure development funds, no other activity has the systemic view of human capital HR has. Unfortunately, while HR in the public sector has a keen affinity for its fellow civil servants, it has not had the compelling economic drivers to create new human capital models, principles, or practices as fast as the private sector. For example, according to the July 1999 GAO report to Congress entitled *Managing for Results: Opportunities for Continued Improvements in Agencies' Performance Plans*:

> *Most of the fiscal year 2000 annual performance plans do not sufficiently address how the agencies will use their human capital to achieve results. Specifically, few of the plans relate—or reference a separate document that relates—how the agency will build, marshal, and maintain the human capital needed to achieve it performance goals. This suggests that one of the central attributes of high performance organizations—the systematic integration of mission and program planning with human capital planning—is not being effectively addressed across the federal government. The general lack of attention to human capital issues is a very serious omission because only when the right employees are on board and provided the training, tools, structure, incentives, and accountability to work effectively is organizational success possible.*
>
> *Although the plans often discuss human capital issues in general terms, such as recruitment and training efforts, they do not consistently discuss other key human capital strategies used by high-performing organizations.*[5]

The good news is that the constantly improving body of knowledge and tools available for knowledge crafting are providing HR leaders and government leaders in general unprecedented human capital strategy options. As the relationship between human capital and knowledge crafting becomes clearer, great strides will be taken.

In any case, it is critical to check the compass of human resources along the way as employees, organizations, and society traverse unprecedented paths. In society and in our workplaces, we are not only experiencing one of the most traumatic social evolutions in the history of work, but we are doing so at a dangerous pace. This was the essence of Alvin Toeffler's visionary thesis in *Future Shock* in 1970:

> *To survive, to avert what we have termed future shock, the individual must become infinitely more adaptable and capable than ever before. He must search out totally new ways to anchor himself.*

> *. . . Before he can do that, however, he must understand in greater detail how the effects of acceleration penetrate his personal life, creep into his behavior and alter the quality of existence.*[6]

During the past decade of the 20th century, HR in the federal government has faced a barrage of external and internal change dynamics. While the private sector has experienced periods of both recession and economic growth, growth has been the dominant trend. In the federal environment, however, the approach to HR has been consistently constricted with regard to investment and resources. Along with downsizing, cost cutting, and unstable budgeting in the federal government, major trends in organizational management, such as business process reengineering, have substantially shifted the HR focus in the federal environment from new generational strategic planning initiatives to reprioritization based on reduced resources.

Attempts to recast the role of HR have included alluring sets of issues that vie for the driver's seat. Issues such as centralization vs. decentralization, in-house vs. outsourced, and transactional role vs. consultative role take on bizarre twists with leaner budgets. Caution is in order here. Employee benefits and employee development costs, for example, should not drive the HR investment. Even though they are essential and dominate fiscally, they should not subtract from the pursuit of new strategic HR initiatives. Invaluable questions may be: When you take away the traditional HR services, what is the HR investment? and What is the cost per employee of the HR strategic R&D efforts? Employees, managers, leaders, and organizations in the federal government need unprecedented HR capabilities, and these require vision and investment.

When a company like PeopleSoft spends $525 million over two years to update its version 7.5 to 8.0, this tends to signal a significant shift in the direction human resource services can move. The direction PeopleSoft is taking discards the client server model and creates a portal-type interface for their more than 100 traditional applications and 59 newer E-business applications. PeopleSoft set out to provide virtual 24x7 capabilities to a more flexible and mobile workforce and, in the process, is creating a more responsive and integrated human resource services environment. This not only follows good practices such as disintermediation, where the lower value intermediate service provider is eliminated, but it also enables employees who are moving to increased self-management. Most human resource offices in the federal government find it impossible to build the business case for developing next-generation HR information systems (HRIS) on their own. As the cost rises because of the sophistication of functionality, it's easy to understand why these systems cannot be easily home grown. Even as the decisions turn to COTS[7] solutions, there are still customization and implementation investment challenges.

In *The ROI of Human Capital,* Jac Fitz-ens, founder and chairman of the Saratoga Institute, presents human capital measurement processes for supporting the value of investing in employee performance. The first chapter is actually entitled "Human Capital: The Profit Lever of a Knowledge Economy." In relation to the knowledge work of organizations he writes:

> *Every employee is an information repository. Knowingly or not, people pick up data in the course of doing their jobs. In many cases, they are not told to do that. What is worse, when they offer data to managers, they are rebuffed with the attitude, You're not paid to think! I believe that the companies that learn how to turn on the information- and intelligence-gathering capability that lies dormant in most employees will dominate the future. And the ROI of human capital in those firms will be astronomical. They will be able to produce much more per person. They will be opening new product lines faster, creating new markets while competitors are reworking old ones, and continually improving life for customers and employees. When that is achieved, management will truly be leveraging the potential of its human capital.*[8]

Jac Fitz-ens presents this book as a summation of years of research at the Saratoga Institute where the client base includes most of the Fortune 100 corporations. The institute's research ranges from dealing with such tough human resource challenges as labor shortages to stepping back and looking at the larger view of management practices during the past 50 years. By their count, researchers at the institute tabulate over 30 major management approaches and 10,000 related books during the period. Given this perspective, Jac Fitz-ens concludes in the last paragraph in his book:

> *. . . we need to support studies aimed at improving the ROI of knowledge management, as well as the effects of information technology on people's work experience. Already, some firms are reforming their supervisory and management practices to deal with the emerging values and dynamics of the new marketplace. We need to know more and we need to know it today.*

Measuring human capital and knowledge crafting ROI with both quantitative and perceptual measures will be insightful in federal agencies, especially as measurements are linked to mission goals and enabling activities. Along with these evaluation efforts, there should be explicit acknowledgment of the assumptions being made about federal employees. In Thomas O. Davenport's book *Human Capital* employees are placed in valuation formulas in an empowering way. Historically, employees are viewed as costs; more recently employees have been valued as assets. Davenport writes:

> *"Workers are assets" has been the dominant metaphor of late twentieth-century management. In some ways, it represents a worthy elevation of employees to the status they deserve. People are, after all, the chief engine of prosperity for most organizations. What other factor of production contributes so much to strategic success. In other ways, however, the asset metaphor falls short of fully expressing the value that people bring to the workplace. . .*[9]

How could the concept of employee as *investor* be translated into the federal sector? There has always existed the view of the federal employee as contributing a public service. This is evidenced by the term *civil servant*. Historically the connotation of civil servant involves being in service to both the public and the nation. Still the same, what does the citizen bring to employment in the federal government? In what ways does a view of a federal employee's capabilities and contributions impact the view of the employee as a knowledge resource and knowledge crafter? Perhaps the concept of a federal employee as a civil servant is the best nomenclature we could want. In any case, employees, management, unions, and leadership need to refresh the finest meanings of this employee label. Moreover, HR needs to help characterize employees as more than simply costs or assets. Careful study would reveal that current views of employees are the drivers of how people are supported, organized, engaged in work, and supervised in the federal workforce.

From a knowledge-crafting perspective, one might say that a core purpose of HR is to provide *know-how* to the organization. At the FAA, HR has striven to move beyond core employee needs and issues to become more attuned to the business and mission imperatives of the organization and the know-how required for effective mission performance. This not only helps HR guide the people processes more intelligently; it also enables HR to respond faster in a consultative manner. Please note that the know-how view cuts an exceptionally wide path through the entire range of HR activities. For example, as one looks at any benefit policy the question may be asked, Do the benefits motivate and empower employees to provide their best know-how in the daily accomplishment of work? As a knowledge-crafting practice, this type of HR question needs to shift to broader questions such as, Will this type of benefit help our employees become more self-managing?

Extending beyond its current reach, HR must become a more viable player in the organization's information technology infrastructure. This involves becoming increasingly high tech and web-centric. Who wants to go there? This is where the visionary HR leadership needs to venture. One of the concepts at the @work Futures Group is called The HR FusionPoint Concept. This term is used to describe a five-step, 24- to 36-month, cyclical process designed to continuously be reused:

- First, HR leaders envision a point on the horizon where they believe certain knowledge processes and technologies would successfully fuse in new ways.

- Second, HR collaborates with other organizational players as partners to identify early adopters and resources.
- Third, prototype opportunities are designed and developed as a test bed for HR's vision.
- Fourth, as the prototype effort comes to fruition, an evaluation is conducted which includes measurement of impact on the organization's mission, new support for human processes, and performance of the technologies.
- Fifth, recommendations are then made to the CIO for appropriate enterprise-wide adaptation.

This process is designed to draw dynamically upon HR's capabilities for supporting electronic government human process development while minimizing HR's need to establish enterprise-wide knowledge management infrastructure resources. As HR engages more extensively in knowledge management, this sort of process will provide a pragmatic approach. What is most important is that HR comes to the table with a leadership commitment to knowledge management infrastructure.

3. THE FAA NETFUSION MODEL

The FAA Team Technology Center was originally established as a premier planning and decision-support center to provide a creative environment, consulting support for advanced meeting processes, and world-class collaboration tools. The motto of the center is *Breakthrough!* because the center helps users work to the edge that is often needed to achieve creative and innovative results. From the beginning, a secondary purpose of the center was to explore processes and technologies that enable virtual work. In the early years of the Team Technology Center research, significant progress was attributed to membership in the Institute for the Future (IFTF) which is based in Menlo Park, California.[10] The IFTF is one of the leading consortiums in the world for tracking and forecasting computer technology trends and their impact on organizations and society. The IFTF provides an invaluable perspective for exploring the edge of new computer technologies and the balance between technologies and human processes. For example, Robert Johansen of the IFTF authored the book *Groupware,*[11] and the IFTF has been a lead researcher of this category of collaborative technologies. Also notable is that the earliest introductions to knowledge management for the Team Technology Center were provided by the IFTF in 1993.

During the past several years, in partnership with the Indian Health Service, a new organization development concept was formulated to respond to rapidly evolving organizational and technological changes. This concept was labeled OD^3. Essentially, OD^3 connotes a new era, as in the Third Millennium, and three strategic focuses for organization development: virtual organizations, knowledge management, and organizational learning. What stimulated thinking in this direction was a question: How can we leverage OD? It was concluded that by relating OD more closely to the other three disciplines, they could all resonate with each other. Currently, in each of these disciplines there are struggles with internal dichotomies of technologies and human issues. Each reflects a struggle for strategic direction. Each reflects the need to dynamically coalesce new concepts, processes, and technologies. With OD^3 as a catalyst, it is possible to foster an integrated evolution, leading to new levels of innovation for each discipline.

Subsequently, the new FAA @work Futures Group was organized to include the Team Technology Center, and a new conceptual approach to research and development was formulated. This new model, the FAA NetFusion Model, builds upon the OD^3 concept and shares a similar core. The @work Futures Group considers models and metaphors as indispensable media for learning and working. The concept of networks is a core aspect of their model and implies dynamic interactions between individuals, groups, parts of organizations, and external relationships. Many different flexible metaphors have been offered to depict modern organizational trends, especially since the mid-1980s. The IFTF itself offered up the idea of a fishnet metaphor.

> *The fishnet is a metaphor we have carefully chosen to express the form of organization emerging from the current turmoil. If we are correct that tomorrow's organizations will look and function like fishnets, then it is important to think of them, talk about them, and create them like fishnets. If we hire pyramid builders or mechanics or road builders to create an organizational fishnet, the results will be disappointing. Fishnets are not made of wood, stone, steel, or concrete for a reason. Unfortunately, many of today's corporate organizations are still being built by people who think they are building rigid structures, not fishnets. Their metaphors, and therefore their tools, are wrong.*[12]

The use of the network metaphor is not intended to advance an alternative to our hierarchical federal organizations. Although there are new design criteria considerations for hierarchical infrastructures, the basic form has merit for serving such a large system as the American public. It may be concluded that the network metaphor is describing only the informal organizational activities in the federal sector. Nevertheless, the network metaphor also may describe secondary organizational architecture that is common and popular in the federal environment. For many years, task forces and ad hoc work groups of various kinds have increasingly worked cross-functionally and across agencies. These types of activities should not be regarded as merely informal alternatives to the formal hierarchy.

The significance of the design of organizational structures is expressed in the words of David Nadler and Michael Tushman in their book *Competing by Design: The Power of Organizational Architecture*:

> *After more than forty years of combined experience with more than fifty organizations of all kinds throughout the world, we've come to realize that organizational design is at once one of the most common—and one of the most commonly mishandled—of all business activities.*[13]

For a global view of the emergence and significance of networks, please refer to the three-volume work of Manuel Castell entitled *The Information Age: Economy, Society and Culture.* In particular, *Volume 1—The Rise of the Network Society*[14] provides a profound analysis of the nature of networking in the global society. For purposes of understanding the significance of networks in the modern organization, one of the most insightful blueprints is found in *The Age of the Network: Organizing Principles for the 21st Century,* by Jessica Lipnack and Jeffrey Stamps.[15] The opening two paragraphs and the final paragraph from their book report:

> *The network is coming of age as a mature, useful, and pervasive form of organization. Networks have been around for a long time, but now they are moving from the informal to the formal, from dealing with peripheral concerns to doing "real work"—getting things done and coping with complexity.*
>
> *Life has become too complicated for hierarchy and bureaucracy. With change as the underlying driver, organizations need more speed and flexibility, greater scope and sharper intelligence, more creativity and shared responsibility.*
>
> *Networks bridge the self and the group, the daily and the eternal, the mundane and the sacred, and carry us into the 21st century.*

Another thought leader who values the network metaphor is Kevin Kelly. He begins the first chapter of his book *New Rules for the New Economy* with:

> . . . *The symbol for the next century is the net. The net has no center, no orbits, no certainty. It is an infinite web of causes. The net is the archetype displayed to represent all circuits, all intelligence, all interdependence, all things economic, social, or ecological, all communications, all democracy, all families, all large systems, almost all that we find interesting and important.*

Implied in the FAA NetFusion Model title is the fusing of networks. At the conceptual level, the @work Futures Group is exploring two primary directions. First, how do people collaborate, create and share knowledge, and learn in networks? Second, how can people networks, learning networks, knowledge networks, and technology networks be fused to create synergistic results? The following sections provide a brief introduction to the domains of the FAA NetFusion Model and examples of ideas and technologies being evaluated.

> Fusion'-zhen *1. merging of diverse elements into a unified whole 2. the union of atomic nuclei to form heavier nuclei resulting in the release of enormous quantities of energy when certain light elements unite*

4. PEOPLE NETWORKS

The first type of network in the FAA NetFusion Model is people networks. Drawing again from Kelly, "The central economic imperative of the network economy is to amplify relationships." Attention to what may be called *knowledge relationships* is part of what is being considered here. This subject is so enticing that the body of literature on social capital is expanding rapidly. Numerous related books are being written for publication. Social capital is the value to an organization that is created in interpersonal relationships.

The @work Futures Group sees people networks linking people with other people and to communities of experts with shared interests throughout the organization to leverage human capital. These networks enable employees, as investors in the organization, to share their talents, commitment, and passion to accomplish their missions. The value-added benefits of this way of interacting are:

- Minimizes barriers of time and distance
- Creates more choices about whom can be called upon
- Makes best experts available to meet mission needs
- Offers 365:24/7 access options for meeting and work
- Provides savings in travel costs and staff time and energy.

To help accomplish the above, the @work Futures Group has eagerly researched collaboration tools that provide a variety of discussion and meeting functionalities.

One software that the @work Futures Group is evaluating is WebIQ, by WebIQ, Inc. of Austin, Texas.[16] Core features of the WebIQ software include a user-friendly meeting set-up capability with dynamic agenda-building resources, various brainstorming templates, and a set of voting tools. Beyond the advanced meeting tool capabilities that WebIQ provides for decision support and decision making, the company has a product strategy to provide increasingly complex decision support tools where sophisticated process control is beneficial or where statistical or quantitative analysis is designed.[17]

The @ work Futures Group has also given extensive attention to creating and sustaining communities of practice. Of this type of community, Etienne C. Wenger and William M. Snyder wrote in the Jan-Feb 2000 edition of the *Harvard Business Review*:

> *Today's economy runs on knowledge, and most companies work assiduously to capitalize on that fact. They use cross-functional teams, customer- or product-focused business units, and work groups—to name just a few organizational forms—to capture and spread ideas and know-how. In many cases, these ways of organizing are very effective, and no one would argue for their demise. But a new organizational form is emerging that promises to complement existing structures and radically galvanize knowledge sharing structures, learning, and change. It's called the community of practice.*
>
> *What are communities of practice? In brief, they're groups of people informally bound together by shared expertise and passion for a joint enterprise.*[18]

In the mid-1990s the Team Technology Center began researching how to create knowledge bases to support networks of professionals around technical subjects. In recent years, this evolved into an approach for a replicable web-based framework for relatively fast and easy support to communities of practice. To this end, several classes of bright and eager students from Virginia's George Mason University's graduate program for organizational learning joined in the research at the center. A set of core web-based resources was identified as:

- A locator to provide convenient contact within and outside the community
- A forum with a range of meeting tools for promote discussion and field requests for expertise
- An events calendar to track major events and professional development opportunities for members of the communities
- A glossary to support a common language pertaining to the subject of interest
- A knowledge center for developing an outline of the subject for capturing shared documents, links, and slides to be used by anyone in the community.

The web provides a rich environment for this type of community to flourish. In relation to knowledge crafting and electronic government, creating web support for informal professional communities of this sort would be a low-cost investment—with a high payoff opportunity—that an HR partner and a technology partner could create together for use across the federal sector. Actually it would be extremely interesting to have an HR community of practice on the web focused on sharing knowledge about the convergence of new HR processes and technologies.

> *Profound changes often happen in simple ways. Take the "+" sign and rotate it 45 degrees. That's all it takes to shift from the Industrial to the Knowledge Economy. And that's all it takes to start to create a vibrant and exciting work environment where people feel engaged as whole persons, and their knowledge, insights and wisdom become the most valuable element in our companies.*
>
> *. . . First, we have to tap our unlimited resources of intellectual and emotional capital in our enterprises. Second, as the Knowledge Economy multiplies peoples' ideas, it engenders new possibilities that further multiply the innovative energies of one another, especially as people learn to be open, honest and collaborative with one another.*[19]
>
> Dr. Charles Savage

So many of these more recent collaboration capabilities are still unfamiliar. But we pursue them as we become increasingly uncomfortable with voids they seek to fill. Working virtually is impersonal and awkward in comparison to face-to-face events, but is that the right comparison? How does meeting virtually match up against no access? When expertise is required for collaboration, we need unlimited choices about whom we can call upon in our organizations and when we call upon them. How will people networking processes and tools evolve? The web has not only created a global forum for new relationships, new networks, and new interactions, but it is also building a new environment for new kinds of relationships, new kinds of networks, and new kinds of interactions. As we push the boundaries of our federal organizations to higher performance levels and to innovation, these are the kinds of questions we should ask, and HR needs to lead the discussion.

5. LEARNING NETWORKS

After several decades of trumpeting the message of life-long learning, we are increasingly hearing that the distinction between work and learning is becoming blurred. While this sounds like the evolutionary impact of employees moving to a higher plane of learning and working, it is initially less progressive than that. Some of the drivers come at us from extremely complex issues like the dearth of talent because of aging population and lower birth rate, overnight obsolescence as a result of breakneck technological advancement, leadership exodus through early retirement, and changing employer-employee relationships. The upshot is a rapidly increasing need for learning resources that employees can use on demand, whenever and wherever they choose to accomplish work.

Nevertheless, amidst the driving need to fill performance gaps with learning and development, there is a reaching for higher order learning that involves creating new knowledge through developing organizational learning capabilities. Organizational learning includes social process that can take place at all levels in an organization. This can happen wherever individuals, work groups, and large organization activities interact intentionally to develop new ways of seeing and perceiving and develop new mental models and insights. This type of intentionality leads to new capacity for knowledge creation and enhanced ability for effective action. Communities of practice and learning networks are likely places for learning about learning. This is largely because of the special affinity of people in these entities, which encourages caring for the learning processes. One of the most useful resources for researching organizational learning is *The Dance of Change: The Challenges to Sustaining Momentum in Learning Organizations*[20].

The @work Futures Group envisions learning networks as learning spaces for multiple approaches to learning. In particular, these networks are intended to support the convergence of learning and work. Value-added benefits of web-supported learning networks include:

- Organization-wide distribution of learning resources
- On-demand availability of learning in the workspace
- User-controlled review and repetition of resources
- Improved work performance
- Less expensive delivery of learning resources.

Government agencies such as the General Services Administration (GSA) and the U.S. Small Business Administration (SBA) are paving the way with on-line learning. For example, Cisco Systems, the worldwide leader in technology networking for the Internet, has an agreement with SBA to produce a six-module online learning program for incorporating the Internet into the day-to-day business of small business. The SBA estimates that there are more than 25 million small businesses in the U.S. An independent consulting firm reports that in 1998, small businesses spent $2 billion on products and services via the Internet.

In 1999 the figure rose to $25 billion and is expected to rise to $118 billion in 2001. The SBA wants to be there to help them out. Perhaps this is why the president of Cisco said, "on-line training will make e-mail look like a rounding error."

In anticipation of a new world of virtual learning, when broadband capabilities drive the Web, the @work Futures Group is watching the development work of Ninth House Network[21], a San Francisco-based company determined to change the face of learning. Ninth House takes its name from the Sumerian Code that dates to 2700 B.C. The Sumerians described life as a journey through twelve houses. In the Ninth House you master higher learning and experience personal limits. Ninth House courses are presented as management development, but when you step back and consider the offerings and the delivery system, you start thinking in terms of this type of training for knowledge crafters in general. Just to whet your appetite, the training courses thus far feature the work of people like Ken Blanchard, Tom Peters, and Peter Senge. Can you imagine Hollywood-quality sitcom episodes? To keep you engaged, they toss in a computer-generated mentor of your preference. Finally, as a member of the Ninth House network, you belong to networks to help you with decision-making resources as you need them.

Many popular sources on knowledge management have posed this question or one similar to it: What do we know about what we know? Perhaps another good question would be: How do we learn what we learn in our organization? Once we start asking these types of questions, eventually the words *learning* and *knowledge* start showing up in the same questions. Furthermore, increasing numbers of the questions are going to be questions that go to the heart of HR's role in the organization.

6. KNOWLEDGE NETWORKS

The @work Futures Group is interested in the full range of the discipline of knowledge management and is particularly keen on knowledge networks because they enable knowledge creation, organization, transfer, and access throughout the organization in unprecedented ways. Speed, volume, and richness of knowledge become hallmarks. Know-how is shared to create the future. The benefits of this type of network include:

- Activities build on past successes and avoid past mistakes
- Best practices are shared and adopted faster
- Knowledge is accessible any time, any place
- Individual tacit knowledge is captured for the benefit of all
- Added knowledge supports richer innovation.

A growing amount of attention within knowledge management is being given to the development of portal technologies. This is largely because portals converge the power of well-selected web-linked resources with individual choice and speed. Space limitations make it impossible to delve into portals here; however, it would be well to mention a platform that the @work Futures Group is evaluating. Lotus is creating a new KM family with K-Station as the first offering. K-Station is a corporate portal that is customizable and personalized. It includes the capability to create discussion databases. The second product, Lotus Discovery Engine, will include an expertise locator and a knowledge mapping tool. Once installed and connected to knowledge repositories, Lotus Discovery Engine can identify affinities between people, documents, and K-Station resources. Both products offer the capabilities to exchange instant messaging if the person you wish to communicate with is online.

Another interesting software tool the @work Futures Group is working with is ProCarta by Domain Knowledge, Inc.[22] of Toronto, Canada. What ProCarta does is extremely practical and very powerful. This tool places the ability to model work processes in anyone's hands, creating both text outline views and flow-charting views. Then the fun begins. Easily visible tables provide related information with the ability to capture all related types of files that would support every task. Particularly significant are the abilities to log actions related to the development of the processes and to keep a journal of changes to the process. With these types of abilities, ProCarta is one of the finest examples of the capability of transferring human capital or tacit knowledge into structure capital or explicit knowledge for use throughout the organization.

7. TECHNOLOGY NETWORKS

> *The Internet and other information and communication technologies are changing the way we work, learn, communicate with each other, and do business. These technologies are shaping our economy and our society in the same way that the steam engine and electricity defined the Industrial Age.*
>
> The White House, Dec 17, 1999

The @work Futures Group is comprised of HR experts in organization development, learning, and collaborative technologies. While this is an unusual blend of coworkers, the HR-technology balance is considered essential to accomplish the research and development work in its charter. As a whole, the research group understands that technology changes the way we work, learn, and share knowledge by providing new infrastructures—new capacity, new speed, new access, and new processes. Most of all, they provide new synergy by converging and fusing our best resources together. They see the value-added benefits of technology networks as:

- New resources for learning, knowledge creation, and work
- Rapid cycles of process improvement
- Fast delivery of new capabilities and updates
- Connectivity—networks become key to innovation
- Lower infrastructure costs.

8. mynetwork.gov: FROM WORKPLACE TO WORKSPACE

The transition from workplace to workspace is happening on many fronts. Over the next two or three years, the proliferation of wireless mobile work will be staggering. Telework is increasing steadily in the federal sector. There is more than a bit of irony in the simultaneous increased expectations for both mobility and availability. Language like *virtual, wireless, ubiquity, pervasive,* and *24/7* is becoming more common. For the @work Futures Group, one of the exciting things that is emerging in this area of social and technology change is the ability to create a highly self-managed workspace for knowledge crafters. The concept for this @work Future Group workspace concept is called *mynetwork.gov.* Functionalities of this workspace include:

- Core self-management tools: calendar, contact info, to do, etc.
- Contracts and management relationships: position and project related
- Organizations and groups: positions and roles
- Network: communities of practice, learning and knowledge networks
- Credentials: education, certifications, professional memberships, resumes, recognition and awards, personal profile with competency listings, employment history
- Portfolio: examples of work and references
- Desired work: special interests for new work opportunities
- "Work Bench": office suite, KM tools, project management tools, modeling and simulation tools, process tools, etc.
- File storage
- Search engines

- Report creation: on-line reports, dashboards
- Communication suite
- Portal service for news, organization intelligence, etc.

The design of this workspace is intended to support the knowledge crafter throughout his or her career. It would reside on the web and would be fully available all the time. In the future, special workstations in offices, hotels, and home environments would support unique functions such as large-screen projection. Otherwise, the user interface will be an extremely convenient wearable system or an easily available public appliance. Certainly the nature of this way of working poses many questions for HR. It is hoped that one of the questions is, How does this support a knowledge crafter's self-management and decision-making?

CONCLUSION

A chapter on HR and knowledge crafting in the federal government only peeks through the keyhole. Who knows exactly where we are headed over the next decade? In any case, the nature of HR will likely change. As a discipline, knowledge management may fade into the background or become part of some other thrust such as a major shift in management science. Whatever happens, knowledge management has raised some fundamental questions for HR about people, structure, human capital, and new technologies that cannot be set aside. Because of the depth of these issues, the Federal Human Resource Development Council launched a community of practice known as the Federal Knowledge Management Learning>Consulting Network in November 1998. This community has conducted learning events each month since its inception, and many members of the community validate the significance of emerging HR issues[23].

Human resource leadership across the federal government needs to attend to the related management issues. One of the finest guides is the book *Working Knowledge,*[24] by Thomas H. Davenport and Laurence Prusak. The authors conclude their work with this statement:

> *Just as balance is necessary in using different approaches to knowledge management, balance is required in trading off knowledge management with other change approaches and with simply getting the day-to-day work done in the organization. . . . Just as we shouldn't undertake any action without examining what can be learned from it, we shouldn't learn anything without relating it to practice. A healthy tension between knowledge and action is the key to organizational (and probably individual) success.*

Hopefully our HR organizations will be knowledgeable enough to help keep the balance. Let us hope they will also be knowledgeable enough about knowledge management to empower our use of human capital in the federal workforce.

Acknowledgments

The best thinking in this chapter reflects that of the team members of the @work Futures Group, the FAA Team Technology Center, and the OD Consulting Group at the FAA. Special thanks to Joe Dinsmore and Giora Hadar at the FAA. Special thanks also to Bernie Dailleboust of the Indian Health Service and Alan Myers of the Health Care Financing Administration for help with developing core ideas related to the future of OD.

NOTES

1. Terkel, Studs. *Working*. New York: Avon Books, 1972, p. xxix.
2. Castells, Manuel. *The Information Age: Economy, Society, and Culture, Vol 1, The Rise of the Network Society*. Cambridge, Mass: Blackwell, 1996, pp. 10–13.
3. Drucker, Peter F. *The Age of Social Transformation* (*The Rise of the Knowledge Worker*). *The Atlantic Monthly,* Nov. 1994, p. 8.
4. Drucker, Peter F. *Managing Knowledge Means Managing Oneself,* Number 16, Spring 2000, *Leader to Leader,* Drucker, Foundation for Nonprofit Management, New York, pp. 8–10.

5. GAO Document B-283190, *Managing for Results: Opportunities for Continued Improvements in Agencies' Performance Plans,* 1999, www.gao.gov.

6. Alvin Toeffler's book *Future Shock,* Bantam Books, New York, 1970 was eventually published in over 50 countries. The sequel, *The Third Wave,* was the first major work to describe the post-industrial society.

7. COTS stands for *Commercial Off-the-Shelf.*

8. Fitz-enz, Jac. *The ROI of Human Capital: Measuring the Economic Value of Employee Performance.* New York: AMACOM, 2000, p. 252.

9. Davenport, Thomas O. *Human Capital: What It Is and Why People Invest It.* San Francisco, Jossey-Bass, 1999, p. 4.

10. The Institute for the Future Web site is www.iftf.org.

11. Johansen, Robert. *Groupware: Computer Support for Business Teams.* Macmillan, 1988.

12. Johansen, Robert and Rob Swigart. *Upsizing the Individual in the Downsized Organization.* Maine: Addison-Wesley, 1994, p. 15.

13. Nadler, David A. and Michael L. Tushman. *Competing By Design: The Power of Organizational Architecture.* New York: Oxford University Press, 1997, p. vii.

14. Ibid.

15. This is the second of an excellent series of five books with extensive information pertaining to virtual work. The first book, *Networking: The First Report and Directory,* was published in 1982, the year Lipnack and Stamps founded The Networking Institute. A fifth book of the latest writings of Lipnack and Stamps will be published in 2001.

16. The Internet address of WebIQ is www.webiqinc.com.

17. "Looking Ahead," *Harvard Business Review,* Sep-Oct 1997. This was a 75th Year Anniversary Issue including Paul Saffo as a panelist about the future with Peter F. Drucker, Esther Dyson, Charles Handy, Paul Saffo, and Peter M. Senge.

18. Wenger, Etienne C. and William M. Snyder, "Communities of Practice: The Organizational Frontier," *Harvard Business Review,* Reprint R00110, 1-800-988-0886, 2000, p. 139.

19. Savage, Charles M., "The Mathematics of the Knowledge Economy," *The Executive Report on Knowledge, Technology, & Performance,* Vol. 4., No. 3, March 1999.

20. Senge, Peter, et al., *The Dance of Change: The Challenges to Sustaining Momentum in Learning Organizations.* New York: Doubleday, 1999.

21. The Web address for Ninth House is www.ninthhouse.com.

22. The Web address for Domain Knowledge, Inc. is www.domain knowledge.com.

23. Contact the author for further information related to the HRDC's community of practice—The Federal KM Learning>Consulting Network. The Federal CIO Council has a sister activity which is providing KM research and learning. Both organizations are working together to develop a government-centric KM Web site at www.km.gov.

24. Davenport, Thomas H. and Laurence Prusak. *Working Knowledge: How Organizations Manage What They Know.* Harvard Business School Press, 1998.

CHAPTER 8

KM and E-Gov
Can We Have One without the Other?

Shereen G. Remez, PhD

In this age of e-everything, we have been so bombarded by promises of e-business, e-commerce, e-gov, and now e-KM, as one former chief information officer (CIO) put it, "You just want to shout: e-nuf!" Is this just another stage or fad? Would adding knowledge management (KM) to the mix really make a difference? Denizens and citizen customers of the federal government alike have been through total quality management (TQM), business process reengineering (BPR), downsizing, rightsizing, belt-tightening, and performance management. Each movement has had its promise and consequences, both positive and negative. But in many instances, as the dust settles on one and a new one arrives, many ask just what lasting impact was achieved? Little wonder then that discussions of e-government and KM are met in some quarters with caution. Is e-government another downsizing effort? Is KM another technology silver bullet that will leave only a smoking gun behind?

Those of us who have been involved in the early stages of e-government and KM feel instinctively that this new wave is real and that it has the potential to deliver government information and services to citizens in better and richer ways. E-gov and KM are not so much about the technology as about strategy and connecting, and they affect not just the "how" but also the "what" and "how much" of government service. Convinced that both e-government and KM are here to stay, our thesis is that they are so intimately linked—as preconditions and enablers of each other—that we will have both, and not one without the other. As it turns out, lessons learned from KM offer important lessons for the future of e-government, and lessons from early experiences with e-business—built as it is on the rise of the Internet—offer useful guidance for the future of KM in government.

There's no retreat from putting the "e" into government—and without KM government isn't e-government.

There is no turning back from putting the "e" into business. Similarly, it is the right time to put the "e" in government, both internally and externally. Any well-run business with prospects for survival, revival, or thriving in the future is fast incorporating Web-based systems and Internet strategies into its operations and business planning. Citizens and businesses that accept Internet-based capabilities from the private sector are increasingly expecting, if not demanding, the same performance from their government. The attraction to easier, better, and faster access to diverse products and services is strong for both consumer and business commerce and is equally compelling when applied to government. Indeed, if the American public's experience so far with the Web is a reliable predictor, the expectation is not just for incremental, but exponential improvement in efficiency and effectiveness of government information, transactions, and relationships. Like it or not, the government of the future is one that will leverage its resources with the power of the Internet.

What many do not take for granted is that efficient and effective government ("e" included) will not be attainable unless the federal enterprise has successfully implemented a functional KM environment.

E-government will depend upon a KM foundation for three reasons. These reasons make sense whether you believe that KM is an innovative new concept or simply a re-casting of several time-tested themes of management.

First, government is inherently a knowledge-intensive business. Given the costs and importance of knowledge in government, it seems unthinkable that a resource-challenged government could be successful in making large-scale improvements in the speed and quality of service without fixing the way it creates, shares, and reuses knowledge. Government depends on timely access to quality knowledge to perform its missions. Major and, potentially, costly risks arise whenever organizations try to operate without it. The tragic bombing of the Chinese Embassy in Bosnia in 1999 illustrates how important having the right knowledge at the right time in the right place can be to a government mission. The address information used to pinpoint the target was outdated, even though electronic.

The cost of finding the knowledge needed to accomplish government objectives is large, and the price of not having sufficient knowledge is nearly always failure. The dependencies and requirements of government for knowledge affect the costs and performance of operations for government and all of its customers and business partners.

Faced with increases in expectations for improvements in service that far outstrip any conceivable increase in resources, the government simply must drive improvements—and generate savings required to support increased service expectations—through better management and more cost-effective performance of its expensive, knowledge-based work. This means KM.

Second, although the federal government is organized vertically by department and agency, much of what federal organizations do is accomplished by common, horizontally integrated functions, aimed at specific customer groups. This is true for most internal government support services, such as information technology, human resources management, and accounting. It is also true in relation to citizen and business groups served by multiple agencies. These shared connections across agencies represent both a need and an opportunity for sharing systems, expertise, and methodologies. For example, more than seventeen agencies were involved in building the "afterschool.gov" Web portal launched in FY 2000.

Third, the levels of government—federal, state, and local—are often blurred in the eyes of the citizen, and success in implementing e-government depends upon integrating these different layers. From a systems perspective, there may be many instances in which the delivery of government service to an individual depends on coordination and action by several levels of government. Sharing knowledge, building connections, and managing shared data across government entities and among local communities are keys to building a better, more responsive public sector.

KM, in the context of e-government, therefore, is leveraging the collective knowledge of agencies to fulfill the missions of the overall federal enterprise. It is getting the right information, at the right time, in the right context to support an identified need, strategy, or action. The federal government is a vast storehouse of knowledge, and many of its employees are experts in any number of diverse subjects, from AIDS research to weather prediction. The real challenge is building an environment where there is a freer exchange of this collective intelligence among federal agencies (horizontal knowledge sharing); an exchange among federal, state, and local governments; and a more accessible exchange between the knowledge stores of the federal government and citizens. This is KM, and it is precisely the kind of activity that is required to catalyze an effective e-government.

KM is not new to government. Some agencies have had major programs that focus on knowledge for years. Vehicles such as Office of Management and Budget (OMB)-sponsored committees, the General Service Administration (GSA) Office of Government-wide Policy, the National Partnership for Reinvention, the Government Information Technology Service (GITS) Board, and the CFO Council have existed precisely to share information across government. But past efforts have not been as comprehensive or enduring as required to build a knowledge-based government. In

FY 2000, the Federal CIO Council recognized the importance of KM by creating the KM Working Group under its Interoperability Committee and by embedding KM as a priority element of its strategic plan for 2001.

What is arguably new is the increased understanding of just how important KM is in enabling better government and what is required to make it happen. Cutting costs and increasing timeliness of knowledge-intensive activities, including delivery of services to the public, are top government priorities. Improving coordination with public and private sector business partners through business-to-government commerce and government-to-government exchange is another important goal. Finally, the result of successful KM will transform many of the processes, and even the roles, of government. For example, modern communications and networking technologies will give citizens unparalleled opportunities for staying informed about and being involved in the ongoing deliberations of government that ultimately affect them. Government may find a role as a convening agent for citizens, experts, and stakeholders in a virtual environment where thousands or even millions of citizens could participate. Building these new communities and nurturing them with available knowledge and resource information would give new meaning to access to government at all levels.

Success in implementing e-business and KM has as much potential as it has distance to go in government.

The good news is that KM offers potentially powerful support for transforming the government into one that harnesses technology to operate better, faster, and cheaper. For example, the CIO Council's Federal Enterprise Information Framework highlights the benefits of reusing and sharing information systems as an alternative to proliferating redundant systems. This better practice can cut costs by an order of magnitude and lead to more efficient systems. When new applications or upgrades are needed, technology refreshment can be available faster and at a far lower cost.

The knowledge embedded in application systems can be shared and reused across many organizations. Sharing and reuse apply equally well to the wide range of other kinds of knowledge resources potentially transferable within the federal enterprise, including coordinating, streamlining, and accelerating joint collaboration, decision making, and action; identifying, sharing, and implementing business solutions; spurring innovation and improvement; and creating new knowledge.

Unfortunately, the cost savings represent more of an estimate of potential opportunities than a reflection of common practice. In reality, a big gap between the possible and the doable is manifest in the early practices and pursuits of both e-government and KM. The challenge is to ensure that the awesome potential for transformation is enough to drive major change in how business is actually done.

E-GOVERNMENT—THE NEXT PHASE IN GOOD GOVERNMENT

In September 2000, a study conducted for the Council for Excellence in Government found the digital revolution is changing the public's future expectations of government, specifically for the delivery of knowledge and intellectual assets.[1] While e-government can simply mean automating current systems with new tools, findings from the study also indicated that most Americans believe the arrival of e-gov has the potential for bringing the government's storehouse of knowledge to where it is needed most. But e-government is not just throwing up a Web site. It is using the power of the Web to build net-based processes throughout the organization and with customers. Electronic knowledge management or e-KM gives government the chance to change its services from delivering the basic goods and benefits to delivering what it knows to those in the public who need it most. According to the study, "By 5-to-1, or 56 percent to 11 percent, the general public anticipates that e-government's impact over the next five to ten years will be positive rather than negative."

Two-thirds of those surveyed in the study initially felt that government investment of tax dollars in making more information and services available on the Internet should be a high or medium priority. However, the proportion grew to 77 percent after those surveyed described the services that can or will soon be available.

Some electronic government Web sites enable users to retrieve medical information from the National Institutes of Health and other agencies, review the voting records of politicians, access Social Security benefit information, and file online student loan applications.

Most important, the study found that "among the more than four in ten (or about 44 percent) Americans who question government's effectiveness at solving problems and helping people," a majority (or 51 percent) anticipate that e-government will have a positive effect on the way that government operates, and two in three believe that e-government will improve their ability to get information from government and government's ability to provide convenient services."

To fulfill Americans' hopes for e-gov and e-KM, in particular, developing an electronic knowledge environment must be addressed. For example, today's public bus riders stand with paper schedule in hand, often waiting many minutes in inclement conditions for buses that are behind schedule. A growing number of these bus riders have a personal digital assistant or text-ready cell phone on hand. In Seattle and some other cities, new antennae ride atop buses signaling their route numbers as they near the bus stop. Owners of coffee shops and cafes near bus stops have even discussed displaying large screens that will also display the incoming bus information. In Washington, D.C., Metro (the area subway system) displays similar arrival information so passengers waiting on the platform will know when their train is coming in "two minutes." The knowledge environment has changed, the public's ability to receive and use "narrowcasting" of specific information has matured, and government also needs to change.

While some believe that the government may have gotten too far ahead of the public with e-KM and e-gov initiatives, George Molaski, CIO at the U.S. Department of Transportation (DOT), disagrees. Mr. Molaski cites DOT's recent decision to allow applications for a federal transportation program to be submitted online. While online applications were not required and not even publicized that heavily, after just six weeks, more than 90 percent of all applications were being submitted online. CNN reported that a recent survey noted that 90 percent of Americans think they will be doing virtually all of their shopping on the Net within ten years. While e-KM and e-gov do face significant citizen privacy and security concerns, the public is ready for some action immediately.

From the broad range of e-commerce, including G to G (government to government), B to G (business to government), and G to C (government to citizens), to citizen services, such as paying taxes online, and perhaps some day, voting, e-gov is evolving by experience rather than by policy. At the same time, e-gov activities and the knowledge sharing that supports them raise significant policy questions: Who owns the information, knowledge, and intellectual property of the government? How does the government handle citizen data? What are the audit and control implications? Who will lead the electronic and knowledge-based revolution in government? What does the future hold for the respective roles of citizens and governments? Many policy issues emerge from the new worlds of e-gov and KM. The world is quickly realizing that information and knowledge are the most valuable government commodities. People want to share in the knowledge that could make their lives better, more productive, richer, and easier. This of course means managing and sharing the vast knowledge resources of the federal government. But can it be done? And how quickly can we expect government to migrate to these new paradigms of government-citizen relationships?

Government-sponsored e-KM also serves another growing need—the need to cut through the "data smog" that increasingly clouds the Internet. Today, for the first time, individuals— rather than publishers and other public sources—are responsible for most of the data generated each year, according to the University of California at Berkeley. Now office workers are responsible for writing more than 80 percent of all original paper documents. The mass of e-mail sent by individuals is five hundred times larger than the entire collection of Web pages. While the government used to carefully screen statistics and information, today's Web surfer often faces a dizzying array of information, much of it inaccurate. By sharing and utilizing more of the government's research and expertise, e-KM can help counterbalance this glut of often unreliable and misleading data, by making vetted information easier to find.

COLLECTIVE UNLEARNING WILL BE KEY TO E-GOV AND E-KM

"It's what we think we know already that keeps us from learning."
—Claude Bernard

Sometimes what you know can be a barrier to what you need to know in order to change and perform more effectively. Large legacy companies, such as the Xerox Corporation, face this challenge in the new economy—and so does the federal government. Most federal agencies are organized vertically. Some of this is mandated by statute. For example, the GSA's Federal Buildings Fund was created to fund buildings, not for technology or travel services. Other barriers are self-imposed, the result of decades of turf building and differentiation. Many agencies share customers, even internally, but refuse to share any customer data.

Challenge #1: Function Follows Form: The Structural Barrier

The federal government is organized like a World War II-era industrial manufacturing plant, with processes that run vertically and sequentially rather than horizontally and simultaneously across an organization.

E-government and e-KM, by contrast, emphasize *horizontal* integration, and e-government is really horizontal government. KM relies upon connections, communities, and context—none of which are vertical. This 90-degree pirouette that government must execute before it can make the entrance onto the electronic stage will require some difficult cultural maneuvering. If government tries to turn too far, too fast, the result could be a cultural headstand—180 degrees, upside-down confusion that will necessitate quick retreat. Citizen concern over privacy plays a strong role in this scenario, as does fear of information intrusion and recreational or professional hacking. But, if government fails to turn fast enough, it may miss the electronic curtain-call completely, resulting in the further disillusionment of citizens who are anticipating and expecting great things from electronic government.

Challenge #2: The Brain Drain and the War for Talent

Beyond the structural barrier to e-gov and KM is the double-edged sword of government downsizing and age creep. During the past decade, the federal government has shed more than 300,000 jobs. Although much, if not most, of the work (and cost) associated with these former positions of government employees has been shifted to contractors, the people and the knowledge they held in their heads within their organizations have left the government. There is also age creep of the federal workforce. The average age of federal employees has risen to 47, and over half of all federal workers will be eligible for retirement within five years. The challenge is obvious. Experienced workers are walking out the door, taking with them knowledge and expertise that cannot be easily replaced. The story goes that the middle-aged lawyer solves a client's problem in 20 minutes by pulling a passage from a legal reference and then bills the client $20,000. The client, naturally, is outraged by the price. In his own defense, the lawyer answers, "You didn't pay for the 20 minutes, you paid for the 20 years of experience that told me where to find that answer." What is the value of those 20 years of experience, and what is the risk to government's ability to perform?

This is a simple illustration, the point is clear—a lot of data and information are out there. But knowledge—the ability to act and leverage that data and information—is much more valuable. The opportunity side of the brain drain is perhaps less apparent, but both e-government and KM will require vastly new ways of thinking and new approaches. The ease and natural ability of a generation raised with computers and eBay and America Online (AOL) simply cannot be taught to most of the federal workforce. The chance to bring in new talent, new ideas, and new attitudes is both a barrier and a boon to e-government.

Challenge #3: Funding: Where Will the Resources for Transformation Come From?

Another barrier to e-government is funding. While many agencies can squeeze out enough capital to invest in specific electronic government projects, it is nearly impossible to amass the dollars needed to launch cross-agency initiatives. Congress is not organized to fund cross-agency initiatives. OMB is not organized to fund or support cross-agency initiatives. The CIO Council is not funded to support cross-agency initiatives. The few cross-agency initiatives that are born require intensive "pass-the-hat" prenatal care that involves crisis intervention and top-down pressure. For example, the funding of FirstGov, the one-stop portal for government information launched by the President's Management Council, is one recent example of pass-the-hat funding to get started; however, a specific appropriation was required from Congress in FY 2001. The CIO Council's activities, which include many cross-agency initiatives, are another example of this "pass-the-hat" funding strategy that stifles high-return investment in e-gov and KM activities alike.

Challenge #4: Citizen Privacy and Security: Who Is Watching the Data?

Finally, the clearest barrier to e-government and KM is the concern of citizens with privacy and security. For example, public concern over "cookies" (small text files used to recognize a repeat visitor and enable Websites to store information on the user's computer) illustrates how new technology can both assist and alarm people. These cookies allow personalization and customization of Websites, an important knowledge-filtering feature. At the same time, cookies can be viewed as an unwanted intrusion and invasion of privacy.

THE HARD LEARNING FROM KM CONTAINS IMPORTANT LESSONS FOR E-GOVERNMENT

What we have learned in KM through dealing with these barriers and obstacles is equally relevant to e-gov. To be successful, a KM program—and in this context an e-gov program as well—requires a balanced approach among four essential components: technology, content, processes, and people. It also requires an emphasis on leadership and the resources required to support the effort and drive the changes required to make KM and e-gov successful.

- **Technology**—One of the big lessons early experience with KM in government teaches is that technology is the easy part of the job. This would appear to be as true in implementing e-government as it is in KM. The truly tough challenges critical to the success of KM and e-government are changes required in leadership, culture, incentive structures, and even organization of the enterprise. Overcoming these challenges will take a change management strategy that includes building a culture of innovation and a robust environment of sharing, both within and across agencies. It will take creating virtual collaborative networks, communities of practice, and communities of interest and strengthening relationships among related government programs and among vendors, who are playing an increasing role in delivering government services.

  Technology alone will not be enough to create e-government—it is only the "e." Agencies will need to examine their strategies to maximize the use of Web technologies in the context of a larger strategy to build knowledge capital, both structural and social. The major advantage of technology, however, is that building a seamless organization, a seamless process, or a seamless face to the customer is immeasurably easier in virtual space than in real life. The technology has given many hope that e-KM and e-gov will be the keys to the next generation government.

To be sure, technology offers unparalleled capabilities at ever-decreasing cost to support both KM and e-gov infrastructure, such as Web-based products and processes; communication and collaborative work tools; and database, content management applications, and advanced technologies that associate metadata with information and facilitate a timely, efficient search for the best, most relevant information required to support the business need. With this kind of capability available, technology is important, if not essential in many cases, but it is not a goal in itself: It is the easy part of doing KM, and, alone, it falls far short of what is required for success.

- **Content**—E-gov and KM also share the need for delivering quality information in as actionable a form as possible: the right information, for the right purpose, in the right format and context, at the right time. This may be a combination of information from many sources, including internal repositories across government, the Web, and other external, licensed sources. It may include knowledge in both explicit and tacit form. In many instances, the most valuable knowledge to be shared is in the heads of people. The challenge is learning how to find and extract that knowledge quickly and efficiently and how to identify and network the right people. Knowledge is not accessing written content in a database, but applying information and data within the human context.

- **Processes**—The structures through which the activities of people and organizations are coordinated and systems through which knowledge is captured, shared, created, and leveraged form the backbone of how most work gets done in the federal government. A great deal of knowledge is embedded in these processes, and automated processes remove that knowledge another step away from people's conscious awareness. Anyone who has used *Turbo Tax* knows that in a year or two they begin to forget how to do their taxes, but they are very efficient in answering tax questions and letting the machine do the calculations. The same thing happens in federal agencies. An example of this became evident during the preparations for Y2K, when most employees could not even remember the manual processes that systems had assumed, making a reversion to manual processing an impossible Y2K back-up plan.

- **People**—Success rests on people and their talents. E-government, and the KM that feeds it, will need decisive, forceful, and persistent leadership to communicate and share the vision, to set performance expectations, to facilitate change where required, to assure appropriate priorities and resources, and to overcome barriers. But leaders cannot do it alone. People will need to feel trusted, empowered, and rewarded for their ideas and actions. Individuals and groups need to act in ways that are good for themselves and for the larger community.

  Those of us in the federal government need to recognize the importance of people. The good news is that personal incentives now are increasingly consistent with the behaviors that will reinforce effective KM within and across government. We are quickly approaching the point where those organizations and people who practice KM most effectively will be the most successful; others will increasingly fail. To stay relevant in a knowledge economy, the government needs to embrace the principles of KM.

- **Leadership**—To move from vision to implementation and to realize the opportunity of government KM—and of e-government more generally—will require clear and persistent focus on strategies for change.

> It is essential first for leadership to initiate change. Top leadership needs to make agency leaders and management responsible for acting as leaders in implementing e-gov and KM and hold them responsible for results.

Kouzes and Posner, in their book *The Leadership Challenge*,[2] offer a framework for the practices and commitments that make leaders effective (see Table 1).

Table 1. The Keys to Leadership—Converting Values to Action

Key Leadership Value	*Key Leadership Action*
Question Current Processes. Don't simply automate or re-tool old work.	Use challenges as opportunities to take risks and institute change. Experiment and learn from mistakes.
Inspire and Evangelize. Build a shared commitment to new goals.	Promote a common vision through individuals' interests and passions.
Enable Individual Action.	Build competencies by giving power away, showing support and assigning critical tasks to others.
Model Behavior and Cultural Change.	Use behavior to express important values. Use small victories to show progress and commitment.
Celebrate the Soul of the Organization.	Recognize individual contributions. Encourage a culture of success.

To succeed, KM and e-gov programs need to be aligned with the business lines that drive programs within and across agencies. The KM and e-gov community as a whole can engage government leadership to work beyond individual agencies and drive initiatives at the enterprise level.

The Internet is, of course, driven in very different ways than the change management strategies outlined above. Beyond the power of the network and all of the enabling technology that goes with it, what drives the Internet are the interests of vertical and horizontal communities that inhabit the Web and the self-interests of millions of people who surf it. Is there a lesson in this market-based approach for KM efforts within government?

This issue is reminiscent of the argument of Nobel Laureate Milton Friedman, who wrote almost 40 years ago in *Capitalism and Freedom* that harnessing the market and the consumption decisions of millions of consumers and citizens is the strongest force for change and progress.[3] Even the written word originated thousands of years ago as a way to track transactions in early commerce. Beyond the change management approach outlined above, government KM and e-gov will take off faster and more effectively the more they emulate the dynamics of the Web and the more fully they address the interests and needs of the people within government who will be implementing change. Several Web lessons may apply:

First, make it easy. No one has to take a two-week course to understand how to buy and sell on eBay. It is intuitive. It is natural. Federal employees need easy-to-use tools for saving, searching, retrieving, finding, sharing, creating, and using knowledge resources. These activities need to be an integral part of the job, not some extracurricular activity.

Second, make it powerful. This means exploiting the power of the network and high quality/specialized databases for depth, breadth, and quality. It means integrating search (all relevant resources, including internal and external people and things) and functionalities as much as possible. And it includes maintaining and enhancing data quality and search precision wherever possible, especially through quality metadata.

Third, make it interesting, engaging, and ultimately rewarding to individual participants. This means offering value for joining in (e.g., giving immediate reward for registering under topics by pushing useful information from external and internal sources to registrants). It also means delivering value for participating and explicitly addressing the "what's in it for me?" question.

KM and e-gov not only *must* happen together—it is inevitable that that they *will* happen together. Like Fred Astaire and Ginger Rogers, the duet is made to order. KM will be the catalyst, the foundation, and the enabler of e-gov. By seeing these two concepts as complementary partners, we can simultaneously change both the structure and the culture of the entire public sector.

NOTES

1. "E-Government: The Next American Revolution." September 28, 2000. This poll was conducted by the survey research firms of Peter Hart and Robert Teeter for the Council for Excellence in Government.
2. Kouzes, James M. and Barry Z. Posner. *The Leadership Challenge.* San Francisco: Jossey-Bass, 1987.
3. Friedman, Milton. *Capitalism and Freedom.* University of Chicago Press, 1962.

CHAPTER 9

Knowledge Management and Document Management in the Public Sector

Elias Safdie

The late noted astronomer Carl Sagan, in a public television series, made the claim that Kepler's laws of planetary motion were known to the ancient Greeks, but that the followers of Pythagoras, for religious reasons, suppressed that knowledge and prevented its codification and dissemination. As a result, that knowledge was lost to humanity for several thousand years.

Fast forward to 1996. The Defense Special Weapons Agency (now known as the Defense Threat Reduction Agency, or DTRA) was facing a very special problem. Some 50 years prior, DTRA was born as a result of the work of another government agency with a more recognizable name: the Manhattan Project. To any trained scientist, the name conjures up images of genius, creativity, and unique knowledge. Oppenheimer, Fermi, and other intellectual giants were an integral part of the work done in the design and production of the first atomic weapons. As of late 1996, the last known individual ever to have built a Cesium clock was in a nursing home, suffering from Alzheimer's. This presented a real and present danger that much of the knowledge gathered in those special times could be lost to humanity for good, much as the laws we now attribute to Kepler were lost. Fortunately, DTRA took a different tack and initiated a program known as "project graybeard." Using multimedia, document management, and Internet technologies, DTRA is capturing as much of this knowledge as possible and has plans to concentrate it in a repository known as DARE. Old notebooks are being scanned and stored as images; interviews with surviving members of the Manhattan Project are being taped; and those tapes are being digitized, indexed, and stored in DARE. DTRA may not realize this, but they have built one of the first systems to manage knowledge.

Many organizations today, both public and private, are attempting to use knowledge management (KM) to help organize, codify, and disseminate the accumulated knowledge in their organizations. They do this to support a workforce and to deliver to managers and decision makers the tools they need to fulfill the goals of the organization. Many of the technologies we use today will be used to manage corporate knowledge. The difference will be in how they are used. For example, the U.S. Department of Defense (DoD) is planning to use technology to manage its knowledge that is gleaned from a publication put out by former Secretary of Defense William Cohen, titled "Defense Reform Initiative: The Business Strategy for Defense in the 21st Century." The publication is available in its entirety at www.defenselink.mil. In this document, Secretary Cohen talks of a program known as Vision 2010. This project has at its core "the ability to collect, process, and disseminate a steady flow of information to U.S. forces throughout the battlespace, while denying the enemy ability to gain and use battle-relevant information." The actual technologies to be used are yet to be determined, but in combination they will constitute a sophisticated system to utilize the knowledge we have to a battlefield advantage. Some other examples of goals, which are delineated in this document, are:

- By January 1, 2000, all aspects of contract processes were to have been paper-free.
- DoD will expand use of electronic catalogs and electronic shopping malls to place buying decisions into the hands of the people who need the product.
- On July 1, 1998, DoD discontinued volume printing of all DoD-wide regulations and instructions and made them available via the Internet and CD-ROM.

DoD is not interested in going paperless for the sake of achieving a technological summit. There are real and compelling reasons for this goal, including the fact that paper has ceased to be an effective medium for disseminating knowledge. Witness the following quote from Secretary Cohen:

> *Computer-based purchasing represents the ultimate "democratization" of the acquisition process—buying decisions are made by the people who need the products. With improvements in technology, particularly the Internet and the World Wide Web, computer users are now able to access information and data on products, often directly from the company itself, and agencies are able to develop interactive electronic catalog systems.*

By disseminating knowledge to those who need it, we empower those individuals to make decisions and further the ends of the enterprise. Likewise, the latest buzzword, *disintermediation*—the act of removing intermediaries from a process—is all about disseminating knowledge and empowering people to be able to take care of their own needs without the aid of intermediaries who "know" what to do on their behalf. Again, from Secretary Cohen:

> *Logistics has long been the linchpin of a nation's military capabilities. Identifying a force's logistical needs and devising and executing a strategy for meeting those needs is often the crux of how effective that force will be in combat. Taking our lead from the private sector, DoD is in the process of applying the latest advances in information technology to the business of supplying our troops. Key to our new system is the concept of just-in-time logistics; merging many warehousing and transportation functions, eliminating the need for stockpiling. The department has made a commitment to provide total visibility into its equipment, supplies, and spare parts all the way from the warehouse in the U.S. to the foxhole in the distant theater. We will track every piece of equipment, every supply shipment and spare parts requisition on a continuous basis.*

Not only in the battlefield, but back at "headquarters," the Pentagon is responsible for much of the planning and policy generation that eventually lead to the acquisition and deployment of weapons systems, military bases, and logistics to the armed forces. Here, plans are afoot to move ATM technology to individual desks and provide access to live video, broadcast video, and remote learning training as a means of disseminating knowledge. To manage all of the logistics of scheduling and broadcasting the right programs at the right time, document management technology will be used. It seems like Secretary Cohen and the rest of the Pentagon are subscribing to Aristotle's observation: "Action without knowledge is folly. Knowledge without wisdom is perilous."

This paper discusses how document management technologies can be used in a knowledge management (KM) environment in the public sector. Examples of best practices are drawn from the author's work in the federal sector, primarily DoD, as well as in the state sector, using examples from public retirement systems, public utility regulation, professional registration, and others.

KNOWLEDGE MANAGEMENT

Definition

There are as many definitions of KM as there are practitioners, consultants, and professional organizations trying to define it. However, the primary definitions revolve around two central themes. The first is a relatively arcane and academic theme that focuses on capturing *tacit knowledge* (defined as knowledge that is held in the minds of members of any organizations and not written down) and transforming the tacit knowledge into *explicit knowledge*. When this is boiled down to its essence, what it means is "let's get the stuff out of people's heads and write it down so all of us can have the benefit of their experience."

This is primarily what DTRA was trying to do in Project Graybeard. As a hypothetical example, let's assume that buried in someone's memory is the fact that during a certain test some of the transponders measuring the effects of the test malfunctioned and gave some erroneous readings, which impacted the initial interpretation of the results. As long as that information stays in this individual's head, the knowledge is *tacit.* As soon as DTRA documents the fact and writes it down, it becomes *explicit.* There are other examples in industry. One organization has a problem in its customer help desk. As an individual deals with more customers and is exposed to more technical product issues, that person develops a great deal of *tacit* knowledge. From a career standpoint, there comes a point when these individuals want to be promoted to other, more responsible areas. While they certainly deserve it, the help desk is then deprived of the benefit of their experience; therefore, management is loath to move them out because they solve problems. On the other hand, if they don't get the promotions they want, many leave the company. The dilemma then is to try to figure out how the organization can take advantage of the experience developed by their better help desk employees and simultaneously retain them and reward them by moving them into more responsible positions. Again, the need to transform *tacit* knowledge into *explicit* knowledge.

A second definition of KM is often viewed as more practical and somewhat less academic. The definition centers around how an organization can get its arms around all of the knowledge and information held, not only in the heads of employees, but also in their filing cabinets, in the hundreds of gigabytes of information in their computer systems, in e-mail systems, in Word documents, in spreadsheets, and so on to enable the organization to meet its goals and objectives. This definition of KM is about identifying, organizing, and disseminating the information collectively held in the organization. Here, two properties distinguish knowledge from information: intimacy and actionability. Intimacy is a measure of how comfortable or how familiar one is with the subject matter. The more intimate one is, the more one can work with the more subtle nuances of the subject, and the better one can adapt or utilize that information over a broader spectrum of situations. This latter observation ties closely to the second criterion—actionability, utility, or applicability. The information must be actionable—it must have significant impact on the subject at hand and must allow the user of that information to take action in pursuit of his or her goal. This definition is much in keeping with Aristotle's "action without knowledge is folly...."

It is important to note that KM is not a technology, although it often utilizes various technologies, in particular document management and analytical applications. Do not fall into the trap of thinking that one can "buy" or "build" a KM system. Organizations cannot buy KM systems any more than they now buy workflow systems. People use workflow to build accounts payable systems, claims processing systems, and the like. Similarly, organizations will use KM disciplines in combination with relevant technology to help organize, codify, and disseminate the accumulated knowledge in their organization. They will do this to support a work force and to deliver to managers and decision makers the tools they need to do their work to fulfill the goals of the organization.

Why Now?

Why is KM important now? Is it just another information technology (IT) fad or an academic exercise? It is important to understand two primary factors that have led to the rise of KM. First are the organizational motivators, and second are the technological enablers that exist today that were not available before.

Organizational Motivators

The byword of today's organizations is speed, followed closely by flexibility. In a rapidly changing environment, organizations must react quickly to a broad range of stimuli. In a poorly organized environment, the information required to make decisions and react to changing environments is simply not available. Decades have been spent creating information and storing it in various forms: paper, tape, disk, optical disk, and more. The sheer volume of the information store can make finding the needle in the haystack a daunting task. Businesses and public-sector organizations desperately need some way to make that information available to be able to access and act upon appropriate information. For example, there is a serious and concerted effort in most departments of revenue to manage the knowledge derived from processing the tidal waves of personal and corporate returns that inundate tax departments annually.

To get an idea of the relative dimensions of these tidal waves of paper, the Office of the Comptroller of the State of Texas receives as many as 144,000 returns a day during the tax monsoon, which can equal 360,000 pages. Over the course of a year, this equates to over 13 million documents. And these are only corporate returns!

Technological Enablers

Ironically enough, technology that caused much of the problem in the first place now becomes an enabler to help solve the problem. Figure 1 depicts the "flow" of technology over time that has on the one hand helped to create the glut of information, and on the other becomes a solution. Individual technologies are depicted as behaving as "feeders" to the main "river" of KM. The headwaters come from two primitive classes of technology. On the one hand is imaging technology that first allowed some control over paper information by allowing documents to be scanned and indexed for subsequent retrieval, and on the other is relational database systems that allow the capture and analysis of transactional information. The upper set of technologies represent those required to deal with unstructured information, while the bottom set are linked to structured data.

Each succeeding technology in the evolution has allowed more and more to be done in terms of organizing and disseminating the information amassed internally and externally. Therefore, the availability of all of these technologies, as well as their increasing affordability, have come together at this time to allow the organization, dissemination, and assimilation of the amassed information. This also allows organizations to meet the demands of speed and flexibility in responding to today's globalized political and socioeconomic systems.

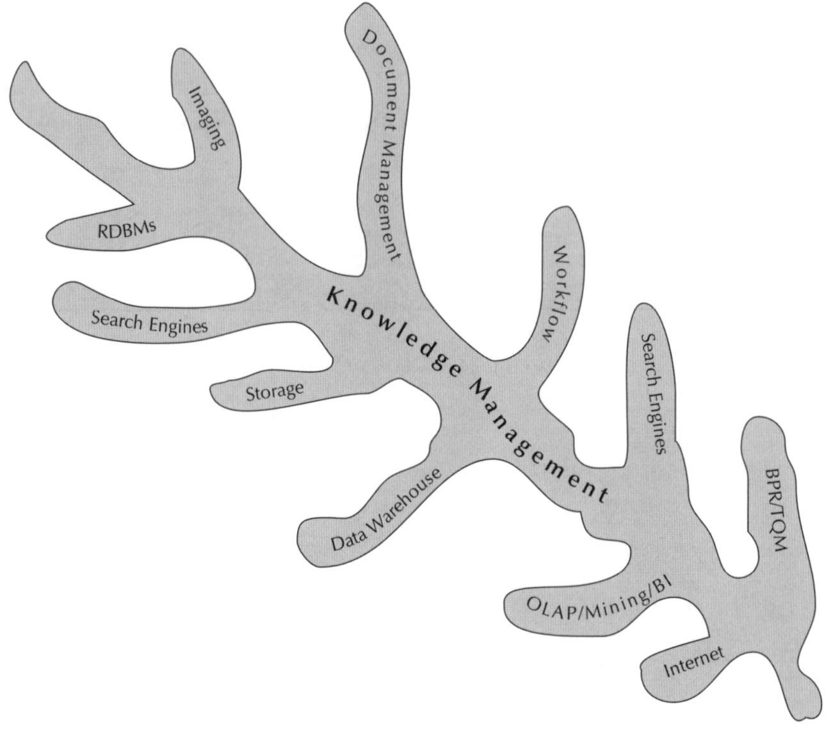

Figure 1. Knowledge Management

DOCUMENT MANAGEMENT

As evident from the "river" of KM (depicted in Figure 1), the top section of technology enablers deal with the unstructured information—information captured in words and pictures—usually in containers called "documents." Here we run into another definitional dilemma. Does a common frame of reference exist with regard to the definition of a "document" and what it means to "manage" them?

Prior to the advent of computer systems, defining a document was relatively easy—information written on a piece of paper. However, with the coming of word processors and other computer devices, the ability to create and manage information in other media gave rise to the concept of "electronic" documents. Xerox's famous Palo Alto Research Center (PARC) has come up with a definition of a document that fits today's technology. According to Xerox, a document is defined as "information structured for human consumption." By this definition, documents can be videotape documentaries, paper user manuals, word processing files, and more. This is the definition used in this paper.

More importantly, this definition underscores the link to KM. If a document is information structured for human consumption, it is intended to satisfy the two criteria of KM: intimacy and actionability. The better structured the information is, the more easily a human can understand it, which in turn means that the human can use that information to make knowledgeable decisions (actions) based on the information in the document. Therefore, the case can be made that document management is a significant enabling technology for KM applications.

The Document Life Cycle and KM

In order to understand what it means to manage documents, it is useful to understand first the life cycle of a document. Typically, a document goes through a number of stages in its useful life, from creation through use and eventual archival or destruction. This is pictured in Figure 2.

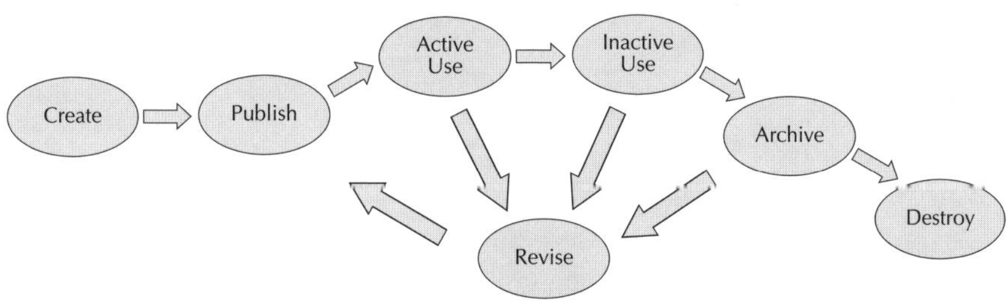

Figure 2. Document Life Cycle

In each phase of the life cycle, different tools and techniques are used to manage that document, and good KM systems take advantage of each tool at the appropriate time to maximize the impact of the document on the organization. These tools are shown in Figure 3.

Creation

During the creation phase, authors determine what kind of document to create, who the intended audience is, and what the intended use will be for the document. If the document has several authors, some kind of control mechanism is needed to determine who will have access to the multiple drafts of the document, and some mechanism is also needed for dealing with multiple comments to make sure they are all appropriately included in the final document. Security services thus are needed to identify authors who have the right to modify the document, and some sort of check-in and check-out procedures are needed to make sure authors do not overwrite each others' edits. Version control is also needed to be able to work with various revisions of the document as the way is made to the final message.

CREATE	PUBLISH	ACTIVE	INACTIVE	ARCHIVE
Capture	Formatting	Search	Search	Search
Edit	Indexing	Device Ind.	HSM	HSM
Import	Security	View		Retention
Check-in	Device Ind.	Edit		
Checkout	Aggregate	Security		
Review		Workflow		
Versioning		HSM		
Signoff				

Figure 3. Tools Required in Each Phase of the Document Life Cycle

In creating the document, information may be included in various forms and from various sources. Scanning capabilities, therefore, are needed to capture images from paper documents; OCR capabilities are needed to translate paper documents into electronic documents that can be edited; import capabilities are needed to add information in various formats from other applications, such as graphics packages or other word processors. Some kind of review and redlining facility are also needed so reviewers can make their comments in line, online, and facilitate the editing process. Finally, authorization to release the document is needed, usually through some form of sign-off procedure.

Publishing

In the final part of the creation process, the document is ready for distribution to the intended audience. However, document management technology provides multiple search and access mechanisms to help the intended audience find what it wants. Simple indexing, full text search (discussed below), and other means are available to help users find the documents they need. However, the documents must be prepared such that these follow-on methods can be used. Depending on the intended use and targeted audience, the document must be structured so that the intended user can find it simply and efficiently in a manner consistent with how they do their work. This is a key element of KM—adapting the search mechanisms and the delivery of the information to the needs of the user within the organization. For example, if a user requires access to information that is chronological (such as the status of a factory order), then the various pieces of information must be indexed chronologically to support the user's demands.

How the document is viewed also impacts the document structure. For example, in paper format, a dual-column document (like a newsletter) is very easy to read. Take that same document and place it on a screen, and it can be annoying to have to continually scroll up and down to get from the bottom of one column to the top of the next!

Active Use

Once the document is completed, it is published and distributed. At this point, the document management characteristics change somewhat. As a research document, for example, the document should not be revisable; therefore, it must be published in a read-only format, such as Adobe's PDF. Depending on the nature of the document, some parts of the document might not be available to all users; therefore, varying levels of security may be needed. As an aside, this is also a consideration in the creation side—if the document has different sections with differing security requirements, these need to be considered in the authoring side.

It is in this phase of the life cycle that document management really exhibits its most significant benefits (e.g., the use of document management may help organizations drowning in paper). A recent survey at a utility regulator identified approximately nine million pages of paper onsite, not including any offsite archived boxes. This paper contained much of the information needed by the employees to perform their jobs, and the timeliness and quality of that information are critical to the quality and timeliness of their output. Yet, finding what is needed when it is needed is often a challenge. Think about the challenge of finding a document in a timely fashion in an environment such as that shown in Figure 4.

How many times have you gone to the records room looking for a document, only to learn it has been checked out? Further, how many times has it been checked out for a long time, perhaps to someone who has left the organization or transferred to another department? How much time is spent looking for paper documents in situations like these? Years ago, a study by Wang Laboratories concluded that the average executive spends more than 20 percent of his or her time searching for information.

Moreover, how much control do you have over the integrity of your documents? If a file that holds several hundred pages is

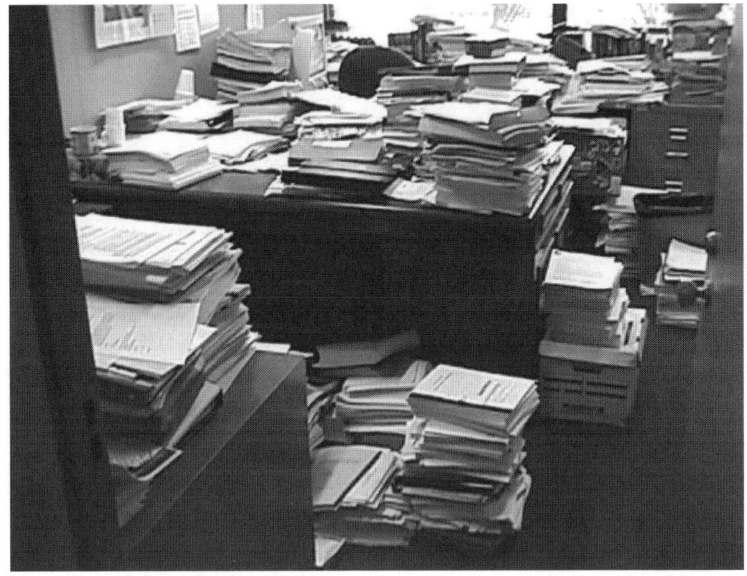

Figure 4. The Need for Document Management

checked out, and it comes back five pages smaller because someone accidentally placed those pages to the side, who would even know that this happened? This phenomenon, known as "folder integrity," is often a major problem in dealing with critical documents.

Because of these kinds of problems, workers often create "shadow" files—personal copies of files that contain duplicates of the original files. The problem is compounded because each shadow file can be slightly different from the original, depending on when each was compiled. This results in people working with incomplete or, perhaps, outdated information. In the case of the utility regulator, it was estimated that nearly half of the nine million pages stored were duplicates of originals.

Imaging Technology. Imaging technology, now several decades old, is a perfect answer for managing the reams of paper at organizations. From a functional perspective, imaging technology is fairly simple to describe.

Simply stated, imaging technology captures a facsimile image of a paper document such that it can be stored and retrieved by computer systems. A digital picture can now be taken of all of those papers using a scanner and managed as information. This has several interesting ramifications:

First, anyone who needs a copy of the document can have it at any time, anywhere in the building, if they are connected to the network. This means no more "out" cards in the records room.

Second, it means no running to the "records room" to get the information (a big advantage when the work is spread out over several floors).

Third, the "folder integrity" problem is eliminated because no one actually removes any paper from the folder.

By applying password protection to certain documents, security procedures can be instituted restricting full access to all of the information in that folder. This is critical in applications such as personnel, where, for example, someone may be interested legitimately in a job description, but may not need to know salaries.

Database technologies can also be applied to simplify finding the documents. For example, if files are only stored by case number (such as for the utility regulator), forgetting the case number makes finding the file impossible. If, however, an "index" system to these documents is built, the case number, as well as the type of case, the attorneys who handled it, the judge who presided over it, and the date of decision can be captured. Workers looking for a document only need to remember any of the indices, and a quick search of the indices can get them to the desired documents rapidly.

Finally, it cuts down on the "shadow file" problem. Human nature will still cause some workers to print off their own copies of the files for their own personal use. Experience has shown, however, that as workers become more comfortable with the technology, they tend to print fewer copies and reduce their need to maintain shadow files.

Full Text Search. Sometimes all of the index elements discussed above are still insufficient to get to the right document needed to solve immediate problems. Access to a document is sometimes needed, but all that might be remembered about the document is that it referred to a specific company or neighborhood, or that it had a specific phrase that had significance in a particular case—for example, all documents related to a particular concept. In these situations, no amount of pre-indexing will be sufficient to help locate the right document. For these situations, the concept of full text search becomes significant.

What is full text search? There are several "flavors" of full text search. For example, individual applications, such as Microsoft Word, Excel, and others, allow users to search *the open document only* for individual words or phrases. While technically this technology is a search of the full text of the document, the concept is broader and more powerful—a search *across all documents* for the occurrence of a particular word or phrase. This technology is seen when using the World Wide Web, with "search engines" such as Excite, Altavista, HotBot, SNAP, and others. The search engine will return a list of documents, perhaps along with their indexes and a brief summary of the document. The results are presented in an ordered list, based on the frequency of occurrences of the desired word or phrase, with the most relevant documents (those with the greatest number of "hits") at the front of the list. Further, "equivalent" phrases or words can be defined by using a thesaurus. For example, if searching for "DoD," we would also like the search engine to return references to "Department of Defense," "Defense Department," and other like phrases; if we search for "AT&T," we would also like to see references to "ATT," "American Telephone and Telegraph," and so on. Other helpful features of this technology include the ability to specify proximity: "give me all occurrences where 'easement' is within five words of 'pipeline,'" and the ability to search for word stems and roots (a search for "scan" also returns references to "scanner," "scanning," "scanned," and so on). Finally, we want to be able to perform logical combinations of words and phrases, such as "give me all occurrences of 'stranded costs' that do NOT mention 'AT&T.'"

A final twist on the concept of full text search is the inclusion of a technology known as "fuzzy logic." Fuzzy logic is an implementation of artificial intelligence that can help users who are unsure of all or some parameters of a search. Usually, this takes the form of helping with misspelled words. The fuzzy logic engine can take misspelled or imprecisely defined search terms and return a list of potential hits, depending on its interpretation of our "fuzziness" or imprecision in formulating the request. For example, if a user is interested in a case where the parent company is in Arizona, and Phoenix is misspelled as "pheonix" or even "fenix," the search engine will infer that the user really means "Phoenix" and will return appropriate documents.

How does full text search work? Those of us who have done text searches on the Web have no doubt experienced the awe of having several thousand documents selected as a result of a query, all in the space of a few seconds! In fact, the search is not done in real time on the documents themselves, but rather on a word index built from all the documents and stored in a separate database. This so-called "inverted" list takes every word of each document and builds tables that identify which words exist on which pages of which documents. Therefore, instead of searching documents for words, the search engine looks through a list of words for documents that contain those words. Secondary indices will then identify the exact pages where those words are found on each document. Thus, when a specific document is brought up as a result of a search, the search engine's viewer goes to the first instance of the word or phrase and allows navigation from instance to instance, according to the predefined tables.

One drawback to this technology is that the inverted list index is often half as large as the set of documents it is indexing; therefore, quite a bit of disk space is needed to implement it. This is somewhat mitigated by the existence of something called a "stop list," which is simply a list of words that are not to be indexed, such as "the, an, at, and, but" and other articles, conjunctions, and so on. Of course, if there is a particular meaning to "AT" (such as the OSD undersecretary for Acquisition and Technology), then "AT" could not be excluded from the stop list.

A second obstacle in full text search is the difficulty that sometimes arises in attempting to utilize some of the more advanced features, particularly the logical combination of words and phrases. Building compound phrases using the logical combination elements of "AND," "OR," "NOT," and "NOR" can lead to misleading results. An interesting example was posed at a conference some years ago, when Prime Ministers Pierre Trudeau and Margaret Thatcher were still in power in Canada and England, respectively. A researcher was using a full text search tool on newspaper articles and wanted to get all stories regarding the politics of Prime Minister Trudeau. Because the researcher did not want any fashion or human interest stories, the researcher wanted to eliminate any articles that referred to Mr. Trudeau's wife, Margaret. Therefore, the query was posed: "give me all references to Trudeau, but NOT Margaret." As a result, the researcher missed a report of an important meeting between Mr. Trudeau and Margaret Thatcher, which was of significant interest to the researcher.

Because of this, as a general rule, it is best to be skeptical of results rather than be overly confident, however, there is no doubt that the inclusion of full text search into a KM implementation will significantly add value to the organization.

Inactive Use, Archiving, Destruction

Finally, today's record retention schedules, used primarily for paper documents, will have to be modified to accommodate electronic documents. This means setting purging requirements into the system to help with the eventual disposition. Hierarchical storage systems, which move information to increasingly cheaper (and slower) storage, are useful for this phase of the document life cycle. Beyond the use of retention schedules and hierarchical storage management systems, the tools required to manage documents in this life phase are the same as those in active use.

Revision

At any point in the life cycle beyond publishing and before destruction, a document may be revised and re-issued. The tools required for these actions are the same as those required in the creation phase.

THE ROLE OF THE WEB

The Internet and, in particular, the World Wide Web are pervasive today, and no treatise of technology would be complete without some mention of the role it plays in both KM and document management. It must be stated up front that this subject is so sufficiently complex and detailed that it could be the sole subject of an entire book, and so this section can only skim the surface of the topic.

That having been said, the roots of the World Wide Web must first be examined to see their obvious links to both KM and document management. The Web is nothing more than a set of protocols by which documents become transportable. Prior to the advent of the Web, researchers on the Internet were faced with a veritable cornucopia of optional formats for storing research documents. In the Unix world, there were .tar, .ps, .troff, .nroff, .gz and others; in the PC world, ASCII, MS Word, WordPerfect, Multimate, and others, as well as multiple image formats (.gif, .tiff, .jpeg), multiple graphics formats, and a host of search engines with names like Archie, Veronica, Jughead, and more. Further, a single topic could lead to a document in one site that was stored in one format (say .troff), which had a reference to another document in another site, which was in yet another format (Multimate). As a result, researchers on the Web spent more time converting formats and trying to render the document than was spent actually researching the topic.

The nature of the issue, then, is twofold. First is the KM issue of researching for intimacy and actionability, and second is the document management issue of indexing and rendering. Clearly, the Web plays into both. However, caution must be taken before leaping to the conclusion that a Website is both a KM system AND a document management system, and that putting documents in a corporate Website is all that is needed to claim victory.

What the Web and its concomitant technology bring to the party is an interconnecting infrastructure that supports interoperability and, through the use of search engines, also helps in the indexing of documents.

These are necessary but insufficient elements of either KM or document management. Remember, the Web was built as a general purpose research engine for an unknown audience. In organizations, there are specific communities of interest that have specific requirements that lead to specific taxonomies on indexing and search tools to make sure that systems are responsive to the needs of the users.

Beyond that, the Web gives no check-in/check-out functionality; no inherent restrictions are made on who places what information in what folder for what reason, leading to significant vulnerabilities. One federal agency that has many departments has just such a problem with its intranet sites. Multiple departments can post multiple copies of the same document, albeit different revisions of that document with the same name.

With no restrictions or processes to coordinate the posting of information, users are left to their own devices to determine which copy of the document they should be using. Clearly this leads to confusion rather than intimacy and inaction rather than action—the antithesis of KM.

The answer, then, is to make sure the advantages of the Web are exploited as a dissemination vehicle, and the advantages of http as a mechanism for hyperlinking taxonomically related documents, etc. At the same time, the limitations of Web technology must be understood and backed up with more robust traditional document management technologies.

BEST PRACTICES IN DOCUMENT MANAGEMENT

Planning/Architecture

Ask anyone who has implemented a document management system what they would change if they could, and the answer will be an unhesitating "more planning." It is critical to understand the business/mission reasons for undertaking a KM/ document management project and what the desired outcome or vision is. Without such a plan, you are much like Alice in her discussion with the Cheshire Cat—"if you don't know where you're going, most any road will get you there."

A good mechanism for developing such a plan is to develop an architecture for the system. A definition of architecture is "the definition of the elements required to solve a problem, and their interactions." An architecture does not have to be technically deep, but it does have to identify all of the elements of the solution and how they interrelate. Figure 5 is a notional model for the elements of an architecture.

The primary element to consider is the mission of the organization. One must understand the mission intimately to ensure that any system furthers those goals and objectives. Business Processes are instituted within the organization to carry out those activities important to the mission. The business processes use both automated and manual procedures. This is important to understand, because too often focus is only on the automated procedures, and some potential enhancements to manual ones are ignored. Users, who perform roles in the processes (refer to the section below titled Reengineering and Workflow), require information to perform their roles (a key point in a KM plan). That information is accessed and manipulated through software applications. The applications sit on technology platforms that are located (centrally or dispersed) across the work locations of the enterprise. Only after understanding all of these elements, along with the strategic drivers

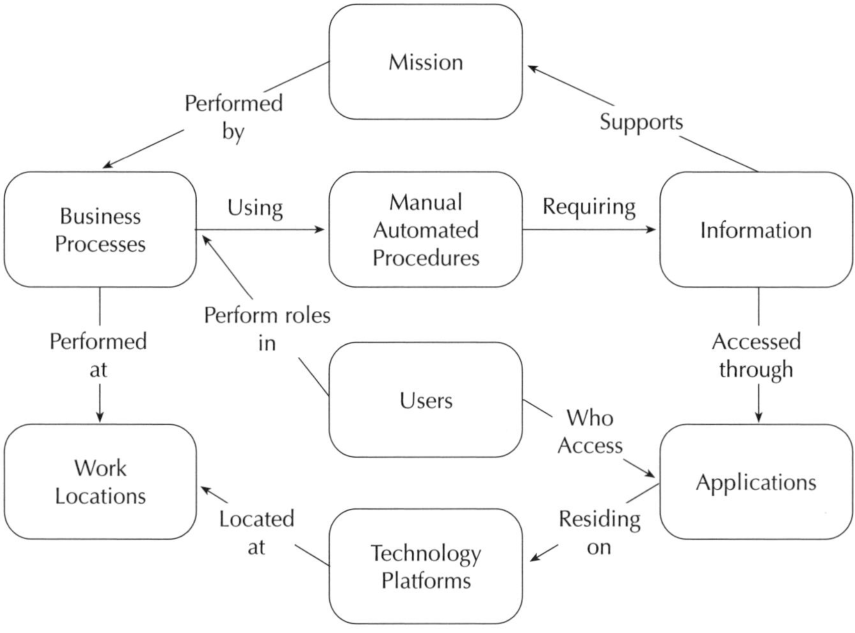

Figure 5. An Architectural Framework

that influence the mission, can an organization put together a cohesive approach to any technology project. This is especially true in KM, because the primary objective of KM projects is to seamlessly integrate the information needed to the right people at the right time to increase the intimacy and effect actionability.

Management Support

Simply stated: do not even attempt to commence a KM project without enthusiastic support from top management. Just as in reengineering efforts, KM efforts will, of necessity, start questioning jurisdictional lines, organizational structures, and existing processes. Many will be threatened by the kinds of questions that arise in these exercises and will try to sabotage the project. If senior management is anything but enthusiastic about the KM project, it will fail.

Reengineering and Workflow

IT has been around for decades, and it remains one of the most contentious functions in any organization. Why? Simply because for most of those decades, IT has been foisted on end users with little apparent regard for what the users needed to do their work. Too often, the attitude was "here's some new technology for you to use—enjoy it." There was no attempt to coordinate the capabilities of the technology with what the users did on a day-to-day basis or how they might use that technology to make those day–to-day tasks more productive, faster, less expensive, and so on.

Over the last few years, information technologists have begun to see the light and have incorporated principles of work analysis into the deployment of IT. This has taken several different forms. For example, some years ago Coca Cola Corporation began sending its programmers on delivery routes with its drivers. This enabled the developers to appreciate what a driver did and how the software they were developing could help the driver in executing his or her assignments, rather than adding a further frustration to an already hectic day.

Government has also bought into this concept. Several years ago, Congress enacted what is now known as the Clinger-Cohen Act, which mandates that no new system can be deployed at DoD without first conducting a process redesign to validate that the technology will indeed solve the business or mission problems it is intended to solve.

Integrating System and Process

One challenge in any project is keeping a balanced perspective between system (technology) requirements and process (business) requirements. Which comes first? Which is more important? How much of the process do I need to know to understand what technology I need?

The answers are not that difficult if the initial architectural model described above is kept in mind. From this perspective, process and mission requirements must drive system and technical requirements.

At the same time, it cannot simply be assumed that the way things are done today is the way they will continue to be done once a new set of tools is acquired. It must be understood that new tools enable new ways of accomplishing objectives.

So what's the difference between a process requirement and a system requirement? Process requirements deal with *what has to be done.* "We need to resolve customer complaints within 24 hours of receipt" is an example of a process requirement. "Customers must be capable of contacting the agency on a 24/7 basis" is another example. The first order of business then is to analyze what has to happen to the existing process in order to meet these process requirements. How long does it take to resolve complaints today? What are the major bottlenecks that prevent meeting this goal? How can we redesign the process to enable us to meet the requirement?

System requirements can then be derived from these process requirements. Systems requirements describe *how technology is used* to meet the process requirements. For example, if it is found that the 24-hour process requirement can't be met because information is not readily available (e.g., it takes two days to look up a microfilmed record), then imaging technology could be implemented to make that information available instantaneously. Internet technology and telephone call centers could help in meeting the second requirement of 24 hour, 7 day availability.

Why Can't the Vendor Do It?

One commonly asked question is: "Because the vendor will be writing the workflow code to its own product, why doesn't the vendor redesign the processes?" It is a good question that has several good answers. The first thing to remember is that the vendor is only expert in the particulars of its product and how certain tasks can be accomplished using that product. The vendor typically does hot have any particular expertise in the nontechnical aspects of any organization's processes. In fact, many vendors will require the client to participate heavily in the design of the workflow to ensure that the client's business needs are represented, just for this reason. Many process improvements that will be discovered may have little to do with technology in general, and even less to do with the specifics of a single vendor's product. Therefore, the skill set required must include people who are expert in process design in general, as well as those who understand the regulations and policies that dictate the organization's process elements. This does not mean that the vendor should not be involved in the redesign effort. Obviously, there will be many areas where appropriate use of the vendor's product will lead to increased efficiencies, decreased cycle times, easier operations, etc. At the appropriate time, it is very important to bring the vendor onto the team.

How Deep Do We Go?

Clearly, then, there is a line of demarcation between what an organization and process redesign can do on its own and what has to be done in concert with the vendor. As a general rule of thumb, high-level functions can be developed without the vendor. We can decide on our own when to use workflow, when to use imaging, when to use e-mail, etc. What the vendor is needed for, however, is *how* to use the specifics of the vendor's package: for example, if there will be an "inbox" icon on the screen to press, or how to get co-workers' e-mail addresses.

Workflow Technology

At this point, instantiating the redesigned processes in a workflow engine can begin. Simply speaking, workflow technology enables the automation of the different business rules that are in use at an organization and that dictate all of the different steps and activities needed to meet the commitments to its constituents, in the right order, at the right time, and by the right people. This is shown in Figure 6.

Workflow's Origins

The concept of workflow is not new. It started in the manufacturing industry about the time of the Industrial Revolution. At that time, Fredrick Winslow Taylor noticed significant efficiency gains might be had if, instead of using one person to build an entire product from start to finish, he could break up all of the individual steps required to build that product. He would then form an assembly line where the work "flowed" past a number of people, each with a single task to perform. This concept has been in operation ever since in the manufacturing world, but only recently (in the past 20 or so years) has the concept been applied to office work. In fact, office work can be thought of in the same way:

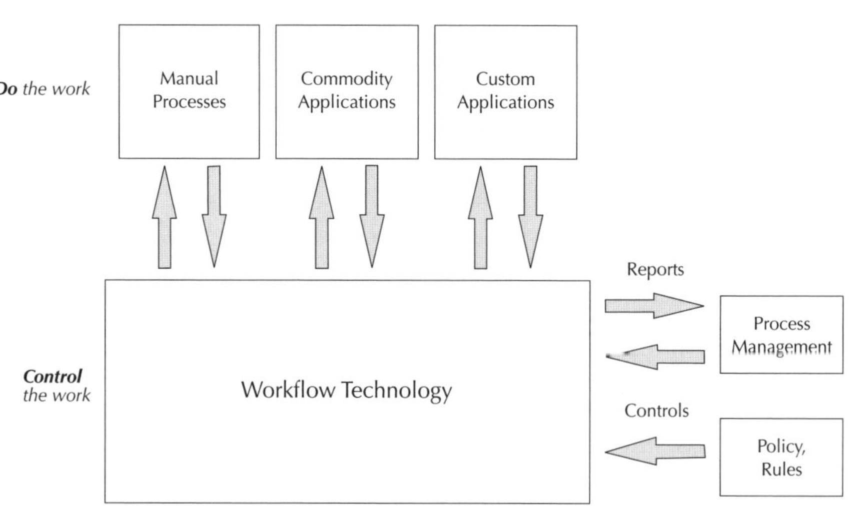

Figure 6. Workflow Technology Controls the Work

for example, to produce a ruling on a tariff application, a number of specialized tasks need to be done in a given prescribed order. Legal specialists need to analyze and render legal positions and recommendations, engineering specialists need to do the same from their discipline, schedules need to be coordinated to accommodate multiple demands, and, in the end, a "product" is created. Clearly it would be inefficient, even impossible, to try to have one person carry out all the tasks from start to finish.

Most organizations today have many applications resident on PCs that help the staff perform the individual steps required to do their jobs. Workflow technology will allow those organizations to control how, where, and when the work gets done.

Rules, Routes, and Roles. Workflow technology, therefore, analyzes the work to be done in the office environment and breaks it into three primary categories: routes, roles, and rules.

- ***Routes*** describe the actual routing of documents and information to realize the finished product. For example, a request for retirement benefits at a public employees' retirement system goes from administration reception to the appropriate department heads for review and approval and then to the appropriate department to begin processing monthly checks.

- ***Roles*** deal with the different activities that individuals are expected to perform in the process. At a utility regulator, a handful of specific roles, such as engineering, administrative, legal, and so on, may be defined—each role being defined as required for certain process steps and not required in others.

- ***Rules*** have to do with the business rules that dictate what work will be done under what conditions. For example, a business rule says that all rate cases must be decided within 11 months. Therefore, workflow technology can track when a case was introduced and provide warnings relative to the different milestones that need to be met.

Note: these three concepts all have to work together to make a process happen. People with specified *roles,* perform particular tasks in keeping with the *rules* of the organization, in a prescribed order, which is defined by the *routes.*

Isn't this just a fancy e-mail system? Can't documents be e-mailed to specific people and accomplish the same thing? This is a common question posed by nearly everyone when they are first exposed to the concept of workflow. The answer is "not really." Work can be e-mailed to other people, and a distribution list can be developed that allows each person on that list to forward their work to the next. However, this is not the same as having a process completely defined within the system so that as soon as the first piece of the process is finished, the system *automatically* knows whom the next recipient should be based on the business rules defined.

In fact, some e-mail–based workflow packages do exist, but they are not as robust as the so-called "production" database-centered system. In fact, the industry has termed the e-mail–based systems "pull" systems because individuals have to pull information from the system in order to do their work; as opposed to the database-centric "push" systems, where the system is in charge and "pushes" work to the appropriate individuals automatically. Some systems even go as far as to open the appropriate applications automatically on an individual's desktop when a new work package arrives, just to save that much more time and make things easier.

The Importance of Metrics. A second major differentiation in the push environment is the ability to track business metrics. How much time is spent researching rate cases as opposed to others? Where should additional resources be added to speed up overall processing? In order to know whether processes are working as well as they might be, those measures considered essential to success must be defined and tracked. Workflow systems allow organizations to define those aspects of the business that are worth measuring and to capture and report those measures automatically, either on a regular basis or an ad hoc basis.

Conversion Strategies

Enterprises have several options with regard to populating document management systems with existing legacy documents. The first option is simply to convert all documents at once, a kind of "Big Bang" approach. A second option is to convert none of the legacy documents and simply start using the system on a "today forward" basis. A third option is to convert legacy documents "on demand" (as they are required).

Each strategy has its benefits and shortfalls. For example, the issues surrounding the Big Bang approach revolve around the costs. Using the utility regulator with more than nine million pages onsite as an example, the costs to convert the documents to images would be on the order of one million dollars. If the organization wanted to OCR the document so as to be able to use full text search as well, the costs would skyrocket to over ten million dollars—many times more than the cost of the system itself.

The "today forward" approach has its downside as well. Documents that may be needed are not available to the staff. It is this drawback that leads to the third option of converting on demand. Of course, this adds time to the process that may not be acceptable.

The tradeoffs among these options are shown in Figure 7, which compares the completeness of information against the time required to build and access the documents.

As demonstrated, some applications, such as the FBI fingerprint identification system, need everything (e.g., fingerprints) loaded and accessible to operate. Some organizations have adopted some unique and very clever conversion strategies. For example, a state retirement system made the following observations after analyzing its traffic flow for several months.

First of all, as shown in the first graph on Figure 8, the agency determined the distribution of its population by age. Next, it determined who was eligible for retirement options according to existing, plus proposed, rule changes and overlaid this on the

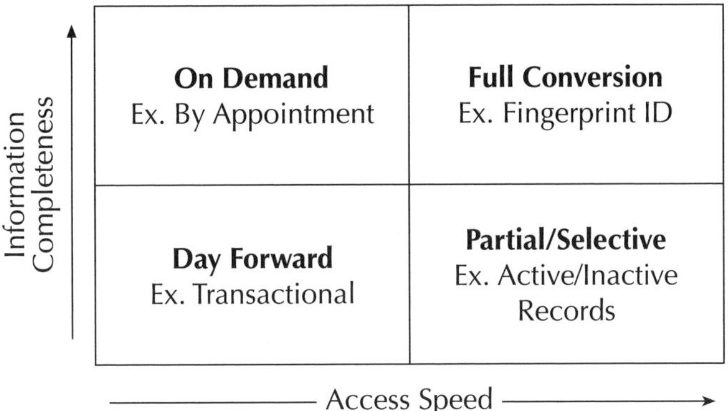

Figure 7.

population distribution, as shown in the second graph in Figure 8. The question, then, became whether the eligibility criteria could become a predictor of who would be using the system. To do this, the agency analyzed its traffic patterns for several months and came up with a distribution that was then overlaid on the previous analysis. This is shown in the third graph in Figure 8. The bar graph shows a strong correlation between the eligibility of a potential user and his or her propensity to visit the retirement agency offices for services. This meant that the agency could effectively *predict* who would be likely to use the services when, and could undertake a phased conversion, thus saving hundreds of thousands of dollars in up-front conversion costs. This kind of predictive utilization analysis can result in many different kinds of strategies that can reduce the time to implementation while simultaneously reducing costs.

Vendor Management

IT projects do not have a good track record of success. In a survey of more than 8,000 projects, the Standish Group (Dennis, Massachusetts) uncovered that only 16 percent were completed on time, within budget, and with all the original features opera-

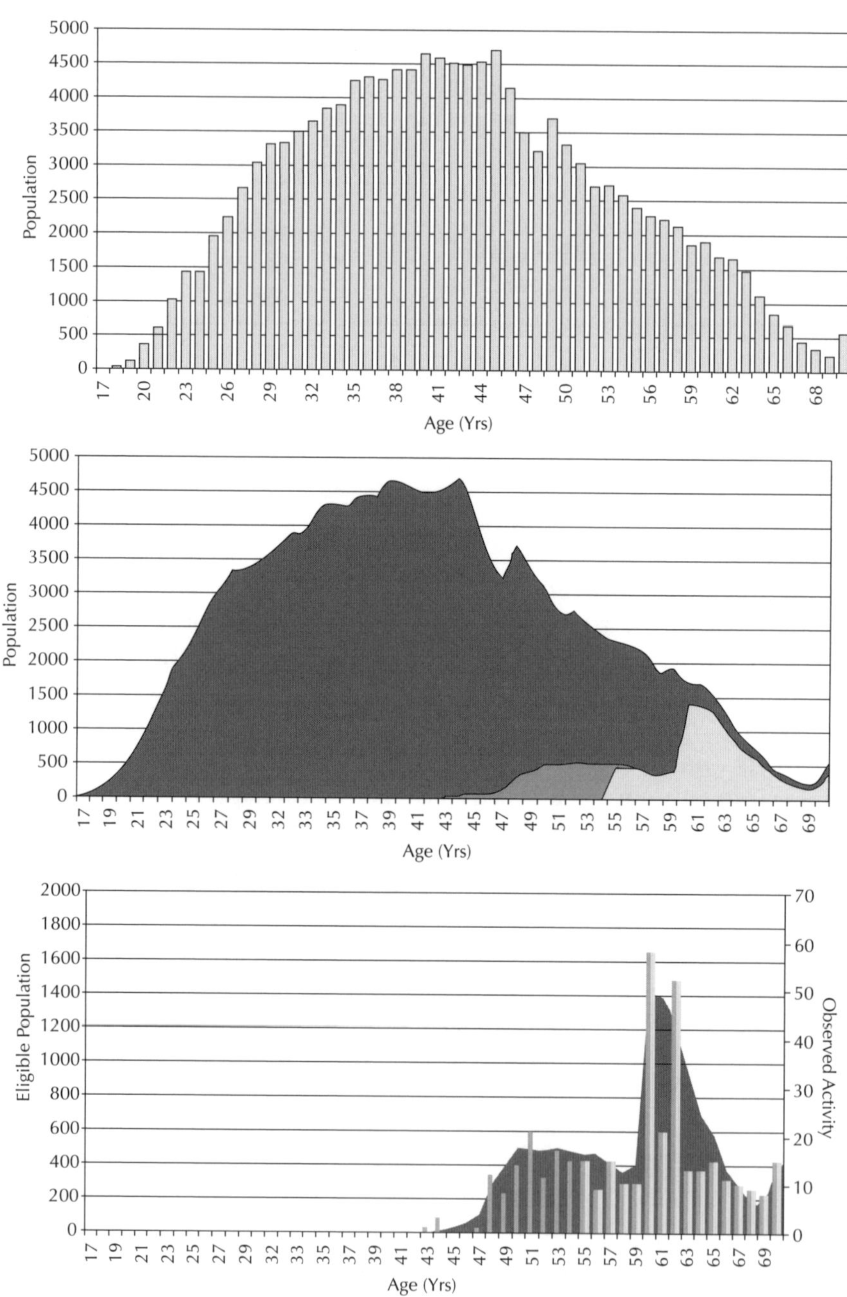

Figure 8. Predictive Utilization Analyses for Backfile Conversion

tional. Fifty-three percent were late, over budget, and had only partial functionality. And 31 percent were canceled before completion. This indicates that chances are less than one in five that you will get what you contracted for, for the money you contracted, in the time you expect it. These are discouraging statistics for anyone intending to implement a document management or KM system.

The obvious questions then revolve around what can be done to bring your project into that 16 percent club. The answers lie in three simple words: plan, communicate, and manage. It is a simple two-step process:

- Plan the work.
- Work the plan.

Unfortunately, in spite of its simplicity, the execution of this concept is elusive to many IT professionals. In fairness, much of the problem lies in the fact that most IT managers are too busy fighting off the alligators to worry about draining the swamp. Therefore, without time and resources available to make this happen, it is too easy to drop everything in the lap of the vendor and hope for the best. Some common-sense techniques and practices that have worked well over the years and that should be considered in your next vendor experience include:

- **Trust but verify.** This famous U.S. policy in the latter stages of the Cold War is an excellent model for working with your vendor. Your relationship has to be one of teamwork, and many IT managers make the mistake of holding back information, laying traps for the vendor, and generally not treating the vendor as a fully integrated member of the team. This cannot only foment a reciprocal distrust on the part of the vendor, but in holding back some political or policy information from the vendor, you might be losing an opportunity to help the vendor help you. Remember that walls work in both directions, and any walls you erect will work against you just as effectively as walls erected by the vendor.

One effective way to make this work is to appoint two co-project leaders, one from the vendor and another from the organization. (Conflict resolution is discussed later in the project structure.) At the same time that the vendor is a team member, you need someone on that team promoting your interests. Remember that the vendor is in business to make a profit, and you will have to live with the results of his or her efforts long after the effort has ended. Some IT managers hire independent consultants to act as the ombudsman for the users on the project. These specialists have the time that many IT and user managers lack to attend meetings, review deliverables, review acceptance tests, etc. and make sure that the results are consistent with the original intent of the customer. They are also motivated to act in the best interests of the customer because they are being paid specifically to do so. This is the "verify" part of the policy, and it is effective. Of course, if you have specialists in house who have the bandwidth to perform this role, by all means use them, but be careful of the skill sets required here. It is critical that this person be capable of dealing with the vendor on a technical and project management level, while simultaneously dealing with the end user at a business and functional level. The person must have good communication and personal interaction skills because much of the job will be helping negotiate potential changes to schedule, price, functionality, or some combination of the three.

- **Keep a channel open.** Communications between you and the vendor must be continuous and concise, written down clearly, and mutually accepted. Every project should start off with a document that details the problem the organization is trying to solve, the scope of the project, the business objectives, and the approach or strategy that will be employed. These are a precursor to a detailed project plan, which must be accepted by both parties prior to commencing any work.

- **Manage the change.** Few things are more important in a project than defining a process for changing the scope, approach, or plan details. As part of this change management process, a log must be maintained recording any proposed changes and whether those changes were driven by user demands or by implementation problems encountered by the vendor that were not foreseen earlier. A mechanism must be defined for determining whether this change carries with it additional fees or not. In keeping with our "Trust but verify" approach, the vendor should legitimately have significant input into the process but not complete power to yell "change of scope" and double the cost. There must be a well-defined chain-of-command to the project, as well as a well-defined escalation procedure to elevate problems to appropriate decision makers.

A Methodology for the Madness

A methodology is a must in any large project. Methodologies provide three useful benefits to any project. First, they define what has to be done and in what order. If the project approach is determined to be a traditional one, the methodology defines the user requirements phase, the architecture phase, the development phase, test phases, etc. If it is to use a prototyping philosophy, the methodology will dictate how to time box the different iterations, and so on. Second, a methodology defines what the deliverables are and how they relate. A methodology might define the need for a functional specification and a preliminary architecture document, for example, and would force the implementation team to justify to management that the architecture document is in fact responsive to the functional requirements document. A methodology might, for example, call for a project review at this juncture to satisfy all concerned that the project is continuing to meet the objectives of the organization. Third, a methodology will define roles and responsibilities for all participants. This is invaluable in building and managing a plan because it spells out for the management team the kinds of skill sets required at which phase of the project and what they have to produce. The methodology-defined deliverables are a good set of milestones for the project planner and manager to work to and are easy to track and simple to gauge their completeness.

No surprises. Regular status meetings are a must. Some managers do not want to hold these weekly review meetings because they feel their people are professionals and should know what they need to do. Status meetings are not about checking up on your people. They are about establishing a forum for interaction, communications, and sharing. The format should be short and sweet. Each person takes two to three minutes to discuss three topics:

- What was accomplished last week?
- What will be accomplished this week?
- What problems have arisen?

Often, the most constructive dialog of the project consists of people responding to each other's status reports, saying things like "Well, if you intend to do X this week, you'd better coordinate with me because I intend to do Y, and we will be conflicting for the same resources." This gives your professionals and team members an opportunity to ply their trade collaboratively. As Schultz's comic character Lucy once said, "Progress happens when we all pull in the same direction." These status meetings afford your team the chance to make some progress.

Structure the team. As part of the chain of command, there needs to be a conflict resolution mechanism that both the vendor and the client can trust. Experience has shown steering committees to be extremely useful. The committee should be made up of senior management of both the client and the vendor. It should meet no more than once a month and should review deliverables, set direction, and resolve conflicts only after other lower-level negotiations have failed. The committee, in effect, is the Supreme Court, from which there can be no appeal of the decision.

Project Planning and Management

Why plan? The only alternative to a well-defined and well-executed plan is failure. Without a clear plan to guide activities, projects turn into collections of chaotic random activity, with individual tasks often working at cross purposes to other tasks. The inevitable side effects of this syndrome include budget over-runs, incomplete projects, and projects that do not deliver the vision.

What is a project plan? A project plan is simply a single document that records everything that needs to be done. A good analogy is that the project plan is the sheets of music (the score) that a conductor uses during a symphony that dictate what instruments are used where and what notes they need to play at what times and in what sequence to perform the piece.

Tools, such as Microsoft Project, allow managers to enter descriptions of all the tasks necessary to complete the project, as well as start dates, projected end dates, resource allocations, dependencies, and more. The plan is a key component of the project management methodology that will be used, in that NOTHING will happen UNLESS it is on the plan.

A project plan is a living document. Reality dictates that at the beginning of any project there are more questions than answers. Accordingly, it is probable that the initial plan will need to be modified as tradeoffs are made during the course of the project. This implies that there will be a change management procedure that will be used to control the changes to the plan and make sure that all changes are well understood, along with their impacts on resources, timeframes, and adherence to the vision.

A typical plan. Below is a high-level summary of a generic project plan:

- **Kickoff**—The kickoff phase of the plan is a critical phase because it introduces a new player to the team—the vendor. During this phase, mutual expectations are set on what will be happening. Communication strategies are agreed to that will keep all team members up to speed on what is happening, as well as making sure that all team members are kept "in the loop."

- **Analysis**—The analysis phase of the project reviews all requirements identified and drives them down several levels of detail. Work redesigns are reviewed and, perhaps, even modified. The analysis also includes conversion requirements, reporting requirements, and specific technology requirements, such as full text search, encryption, and OCR.

- **Design specification**—Once the requirements are defined, specification of the design details, including screen layouts, business rules, and data structures, can begin. The vendor will likely produce a functional specification that defines all known requirements. The functional specification will be, perhaps, the most significant document produced in the planning process because it will be the document of record to determine if the final delivered product meets the stated needs of the organization.

- **Development**—The development phase of the plan will take the specifications and drive them down into code. At this point, the "concrete" starts to set, and changes become more and more difficult (and expensive) to make.

- **Procurement**—Once the code is developed, the hardware it will operate on is purchased, as well as all software licenses needed for the system.

- **Installation**—After the hardware and software arrive, system installation can begin, with assurance that the infrastructure is operational before customized software is added.

- **Conversion**—Many of today's existing databases reside on legacy mainframes, so a conversion program will have to be run to make all of the historical data available to the new system. Note: the conversion is held off until the last possible moment to make sure that all data are available to convert.

- **Acceptance testing**—The acceptance test ensures that the delivered system is consistent with the requirements.

- **Production/deployment**—Finally, the finished system is available for all of the staff to utilize.

CONCLUSION

As the "KM river" analogy demonstrated, document management is an integral part of any KM initiative. The key to success can be summed up in three words: understand, understand, and understand. First of all, an organization must understand the needs of the community it is serving: who needs to see what documents when; and what factors are significant in the way they search for information among and within the documents. Second, the organization must understand the workflow associated with the various documents. Finally, it is imperative that a clear understanding of the technology and its limitations be developed in order to apply the appropriate technology to the appropriate problem. The road to success is not simple nor the same for every organization, but the payoff will come with some planning and some patience.

CHAPTER 10

A Systems Approach to Engineering a Knowledge Management System

Michael Stankosky, ScD
Carolyn Baldanza

The purpose of this chapter is to show how systems thinking, a systems perspective, and proven systems engineering best practices ensure successful design and implementation of a knowledge management system (KMS). The chapter treats knowledge and knowledge management (KM) definitions, presents a historical evolution of systems thinking from the 1970s to the current day, highlights the value and importance of the systems approach to KM, suggests a systems engineering methodology for engineering a KMS, and, finally, discusses the future of KM.

KM DEFINED AND EXPLORED

Let's begin by defining *knowledge* and *knowledge management.* Although many definitions are floating around, the following definitions are the result of three years of KM research by Chauvel and Despres:[1]

Knowledge is:

- The cutting edge of organizational succcess (Nonaka, 1991)
- The engine transforming global economies (Bell, 1973, 1978)
- Leading us toward a new type of work with new types of workers (Blackler, Reed, and Whitaker, 1993)
- The element that will lead to the demise of private enterprise capitalism (Heilbruner, 1976)

- The sum total of value added in an enterprise (Peters, 1993)
- The "mobile and heterogeneous [resource that will end the] hegemony of financial capital [and allow employees to] seize power" (Sveiby and Lloyd, 1987)

Knowledge results in:

- The "learning organization" (Mayo & Lank, 1995)
- The "brain-based organization" (Harari, 1994)
- "Learning partnerships" (Lorange, 1995)
- Obsolete capitalists economies and radically different societies (Drucker, 1993)

Conclusion:
Knowledge is fast becoming a primary factor of production (e.g., Handy, 1989, 1994; Peter, 1993; Drucker, 1992).

Source: Theseus International Management Institute, February 2000

The above definitions are by no mean all inclusive. In any case, we prefer Wiig's definition of KM: "Knowledge management is the systematic, explicit, and deliberate building, renewal, and application of knowledge to maximize an enterprise's knowledge-related effectiveness and returns from its knowledge assets." Our preference stems from his use of the operative words that indicate what engineering a KMS is all about: "systematic, explicit, and deliberate." We develop this more later in this chapter. (It is important to note up front that this is not a discussion about "knowledge"—rather, a discussion about knowledge *management* (KM). Here the operative word is *management*. We have seen data, information, and information systems all being managed. But the question remains, can knowledge also be managed?

What is knowledge?

"Knowledge is information that changes something or somebody—either by becoming grounds for action, or by making an individual (or an institution) capable of different or more effective action."

Peter F. Drucker in *The New Realities*

What is knowledge management?

"Knowledge management is the systematic, explicit, and deliberate building, renewal, and application of knowledge to maximize an enterprise's knowledge-related effectiveness and returns from its knowledge assets."

Some say KM is a fad, but it has lasted nearly a decade as a distinct concept. It is beyond the fad stage (historically, fads normally last five years). KM, however, originating around 1991, is still a relatively new concept—although Peter Drucker talked about the "knowledge worker" decades ago. Still, many organizations say that KM is nothing new and has been around for decades. According to the Corning Corporation, which has a robust KM program, it has been practicing KM for over 125 years now.What is new is the emphasis on KM as a concept, with its accompanying definitions, uses, taxonomies, experts, consultants, practitioners, and relabeled information technologies. Hundreds of books are written on the subject, and a conference is held each month. KM institutes and consortia have sprung up, and even within academia one can find many courses and research on the subject. Despite all this, there persists a vague notion as to what it is, how to do it, how to measure it, and what its value is to the organization.

Although some organizations are effectively measuring their KM programs, there is still debate and confusion as to what KM is and what its value is. This is because KM lacks first principles and a theory or body of knowledge. Knowledge management is analogous to gravity in that it was not until Sir Isaac Newton articulated the laws of motion and energy in the 17th century that we had the laws of motion we are familiar with today. In fact, without his articulation of them, we would not have experienced the industrial age. Keep in mind, however, that gravity existed well before Newton came along. What he did was take an observable phenomenon (i.e., falling apples) and deduce the laws of motion and energy that we are familiar with today.

The same is now true for KM. It has been around for a long time, but it only began to manifest itself as a distinct concept in

1991, when the first chief knowledge officer (CKO) was appointed. Many definitions, models, technologies, and processes have emerged since that time, almost to the point of making it truly hard to define KM. The good news is that whatever an organization decides KM is, for the most part one can find enthusiasm, pay-offs, and knowledge sharing. Although the impetus behind KM projects is to attempt to at least "get something started" or to "do something useful," there are still no organized, commonly accepted principles or references to fall back on. Without knowing all the inputs and processes, any efforts have led to time-consuming exercises, frustration, limited success, and often disappointment in the final results. Conversely, there are enough success stories to justify and sustain KM programs and enough best practices to document what works and what does not.

The time has come for the development of "first principles" and the making of KM into an academic discipline. Without this framework, there are not only no criteria by which to judge its value, but also no definitive guidelines for designing and implementing a knowledge management system.

It is interesting to note from a historical perspective that KM represents the near end of an evolution of several management concepts, systems, and technology elements, as depicted in Figure 1. We see the various management concepts, systems, and technology elements all culminating in knowledge.

Another way of looking at this evolution is from a hierarchical perspective, similar to Maslow's hierarchy of needs theory. In that theory, an individual's needs are arranged hierarchically, from the lower level physiological needs to the highest level need, the need for self-actualization. The point here is that in achieving the highest need, the lower needs remain and are part and parcel of the fabric of the human being.

Figure 2 hierarchically displays systems thinking (at the bottom) all the way to knowledge management engineering (near the top). The other evolving disciplines, software engineering and systems engineering, from which emerged best practices

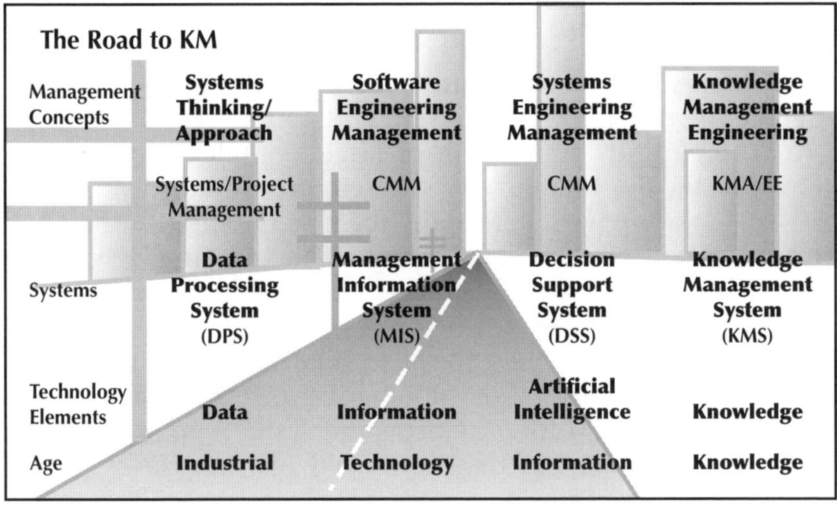

Figure 1. Evolution of Knowledge Management

known as a capability maturity model (CMM), are depicted in their position in the hierarchy and according to the time sequence in which they were developed. They continue to be part of the fabric of a KMS, especially in its design and implementation, similar to what we discussed with Maslow's hierarchy.

Where is all this leading? We have evolved from the bottom up to where we are today. Had we had KM "first principles" earlier, then we would have learned a long time ago how to design and implement a KMS from the top down, without having to deal with the cacophony that surrounds us today. We see the U.S. government, for example, undertake a great movement in electronic government (e-gov). KM is a fundamental part of it because one objective of e-gov is to share knowledge across all agencies to better serve the citizen. Yet there are no definitive guidelines or first principles to evaluate the thousands of acquisition proposals that will eventually come to the agencies for award. Will they award on the basis of the leading-edge KM technologies or to the organization that has the best processes for a KMS? Or maybe award will be based on some other criterion that has no sound basis.

To amplify this point, Figure 2 has a percentage next to each engineering discipline (i.e., 80, 40, and <10 percent). This represents the current failure rates of large, complex software programs, using the best practices heretofore noted (i.e., CMMs). Notice that when we superimpose the systems engineering CMM on the software CMM, the failure rate is halved. Finally, when we impose the enterprise engineering (EE) model, it is less than 10 percent. It stands to reason because software supports a system and a system supports the enterprise. It is important to start from the top down in software development. However, before we had a KMS/EE or a CMM for enterprise and systems engineering, respectively, software was first developed without the benefit of

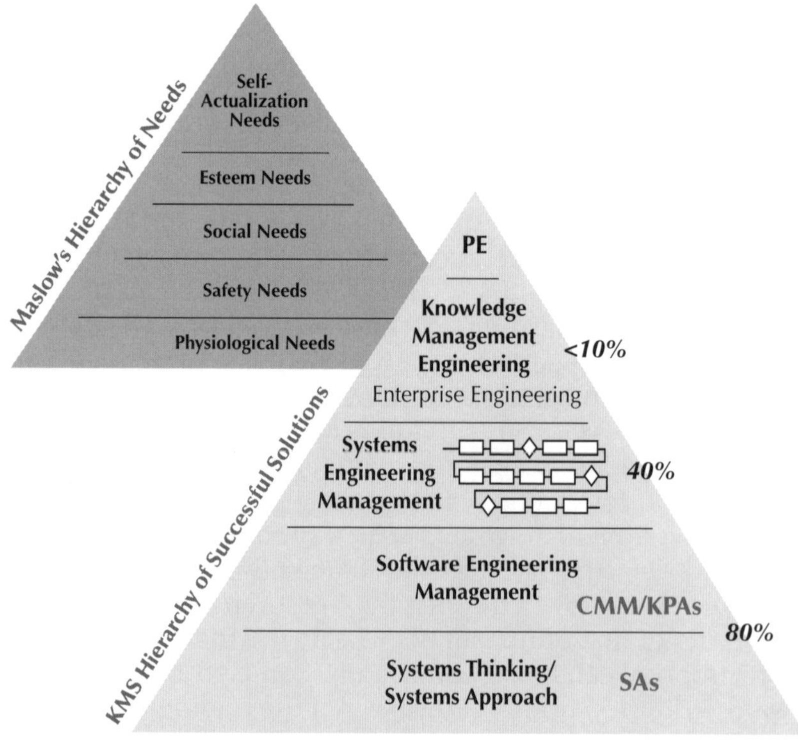

Figure 2. Hierarchy of Successful Solutions

truly knowing what systems and enterprise the software had to fit into. Yes, in a sense we knew, but we did not have the rigor of systems engineering and, eventually, KMS engineering to guide us as we were doing our software engineering. (We are doing KM engineering without that benefit because KMS engineering does not yet exist as a CMM-like model.) Imagine the financial and program consequences if such an approach worked and was fully implemented. Unfortunately, the newspapers recently reminded us of the large system development failures by the largest corporations, despite use of the best practices in software engineering.

THE BIRTH OF A BODY OF KNOWLEDGE: THE FOUR PILLARS

What is the next step? We do need first principles (i.e., a body of knowledge) for KM, and this function should be the responsibility of the universities. Even an Isaac Newton had to rely on them to take his first principles and subject them first to the rigors of the scientific method and, second, to develop the body of knowledge about mathematics and motion from which the many applications we see around us were spawned.

The George Washington University (GW) is attempting to do this. The university approved a degree-granting program, with a concentration in KM, starting in the 2000 academic year. More than 25 doctoral students signed up within the first year, several transferring from other doctoral programs. It was to this body of researchers that the challenge was given to create a body of knowledge for KM similar to its precursor disciplines of systems management and systems engineering.

Preliminary research indicated that, given all the readings, practices, conferences, and findings to date on KM, one could group all the key elements of KM into four pillars, similar to Newton grouping his observations about gravity under the laws of motion. (Refer to Figure 3.)

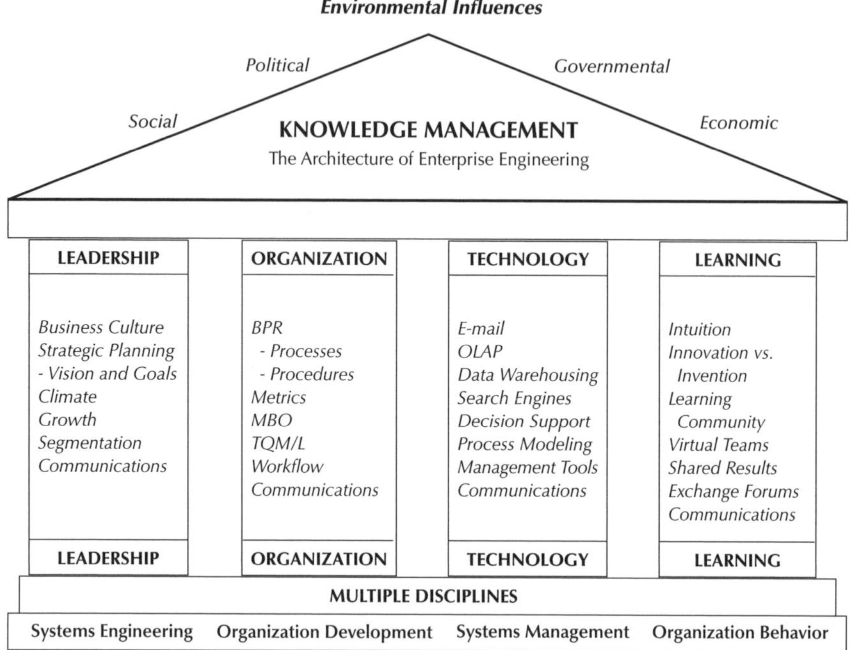

Figure 3. KM Pillars—Key Principles Around KM

The number "four" was not sacrosanct; the apples just fell that way. The challenge was to label each pillar to encompass the many key subelements under each. Table 1 highlights some of the key elements, subelements, and related disciplines that are grouped under each pillar. This was not only validated in a doctoral dissertation by Dr. Frank Calabrese,[2] but also became the foundation for a research map highlighting the principal functions of a KM System: knowledge assurance, representation, transfer, and utilization. (Refer to Figure 4.) This map guides all the doctoral students, who have taken a piece of the map as their research project.

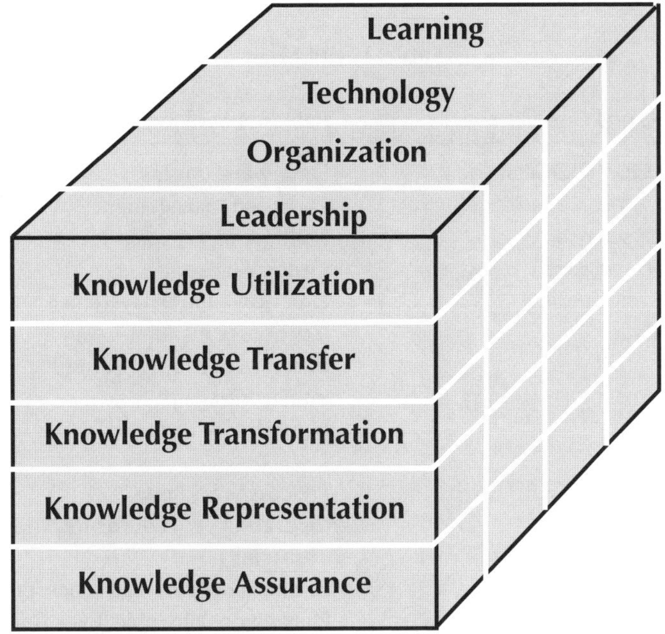

Figure 4. Principal Functions of a KM System

As Dr. Calabrese stated in his dissertation: "This research is based on the belief that KM is not a fad, rather, on the premise that managing an enterprises' knowledge resources (i.e., KM) can be more effectively achieved by creating KM programs using a defined framework of key elements and key subelements."[3]

When the four pillars were showcased, many people agreed with them; however, others often asked the question: Which of the four is the most important? In asking that question, they misunderstood what was being said (i.e., all four make up the "foundation" of a KM system). Without all of them in some kind of harmony, a KMS does not exist. Take away one, and the chances of KM systems succeeding in the long term are doubtful. All four form the essence, the core, and the fabric of a KMS. They cannot be separated.

Table 1. KM Pillars

Key Elements and Disciplines	*Representative Key Sub-elements*
TECHNOLOGY/TOOLS Disciplines: • Computer science • Operations research • Electrical engineering • Math/statistics • Logic • Management information systems	Data warehousing Database management SW Multimedia repositories GroupWare Decision support systems Corporate intranet Business modeling systems Intelligent agents Neural networks, etc.
ORGANIZATION/CULTURE Disciplines: • Psychology • Operations research • Organization development • Philosophy • Socio-linguistics	Process workflows Operating procedures for knowledge sharing Business process reengineering (BPR) Management by objectives (MBO) Total quality management (TQM) Metric standards Hierarchical, centralized, decentralized Matrix-type organization Open/sharing Closed/power based Internal partnering vs. competing type culture
LEADERSHIP/MANAGEMENT Disciplines: • Operations research • Management science • Psychology • Philosophy • Logic • Linguistics • Management information systems • Behavioral profiling	Strategic planning Vision sharing Specific and general goals and objectives Executive commitment KM programs tied to metrics Formal KM roles in existence Tangible rewards for use of KM Special recognition for knowledge sharing Performance criteria include KM items

continues

Key Elements and Disciplines	*Representative Key Sub-elements*
LEARNING ENTERPRISE Disciplines: • Cognitive psychology • Organization development • Systems engineering • Management philosophy • Personal mastery • Introspection	Tacit and explicit knowledge understood Sharing vision/team learning Management support for continuous learning Knowledge captured and distributed KM values and principles formally encouraged Virtual teams/exchange forums in use Communities of practice/shared results are active Innovation encouraged/recognized/rewarded

During the 1970s and 1980s, technology was an enabler to achieving an enterprise's objectives. Today, that is no longer the case. Technology is systemic—it is such a fundamental part of the system that the enterprise of today cannot function or survive without it.

To underscore that, we redesigned the four pillars into four spheres. (Refer to Figure 5.)

We use the analogy of a juggler who has four balls in the air at one time. If the juggler drops any one of them, the game is over. What we do not know at this stage in our research is the relationship among the four. Depending on the life cycle of the enterprise, we suspected that one or several would be dominant. In April 2000, we presented this concept at the International Council on Systems Engineering, Mid-Atlantic Regional Conference. Essentially, the elements are interconnected and build upon each other for successful enterprise engineering. But what constitutes alignment for the organization, its enterprise, or a process is not so much to have a perfect alignment among these elements as it is to develop a construct suitable to the business strategy and to the environmental influences that impact that strategy on a day-to-day basis.

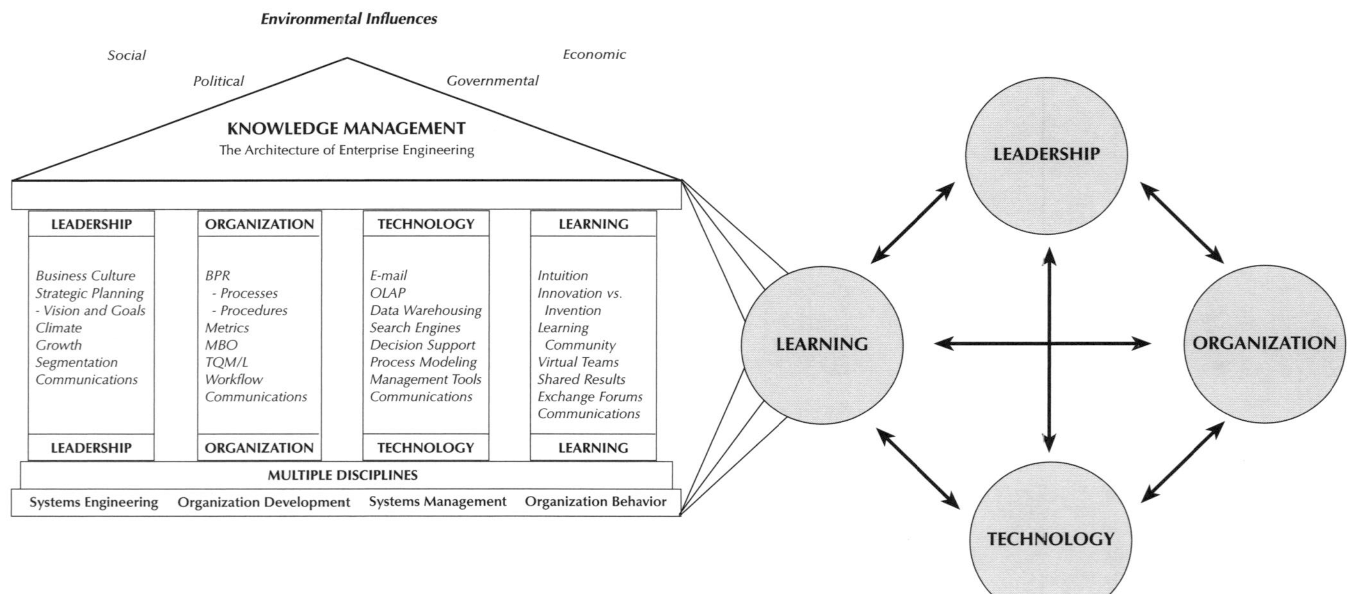

Figure 5. Evolving Pillars—Interrelated Spheres

For example, too much emphasis on technology without incorporating the other critical elements (i.e., leadership, organizational structure, and learning) can easily result in a failed system. Conversely, an enterprise can also place too much emphasis on strategy (i.e., through leadership) and organization, and not necessarily capitalize on technology to implement that strategy or provide a continuous learning environment.

KM research at GW continues at a rapid pace:

- From defining and validating first principles
- To prioritizing KM objectives, both in government and industry
- To building models for each pillar and analyzing the relationships within and between each
- To creating processes for various levels
- To evaluating metrics and returns on investment (ROIs) from KM systems
- To listing and evaluating various KM tools and how-to's for ease of implementation
- To building a theory of information security/assurance so that we can design it into an MS rather than think about it as an afterthought.

All this is being done concurrently. The researchers meet periodically to share their results and see how they impact one another's research. Outside experts are called in to review and comment. Everything is baselined and referenced to what is happening in the "real" world. In fact, many of the researchers themselves are in significant KM leadership positions in government and industry.

One of the major outputs from this research, beyond validating a body of knowledge, are guidelines for designing and implementing a KMS. The most cited major barrier to KM success is "culture." Our approach is to work with the existing culture through various strategies. Many enterprises' cultures are built up over decades and are their defining attribute. As such, they should not be changed. Instead we must figure out how to exploit them. In the case of a KMS, if the culture of an enterprise can be classified similar to how a personality (à la Myers-Briggs) is classified, then we should be able to ascertain which of the variations of the four pillars are user-friendly to that type of culture. Then if an enterprise wishes to change its culture, it can use the pillars as "enablers" of the particular type of culture it desires. This is the ultimate goal of the KM research at GW. We believe this type of approach can be effective and addresses the ever-present problem of "culture."

SYSTEMS THINKING/SYSTEMS APPROACH TO ENGINEERING A KMS

We now turn to the systems thinking/systems approach and KM. Peter Senge was the first person to summarize, popularize, and integrate the notions of the learning organization and systems thinking in his book, *The Fifth Discipline*, written in 1990.[4] His thesis was that by using a systems perspective, the organization learned and, consequently, improved both its efficiency and effectiveness. In some ways, Senge presaged the knowledge era, where the expectation is that knowledge can be managed. One objective of a KMS is to tap into and share the tacit knowledge already acquired in an enterprise. Many agree that 80 percent of an enterprise's knowledge is tacit (i.e., not formalized or documented in such a way as to be available to the rest of the enterprise). Hence, if we can build a system to capture any part of that 80 percent, the research then has great value to that enterprise.

The KM research noted above at GW is conducted in the School of Engineering and Applied Science and resides in the Department of Engineering Management and Systems Engineering, an interdisciplinary department that blends technology with management considerations. It is only natural, therefore, that one of our research objectives is the application of this loosely defined science or body of knowledge to real-world applications.

We noted in Figure 1 that the evolution of the concepts of systems management and systems engineering grew out of the complexities of the space age. In the late 1960s, that industry challenged the University of Southern California to create an academic program to guide and tackle the complexities of systems development. We now rely on those proven concepts to address the challenges of the knowledge age, perhaps more complex than space itself. While there are many aspects of the systems approach to engineering a KMS (depicted in Figure 6), this discussion highlights only one—that of systems engineering, a discipline followed throughout many large U.S. corporations. In fact, several of such companies define themselves as a systems engineering and integration (SE&I) corporations (also note the name "Systems Engineering" in our Department).

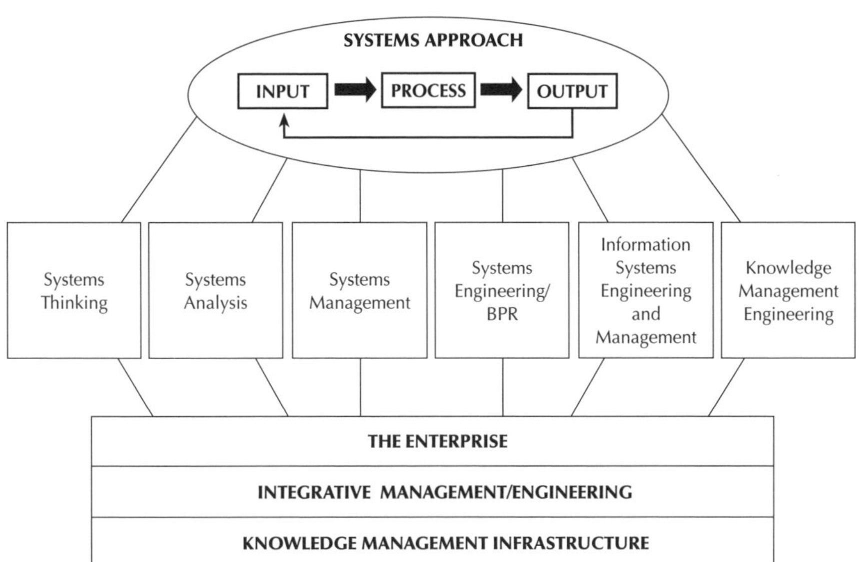

Figure 6. Systems Approach—Engineering a KMS

We do not intend to cover systems engineering in detail here (a book is in progress on this subject). However, a systematic, widely accepted methodology employing the concepts of systems thinking and systems approach is both useful and necessary to designing and implementing a complex system, such as a KMS.

Listed below are accepted definitions of systems thinking, systems approach and systems engineering.

> **Systems thinking** encompasses a large and fairly amorphous body of methods, tools, and principles, all oriented to looking at the interrelatedness of forces, and seeing them as part of a common process—an integrator of the other "disciplines" that continually remind us that the whole can exceed the sum of its parts.
>
> Senge

> A "**systems approach**" is basically a recognition that all the elements of a system must interoperate harmoniously, which in turn requires a systematic and repeatable process for designing, developing, and operating the system.
>
> Eisner, 1998

> **Systems engineering** is an iterative process of top-down synthesis. Development and operation of a real-world systgem that satisfies, in a near-optimal manner, the full range of requirements for the system.
>
> Eisner, 1988

To illustrate how to employ the systems approach and systems engineering methodology in designing and implementing a KMS, refer to Figure 7.

The first step is to delineate the environment of the enterprise, both internal and external. If we are to "share" our knowledge throughout the enterprise, we need to identify at the outset with whom we are willing to share it.

Second, list the enterprise's core strategic objectives (in a measurable format). The enterprise needs to know when it succeeds and, hence, the importance of the metrics upfront. Also at this stage, list the critical information/knowledge needs to achieve the objectives. This prevents the enterprise from chasing irrelevant and unfocused information/knowledge. Otherwise, you may end up searching for, managing, and guarding your trash.

Third, the four pillars must be factored into every design part of the KMS. They may not be as evident throughout, but they must be there. For example, in the next step, we will see a high-level functional architecture develop from these inputs. In this architecture, all the key and sub-elements noted in Tables 1 and 2 and derived from the four pillars *must* somehow be factored in for the KMS. (Just like the automobile engineer who, when he designs a car and puts it into motion, must take into account one of Newton's laws: "A body, once in motion, remains in motion, unless acted upon by some outward force." In this case, he designs a "brake.")

Fourth, as a process, a high-level functional architecture, with its waterfall subordinate architectures (each of which is subordinate to and depends on the higher one for definition) are designed based on the inputs. Again, these architectures must have an audit trail back to the inputs, especially to the four pillars and the measurable objectives of the enterprise. The subordinate ar-

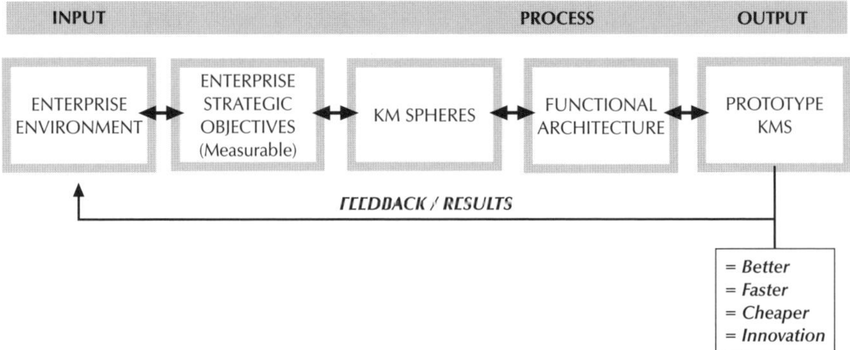

Figure 7. KMS Systems Approach and Systems Engineering Methodology

chitectures are: (1) operational, which describes the "operations" and organizational structures of the enterprise; (2) information, which deals with the sources and functions (noted in our research map, Figure 4, above) of the critical/vital information and knowledge needs of the enterprise; (3) systems that provide us with the various infrastructure and other systems, both human and technological, to support the enterprise; and (4) technical, which becomes a basis for standardization, commonality, and configuration management to drive our systems and information architectures.

If all is designed well, the output should be a KMS to fit the culture and support the objectives of the enterprise. A prototype KMS is recommended, both to assess the effectiveness of the architecture and provide a feedback mechanism. The final outputs will be doing things better, faster, and cheaper, as well as *innovation*. Both are the ultimate competitive advantages.

TRANSITIONS TO THE FUTURE

During the past decades, we saw many beneficial management concepts and technology solutions come and go, such as management by objective (MBO), total quality management (TQM), business process reengineering (BPR), management information systems (MISs), strategic planning, and, recently, enterprise resource planning (ERP). Some were disasters for the enterprise. Many were time and resources wasted rather than wisely spent. A few metamorphosed into the current management practices of the day and lost their identity. Others saw a rebirth, such as TQM/Six Sigma, currently implemented with a vengeance by General Electric Corporation. If these were so good, why didn't they work? Our hypothesis is because they lacked a framework in which to operate and thrive. Further to our discussion, it is because they lacked an enterprise/knowledge management framework/system, underwritten by a systems perspective—similar to a jigsaw puzzle, wherein the pieces are hard to put together without a mental picture.

Today, a well-engineered KMS, using the systems approach, represents the future growth and dynamism of the enterprise, especially given the global and networked world within which we operate. We all have a stake in ensuring we have a validated body of knowledge from which to operate. These "first principles," like those of Newton's, will drive the knowledge age as surely as Newton's drove the industrial age. Everyone in government and industry has a major stake in the outcome. And, if it is not in KM, we had better find it elsewhere, for the future well being of the enterprise depends on it.

NOTES

1. Chauvel, D. and Despres, C. A. *Thematic Analysis of the Thinking in Knowledge Management.* The Theseus Institute, Sophia Antipolis, France, 1999.
2. Calabrese, Francesco. *A Suggested Framework of Key Elements Defining Effective Enterprise Knowledge Management Programs.* Washington, D.C.: The George Washington University, 2000.
3. Maslow, A. H. *Motivation and Personality.* New York: Harper, 1954.
4. Senge, Peter. *The Fifth Discipline: The Art and Practice of the Learning Organization.* New York: Doubleday/Currency, 1990.
5. Wiig, Karl M. *Knowledge Management Foundations: Thinking About Thinking—How People and Organizations Create, Represent, and Use Knowledge.* Arlington, TX: Schema Press, 1993.

PART III

Leading Knowledge Management

In Part II we dealt with aspects of knowledge management that link us with the advent of electronic government. In this section, *Leading Knowledge Management,* we start to address the question: How do we provide the direction or management to make it happen? This section focuses on topics such as: managing change, communities of practice, competencies of the CKO, and attempting to measure the return on investment of knowledge management initiatives.

In "Who Will Lead the Knowledge Revolution?" by Shereen Remez, and "Leadership and Knowledge Management" by Joe Williamson, Vice President Knowledge Services, EDS Federal Government, we open squarely on the core issue of this section: leadership and leading knowledge management.

The CKO is a fairly new executive in the enterprise and has been the object of much interest and speculation. "Should there be a CKO?" "Who should hold the job?" "What previous experience should that individual have?" These are some of the questions being asked throughout the industry and Bob Neilson, professor and CKO at the National Defense University, attempts to provide some of the answers in "Knowledge Management and the Role of the CKO."

"Managing Change in a Knowledge Environment" is the vehicle chosen by the Department of the Navy's Alex Bennet to address the critical issue of change management in KM. She looks at the difficulties in managing change under the new realities of the marketplace and underscores the need to handle the challenge in order to be productive and competitive in the marketplace.

At some point, every knowledge management initiative has to be financially justified. In "Knowledge Management: The Business Proposition for Government Organizations," Kelvin Womack, a principal with KPMG Consulting, provides us with a methodology and suggested metrics.

Leadership in knowledge management inevitably leads us to the issue of communities of practice. They are the essential building blocks for knowledge management environments. Cathy Hirsh, Vice President, IT Consulting, AMS, and her colleagues, Mark Youman and Susan Hanley, now CKO of Plural, draw from their AMS experience in addressing the topic: "Creating Knowledge-Based Communities of Practice."

The last chapter in this section addresses the question of leadership as we attempt to garner knowledge about our customers. Every organization has customers, whether they are in the private or public sector. Furthermore, it is well established that the raison d'etre of an enterprise is to serve its customers. To do this in a superior manner, it is essential to know them well. In "Harnessing Customer Knowledge: Merging Customer Relationship Management with Knowledge Management," Oracle's Tim Cannon presents a strong case for linking the two disciplines.

CHAPTER 11

Who Will Lead the Knowledge Revolution?
An Examination of the Differing Roles of CIO and CKO

Shereen G. Remez, PhD

> *CKOs focus on what's in people's heads—their intellectual assets. However, successful CKOs focus on what's in people's hearts—their desire to learn, improve, and share their knowledge with those they trust.*
>
> Jon Powell, CKO, Plural

> *The role of the CIO is not dictator, but one of gardener. . . The CIO nurtures good ideas and prunes out bad ones.*
>
> Timothy Hoechst, VP, Technology, Oracle

Now that virtually 100 percent of *Fortune 500* companies have chief information officers (CIOs) and 25 to 30 percent have chief knowledge officers (CKOs), perhaps it is time to answer the question of distinctions, similarities, and overlap between the two roles.

In the federal government, CIOs emerged officially with the passage of the Clinger-Cohen Act in 1996, mandating the appointment of CIOs in every major executive agency and enforcing the high level of EL-4 or equivalent, as well as the direct reporting authority to the secretary or agency head. In the private sector, the CIO concept has been around for nearly five years, with varying reports of success and failure, not to mention frequent job mobility.

CKOs, on the other hand, as we glide into the new millennium, are few and hard to spot in the federal government, and the concept of CKO is more cutting edge than mainstream at the federal level. Looking at the *Fortune 500*, by contrast, we find that 80 percent of CKOs are spending significant dollars on knowledge management (KM), and more than 25 percent of major firms, such as General Electric, Dow Chemical, and Chevron, have designated CKOs as a focal point for their initiatives.

If the history of chief financial officers (CFO Act, 1990) and CIOs (Clinger-Cohen Act, 1996) repeats itself for CKOs, aspirants should be polishing resumes in anticipation of either legislation or an executive order during the first year or two of the new millennium.

This chapter, however, focuses on the respective roles of CIO and CKO—what each has in common and where each differs in both perspective and responsibility. Ultimately, the two must work together if a new vision of government that is both electronic (high-tech) and friendly (hi-touch) is to be achieved.

HISTORY OF THE CIO VS. THE CKO

The role of CIO originated in the private sector, presumably out of the frustration most chief executive officers (CEOs) felt about their information technology (IT) investments. Bemoaning a lack of alignment with business objectives, many companies sought to recapture control over the billions of dollars spent on IT without much evidence of the long-promised productivity gains. Roger Smith, CEO of General Motors, once said, "If I had all the money we wasted on failed information technology systems, I could just have bought Nissan and Toyota outright."

CIOs were supposed the bridge the language gap between the lexicon of business and the secret code of IT. Most CIOs, at least at the outset, came from the IT world, and many had a difficult time making the environmental transition from "techy" to boardroom. In fact, a common joke around the CIO community was that CIO stood for "Career Is Over!"—and many CIOs became easy targets for failed system ventures. Today, the job remains an extremely challenging one that requires both business acumen and the constant refreshing of technology expertise. And, in today's fast-moving world, the problems continue to plague systems that take longer to build, buy, and implement than top management takes to make new business decisions that render existing systems less than "state-of-the-art," if not totally inadequate to handle their new business strategy.

The role of CIO remains one of balancing the sometimes rocky marriage between business goals and the productivity that technology systems are supposed to deliver. These technology approaches are constantly evolving as well—historically, from mainframes to client server to Web-based, from centralized databases to distributed databases, from a strong emphasis on control and centralized management to decentralized LAN-based management and then back again. And, today, the concurrent growth of Internet-based business strategies that involve partners, customers, internal systems, and a multitude of vendors must be tempered with an increasing awareness that openness can also increase the vulnerability to security threats.

The CIO must be a full-business leader with a strong "seat at the table." His or her major role is to ensure that the technology investments made by the company or agency fully support the business strategy. Today, many business strategies are also technology driven. Pete Solvik, CIO at Cisco, has said that every corporation in today's world must have an Internet strategy or risk extinction.

CHIEF KNOWLEDGE OFFICER

The CKO's role has emerged over the past five years as the economy has moved from a reliance on "manpower" to a reliance on "mindpower." Where physical muscle once drove the Industrial Age economy, a rapid shift is now being made to mental muscle, where "know-how" and "know-who" are more important than the production of goods. We have moved from an economy of "hands" to an economy of "heads." These CKOs have the role of leveraging corporation or agency knowledge in ways that were previously unknown or simply overlooked. According to Tom Davenport, KM guru at Andersen Consulting, CKOs should: "Combine an orientation to the structured, explicit knowledge with an intuitive feel for precisely how cultural and behavioral factors may impede or enable the leveraging of knowledge in an enterprise." Davenport talks about how difficult it is to find a combination of hard skills and soft skills in one person. However, corporations are increasingly recognizing that their people and what they know are far more valuable that the physical assets of enterprise. Peter Drucker, world-renown management guru, said in the *Harvard Business Review*, "The knowledge worker is fast becoming the most valuable asset of any corporation" (or agency). And Larry Prusak of IBM observed that "The only thing that gives an organization a competitive edge—the only thing that is sustainable—is what it knows and how fast it can know something else."

To be effective, CKOs, like CIOs, need to earn a "seat at the table"; however, their seat may be newer and upholstered in the knowledge assets of the corporation—perhaps built on rollers to symbolize the agility, flexibility, and mobility a CKO must display in the rapidly evolving world of knowledge. Like the technology czars, the knowledge czar must ground his or her leadership in the world of business requirements and results. A demonstrated "ROI" (return on investment) is as important for knowledge management as it is for IT systems. And, like technology for its own sake, knowledge for its own sake is anathema to good business strategy.

The CKO, while striving for new and creative ways to maximize the know-how of the corporation, must stay grounded in the reality of business practice. He or she is, in a sense, a translator between the world of knowledge, innovation and ideas, and the world of missions, objectives, measurements, and finance. Just as the CIO must bridge the gap between technology and the business, the CKO must build a bridge to a new way of doing business. One part evangelist, all parts business strategist, the CKO needs to rally the enterprise around an idea—and that idea is that knowledge truly is powerful and productive.

ROLES OF THE CIO VS. CKO

The CIO is traditionally responsible for capital planning (the expenditure of funds for IT), the selection of products for the infrastructure (e-mail, enterprise desktop applications, operating systems, Web products, etc.), the Internet, information architecture, security, systems design and implementation, quality assurance, data/information management, IT training, enterprise applications (ERP), and emerging technologies. These are all technical or financial skills. The outstanding CIO, however, is more than a technocrat. He or she must be a leader and a catalyst for change—the technical Moses who will lead the organization out of the desert of status quo and into the promised land of e-business and e-government.

The CKO, on the other hand, focuses on intellectual capital, human capital, social capital, structural or corporate capital, tacit knowledge, best practices, communities of practice, communities of interest, knowledge portals (also known as enterprise information portals), data warehouse initiatives, and new KM technologies. The CKO tries to identify what the enterprise needs to know to do the work, what it already knows that can be shared and leveraged, and, most importantly, what it doesn't know that may result in lost business or failure. The outstanding CKO must not be mislead by technology, because technology alone will not deliver KM nor e-government. The CKO must also be a dynamic leader with vision—always throwing out his/her rope to lasso the organization to the knowledge economy and gently but firmly pulling the enterprise toward that vision.

Although both professionals arrive with varying backgrounds, the majority of CIOs have a strong technical background—many have been techies who have worked their way up from programming to Director of Technology, Information Resources Manager, CIO, or Chief Technology Officer. Many have a business background, having served in a company as a senior management official.

The backgrounds of CKOs may be in consulting, organizational psychology, human resources, technology, library science, or academia (usually with some business background). Some CKOs have been CIOs, and some CKOs are CIOs doing double duty. Many CKOs have been involved in "learning" in the organizational sense for years. They are people with a rounded combination of experiences, both in technology and human interaction.

Both CIOs and CKOs must be extraordinarily entrepreneurial and visionary, obvious skills for a leader in the 21st century. Both must be well respected in their enterprises, senior executives who have a credible track record and history of success. Both must have the ability to form relationships and alliances, and both must be interested in being a "change agent" rather than maintaining the status quo. Both must be strong in the face of changing political winds and the rough seas of internal politics because the bureaucracy inevitably challenges the novel and rewards those who have the courage to innovate with growing barriers to success.

However, the CIO should not be the CKO, even though technology is a large part of today's KM field. IT is necessary but not sufficient for KM. It supports and enables the identification, gathering, storage, and dissemination of knowledge, but it is neither creating nor applying knowledge itself—that is reserved solely as a human endeavor. KM is about people, not computers.

CIO COMPETENCIES VS. CKO COMPETENCIES

The Federal CIO Council spent a great deal of time and collective energy developing a list of competencies required for the CIO in the federal government. In the spring of 2000, the first class graduated from the Federal CIO University, a program designed to develop these skills and competencies. As shown in Chart 1, CIO Competencies, it is essential that the CIO have a complete understanding of technology and technology issues, including today's complex e-commerce world and the growing world of information assurance and security. Equally important, the CIO must have the skills to form trusted relationships with the head of the agency, the CFO, and other important program officials. Because IT permeates virtually every government activity, from mission-critical to administrative support, the CIO must have a solid grounding in the business of the agency. Thus, the CIO at the National Institutes of Health (NIH) needs to understand the business of health research and development, and the CIO at the National Aeronautics and Space Administration (NASA) must have a working knowledge of aerospace exploration, technology, and research.

Security is becoming one of the most critical competencies of CIOs as world network traffic grows exponentially, as web-based work permeates the organization, and as Internet terrorism threats increase. CIOs, like all leaders, must have vision. They need to see the future, have the passion to shape and articulate it well to doubters, and inspire all agency employees to move toward it without fear. Most important, they must persuade top management that the future is real—real enough to invest in. Selling the promise of new technologies—from portals and e-business to public key infrastructure (PKI), from enterprise resources planning systems to data warehouses—is more than challenging. Difficult to explain both technologically and in business terms, these bold initiatives must garner top management commitment and extensive new resources. The CIO must be prepared to deal with the failures and setbacks that he or she will undoubtedly encounter along the way. It is no wonder that many wary CIOs, especially in the complex federal environment, adopt a "wait and see" attitude rather than risking failure by being too far out on the edge of technology.

According to a recent study of 1,400 CIO members of Gartner's Executive Programs, today's CIO is now mutating into four different possible CIO roles:

1. **The Strategic CIO:** This position is responsible for top-level business strategy rather than day-to-day implementation. This is the position most likely to migrate to CEO and is truly a "seat-at-the-table" role.

2. **The Chief Infrastructure or Technology Officer:** This role concentrates on delivery, implementation, and cost containment. Outsourcing is often a large part of this type of CIO's responsibility, such as for seat management or data center outsourcing.

3. **The Technology Opportunist:** This role evolved from the explosion of e-business and emerging technologies that are driving new business ventures and new value propositions for ongoing enterprises. Online customer transaction services and reverse auctions are examples within the federal government. The emphasis on e-government will stimulate an increasing need for this type of CIO.

4. **The Business Line Leader:** This CIO is responsible for a specific mission area and may emphasize IT delivery and implementation within a particular business (e.g., supply chain, telecommunications, or student loans).

Chart 1. Ten Core Competencies for CIOs

These are the big ten core competencies that serve as the basis for training programs offered by the Federal CIO Council through the General Services Administration (GSA). These Clinger-Cohen Core Competencies are endorsed to serve as a baseline to assist government agencies in complying with Section 5125(C)(3) of the Clinger-Cohen Act.

1.0 Policy and Organizational

- 1.1 Dept/agency missions, organization, function, policies, procedures
- 1.2 Governing laws and regulations (e.g., Clinger-Cohen, GPRA, PRA)
- 1.3 Federal government decision-making, policy-making process, and budget formulation and execution process
- 1.4 Links and interrelationships among agency heads, COO, CIO, and CFO functions
- 1.5 Intergovernmental programs, policies, and processes
- 1.6 Privacy and security
- 1.7 Information management

2.0 Leadership/Managerial

- 2.1 Defining roles, skill sets, and responsibilities of senior IRM Officials, CIO, IRM staff, and stakeholders

2.2 Methods for building federal IT management and technical staff expertise
2.3 Competency testing—standards, certification, and performance assessment
2.4 Partnership/team-building techniques
2.5 Personnel performance management technique
2.6 Practices that attract and retain qualified IT personnel

3.0 Process/Change Management
3.1 Modeling and simulation tools and methods
3.2 Quality improvement models and methods
3.3 Techniques/models of organizational development and change
3.4 Techniques and models of process management and control
3.5 Business process redesign/reengineering models and methods

4.0 Information Resources Strategy and Planning
4.1 IT baseline assessment analysis
4.2 Interdepartmental, inter-agency IT functional analysis
4.3 IT planning methodologies
4.4 Contingency planning
4.5 Monitoring and evaluation methods and techniques

5.0 IT Performance Assessment: Models and Methods
5.1 GPRA and IT: Measuring the business value of IT
5.2 Monitoring and measuring new system development: When and how to "pull the plug" on systems
5.3 Measuring IT success: practical and impractical approaches
5.4 Processes and tools for creating, administering, and analyzing survey questionnaires
5.5 Techniques for defining and selecting effective performance measures
5.6 Examples of and criteria for performance evaluation
5.7 Managing IT reviews and oversight processes

6.0 Project/Program Management
6.1 Project scope/requirements management
6.2 Project integration management
6.3 Project time/cost/performance management
6.4 Project quality management
6.5 Project risk management
6.6 Project procurement management

7.0 Capital Planning and Investment Assessment
7.1 Best practices
7.2 Cost benefit, economic, and risk analysis
7.3 Risk management—models and methods

- 7.4 Weighing benefits of alternative IT investments
- 7.5 Capital investment analysis—models and methods
- 7.6 Business case analysis
- 7.7 Integrating performance with mission and budget process
- 7.8 Investment review process
- 7.9 Intergovernmental, federal, state, and local projects

8.0 Acquisition

- 8.1 Alternative functional approaches (necessity, government, IT) analysis
- 8.2 Alternative acquisition models
- 8.3 Streamlined acquisition methodologies
- 8.4 Post-award IT contract management models and methods, including past performance evaluation
- 8.5 IT acquisition best practices

9.0 Technical

- 9.1 Information systems architectures client/server, collaborative processing, telecommunications
- 9.2 Emerging/developing technologies
- 9.3 Information delivery technology (Internet, Intranet, kiosks, etc.)
- 9.4 Security policy, disaster recovery, and business resumption
- 9.5 System life cycle
- 9.6 Software development
- 9.7 Data management

10.0 Desktop Technology Tools

CKO COMPETENCIES

The CKO has a holistic role to play in the organization. Like the CIO, his or her reach is enterprise-wide and horizontal rather than vertical. But, perhaps even more than the CIO, the CKO needs to have a new vision for the workplace and be exceptionally talented and skilled in communicating that vision to the secretary of the department and other leaders, to top management, and to employees. The CKO is trying to instill the idea of knowledge flow, not just knowledge collection, and this concept is not well understood by most government entities. "This is about swimming, not about building swimming pools", says Michael Helfrich, former Vice President of Knowledge Management at Lotus.

The Knowledge Management Working Group of the Federal CIO Council, co-chaired by Alex Bennet and Shereen Remez, has endorsed these preliminary competencies for the CKO. These competencies were developed under the leadership of Dr. Robert Nielson, CKO of the Information Resources Management College of the National Defense University. Two brainstorming sessions were held with public- and private-sector leaders. The results, as shown in Chart 2, CKO Competencies, show that many of these skills are both hard to measure and identify and hard to teach. They are tacit skills that must be hired, not learned on the job. As Tom Davenport of Andersen Consulting writes: "CKOs have three critical responsibilities: creating a knowledge management infrastructure, building a knowledge culture, and making it all pay off economically." CKOs must be technologically sophisticated, organizationally aware, and financially responsible to the enterprise. Like many "new economy" job titles, the CKO is an eclectic mix of know-how, know-what, and know-who—a leader who can turn the ambiguity and speed of the modern business and government environment into opportunity for growth and change.

Chart 2. CKO Competencies

1. Leadership and Management
- Ability to influence top management
- Skill in diplomacy
- Ability to motivate large numbers of people; serve as model
- A recognized and respected individual who engenders trust
- Exceptional energy and persistence

2. Strategic Thinking
- Has a clear vision and sticks to it
- Understands and uses systems/holistic thinking
- Knows the business imperative and aligns KM with the business
- Understands the unique skills needed to leverage knowledge effectively
- Understands and focuses on the customer

3. Communications
- A great storyteller of corporate stories and lessons
- An avid communicator, especially around new ideas
- Ability to persuade and form coalitions across enterprise

4. **Tools and Techniques**
   - Understands KM tools and technologies (e.g., portals, intelligent and collaborative software, search engines, data warehouse)
   - Understands the uses, applications, and comparative effectiveness of different KM tools
5. **Personal Knowledge and Cognitive Capability**
   - Understands the organizational culture
   - Knows and aligns with the organizational mission
   - Understands business process re-engineering and measurement
   - Knows KM concepts and strategies
   - Knows new organizational structures and new ways of organizing
6. **Personal Behaviors**
   - Innovator and risk-taker
   - Learns and shares information
   - Is a team player
   - Is committed to knowledge acquisition and sharing

In today's world, when KM is still a somewhat new and somewhat fuzzy concept, the CKO must a catalyst, capable of changing the enterprise perspective. CKOs need to "think globally, but act locally," keeping in mind a vision for the knowledge-centric enterprise, while sponsoring smaller, local points of activity that demonstrate knowledge-sharing as a business strategy. As the chief architect of the knowledge environment, the CKO needs to work closely with the CIO to ensure that the information infrastructure supports the knowledge flow. Obviously, standardization of technology at all levels, from portal applications to operating systems, is helpful to the electronic exchange of information.

Most importantly, the CKO needs to be a people-centric leader. Knowledge exists in people's minds, and the willingness to share knowledge is a function of the organizational culture. Cultural change is, therefore, a function of the CKO's ability to lead, persuade, model, and inspire others within the organization at all levels to embrace the concept of knowledge with the same enthusiasm previously reserved for bricks and mortar. Helpful in this leadership role is the ability to use corporate storytelling to get the point across. Reams of statistics, performance measures, and justifications often do not stack up to success when vying for scarce resources or convincing top management that knowledge is vital. One good corporate story told well is worth a thousand statistics and can often inspire others to see what was before shrouded in mystery and confusion.

DOs AND DON'Ts

Many myths surround this new area of endeavor. Here are a few of them dispelled by early experience of the CKO community within government.

Myth: ***There is no need for a separate CKO position.*** The fact remains that IT does not equal KM. As Larry Prusak of IBM has said, "If organizations could be as smart as they want to be simply by building a repository and issuing everyone a laptop, they would have done that years ago." The implication of the equation IT ≠ KM is that successful organizations will rely on a focal point, a CKO, for their knowledge activities. The risk of combining KM with IT is that of reducing knowledge to servers, software, and networks. KM is really about people, not about technology. Exactly how this is organized depends on the culture of the enterprise, but the leader of this change must be seen as having "a seat at the table."

Myth: ***A knowledge culture can be created by executive mandate.*** The fact is that an agency or department cannot change overnight. A knowledge culture represents a radical overhaul of current systems for organizing work, rewarding and punishing sharing, and funding. Although support from the top is absolutely necessary for KM to work well, it cannot be ordered in a memorandum to all employees. The private sector has paved the way for government by building organizations for the new economy that are flexible, allow for partnerships even among competitors, and reward innovation.

In government, the best approaches are shaping up as "top down, bottom up," with lots of lights in the middle. The CKO's role is to stimulate that enthusiasm and support at all levels of the organization.

Myth: ***Standardization inhibits flexibility and creativity.*** Many capable innovators mistakenly feel that standardization is anathema to innovation and knowledge creation. Counter-intuitively, perhaps, CKOs are better served by being the staunchest supports of the efforts of CIOs to create standard architectures and infrastructures that support "plug-and-play" knowledge technologies. As Kurt Zimmer, Chief of Information Technology Consulting at Gartner, has often said, "There are a lot of good technologies out there—pick one and standardize on that." Knowledge-sharing across e-mail, files, databases, and applications is often hampered by problems of interoperability.

The CKO and CIO must work together to convince the organization that, when it comes to supporting technology, less is actually more.

Myth: ***Technology alone will solve the problem.*** This "build it and they will come" philosophy has been disproved in the IT world, and it is being re-tested with similar results in the KM world. Business problems and business challenges that lend themselves to KM interventions turn out to be about 80 percent people and 20 percent technology. It is true, as Mike Turillo, CKO of KPMG, has said, "You can't have knowledge management without technology." But so is the converse: "You can't have knowledge management without people." The people/technology equation is the yin and yang of successful knowledge management. The outstanding CKO will spend about 80 percent of his or her time on people, and 20 percent on technology.

Myth: ***Knowledge management is more a private-sector concept and creates just another stovepipe in the government.*** While it is true that the private sector has embraced knowledge management earlier and seems to have built whole businesses based on intangible assets, such as intellectual assets, the growing interest in e-government will add velocity to the KM movement. Following the pattern of CFOs, CIOs, and now CKOs, it is a matter of government finding the right flavor of KM to meet its needs. Already many government agencies are advertising CKO positions, some even reporting to CIOs or CFOs, and a few in programs, libraries, or human development offices. The successful CKO will build knowledge sharing and management into the mission of the agency, cascading into the actual processes used to perform mission critical tasks. That way, there is little risk of building a "knowledge empire," which could become another stovepipe. Knowledge is not a separate entity from business, but it is not "business as usual.

Myth: ***Knowledge management is a fad, and so "CKO" is a passing phase.*** Like all major management change, there is the natural life cycle of new and strange, eye-opening and exciting, over-promising and disappointing, and finally integration into organizational culture and process. Time will tell how much the federal government needs an enduring position of CKO, or for that matter, knowledge manager and knowledge worker. However, government's business for the people it serves is predominantly information-based: citizens want to know about their benefits, and they need information on how to get a passport, how to file taxes, or what research exists on diseases such as cancer. Today, it is still very difficult for citizens to find what they are looking for. Complementing its external role as a source of trusted knowledge, government's internal role also relies on many processes that require a knowledge of best practices and the exchange of information across government entities and with suppliers and partners. This supports the notion that at least for the next decade government will need leaders who both understand and can move government in a direction that allows for sharing across agencies, within agencies, and between government and those it serves.

CONCLUSION: YOU CAN'T HAVE ONE WITHOUT THE OTHER

The CIO has many important roles within the organization: IT architect, systems implementation, e-business, capital planning and investment, and more. But the move to a knowledge economy worldwide necessitates the creation of a new economy hybrid: the CKO. The CKO knows technology but is not bound to it; the CKO focuses on knowledge, its content, its value, its application, and its flow. No one leader could possibly do justice to both jobs.

Like the old song says, "Love and marriage—ya can't have one without the other." Likewise, as the vision of e-government becomes more like reality, the CKO and CIO will need to work together like the corporate partners that they are to help the organization successfully navigate the rough waters of radical change. As humans and machines grow nearly indistinguishable, it will be important for knowledge workers to adjust to the virtual world and to shape it with their own shared values and common issues. Rather than creating structure to "fix" each new challenge, the CKO and CIO will work together to create an environment that allows and encourages the sharing and reuse of knowledge and the connections between people who need government knowledge and those who have it.

The bottom line is that the federal government needs both; CIOs, in particular, should be attuned to the growing need for knowledge management and the CKO.

BIBLIOGRAPHY

Davenport, Thomas H. and Prusak, Laurence. *Working Knowledge*. Harvard Business School Press, 1998.

Liebowitz, Jay. *Knowledge Management Handbook*. CRC Press, 1999.

Peters, Tom. *The Circle of Innovation*. Alfred A. Knopf, Inc., 1997.

Senge, Peter. *The Fifth Discipline Fieldbook*. Doubleday/Currency, 1994.

Stewart, Thomas A. *Intellectual Capital*. Doubleday/Currency, 1997.

Wheatley, Margaret J. *Leadership and the New Science*. Berrett-Koehler, 1999.

Zack, Michael H. *Knowledge and Strategy*. Butterworth-Heinemann, 1999.

CHAPTER 12

Leadership and Knowledge Management—Perspectives

Joseph Williamson, PhD

The last two decades have seen remarkable changes in how organizations sustain competitive advantage. Increased competition, the explosion of Web technologies, and demands for improved products and services have created dramatic changes in the structure, goals, objectives, and outcomes of organizations—changes that have not been limited to the private sector. In fact, it is the same market forces that demanded improved efficiencies from the private sector that are now demanding changes in the public sector. The old way of doing business is out; public-sector organizations see themselves as service providers for the general public. Future public administrators and their organizations will see themselves as part of a network, their role being to guarantee the fulfillment of public tasks in concert with other participants.

For over a decade the idea of reinventing government has been on the agenda for many public-sector institutions, particularly in the United States, Europe, New Zealand, and Japan. The United States is in the midst of an enormous transformation from an industrial economy to a post-industrial digital economy. The digital economy has brought with it a fundamental shift in the driving forces that generate change. Communications between individuals, individual to corporation, corporation to government, government to government, and government to individual form the basis of all relationships within a given culture. The power of the computer, fueled by an explosive expansion of communication technologies, has given people access to information that is profoundly affecting all those relationships.

Competition among federal agencies and departments, states, counties, cities, school districts, and universities for economic development, grant funding, and the best students, teachers, and employees has forced a re-examination of the way the public sector operates. At a time when both private and public organizations are being forced to do more with less, there is an impatient demand for greater accountability and improved services. Tugging the public sector through this efficiency revolution is the information technology (IT) industry.

This is highlighted when one compares industrial-age and knowledge-based organizations: industrial-age organizations are characterized by separate, inward-looking departments that operate in a supply-to-production and functional way; knowledge-based organizations envision an integrated, synergetic organization that operates internally on an interdisciplinary basis and externally in a demand- and outcome-related way. Demand fulfillment and demand creation extend the enterprise from its suppliers' suppliers to its customers' customers. Also, the role of electronic settlement has become more important with the advent of increased communication. This can greatly affect the enterprise's efficiency in dealing with clearing houses and settlement information. Such an organization looks to cooperate with private partners, the service and voluntary sectors, and the general public to guarantee the fulfillment of its tasks and services (see Figure 1).

The real world is not as simple as the picture just painted. In reality, organizations conduct business in the complex world of their value chain, which involves a large number of other enterprises. In fact, it involves an entire trading community. This set of business partners that are electronically connected can be referred to as an "electronic trading community." This typically includes business partners across the entire supply and distribution chain and, ultimately, the links to customers.

Even those in the public sector who compare their services to those offered by private or public bidders and who have trans-

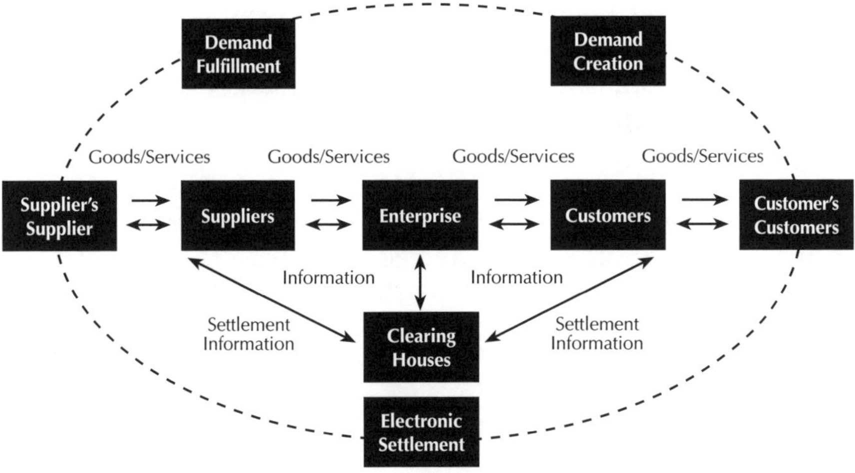

Source: Gartner Group, EDS Electronic Business

Figure 1. Electronic Trading Communities

formed their administrations into service enterprises are still following the old, time-honored practices when it comes to their dealings with other branches of government and with the public.

The first attempts at transformation have been primarily aimed at internal administration processes (process reengineering) and contain elements such as product plans, budgeting, contract management, controlling and reporting, technically supported information processing, and employee guidance and participation. More and more governments are striving for customer orientation, particularly in offices dealing with the public.

In a sense, public-sector organizations have a monopoly on their services. In most cases, the public cannot switch to alternative "bidders." In the private sector, competition guarantees higher standards and receptiveness to change. Public-sector organizations will only achieve lasting success if they are linked with competition or at least with tools that closely resemble competition. Employee empowerment, decentralization, delegation of responsibility, and competition between public and private bidders are absolutely essential if the public sector is to evolve and renew itself.

What is interesting is that almost all the technologies that will make e-government possible are already working for e-business. For example, applications for enterprise resource planning, customer-relationship management and supply-chain management, business intelligence and data-mining tools, and Internet procurement and payment systems are all available now and need very little adaptation for public-sector use. In the same way, the security protocols, the multi-layered firewalls, and the public key infrastructures needed for authentication and the protection of data are already available off-the-shelf.

KNOWLEDGE MANAGEMENT

Technology solutions exist, but governments have historically been deficient in sharing information and data among agencies, to say nothing of sharing the same information with other levels of government. So perhaps the approach to transformation from an industrial-age government to electronic government requires more than just technology. Knowledge management (KM) is an integrated, systematic approach for identifying, managing, and sharing all of an enterprise's information assets, including databases, documents, policies, and procedures, as well as previously unarticulated expertise and experience resident in individual workers. Industries, such as the airline, engineering, pharmaceutical, and utility industries, are realizing the value in utilizing KM to share experience, to share information, to distribute expertise, to communicate, and to accelerate learning.

Fundamentally, KM makes the collective information and experience of an enterprise available to the individual, who is responsible for using it wisely and for replenishing the stock. This ongoing cycle encourages a learning organization, stimulates collaboration, and empowers people to continually enhance the way they perform work. The KM focus is knowledge sharing as a means of sustaining competitive advantage.

Knowledge, unlike other commodities, changes and grows as it passes through individuals, groups, and society as a whole. Not only have communications networks and computing power been the technological driving forces in the rapid expansion of information, but also their capacity and power are expected to double every two to three years for the next several decades.[1] Because of the communication network expansion and the increase in computing power, digital-age tools of speed and precision are replacing the tools of the industrial-age of mass production and standardization. The rapid transfer of knowledge through people and organizations is forcing information-age organizations to more precisely identify needs and to develop products to meet those needs quickly and accurately.

Web-centric enterprises are dramatically extending knowledge-leveraging opportunities. Internet technology—with its global 24/7 reach, public telecommunications access, platform independence, hyperlinked multimedia environment, low cost, and ease of use—enables a wide and deep participation in these electronic communities. Such electronic communities produce extraordinary volumes of valuable information. Moreover, users not only consume but also contribute information and knowledge. The aggregation of this information into new patterns is an ever-increasing source of value-added service, competitive differentiation, and revenue. The ability to share corporate knowledge—the discipline of KM—is a sustainable competitive advantage.

Success in the discipline of KM requires enterprises to fully leverage their intellectual capital: the collection of information, knowledge, and experience that allows them to perform their mission and to adapt to constantly changing requirements. By managing intellectual capital effectively, organizations can create a climate in which information sharing and continuous learning are normal parts of doing business.

A BRIEF HISTORY OF KM

The KM field is partly an outgrowth of the field of information management (IM) or management of information systems (MIS). These latter fields are primarily concerned with developing organizational designs and technological systems to improve the management of information within an organization. This aspect of KM is typically thought of as the technical side of KM, or the "data-information-knowledge chain," and is usually the first aspect seized upon when one begins to look at KM as an enabler of transformation (see Figure 2).

KM AND THE STRATEGIC IMPORTANCE OF KNOWLEDGE

The KM field is also partly an outgrowth of a field of management concerned with the strategic importance of knowledge to the competitiveness of the firm.

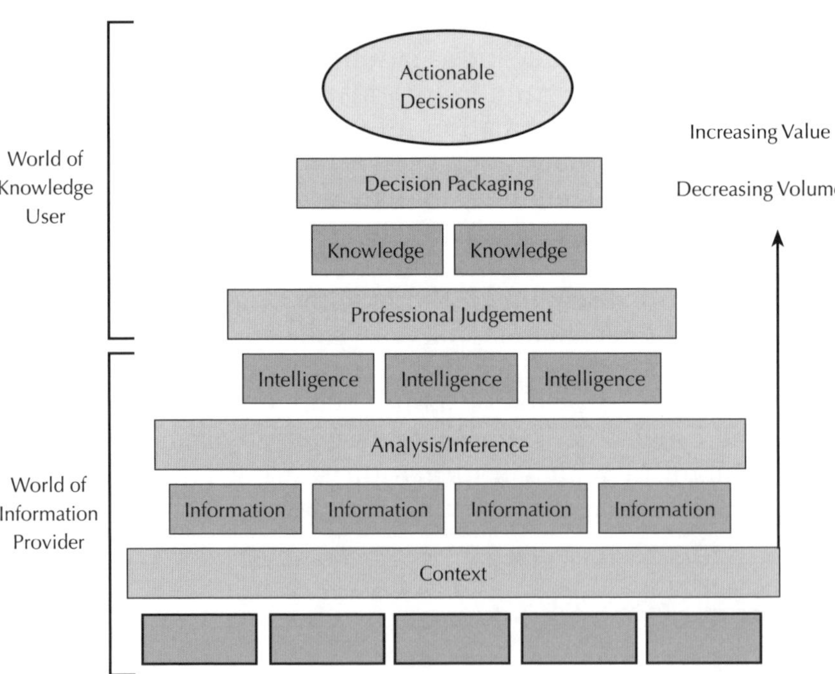

Figure 2. The Technical Side of Knowledge Management: the "Data-Information-Knowledge Chain"

Today, no single technology or discipline will provide all of the elements necessary for a diverse group of experts or a community of trading partners to maintain a rewarding and sustainable virtual interaction. E-business isn't just adding new tools and capabilities to the business arsenal—it's changing the way businesses define themselves.

The traditional "bricks and mortar" business looked within its four walls for solutions. Individual divisions within an enterprise likewise found themselves trapped within their own "walls." Marketing and production areas, for example, could not easily share vital customer information they had gathered separately. Networking and databases began the task of breaking down those walls so that an enterprise could share data within its organization or with an individual supplier or partner. Now the Internet and e-commerce are completing the task by enabling extended enterprises to simultaneously share information, goods, and services across an *entire* supply chain, from their suppliers' suppliers to their customers' customers—wherever across the globe each may be.

However, the technology-enabled extended enterprise may merely represent "low-hanging" fruit. Among the many impediments to successful, thereby sustained, extended enterprise are broad issues of data and information overload, lack of awareness of others' activities, lack of context about the purpose and history of shared objects, lack of appropriate feedback and acknowledgment of contributions to the extended enterprise, disorientation, unbalanced participation, and problems with bringing new team members into a complex and established collaborative environment.

KM AND LEARNING

The KM field is also partly an outgrowth of a field of the notion of "learning," for it has traditionally been concerned with the shallower notion of "creating knowledge" that has a productive value.

The term "organizational learning" was coined and popularized by Chris Argyris and Donald Schön in the late 1970s.[2]

The notion that organizations or systems facilitate learning (and later have a learning capacity in their own right, much like an individual) evolved throughout the 1960s and 1970s, particularly in literature dealing with "systems theory."

In the ideal learning organization, all members are fully engaged in the organization's processes, precisely because it is people who learn and apply learning. The reason is simple, at least in theory. Organizational dynamics—structures, procedures, and practices—are at best enabling. Organizations cannot learn independently of their members. But the organization is not merely a form; it is a living organism of its members interacting with one another in the context of their external environment. It is, in this sense, that we can speak of an organization as a learning organization: its basic processes, whereby the members do the work of the organization, either advance the learning capacity of the organization, and thus its collective knowledge, or they do not (see Figure 3).

The ultimate purpose of learning is to apply knowledge in practice; knowledge, therefore, is always linked to action. Public-sector organizations that seek to function as learning organizations

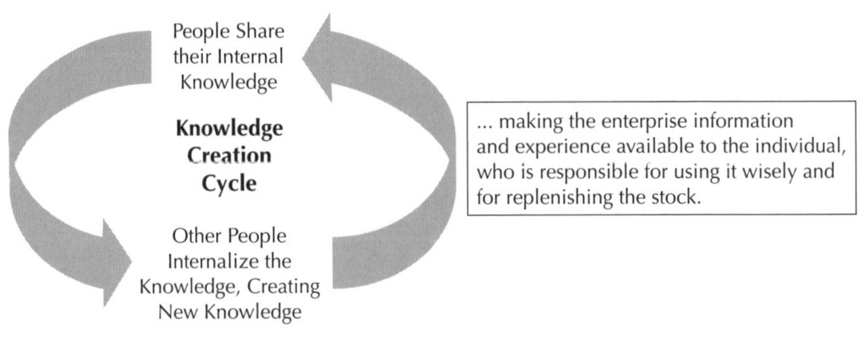
People Share their Internal Knowledge
Knowledge Creation Cycle
Other People Internalize the Knowledge, Creating New Knowledge
... making the enterprise information and experience available to the individual, who is responsible for using it wisely and for replenishing the stock.
Ongoing cycle:
• Encourages a Knowledge Based Organization (KBO)
• Stimulates collaboration
• Empowers people to continually enhance the way they work

Figure 3. Knowledge Management and Learning

make space for knowledge to be public (that is, available and accessible, if only within the confines of its own organization) and thus subject to the broadest possible range of critical analysis, comment, and discussion. An organization committed to organizational learning, if well managed, can govern the politics of ideas in ways that encourage its members to engage in dialogue and discussion that are not only civil but place the highest premium on promoting, as best as possible, the public interest.

Adaptive and Generative Learning

Peter Senge (1994) makes a distinction between learning that helps one cope ("adaptive learning") and learning that helps one create ("generative learning").

In addition, a learning organization is also well managed when the organization acknowledges that "tacit" knowledge, which is based primarily on practical or subjective experience, but without a theoretical explanation to support its claims, can be every bit as important in a learning organization as "explicit" knowledge, which is based on quantitative or empirical foundations.

KM FOUNDATION OF E-GOVERNMENT

The way to e-government divides into three distinct steps:

- Step One—*Knowledge Management:* This step typically starts as pilot programs or as initiatives championed within a particular department or agency. Typically, they go after automation for operational effectiveness focus and information or KM focus. The focus is internal, but it is on the people and the processes. They begin to challenge traditional working practices and processes.

- Step 2—*E-commerce*: This step has an external focus of connecting to trading partners and to customers, communicating for process improvement, and on transactions. At this point, Websites allow a formal, quantifiable exchange of value to take place. It might be renewing a license, paying a fine, or enrolling in an educational course. Several hundred such sites operate mostly at the state or local government rather than federal government level. More sophisticated versions can guide applicants through making a claim for benefits or filing a tax return, such as the United Kingdom's Inland Revenue site. They continue to transform traditional working practices and processes.

- Step 3—*E-government*: This step integrates the complete range of government services and provides a path that is based on need and function, not on department or agency. The focus in this step is on collaboration for enhanced service, the community development imperative, and new products and services.

LEADERSHIP

We have learned that:

- A *KM environment* will only work if focused on *learning*.
- Learning will only work if it focuses on *performance and results*.
- None of this will work without the right kind of *leadership*.

Leadership may be defined as the process of giving meaningful direction to collective effort and causing willing effort to be expended to achieve collective goals.[3] One difficulty in appreciating the role that leadership can play is that we are used to the "military" image of traditional hierarchical leaders. However, when leaders act as mentors, teachers, and stewards, they fill roles that are much more effective than the traditional hierarchical leader model.

LEADERSHIP VS. MANAGEMENT[4]

Leadership and management are two distinctive and complementary systems of action.[5] Both are necessary but have different purposes. Management is concerned with coping with complex modern organizations and brings a degree of order and consistency to the quality and profitability of products. Leadership, by contrast, is about capitalizing on change.

Leadership	*Management*
Planning Organizing and Staffing Controlling and Problem Solving	Setting a Direction Aligning People Motivating People

Companies manage complexity by planning and budgeting, establishing plans to get there, and then allocating resources. By contrast, transforming an organization begins by setting a direction and developing a vision of the future along with strategies for producing changes needed to achieve that vision. Management achieves its plans by creating an organizational infrastructure and set of jobs for accomplishing plan requirements, staffing the jobs with qualified individuals, communicating the plan, delegating responsibility, and developing systems to monitor implementation. Leaders align people by communicating the new direction to those who can create coalitions that understand the vision and are committed to its achievement.

Management ensures plan accomplishment by controlling problems through reports, meetings, etc.—calculating variances and then planning and organizing to solve the problems. For leadership, however, achieving a vision requires motivating and inspiring—keeping people moving in the right direction, despite major obstacles to change.

LEADERS

Leaders can build an environment that is conducive to learning in three ways—creating a picture of the future, generating motivation to act, and helping people to act by backing them up.

Create a Picture of the Future

The first way to build an environment that is conducive to learning is by articulating guiding visions. Visions are different from campaign slogans or management buzzwords. They are developed gradually, often over many years, through reflection on an organization's history and traditions and on its long-term growth and opportunities (see Nadler and Tushman[6]).

They represent a picture of the future or a desired future state with which people can identify and that can generate excitement. By creating vision, the leader provides a vehicle for people to develop commitment, a common goal around which people can rally, and a way for people to feel successful.

This is accomplished through a range of different actions, the most profound being the articulation of a compelling vision in clear and dramatic terms. The vision needs to be challenging, meaningful, and worthy of pursuit, but it also needs to be credible. People must believe that it is possible, even if difficult, to succeed in the pursuit of the vision. Vision is also communicated in other ways, such as through expectations that the leader expresses and through the leader personally demonstrating behaviors and activities that symbolize and further that vision.

Generate Motivation to Act

A second way to build an environment that is conducive to leaning is to generate a motivation to act. Different leaders engage in motivating in different ways, but some of the most common include demonstration of their own personal excitement and energy, combined with leveraging that excitement through direct personal contact with large numbers of people in the organization. They express confidence in their own ability to succeed. They find and use successes to celebrate progress toward the vision.

Very successful leaders demonstrate the ability to listen, understand, and share the feelings of people in the organization. They express support of individuals. Perhaps most importantly, the effective leader tends to express his or her confidence in people's ability to perform effectively and to meet challenges.

Help People to Act—Back Them Up

A third way to build operating environments for learning lies within the leadership team itself. It is important that leaders recognize that they, also, must change, and that many of the skills that have made them successful in the past can actually inhibit learning. They must provide considerable attention to the learning infrastructure. In a world of rapid change and increasing interdependence, learning is too important to be left to chance. "What we lack is infrastructure for learning."[7]

If no ongoing learning infrastructure support is available, how do we:

- Achieve accelerating growth objectives?
- Attract and retain profitable clients?
- Attract and retain talented employees?
- Reduce long learning curves?
- Maintain a corporate memory?
- Extend and improve business relationships?

- Address data and information overload?
- Rapidly develop new product and service offerings?
- Make the most out of our technology investments?
- Repeat success and avoid reinvention?
- Differentiate our business in a fiercely competitive environment?
- Ensure that we are leaders in our industry?

People can benefit significantly from leaders who can be protectors, mentors, and thinking partners. When dramatic improvements achieved in one line organization threaten others, leaders can help manage the threat. Alternatively, leaders can make sure that new innovative practices are not ignored because people are too busy to take the time to understand the processes involved. By working in concert with internal champions, leaders can help connect innovative local leaders across the enterprise. They also play a mentoring role in helping the local leaders understand complex political landscapes and communicate their ideas and accomplishments to those who have not been involved.

MULTIPLE LEADERS

An executive steering committee is typically formed to facilitate the vision of making information and knowledge available to those who need to use it. The executive steering committee will serve as a forum to provide the strategic direction and priorities for institutionalizing learning, sharing information, and identifying cross-functional issues or opportunities that exist in the organizational transformation. Education and training are significant parts of the transformation; therefore, the executive steering committee will also oversee the introduction of learning management systems. Committee members come from across the value chain and are the leaders for their communities of interest with a thorough understanding of KM potential benefits.

Specifically, an executive steering committee will:

- Serve as a catalyst for institutionalizing KM
- Identify and resolve issues regarding KM
- Prioritize requirements and recommend funding strategies
- Resolve conflicting priorities among functional requirements and development and support requirements
- Ensure that KM goals and objectives for KM are coordinated and integrated.

In summary: It's about "people"—not just technology."

NOTES

1. Negroponte, Nicholas. *Being Digital.* New York: Knopf, 1995, pp. 21–36.
2. Argyris, C. and Schon, D. Organizational Learning: A Theory of Action Perspective. Reading, MA: Addison-Wesley, 1978.
3. Jacobs, T.O. and E. Jacque. "Leadership in Complex Systems." *Human Productivity Enhancement.* J. Zeidner (ed.). New York: Praeger, 1990, p. 281.
4. Adapted from Watson, Carl. The Institute for Leadership Dynamics, 1998, www.leadership-dynamics.com.
5. Kotter, John P. "What Leaders Really Do?" *Harvard Business Review,* May–June 1990.
6. Nadler and Truman. *California Management Review,* Winter 1990.
7. Senge, Peter M., et al., *The Fifth Discipline Fieldbook.* New York: Doubleday, 1994, p. 34.

CHAPTER 13

Knowledge Management and the Role of the CKO

Robert E. Neilson, PhD[1]

Much of the discussion surrounding the emerging field of knowledge management (KM) is like stirring a vat of jello with a slinky—little firms up. KM concepts seem to float in a jello-like environment without form, density, or direction, making it difficult for practitioners to grasp key KM concepts. A common refrain in corporate boardrooms and executive offices in federal agencies is, "I'd be happy to embrace KM if I only knew what it is and how it will help us meet enterprise objectives."

This refrain is understandable because the theoretical bases underlying knowledge management are unclear and are still emerging.[2] Additionally, there is little consensus regarding the competencies needed by those individuals charged with leading KM initiatives. An alphabet soup of acronyms has sprung to life, giving organizational legitimacy to individuals who are charged with the task of valuing, leveraging, or reusing tacit and explicit knowledge. CKO, CTO, CLO, KA, KM, and KE represent a sampling of the acronyms associated with the field of KM.[3] But what do these people do? Are these people competent to execute tasks that drive business results? How would you recognize a "third-degree black belt" CKO if you bumped into one in the hallway? The purpose of this chapter is to throw some "conceptual cement" into the "KM vat of jello" to firm up some KM concepts and contribute some thoughts and ideas regarding what competencies and skills CKOs need to survive and flourish.

More specifically, the purpose of this chapter is to:

1. Establish a rationale justifying why managing knowledge is a significant factor of production in knowledge-based organizations

2. Review selected studies that identify the competencies, skills, and behaviors of those individuals charged with the task of implementing a KM vision

3. Present the results of brainstorming sessions involving public- and private-sector CKOs or equivalents who responded to four key questions associated with knowledge management.

WHY MANAGING KNOWLEDGE IS A SIGNIFICANT FACTOR OF PRODUCTION IN KNOWLEDGE-BASED ORGANIZATIONS

First, from an economic standpoint, traditional factors of production—land, labor, and capital—no longer occupy center stage as a means of leaping forward. To paraphrase Drucker and Thurow,[4] knowledge has become the key economic resource; with everything else dropping out of the equation, knowledge has become the primary source of competitive advantage. Competitive advantage depends on the intelligence with which knowledge is used throughout the enterprise. Second, with the growth in the number of people using the Internet, coupled with the rapid expansion of the wired and wireless global information infrastructure, avenues to link people and ideas to produce new products and services grow exponentially. Third, the characteristics of digital media are inherently different from those of physical or tangible products. The ease with which media in digital form can be replicated, transmitted, modified, and manipulated is inherently different from physical works (e.g., books or journals) that rely on traditional means of production (printing) and distribution (physical delivery). Explicit and tacit knowledge about a product or service is as important as the product or service itself because it serves as a basis to improve or develop new products or services. Hence, knowledge has emerged as a formidable factor of production—a "capital."

Figure 1 illustrates how the combination of human, intellectual, social, and structural capital is the fuel that propels knowledge-based enterprises to meet enterprise goals or missions.[5]

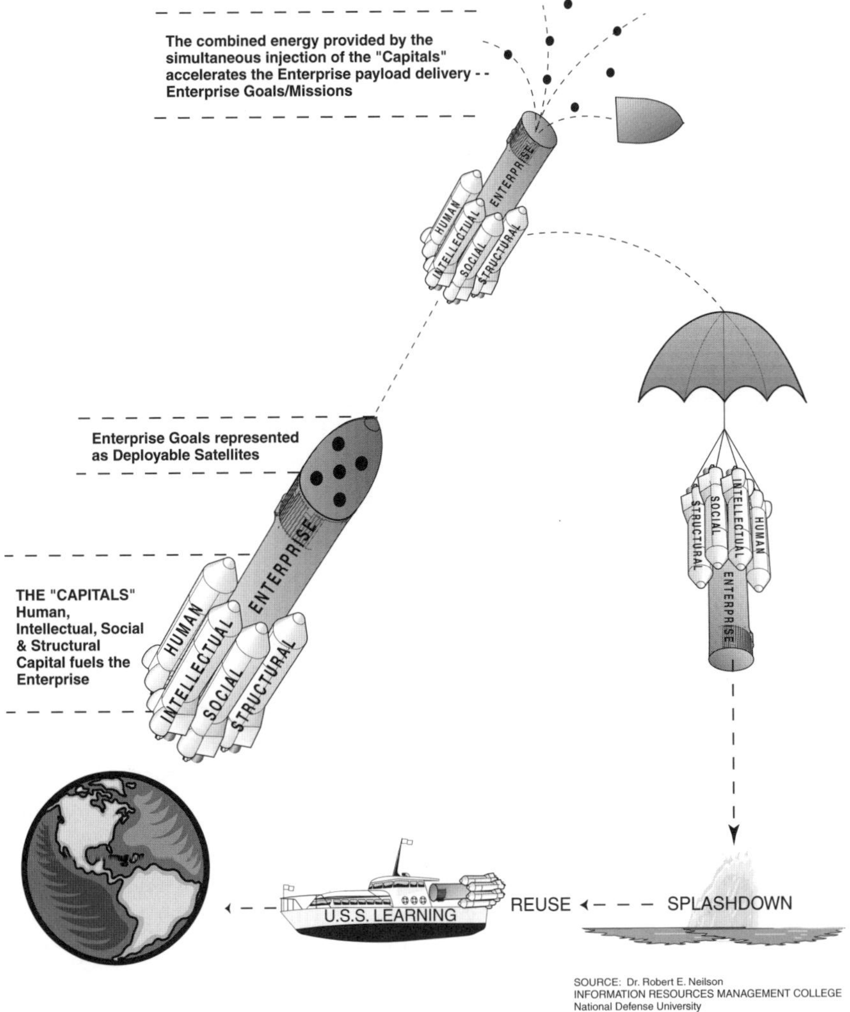

Figure 1. KM: Accelerating the "Capitals" to Propel the Enterprise

It takes the injection of highly volatile liquid nitrogen to propel a rocket into space to deliver payloads. Similarly, it takes the simultaneous injection of human, intellectual, social, and structural capital to propel an enterprise forward at ever-increasing speeds to meet global enterprise goals or missions. Those enterprises that can create and apply knowledge faster than their competitors or adversaries have a distinct advantage. The dynamic mixing of human, intellectual, social, and structural capital provides the fuel for creating and using knowledge.

Key factors in rocketry and knowledge-based organizations are reuse of components and learning from each mission. It makes no sense to discard fuel tank stages of rockets if they can be reused. It also makes no sense to discard the human, intellectual, social, and structural capital in organizations when each factor of production may be in short supply. The object is to learn, reuse where applicable, and innovate ways to deliver "payloads."

It is interesting to note that there may be alternate ways to deliver payloads into space other than using rockets. Likewise, enterprises need to be cognizant that "hitching" your "capitals" to a single rocket design may spell disaster for the enterprise if the organization fails to experiment with new modes of propelling payloads that may supersede rocketry. Hence, innovation should continue unabated.

WHAT COMPETENCIES, SKILLS, AND BEHAVIORS ARE NEEDED BY THOSE CHARGED WITH IMPLEMENTING A KM VISION?

Michael J. Earl and Ian Scott, Dede Bonner, and Angela Abell and Nigel Oxbrow attempt to identify competencies and skills that CKOs (or those charged with implementing a KM vision) need.[6] Earl and Scott's seminal article, "What Is a Chief Knowledge Officer," found that there is little or no job specification for CKOs, but their organizational goals are fairly clear. A CKO's task is to correct one or more of the following perceived deficiencies:

- Inattention to the explicit or formal management of knowledge in ongoing operations
- Failure to leverage the hidden value of corporate knowledge in business development
- Inability to learn from past failures and successes in strategic decision making
- Not creating value or "making money" from knowledge embedded on products or held by employees.[7]

These deficiencies suggest that organizations are doing an inadequate job of managing or leveraging their intellectual assets. Chief information officers (CIOs) seem to focus their energies and activities on managing physical rather than intellectual assets. CIOs are rarely fired if they can: (1) keep networks running without disruption; (2) furnish near state-of-the-art computer equipment and applications on a reasonable lifecycle to ensure that the information technology provides a means to meet business objectives; and (3) provide robust security to protect networks from physical destruction and a myriad of threats delivered via cyberspace. The primary activities listed above deal with physical assets, something you can touch and feel. Leveraging intellectual assets—intangible assets in the form of data, information, and tacit and explicit knowledge—resides somewhere "down the food chain" of critical activities for CIOs. To summarize Earl and Scott, "Most CIOs have demanding enough agendas without adding the ambiguities of the CKO role."[8]

Bonner, in an article appearing in the February 2000 issue of *Training & Development* titled "Enter the Chief Knowledge Officer," surveyed 18 large public and private sector organizations to ascertain roles, responsibilities, and activities of CLOs and CKOs. Bonner found that CKO and CLO roles are strikingly similar. The following activities were most often cited by both groups:

- Align and integrate diverse functions or groups

- Use previous best practices or design benchmarking studies
- Develop a culture of acceptance of organizational learning, continuous learning, and KM
- Have a customer orientation
- Create knowledge-content activities to enterprise objectives
- Leverage corporate-wide learning
- Establish partnerships with senior managers
- Conduct strategic planning and implementation
- Be a visionary and champion for organizational learning and KM.

More importantly, CKOs engage in activities associated with a series of power verbs, including: align, benchmark, design, develop, identify, implement, integrate, leverage, partner, and plan. These verbs indicate that CKOs and CLOs may need to possess a diverse mix of skills and behaviors that rely more on personal influence, persuasion, interpersonal skills, and flexibility than on a more directive mix of skills associated with traditional chief executive officer (CEO) and chief organizational officer (COO) roles and responsibilities.

Based on a review of seven case studies, Abell and Oxbrow maintain that providing a new role, with a new title, as a mechanism for emphasizing KM as a new corporate approach, rather than as initiative, is gaining ground.[9] A host of roles and titles is emerging. Additionally, a KPMG study indicated that in 100 leading companies almost all thought KM was "here to stay," and many were taking steps to implement KM concepts.

What background and skills are necessary for those charged with implementing a KM vision? Abell and Oxbrow report that CKOs need to view organizations holistically and should possess a mix of hard and soft skills characteristic of a leader of a strategic change management program.[10] They divide these skills into two major categories: (1) skills to develop the vision and (2) skills to plan the program. Table 1 lists recommended CKO skills.

Table 1. Recommended CKO Skills

Skills to Develop the Vision	*Skills to Plan the Program*
• Business knowledge	• Organizational development
• Political understanding	• Information and IT strategy
• Risk analysis	• Financial planning
• Influencing skills	• Communication
• Leadership	• Innovation
• Creativity	• Risk management
• Presentation skills	• Flexibility and openness to all issues
	• Managing across boundaries
	• Helping individuals to self-manage
	• Ability to release the full potential of people

What these three selected studies indicate is that managing knowledge is increasingly a factor of production. Individuals charged with the task of implementing a KM vision need a mix of hard and soft skills but must link their efforts to a business value proposition. Lastly, there is still a perceived deficiency in leveraging the hidden value of corporate knowledge in business development or in ongoing operations. Most of these studies focused on private industry. Are the results of these studies applicable to the public sector? Is there a difference in the roles and responsibilities for CKOs in the private sector versus the public sector?

RESULTS OF BRAINSTORMING SESSIONS INVOLVING PUBLIC AND PRIVATE SECTOR CKOS

To ascertain if differences exist in roles and responsibilities between public and private sector CKOs, two separate automated brainstorming sessions were conducted in May and June 2000 at the Information Resources Management College of the National Defense University.[11] The first group included CKOs or equivalents from the federal government. The second group included CKOs or equivalents from the private sector, primarily from IT and consulting businesses. Each group was asked to brainstorm ideas responding to four questions:

1. Why is KM important to your organization?
2. What is the role of a CKO in a public sector organization?
3. What competencies make a CKO successful?
4. What are the most important personal attributes CKOs must bring to the job?

The framing of the first question, "Why is KM important to your organization?" was intended to elicit higher-order responses by asking for a rationale justifying KM investments. With continuing controversy surrounding the role of a CIO in federal agencies, introducing CKOs in public organizations may muddy the waters regarding their contribution to mission objectives—hence question number two, which focused on the role of a CKO in a public organization. Question number three attempted to probe beyond existing literature that reports on "what CKOs do." The attempt was to determine which competencies help make CKOs successful. Last, recent research shows that CKOs come to the position from diverse academic backgrounds and have cross-functional experience in enterprises. It seems that the more diverse the better. Consequently, question number four was included to determine the most important personal attributes that CKOs must bring to the job as a result of varied academic backgrounds and experiences.

Figure 2 is a hub-and-spoke diagram that displays the combined findings of both brainstorming sessions.[12] The central question is located in the center of the diagram, with enabling verbs located in oval shapes located on the spokes. The main idea or activities are located in rectangular boxes at the end of the

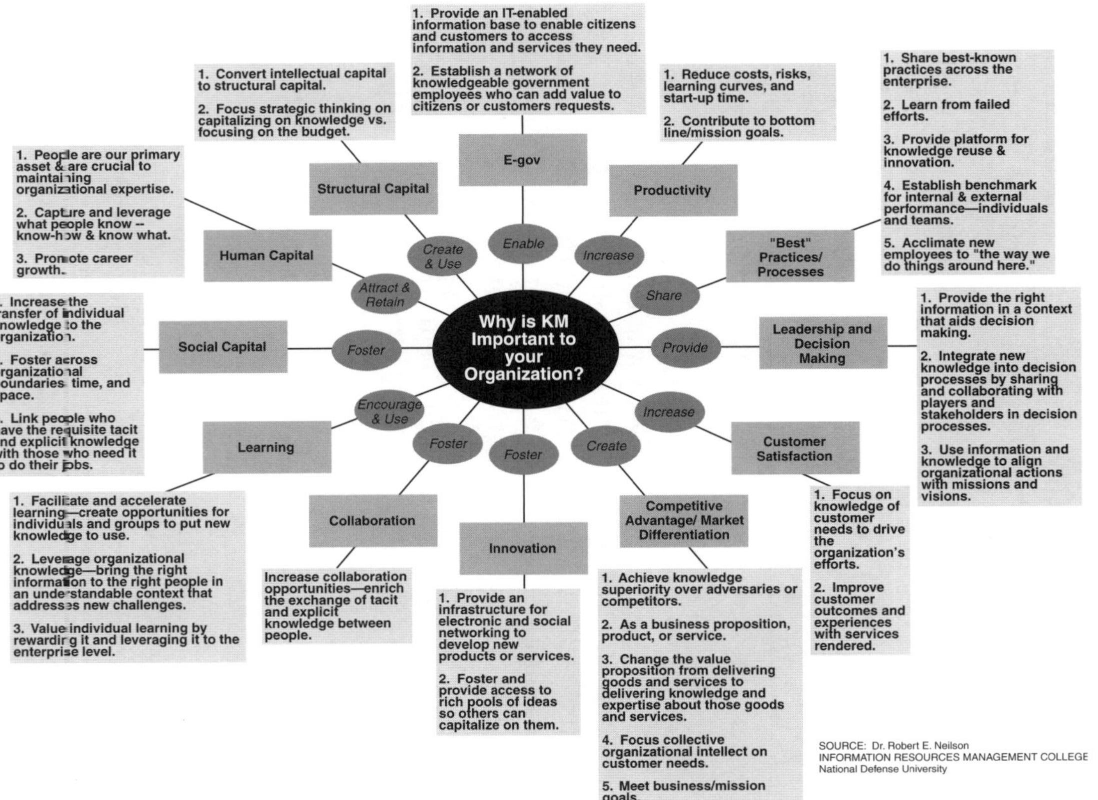

Why is KM Important to your Organization?
Enable
E-gov
1. Provide an IT-enabled information base to enable citizens and customers to access information and services they need.
2. Establish a network of knowledgeable government employees who can add value to citizens or customers requests.
Increase
Productivity
1. Reduce costs, risks, learning curves, and start-up time.
2. Contribute to bottom line/mission goals.
Share
"Best" Practices/ Processes
1. Share best-known practices across the enterprise.
2. Learn from failed efforts.
3. Provide platform for knowledge reuse & innovation.
4. Establish benchmark for internal & external performance—individuals and teams.
5. Acclimate new employees to "the way we do things around here."
Provide
Leadership and Decision Making
1. Provide the right information in a context that aids decision making.
2. Integrate new knowledge into decision processes by sharing and collaborating with players and stakeholders in decision processes.
3. Use information and knowledge to align organizational actions with missions and visions.
Increase
Customer Satisfaction
1. Focus on knowledge of customer needs to drive the organization's efforts.
2. Improve customer outcomes and experiences with services rendered.
Create
Competitive Advantage/ Market Differentiation
1. Achieve knowledge superiority over adversaries or competitors.
2. As a business proposition, product, or service.
3. Change the value proposition from delivering goods and services to delivering knowledge and expertise about those goods and services.
4. Focus collective organizational intellect on customer needs.
5. Meet business/mission goals.
Foster
Innovation
1. Provide an infrastructure for electronic and social networking to develop new products or services.
2. Foster and provide access to rich pools of ideas so others can capitalize on them.
Foster
Collaboration
Increase collaboration opportunities—enrich the exchange of tacit and explicit knowledge between people.
Encourage & Use
Learning
1. Facilitate and accelerate learning—create opportunities for individuals and groups to put new knowledge to use.
2. Leverage organizational knowledge—bring the right information to the right people in an understandable context that addresses new challenges.
3. Value individual learning by rewarding it and leveraging it to the enterprise level.
Foster
Social Capital
1. Increase the transfer of individual knowledge to the organization.
2. Foster across organizational boundaries, time, and space.
3. Link people who have the requisite tacit and explicit knowledge with those who need it to do their jobs.
Attract & Retain
Human Capital
1. People are our primary asset & are crucial to maintaining organizational expertise.
2. Capture and leverage what people know -- know-how & know what.
3. Promote career growth.
Create & Use
Structural Capital
1. Convert intellectual capital to structural capital.
2. Focus strategic thinking on capitalizing on knowledge vs. focusing on the budget.
SOURCE: Dr. Robert E. Neilson
INFORMATION RESOURCES MANAGEMENT COLLEGE
National Defense University

Figure 2. Importance of KM to Your Organization

spokes. Detailed information for each main idea or activity is located at the periphery of the diagram.

The findings indicate a particular emphasis on the "capitals." Attracting and retaining human capital, fostering social capital, and creating and using structural capital were heavily emphasized by both groups. The private-sector CKOs most heavily emphasized the need to attract and retain human capital to ensure that they remain competitive. Both groups stressed the need to share best practices/processes; however, they tempered that notion with the idea that innovation, collaboration, and learning are the activities that will propel the organization forward. Simply relying on sharing best practices will yield short-term results. All participants agreed that KM efforts need to be linked to business goals or mission objectives. The public sector CKOs look to KM initiatives to provide a foundation for electronic government, while the private sector CKOs made little mention of using KM as a basis for electronic business. Lastly, both groups recognized that the ultimate goal of any KM efforts is to satisfy customers by providing the leadership with the right information at the right time to make critical business decisions.

Examining the content shown in Figure 3 indicates that CKOs in the public sector play a markedly different role from that of a CIO. While CIOs focus much of their activity on physical computer and network assets, CKOs focus their efforts on an integrated set of activities that addresses organizational behaviors, processes, and technologies.

Critically analyzing the content for each activity indicates that a CKO's role involves leveraging the "soft stuff" in organizations. Creating a knowledge-sharing culture, championing communities of practice, providing leadership and strategy, and using incentives and rewards are activities that are the province of the CKO. These activities, however, are tough to measure using traditional and generally accepted business metrics. They mirror the activities of the successful CEOs. Some pundits remark that CKOs are CEOs-in-waiting. CKOs must also possess a working knowledge of the tools and technologies to leverage the extant intellec-

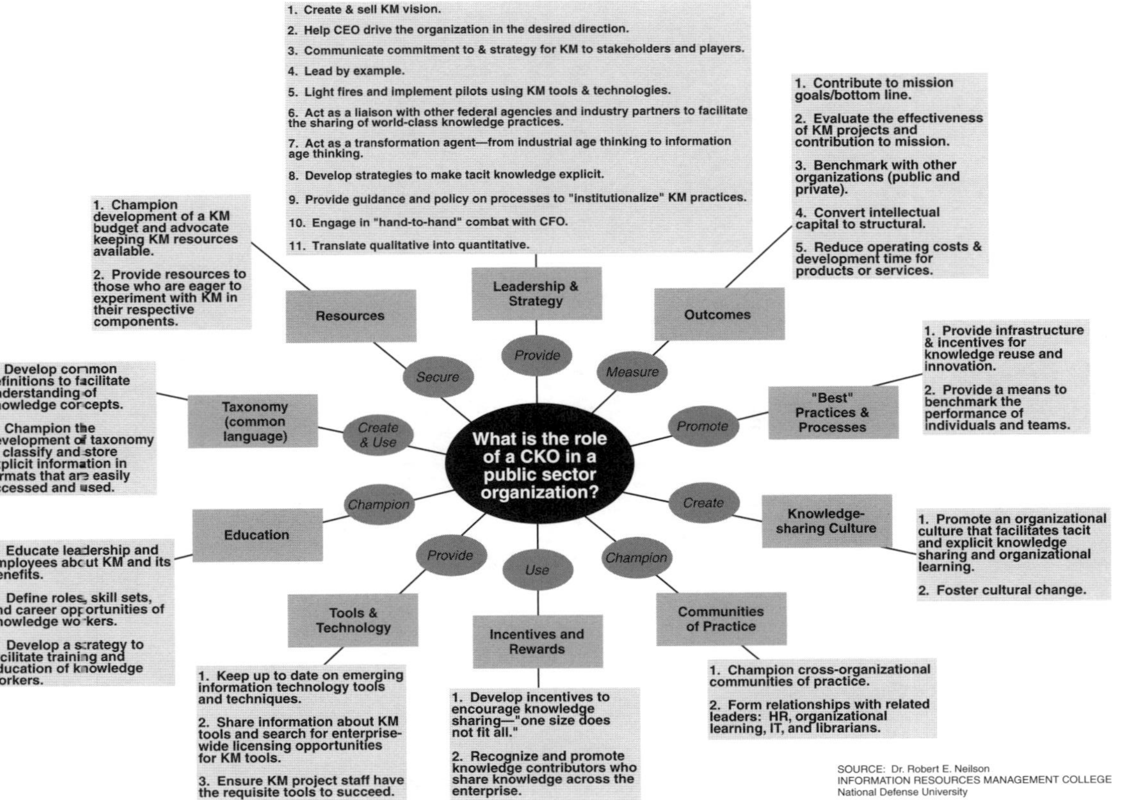

Figure 3. Role of the CKO

tual base in organizations, but they are not necessarily technologists by training. In sum, their role is to coax, cajole, and provide incentives to deliver value to the organization using existing and unexploited explicit and tacit knowledge sources.

Frequently, CKOs fulfill their role by experimenting and partnering with business units. Additionally, they are charged with the task of charting clear processes, classification schemes, and tools to access and use existing data, information, and explicit and tacit knowledge in a manner that promotes sharing across time, space, and boundaries.

In the beginning of this chapter, a key question was posed: "How would you recognize a third-degree black belt CKO if you bumped into one in the hallway?" Figure 4 illustrates six major competency areas that CKOs or aspiring CKOs should possess.

Of all the competency areas, both public- and private-sector CKOs thought that successful CKOs must think holistically and strategically and must be able to communicate the value of KM convincingly to skeptical audiences. CKOs need to move beyond what Davenport and Prusak call "serious anecdote management" and translate the qualitative benefits of KM projects into quantitative benefits to win the hearts and minds of chief financial officers (CFOs).[13] Otherwise, many KM projects will fall into the management fad *du jour* category, much like total quality management and business process reengineering. In addition to the requisite leadership and management capabilities and a working knowledge of tools and technologies, existing and aspiring CKOs need to possess an *a priori* personal knowledge base and cognitive capabilities as specified in Figure 4. Without a personal knowledge base and demonstrated personal behaviors, newly appointed CKOs will have difficulty "selling" KM concepts to senior management. They will lack credibility.

Last, participants in the brainstorming sessions were asked: "What are the most important personal attributes CKOs must bring to the job?" Figure 5 illustrates the results.

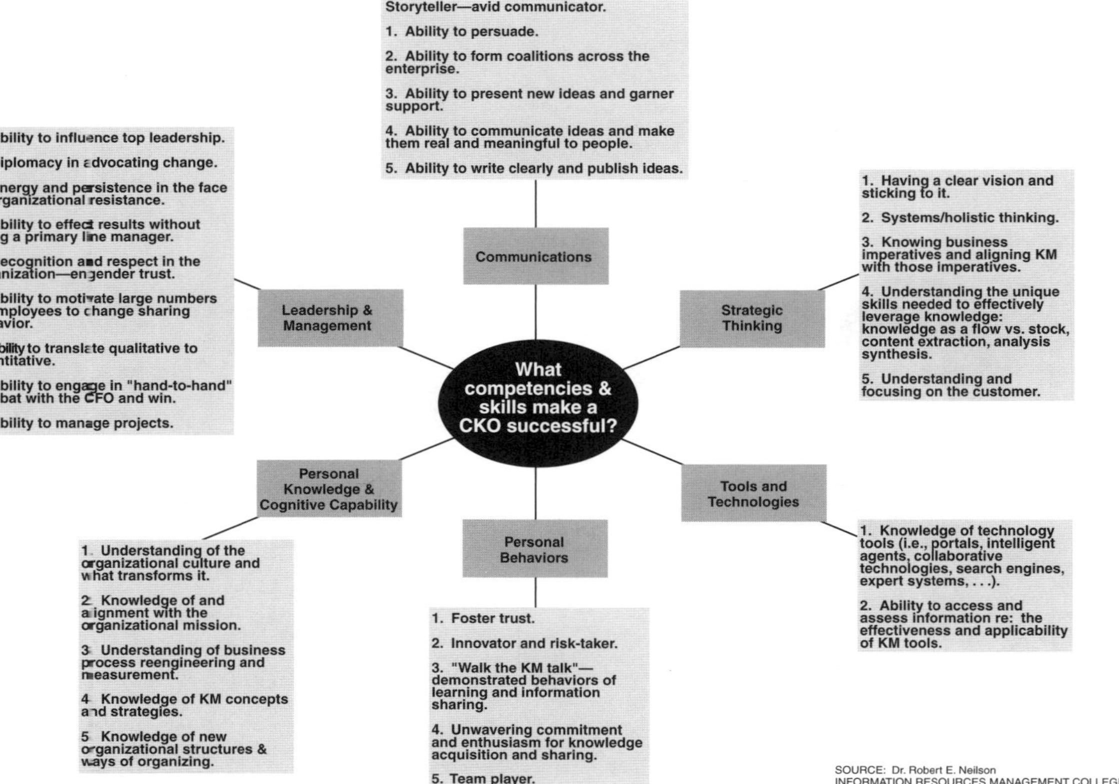

What competencies & skills make a CKO successful?
Communications
Storyteller—avid communicator.
1. Ability to persuade.
2. Ability to form coalitions across the enterprise.
3. Ability to present new ideas and garner support.
4. Ability to communicate ideas and make them real and meaningful to people.
5. Ability to write clearly and publish ideas.
Strategic Thinking
1. Having a clear vision and sticking to it.
2. Systems/holistic thinking.
3. Knowing business imperatives and aligning KM with those imperatives.
4. Understanding the unique skills needed to effectively leverage knowledge: knowledge as a flow vs. stock, content extraction, analysis synthesis.
5. Understanding and focusing on the customer.
Tools and Technologies
1. Knowledge of technology tools (i.e., portals, intelligent agents, collaborative technologies, search engines, expert systems, . . .).
2. Ability to access and assess information re: the effectiveness and applicability of KM tools.
Personal Behaviors
1. Foster trust.
2. Innovator and risk-taker.
3. "Walk the KM talk"—demonstrated behaviors of learning and information sharing.
4. Unwavering commitment and enthusiasm for knowledge acquisition and sharing.
5. Team player.
Personal Knowledge & Cognitive Capability
1. Understanding of the organizational culture and what transforms it.
2. Knowledge of and alignment with the organizational mission.
3. Understanding of business process reengineering and measurement.
4. Knowledge of KM concepts and strategies.
5. Knowledge of new organizational structures & ways of organizing.
Leadership & Management
1. Ability to influence top leadership.
2. Diplomacy in advocating change.
3. Energy and persistence in the face of organizational resistance.
4. Ability to effect results without being a primary line manager.
5. Recognition and respect in the organization—engender trust.
6. Ability to motivate large numbers of employees to change sharing behavior.
7. Ability to translate qualitative to quantitative.
8. Ability to engage in "hand-to-hand" combat with the CFO and win.
9. Ability to manage projects.
SOURCE: Dr. Robert E. Neilson
INFORMATION RESOURCES MANAGEMENT COLLEGE
National Defense University

Figure 4. CKO Competencies and Skills

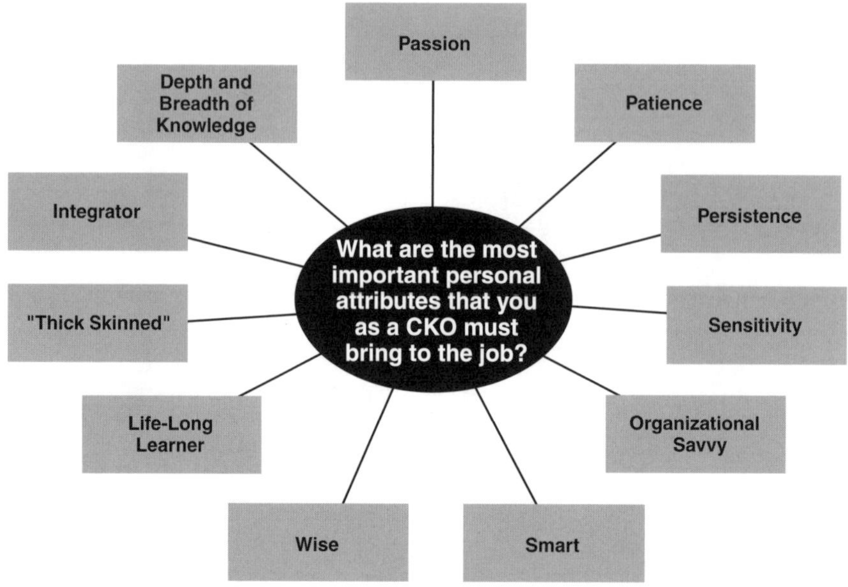

Figure 5. CKO Personal Attributes

With the exception of "life-long learner," most of the remaining personal attributes do not discriminate between CKOs and other senior executive positions. Perhaps in future research, CKOs should address a more precise question that asks them to identify those unique personal attributes they should possess *in addition to* personal attributes typically associated with senior leadership positions.

POTENTIAL USES OF FINDINGS FROM BRAINSTORMING SESSIONS

Looking to the future, there are several potential uses for the results of the brainstorming sessions. First, in the absence of more definitive research, the results could be used as a basis for developing a federal CKO competency model. The CKO competencies and skills shown in Figure 4 are a first step in answering the question posed earlier: "How would you recognized a CKO if you bumped into one in the hallway?" Second, an important task is developing the next generation of human capital who will lead KM efforts in the federal sector content. The results of the brainstorming sessions, coupled with complementary studies, may help form the basis for KM curriculum development and, possibly, CKO certificate or certification programs. In addition, the results could help human resources personnel working with senior executives craft better job descriptions for CKOs. Last, the result could aid in developing assessment instruments to determine if organizations are ready to embark on KM initiatives.

SUMMARY

The results of the brainstorming sessions seem to confirm many of the findings of previous studies and surveys. CKOs are springing to life in public and private sector organizations, addressing a perceived unmet need to capitalize on knowledge-based assets. They possess a different mix of hard and soft skills than that of CIOs. Many reasons for embarking on KM initiatives are the same in public- and private-sector organizations. Problems endemic in large knowledge-based organizations are endemic in large organizations, whether public or private. One key difference became evident between public- and private-sector CKOs. Public-sector CKOs look to KM as a basis for electronic government. Many functions of government are associated with collecting, analyzing, or disseminating data and information. In a logical extension of these functions, perhaps collecting, analyzing, and disseminating explicit and tacit knowledge should be added to the list.

In 1787, James Madison, writing in the *Federalist Papers* said, "To give information to people is the most certain and legitimate engine of government." Extending Madison's notion, the time may have arrived where providing access to information *and* knowledge may be the most certain and legitimate function of government.

NOTES

1. Dr. Robert E. Neilson is the CKO and a professor at the Information Resources Management College, National Defense University. He can be reached at neilson@ndu.edu. Special thanks to those who participated in the brainstorming session or who were kind enough to offer comments on initial drafts. They include: Dr. Shereen Remez, GSA; Dr. Clinton Brooks, NSA; Alex Bennet; Navy; Miriam Browning, Army; Doug Weidner, Litton/PRC; Carl Hansen, SRA; Jay Chatzkel, Progressive Practives; Edward Allard, DOE; Andrea Alterman Hassan, CSC; Rick Pfaltz, Pinnacle; Tom Beckman, IRS; Peter Engstrom, SAIC; Harriet Riofrio, OSD; and Drs. Jay Alden and Jerome Paige, IRM College, NDU.

2. To move the field of knowledge management from the fad stage to a discipline with more substance, Robert de Hoog et al. propose a theoretical framework for KM using simulation gaming anchored in a specific process model. (See Robert de Hoog et al. Investigating a Theoretical Framework for Knowledge Management: A Gaming Approach. *Knowledge Management Handbook,* ed. Jay Liebowitz. Washington, DC: CRS Press, 1999.)

3. CKO—chief knowledge officer; CTO—chief technology officer; CLO—chief learning officer; KA—knowledge architect; KM—knowledge manager; and KE—knowledge engineer.

4. Drucker, Peter. *Managing for the Future.* New York: Truman Talley Books, 1992. Thurow, Lester C. *Building Wealth: The New Rules for Individuals, Companies, and Nations in a Knowledge-Based Economy.* New York: Harper Business, 2000.

5. *Human capital* is all individual capabilities—the knowledge, skill, and experience of the organization's employees and managers. *Intellectual capital* includes the intangibles, such as information, knowledge, and skills, that can be leveraged by an organization to produce an asset of equal or greater importance than land, labor, and capital. *Structural capital* is the processes, structures, and systems that a firm owns, less its people. *Social capital* is the goodwill resulting from physical and virtual interchanges between people with like interests and who are willing to share ideas within groups that share their interests.

6. Earl, Michael J., and Ian Scott. What Is a Chief Knowledge Officer? *Sloan Management Review* 40:2, 1999. Bonner, Dede. Enter the Chief

Knowledge Officer. *Training & Development,* February 2000. Abell, Angela and Nigel Oxbrow. *People Who Make Knowledge Management Work: CKO, CKT or KT?* in *Knowledge Management Handbook*, ed. Jay Liebowitz, Washington, DC: CRS Press, 1999.

7. Earl and Scott.
8. Earl and Scott.
9. Abel and Oxbrow.
10. Abel and Oxbrow.
11. The results of brainstorming sessions represent the view of participants. Although the results of the sessions seem to confirm the results of similar studies, more rigorous research should be conducted to see if the findings contained in this study can be generalized to a larger universe.
12. The results of brainstorming sessions are also located at: http://www.ndu.edu/ndu/irmc/km-cio_role/km-cio-role.htm. The four key questions are hotlinked to graphic illustrations created in Shockware. Roll your cursor over the boxes at the end of the spokes, and the detailed content will appear.
13. Davenport, Thomas H. and Laurence Prusak. *Working Knowledge.* Boston: Harvard Business School Press, 1998.

CHAPTER 14

Managing Change in a Knowledge Environment

Alex Bennet

Most organizations today exist in a knowledge environment. As the globe shrinks and information traffic covers Mother Earth, data, information, and knowledge will significantly impact every individual and every organization. These forces, residing external to the millions of firms, government agencies, and not-for-profits, will play a significant role in both forcing internal changes to ensure survival and, at the same time, challenging change management as it works to effectuate those changes. This chapter looks at the difficulties in managing change on this new landscape—change that is needed to make organizations capable of operating competitively with a high-quality output over the long haul.

The chapter first looks at generic characteristics needed to survive in a knowledge-intensive world (i.e., what an ideal knowledge organization would look like). The challenge of moving a bureaucracy or its variant to the ideal knowledge organization is then considered. In other words, the chapter looks at change management, offering some new and some not-so-new ideas that a change agent should consider. Several new models are presented to provide the reader different perspectives on the change problem. While each view taken by itself is useful, it is rarely enough. Change management is a systems problem, and orchestrating change is a complex process requiring multidimensional understanding of both the system being changed and the change process itself.

The use of tools to support change management is strongly endorsed based on the author's six years of experience in developing and implementing a number of them in support of a change process encompassing a 900,000-person organization. References are sprinkled throughout the paper for readers interested in further research.

THE INTERNAL KNOWLEDGE ENVIRONMENT

A good knowledge organization is one built on quality knowledge systems—systems that provide the right information to the right people at the right time, taking into account the way information is received, and perceived, to ensure that information flows freely and quickly. In other words, an internal environment where the technology is conducive to human use and where people want to share their own expertise and reap the benefit of others' experience. Individuals who are part of this environment will themselves become open systems by being both producers and learners of knowledge. They will have the ability to focus their attention on what makes the greatest difference and on what helps achieve the greatest good, defined in terms of the organization's mission and vision.

The above environment comes from what we have learned about ecologies that create and nurture innovation and the sharing of ideas. Environments conducive to innovation flourish best under decentralized organizational structures that, through their supporting infrastructure and inherent interpersonal relationships, create a natural expectation and acceptance of the responsibility all members have for initiating new activities. These organizations have simple processes for exploiting new ideas (including champions and resources) and encouraging and rewarding experimentation (via tolerance for failure and loose deadlines, with minimal surveillance, evaluation, and administrative interference). Effective communications among all levels leads to the sharing of understanding—through both success stories and lessons learned—as a natural part of the culture.

The ideal knowledge environment builds on these learnings to include the need for effective *continuous and interpersonal* communications at all levels and the use of team-based structures. Continuous and interpersonal communications create an essential framework within which creative thinking, brainstorming, inquiry, dialogue, debate, scenario planning, discussion, and rational analysis are encouraged. These are the ways in which synergy can create new thinking and paradigm shifts.

Recent research has indicated a correlation between a preschool age child's intelligence level and the amount of time the child spends with parents in interpersonal communication. A similar phenomenon may hold for organizational intelligence (i.e., workers will be more creative, thoughtful, and act smarter when they spend time interacting with each other within the framework of a clear vision or goal).

The idea of creating an optimum knowledge-based organizational environment has at its foundation cohesive subgroups or teams and networks of relationships where open and free exchange of ideas is the norm. The advantage of teams (as for any form of small collaborative group) is that individuals can get to know each other, developing trust and effective interpersonal relations that generate information and knowledge sharing through brainstorming, problem solving, and decision making. Team learning can then occur naturally through the process of responding to changes in the external environment. As teams develop their own centers of learning and as people move around within the organization, the seeds of team efficiency will expand throughout the organization and generate the desired knowledge environment. This is only one factor in creating the desired change. (See Bennet, 1997, for details on team innovation, learning, and management.[1])

Taking another view of the ideal knowledge organization, consider the concept of the intelligent complex adaptive system (ICAS). The ICAS represents an organization with an internal environment that combines the traits of teams, organizational intelligence, complexity, and adaptability. Taken together, these will lead to an open, knowledge-creating, knowledge-sharing, and knowledge-applying organization.

The above discussion assumes knowledge organizations with ideal internal environments. In the very human world that starts the 21st century, organizations are at some level between the bureaucracy and the knowledge organization. Note: Even the "knowledge organization" does not imply a state of perfection on this continuum. A "perfect" state presupposes something completed and fixed, beyond change and so beyond motion, further development, and creativity. To survive, the knowledge organization will have to re-examine itself and its external environment constantly and, after doing so, continuously adapt and redirect its thrust. In other words, as De Geus has noted, it must be a living organization.[2]

THE CHANGE APPROACH

Where an organization lies on this spectrum or continuum from bureaucracy to ICAS very much drives the approach required to manage change (see Figure 1). At the left end of the spectrum, you would work through the chain of command and mandate compliance and, based on the Weberian bureaucratic model, share as little information as necessary to accomplish the desired change. Weber believed that "Every bureaucracy seeks to increase the superiority of the professionally informed by keeping their knowledge and intentions secret."[3]

At the other end of the spectrum, the change manager's job is to demonstrate value and to educate, letting the organization itself build the response and implementation strategy appropriate for each organizational element. In exploring the application of the science of complexity to organizations, Stacey suggests three basic needs for a complex adaptive organization. These are to provide workers with (1) a clear rationale for new direction, (2) a strong set of values they can share and operate within, and (3) the freedom to self-organize.[4] The precept is that the workers know what needs to be done, and, given direction and values, they are able to organize themselves better than management can dictate. This approach is consistent with some findings in complexity theory but has not been widely tested. It would work only with organizations already in an advanced state of empowerment and knowledge sharing (i.e., on the right side of the spectrum). Although some present-day world-class firms exhibit elements of this self-organizing approach, most of today's organizations have a long way to go.

This same concept of change management for a knowledge organization surfaced in a five-year study involving over 2,500 individuals in 460 companies. The Jensen Group study on "Changing How We Work" found that "God's reality is that if we designed knowledge management structures that created meaning, drove understanding, integrated content, and facilitated conversations, change would change itself—at the appropriate speed."[5] The study goes on to conclude that change management is, in reality, an "artificial solution imposed on an [sic] dysfunctional corporate knowledge system."

Success occurs over time, and comes with many faces. In fact, there is danger in premature convergence, for it can limit potential. As much as we are inclined to desire change at Internet speed, there is a natural pace and rhythm of change that is specific to each organization.

Figure 1 shows that as we move from the bureaucratic structure to the knowledge organization, both individual and organizational learning increase, and resistance to change decreases. However, we must be careful and not fall into the trap of believing that knowledge organization structures do not resist change. Knowledge organizations, being adaptive and learning, are much more comfortable with new ideas, products, and organizational structures than a corresponding bureaucratic firm. However, if the anticipated change is perceived as affecting, or may affect, a worker's job security, organizational status, physical location, or career opportunity in any negative way, resistance can be strong, subtle, and possibly invisible in either organization. Fear and psychological loss drive behavior far more than rational thought. How an individual defines "loss" is highly dependent on the degree of the individual's learning and flexibility, with the feelings of loss inversely related to learning and flexibility.

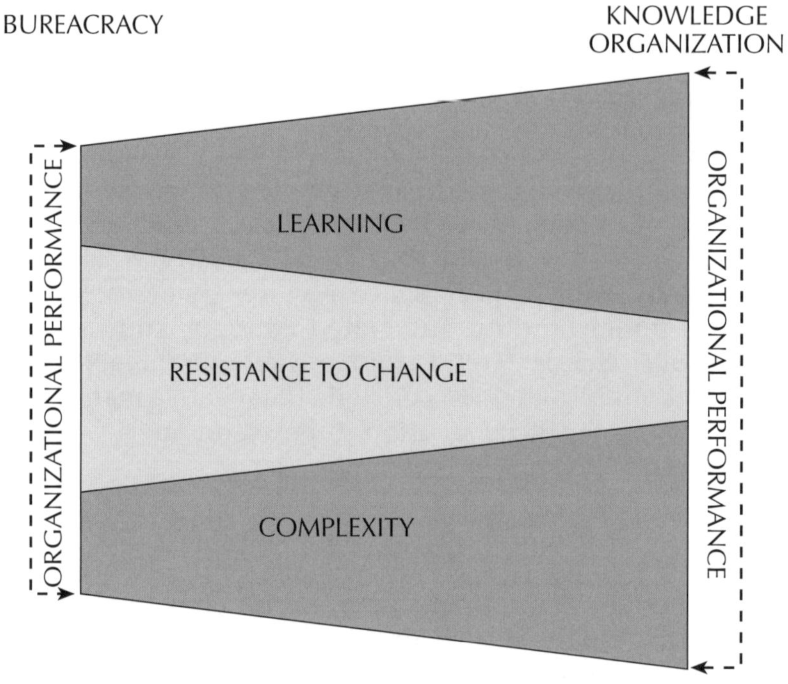

Figure 1. From the Bureaucracy to the Knowledge Organization

Figure 1 also shows that as we move from the bureaucratic structure to the knowledge organization structure and individual and organizational learning increases, complexity increases. We have all seen and experienced what appear to be incredibly complex bureaucratic organizations. In many ways, this is a mirage. Frustration is not complexity. Because of the hierarchical structure and base of command and control in a bureaucratic organization, there are fewer directions to go, less variety in decisions and actions, and less potential to bring to bear than in the knowledge organization based on teams and knowledge sharing. Bureaucratic organizations were designed for stable, repetitive, error-free processes meeting their design objectives. In contrast, knowledge organizations flourish on new ideas and change. The amount of potential in a knowledge organization is limited only by the number and quality of ideas generated, and the array of possibilities is limited only by the resources available.

Because of its multiple communication networks, feedback paths, and constant variation of team structures, complex structures, such as the knowledge organization discussed above, have the ability to learn, adapt, and take on a far broader variety of actions than a bureaucracy. Thus, although they are more complex than bureaucracies, they can use that complexity to respond more quickly and more effectively to a nonlinear, dynamic, knowledge-laden external environment.

THE CHANGE PROCESS

We have learned through the years that when organizational change is mandated and certain actions occur in response to that mandate, individual behavioral change is highly dependent on the individual's receptivity to change and to the incentive to exchange old behaviors for new ones. Receptivity to change is affected by a combination of internal and external information and current beliefs, all of which are subject to continuous examination and update. This means that all incoming information is colored by current beliefs and feelings. It also means that all incoming information, whether originating from the nonconscious mind of the individual or from the external environment, is under continuous examination, and as a result, the individual's beliefs themselves are also subject to continuous reexamination (see Figure 2). This powerful process goes on at various levels within all learning individuals.

This process also operates continuously and invisibly in a learning organization. Incoming information is continuously examined in light of the organization's structural capital (i.e., that explicit information and knowledge within the organization). It

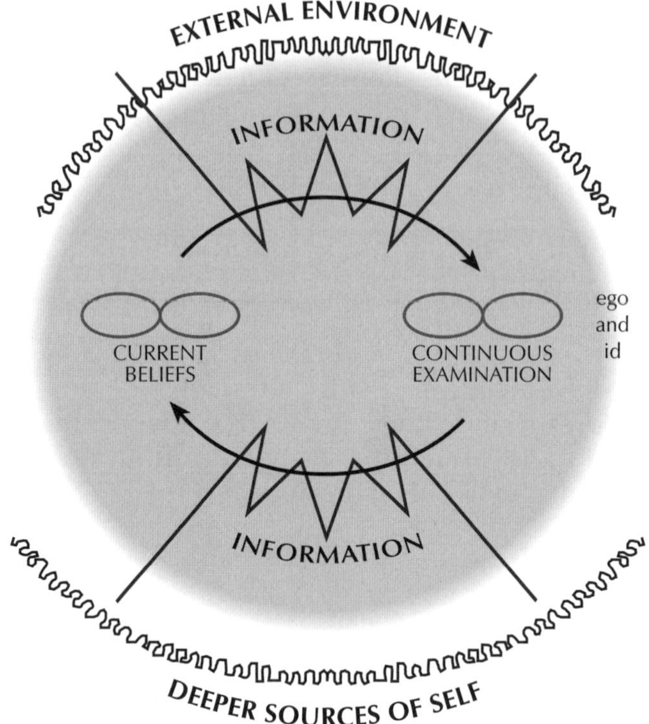

Figure 2. Cycle of Continuous Examination

is then considered in relationship to the belief set (in a healthy organization reflected in the mission, vision, and strategy) and to the organizational culture (through values, behavior, and expectations). Any new information needs to be made sense of in these terms before it will be embraced by the organization. And, the mission, vision, and strategy should always be under continuous examination in light of incoming internal and external information. This under-the-looking-glass approach reduces what we call "resistance to change" because both "old" and "new" information and knowledge are subjected to it.

From psychology (Freudian theory) we get the concept of the ego, that aspect of personality that encompasses the sense of "self" in contact with the real world. To represent the instinctive aspects of personality, Freud uses the concept of the id.[6] Viewing an organization as having a culture, an emergent characteristic similar to personality in an individual, we can extrapolate that culture is made up of both an ego and an id. The ego provides that portion of the inner identity of the organization that faces the world with rational thinking, and the id represents past experience and beliefs converted to instincts and emotions through time.

The culture (ego and id) of the organization is a powerful energy force. While the organizational ego serves as the watchtower and processor for incoming information, the id provides the energy and spirit for action and resolve. Ego represents the rational, objective part of culture, and id represents the emotional, subjective part. Whether viewed in the individual or organizational setting, the ego and id can be strong advocates or barriers to change, and both must be recognized and dealt with. An organization can be changed and turned in literally endless directions by recognizing and dealing effectively with both organizational ego and id.

All too often, senior managers of today's organizations believe that because their workforce is empowered and flexible, they need deal only with the ego side of culture, providing a set of reasons why change must occur and some plan to accomplish that change. They may consider the id side as touchy-feely and, therefore, unnecessary. Freudian theory reminds us that people act consistently with their personal knowledge, beliefs, and feelings—especially in times of possible danger, and all significant organizational change will be perceived as threatening to some workers. Change must be addressed in terms of both the ego and the id.

A first step to receptivity is gaining attention. As the environment bombards the senses, attention itself rapidly becomes a scarce resource. Information doubles every eighteen, nine, or three months (depending on which study you read). Currently, there are more than 800 million Web pages, and Internet traffic is doubling every 100 days. By the time you read this chapter, these figures will have doubled.

Marketing experts have studied potential buyer response for decades. A lot of what they have learned carries over to the art of managing change in either government or the private sector. The importance of product names transfers to the perceived trustworthiness of information dependent on the sender. Market segmentation and customization map to the personalization of information as seen by its recipient. Product appeal and advertising campaigns relate to evoking emotion with the information sent. And, finally, the importance of product value becomes the receiver's real or perceived need for use of the information. To get someone's attention, something of perceived value (to them) must be offered in return. When addressing effective knowledge management, Tom Peters says the crux of the issue is not information, information technology, or knowledge per se. "It's how . . . you get busy people . . . to want to contribute [or use information] . . . the answer turns out to lie more with psychology and marketing than with bits and bytes."[7]

Sensory inputs provide the stimuli for the culture's attention or inattention. The external senses provide what Thomas Reid, a Scottish philosopher who lived, thought, and wrote over 200 years ago, called a conception and an invincible belief of the existence of external objects.[8] Reid credited a "double province" to the senses: to make us perceive and to make us feel. Reid uses the smelling of a rose as an example. When we smell a rose, two separate and parallel things happen: a sweet, subjective smell enters through our olfactory system, *and* we perceive the external and objective presence of a rose. What Reid is getting at is that the sense of smell is something that directly affects us as individuals, a subjective experience, a feeling. But the perception of an external presence provides us with objective facts to make judgments about the external objective world.

The culture of the organization, then, carries the residue (memory) of feelings about the organization and the external world. At the same time, it is constantly under the influence of its own belief set, which is itself being continuously examined as new external and internal information flows within the organization. Thus, in the regular course of events, the organizational ego will modify itself and change or flow into a somewhat different ego. Such is the usual process with cultures. They change slowly, never losing all of their history nor accepting all of the new ways, with the id portion taking longer to adjust to the new changes than the ego. When an organization's culture undergoes traumatic shock, such as massive layoffs, mergers, or impending dissolution, there is a frantic attempt to create alternate stories or self-images to handle the situation. But egos have their id partners that carry the memory of the images and experiences of traumatic shock. If all humans behaved rationally, there would be very few overweight people, no smokers, and wars would be history. If organizational cultures followed their egos, most would be high-performance, knowledge-centric, and adaptive. However, such organizations are rarely found.

The classic belief has been that organizations do not change without undergoing a traumatic emotional experience. While this may be true in the bureaucratic structure, as organizations adapt to knowledge environments, there may well be new learnings that will allow change without this historic need for trauma.

Once attention is gained, individual learning styles significantly contribute to each worker's ability to take in information, its context, and its meaning. Nonaka and Takeuchi[9] identify and discuss the four modes by which knowledge is transferred. These modes use some combination of tacit knowledge (which is internalized in each of us) and explicit knowledge (which can be codified in some form of media). The four quadrants are aligned to preferred learning styles: tacit to tacit (individual learning through apprenticeship); tacit to explicit (group learning); explicit to explicit (organizational learning); and explicit to tacit (enterprise learning). While each individual has a preferred learning style and each area of knowledge has its natural habitat, the challenge is to create a dynamic environment that permits all knowledge forms and all learning styles and perspectives to share understanding and create innovative solutions.

Even if individual attention is gained and the material presented in a variety of ways, taking into consideration learning styles and modes of receptivity, unless the receiver is operating in a processing mode consistent with the knowledge content, very little will be acted upon. Recent psychological studies show that the focus of an individual's attention changes, on the average, every 40 minutes. That means attention alone will not carry the day. Long speeches, videos, or meetings will not of themselves produce the desired paradigm shift in either individuals or the organizational culture. So what now?

Given the discussion above, it may be surprising that organizations can and do change. But of course they do. We offer the following as considerations when stimulating change:

- Knowledge organizations, like people, have an internal belief structure and an instinctual history that is constantly examining itself based on the flow of information from both internal and external sources.
- The organizational culture (i.e., its ego and id) has the ability to turn the organization in literally endless directions.
- The level of learning within an organization is inversely proportionate to the expected resistance to change.
- As the external environment becomes more complex, the bureaucratic organization is more difficult to control, and its efficiency decreases.
- As organizations become more knowledge-based and true collaboration and empowerment occur, internal complexity increases, which can be used to support change.

ELEMENTS OF CHANGE

We and our organizations are affected by changes in our environment, and to various degrees we can exert influence on that environment. We now consider planned change, where we strive to create the future reality of our organization.

A preparatory tenet for planned change is to determine if the need for change is real and the time needed is available. Is there a good business case for changing, and has a viable strategy been developed? A second tenet is the willingness to let change beget change. Change can be initiated and orchestrated, but it cannot be rigorously controlled. The end-state is never precisely predictable. What frequently happens is that resistance is proportional to the level of control of the change process. Remove people's say in the change, and you remove their motivation to cooperate.

A third tenet is the intention to see it through. False starts will generate confusion, produce discretions in both efficiency and effectiveness, and embed themselves in the cultural memory. Start change with the intent, energy, and resources to see it through, yet with a strategy flexible enough to meet the second tenet above.

The first element of planned change is a clear understanding of where the organization currently is (value and values, structure and processes, strengths and weaknesses) and what the desired state of the future is (vision and mission, opportunities and strategies). What's different in a knowledge-based organization is that this crucial first step is the most important instrument of change. If the need for change can be communicated, understood, accepted, and aligned across the organization, supported with implementation tools (which invite change in a nonthreatening way) and incentives, change momentum will be well underway.

The value of change is made visible through the use of cross-organization and cross-product teams to define the vision, the effective use of diverse modes of communicating that vision, and continuous commitment from senior and middle management to that vision and to the employee's welfare. The fluid exchange of ideas and understanding across the organization, built from the belief set of the organization, will determine what change will occur. That means: (1) exchange at every level of the organization, horizontal and vertical, and (2) a focus on building a common understanding of the context (the need for change and the vision of the future) and defining pathways and connections to get there. Ultimately, this comes down to individuals, their relationships with each other, and the data, information, and knowledge they have access to accept and apply.

Tools are critically important to change management and can be used as both motivators and long-term facilitators. Tools may provide guidance on how to get from here to there (policies, guiding principles, instructional material); road maps that provide for process change (methodologies such as scenario planning); technology (from collaborative software to simulations); and communities and forums for the active exchange of successes and lessons learned. People and dollar resources, such as change champions and seed funding, can be instrumental in speeding up the journey.

Motivation is increased through tools that demonstrate the potential for greater efficiencies and effectiveness, with the associated rewards of personal productivity, better products, and higher customer satisfaction. Because tools are objective in that they do not carry the connotation of "past wrongs," they offer "new opportunities" to improve performance without the emotional baggage of "I must not have been doing it right before!" Tools do not challenge internal belief systems or past behavior; rather they encourage change through taking advantage of an opportunity—especially when the user has the freedom of choice.

Facilitation occurs where tools encourage and foster better communication and collaboration. If people start talking and listening, they will learn better and be more willing to change. Some tools act as an independent focal point for discussions, debate, and inquiry. These "shared spaces" provide effective ways to bring people's perspectives together and communicate with a common focus and language.

Scenario planning is helpful because its process encourages creative, yet self-consistent, thinking, and it gives the group an idea of what the future could look like, for example, a direction to move toward. This ensures that change is directed and purposeful, providing a vision to spark the emotions and encourage dreams.

A simple and perhaps surprising tool is the use of space to foster communication and the sharing of understanding, which in turn facilitates change. The frequency and amount of conversation among workers are exponentially related to the closeness between their offices; the closer their offices, the more they talk to each other. By placing change agents throughout the organization, or having supervisors and managers spend more time managing by walking around, employees will have greater opportunity for face-to-face dialogue to reduce their fears and better understand the need for change and its impact on their work and job security.

In addition to cognitive tools, such as lateral thinking, synectics, synthetic analysis, and dialogue, systems thinking has been found to be very useful in helping people comprehend the complex relationships that exist in their organization and to identify feedback and circular patterns of cause and effect that may either stifle or accelerate organizational change. (See the articles by Bohlin and Brenner, 1996,[10] and Rooke and Torbert, 1999,[11] in *The Systems Thinker*.)

System dynamics (a form of advanced simulation) can change fundamental belief systems objectively as groups work together to build a common understanding of how their organization really works. System dynamics models provide the opportunity to experiment with cause and effect in simulated current or future organizations through sensitivity analyses and flight simulation runs. Groups of managers have used modeling to identify serious problems in their organization, recognize their own paradigm errors in how the organization really works, and develop and simulate correction strategies. (Vennix, 1996,[12] and Morecroft and Sterman, 1994,[13] offer in-depth discussions of this process; Bennet, 1997,[1] includes an Integrated Product Team flight simulator.) The bottom line is that group and personal experimentation help create willingness and a rationale for understanding and supporting change.

Another valuable tool an organization has for change is shared ideas using collaborative technology.[14,15,16] The more these mental implements are used, the more ideas are available for use, and the more opportunity for the organization to develop and fulfill its own unique competitive advantage.

Incentives certainly include high-visibility reward and award systems. They also include reinforcement from leadership. An essential positive incentive that comes out of the Total Quality groundwork is leadership walking the walk. Leaders (including middle managers) must be a proactive part of the change process, consistently presenting the vision, clarifying the path and acting as role models for all employees. Organizational awareness of potential negative actions can also be an incentive. Because there will always be individuals who resist change, leadership must be prepared to take swift corrective action where fear of change turns into active and overt rebellion. While some may find this idea of "carrying a big stick" outdated, it is a mental tool for those still on the growth road toward becoming continuous learners.

It would be nice if we could paint that clear vision, snap our fingers, and achieve the desired end state, but the reality is that a transformed organization does not just happen. In many ways, organizations evolve like living organisms. They grow much like a human child. A concerned parent has a great deal to do in a child's early years with relating information and incentivizing behavior; but as the child grows older self-incentives and incentives from the external environment take priority; and the parent role becomes one of information sharing, guidance, and dialogue. When the child enters adulthood, the parent serves more in the advisory capacity. During this cycle, growth visibly occurs in small chunks, with the parent first focusing on life-threatening issues, then working with the basic qualities of the genes and environment (ego, capability, and value set) to create emergent characteristics that affirm and mold the belief set. Along this growth road, benefits accrue for both the child and parents as they learn about what it is to be human through each other's eyes. This metaphor offers insights for the growth of organizations from the first "Eve" (the first homo sapien) of 117,000 years ago through the bureaucratic organization to the beginnings of the knowledge organization. The growth cycle in individual organizations can also reflect this metaphor, as well as the change effort itself. While dependent on the environment, change behavior reflects its place in the growth cycle. For every change there is a time.

EMERGENT CHARACTERISTICS

As organizations change and take on new forms, they often do so through the creation and development of what systems theorists call emergent characteristics. These represent new properties that are totally different from the properties of the old structure, and they cannot be directly derived from the lower levels of the organization. For example, social organizations emerge from individual actions, and knowledge sharing arises from changes in behavior and new technology; yet social organizations and knowledge sharing are phenomena that are very different from individuals or technology. The connection between the early organization and its current emergent properties is extremely complex and difficult to follow via cause-and-effect chains. It is also difficult to predict the precise nature of the emergent characteristics. This is one reason why planned change is so difficult and the change process so hard to control. For example, it is easy to create a vision of a team-based organization with high employee empowerment. But the exact details of the best team structure or the specific way that employees should be empowered are very hard to predetermine. People are not machines, and their variability and self-determination are essential for their efficacy. Thus, while a desirable emergent characteristic can be nurtured, it cannot be decreed.

Emergent characteristics can be best understood in relation to a clearly defined vision prior to the anticipated change. Emergent characteristics usually make up the key factors that will make the vision a reality, as well as providing local indicators or measures of success. Emergent characteristics grow from ideas—ideas that emerge from individuals in relationship with each other. These organizational ideas, much like the individual model shown in Figure 2, are constantly examined in light of new information (both internal and external). And these ideas, even while affected by their environment, are also constantly altering and creating their environment.

What do these emergent characteristics look like? Some examples that relate to the knowledge organization are: community, knowledge sharing, knowledge repositories, organizational flexibility, and organizational learning. As discussed above, it may be impossible to identify the lower-level causative elements that lead to the creation of these emerging characteristics.

Community. Community is formed through networks based on relationships. Teams, flexible work groups, and communities of practice (COPs) and interest (COIs) are ways of building community. What is specific to COPs and COIs—recently coined labels to describe a particular way of working in the world—is that they are organized around a shared domain of knowledge. COPs and COIs cross operational, functional, and organizational boundaries and focus on value added, mutual exchange, and continuous learning. While aligned with the strategic direction of the organization, they are maintained by making connections and providing added value for their participants. Critical factors to success include a sense of urgency, trust, respect, personal passion, open communications, and the participation of key thought leaders. The exact nature, form, and participation level of COPs and COIs are dependent on the needs of the organization and the benefits to their members.

Knowledge Sharing. The sharing of knowledge is not natural to the organic growth of the bureaucratic organization. During the knowledge lifecycle, an individual uses data and information to create new knowledge built on context and understanding. As knowledge is shared across the competitive base, this knowledge is: (1) used to improve products and (2) used alone or in combination with other knowledge to create new ideas or new knowledge (i.e., the innovation process). New knowledge (ideas and innovation) is one of the positive results of sharing knowledge. Another positive result is the efficient availability of the best knowledge to decision makers. The negative potential of sharing knowledge is its potential decay or loss of value as time elapses, needs change, and new knowledge comes into demand (see Figure 3).

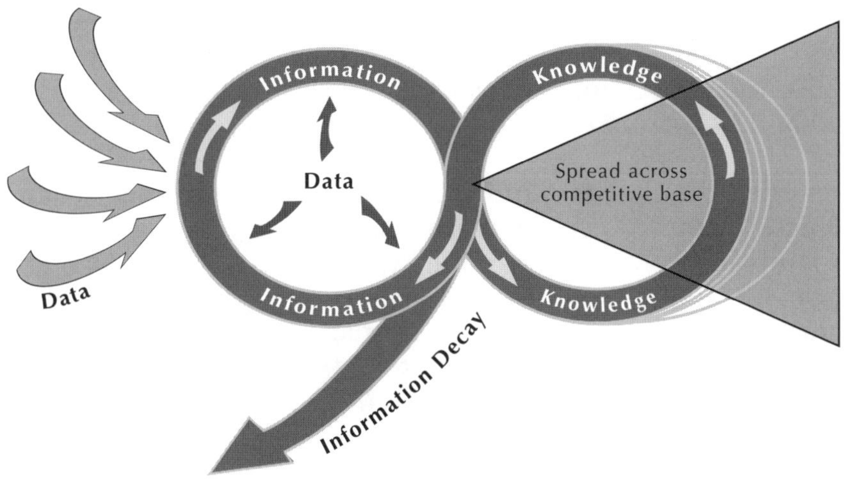

Figure 3. The Knowledge Lifecycle

It now becomes clear why, historically, managers have always considered their knowledge as a source of power. It is also clear why the knowledge organization of the future—living in an environment with easy access to unlimited data and information—will consider knowledge shared as their source of power. These knowledge organizations will succeed based on the continuous influx of new ideas and innovation and their superior ability to create, find, and apply knowledge at the time and place where it is most powerful.

Knowledge Repositories. Knowledge repositories, automated libraries, computer services, and databases offer a capability for not only storing huge amounts of data and information but also for efficient and semi-intelligent retrieval and assemblage capability. As search algorithms, intelligent agents, and semantic interpreters become more powerful, employees will be able to rapidly retrieve information needed for problem solving and decision making. Although knowledge repositories may appear to be technology driven, they require a great deal of human effort to input the right information and motivate people to make effective use of them. Both of these require culture changes that, if successful, will result in a new organizational strength. The value of the knowledge repository is not so much in what resides in it but in what flows in and out of it to and from decision makers.

Organizational Flexibility. Another desired emergent characteristic of the knowledge-based organization is the ability to respond quickly to changes in the external environment. Organizational flexibility requires workforce empowerment, clear vision and values, and willingness by management to encourage prudent risk taking. A "freedom to take action" environment, coupled with open communications and fast, small, self-organized teams will result in opportunity making and taking.

Organizational Learning. Effective organizational flexibility also requires continuous learning, the fifth emergent property discussed here. Lifelong learning, changing, and forgetting lie at the foundation of progress in the modern world and may well be the ultimate separators between success and failure for individuals, public organizations, and private industry. Without learning, change is likely to be wasteful or irrelevant; with learning, change carries the opportunity for improvement.

THE STRATEGIC INITIATIVE PULSE

Change can be managed through a set of strategic initiatives designed to bring about specific emergent characteristics. The timing of these strategic initiative thrusts should correlate with the system's ability to recognize value and begin implementation. Each organization has a receptivity rhythm that can be monitored based on feedback loops.

The model in Figure 4 demonstrates the strategic initiative pulse (SIP) that was developed over three years of study of the

U.S. Department of Navy (DON) Acquisition Reform Office implementation approach. It is loosely analogous to Isaac Newton's fundamental laws of motion, stating that to maintain a change in motion you must have a continuous force. If the pressure for change is a constant, change itself will accelerate. As a construct for understanding the SIP, we will artificially divide the organizational system into three categories of people, forces, or levels: the proactive forerunners, the doubting Thomases, and the resisters (including "rocks" who will rarely change).

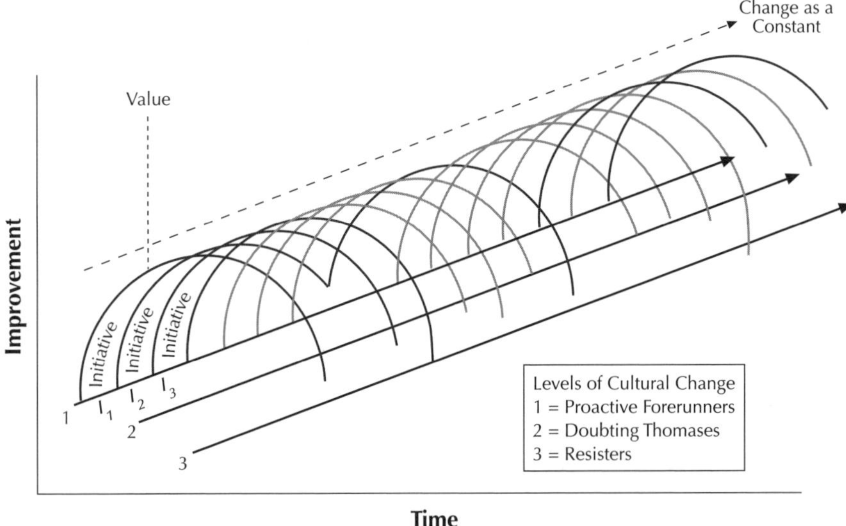

Figure 4. The Strategic Initiative Pulse

Assuming cohesive thinking and compatibility between the organization's needs and the change initiative, introduction of a new initiative (I_1) requires consistent, constant pressure at all levels of the organization. Over time, this pressure will result in recognition of the value of the change initiative by the organization. It is at the point of value recognition that the organization's proactive forerunners embrace the initiative and begin implementation

If the proactive forerunners appear to be successful with I_1, implementation of the initiative quickly cascades down through the ranks of the doubting Thomases. The greater the appearance of I_1 success by the proactive forerunners, the faster the cascade through the doubting Thomases. Then the hard work begins. The consistent, constant pressure must continue as slowly, slowly, the top layer of resisters opens up. How long and how far down into the resister layer the system can continue this I_1 push is dependent on the resources of the change effort. For at some point behind I_1's introduction, and prior to system value recognition, I_2 has been introduced and is requiring the same consistent, constant pressure for success. Then, near the value recognition point of I_1, and while I_2 is still in need of consistent, constant pressure, I_3 has been introduced into the organization. As demonstrated in Figure 4, to achieve continuous change, value recognition points are reinforced by overlapping change efforts.

Here is where the intelligent learning system comes into play, built on open feedback loops. It is best explained by example. When U.S. Department of Defense (DoD) Secretary Perry mandated the use of integrated product teams (IPTs), within 48 hours DoD teams of every type began calling themselves "IPTs," while struggling to figure out exactly what IPTs were.

Within a couple of weeks of announcement of that policy, the DON Acquisition Reform Office posted draft IPT guidelines on the Internet. During the following two weeks, more than 600 e-mails, phone calls, and personal dialogues ensued among the staff asking: "When will the final guidelines be issued?" Approximately six weeks into the change process, a second "draft" version of the IPT guidelines was posted virtually. Over the following two weeks, a flurry of questions ensued, but this time those questions numbered in the dozens instead of the hundreds. Three months into the change process, you began to see programs differentiating between IPTs and other types of teams. When a third set of "draft" guidelines was virtually posted, the two dozen responses were focused more on how to improve the guidelines than on asking "When do the final guides come out?" These response patterns, observed over a three-year period, could eventually be granulated down to sub-elements of the organization, each of which had a different culture and a different receptivity rhythm.

The response patterns demonstrated that initiatives too closely introduced failed to work through the organization (see Figure 5). This, of course, is partially due to the reduction of consistent, constant pressure, which is difficult to sustain when multiple initiatives are simultaneously introduced. Conversely, if too much time elapsed between change initiatives, the initial buildup to the point of value recognition became slower and more difficult (see Figure 5). As change behavior becomes embedded in the organization, the organization once again becomes static and slower to respond to change.

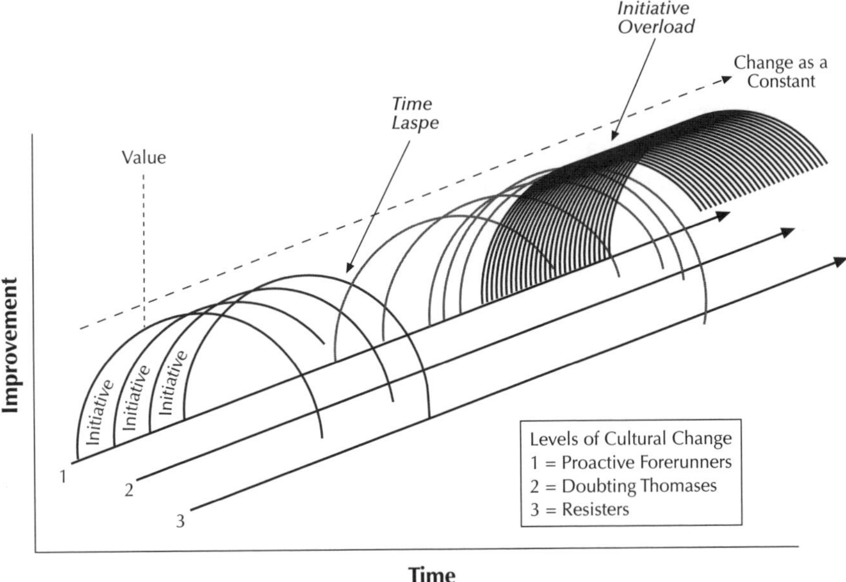

Figure 5. The Strategic Initiative Pulse Pattern

As demonstrated in the SIP, change requires aggressiveness in terms of continuous, constant pressure (or force). This implies the power of energy directed into action. The transformation of any idea into realization is the result of this creative aggression.

SUMMARY

It is clear that there is no one simple solution to change and that every change effort is context sensitive. It is also clear that the change approach is dependent on where an organization lies on the continuum from a bureaucratic organization to a knowledge organization.

We looked at the internal knowledge environment of an organization in terms of an intelligent complex adaptive system (ICAS). We viewed organizational change and learning through the lens of an individual change and learning model. We explored elements of change and discussed the creation of emergent characteristics. Finally, we looked at one model for orchestrating organizational change initiatives.

The last summary paragraph of a chapter offers the author one final opportunity to share the knowledge and passion so important to sharing ideas. My final words are these: vision your reality, then act accordingly, as if that reality is today.

NOTES

1. Bennet, D. *IPT Learning Campus: Gaining Acquisition Results through IPTs*. Alexandria: Bellwether Learning Center, 1997.
2. De Geus, A. *The Living Company*. Boston: Harvard Business School Press, 1997.
3. Gerth, H. and C. Mills (ed. and trans.). From Max Weber: *Essays in Sociology*. New York: Oxford University Press, 1946.
4. Stacey, R. *Complexity and Creativity in Organizations*. San Francisco: Berrett-Koehler Publishers, 1996.
5. The Jensen Group. *Changing How We Work: The Search for a Simpler Way*. Northern Illinois University College of Business, 1997.
6. Gerow, J. *Psychology: an Introduction*. New York: Harper Collins, 1992.

7. Peters, T. *Liberation Management.* New York: Alfred A. Knopf, 1992.
8. Reid, T. *Essays on the Intellectual Powers of Man* (ed. D. Stewart). Charlestown: Samuel Etheridge, 1785, 1813.
9. Nonaka, I. and H. Takeuchi. *The Knowledge-Creating Company: How Japanese Companies Create the Dynamics of Innovation.* New York: Oxford University Press.
10. Bohlin, N. and P. Brenner. "The Learning Organization Journey: Assessing and Valuing Progress." *The Systems Thinker,* Vol. 7, No. 5, pp. 1–5, 1996.
11. Rooke, D. and W. Torbert. "The CEO's Role in Organizational Transformation." *The Systems Thinker,* Vol. 10, No. 7, pp. 1–5, 1999.
12. Vennix, J. *Group Model Building: Facilitating Team Learning Using System Dynamics.* New York: John Wiley & Sons, 1996.
13. Morecroft, J. and J. Sterman (eds.) *Modeling for Learning Organizations.* Portland: Productivity Press, 1994.
14. Schrage, M. *Shared Minds: The New Technologies of Collaboration.* New York: Random House, 1990.
15. Coleman, D. *Groupware: Collaborative Strategies for Corporate LANs and Intranets.* New Jersey: Prentice Hall, 1997.
16. Skyrme, D. *Knowledge Networking: Creating the Collaborative Enterprise.* Oxford: Butterworth Heinemann, 1999.

BIBLIOGRAPHY

Auyang, S. *Foundations of Complex-System Theories.* Cambridge: Cambridge University Press, 1998.

Berger, L. *In the Footsteps of Eve: The Mystery of Human Origins.* Washington, D.C.: National Geographic, 2000.

Bohm, D. *Unfolding Meaning.* New York: Routledge, 1985.

Ellinor, L. and G. Gerard. *Dialogue: Rediscover the Transforming Power of Conversation.* New York: John Wiley & Sons, Inc., 1998.

Holman, P. and T. Devane (eds.) *The Change Handbook.* San Francisco: Berrett-Koehler Publishers, Inc., 1999.

Humphrey, N. "How to Solve the Mind-Body Problem." *Journal of Consciousness Studies*, Vol. 7, No. 4, pp. 5–20, 2000.

Kao, J. *Entrepreneurship, Creativity & Organization.* New Jersey: Prentice Hall, 1989.

Senge, P. *The Fifth Discipline: The Art & Practice of The Learning Organization.* New York: Doubleday, 1990.

Van der Heijden, K. *Scenarios: The Art of Strategic Conversation.* West Sussex, England: John Wiley & Sons.

CHAPTER 15

Knowledge Management
The Business Propositon for Government Organizations

Kelvin K. Womack

Two key questions typically faced by government and nonprofit organizations in implementing knowledge management (KM) are: Why do it? and How do we forecast and measure its value to the organization? These are daring questions for commercial and nonprofit oriented entities. They are particularly challenging for public sector organizations for several reasons:

- Government managers are just beginning to grasp the value of knowledge as a key resource. This is a prerequisite to understanding how to leverage knowledge for business impact.

- Government organizations often find it difficult to draw comparisons with commercial organizations that have shown bottom line results from installing KM disciplines.

- Public sector organizations often do not see the linkages between KM and performance.

- Sometimes there is a perception that government business is unique and does not lend itself to new disciplines such as KM.

Despite these challenges and others too numerous to list, it is clear that KM is a discipline whose time has come within the government. Why is this true?

- As service providers to the public, government relies heavily on the know-how of its workers. Most of the workers' output results from mental rather than physical labor.

- The drive for improved performance and results within government makes it imperative that the government be efficient in its collective mental labor. This includes improving the rate at which we learn efficient ways of performing work.

- Technology, particularly computers and the Internet, has provided powerful new tools for sharing thoughts and ideas in ways that were not possible until now.

- The U.S. federal government is facing a tremendous management challenge due to an aging workforce and impending retirements over the next decade. This drain of expertise presents an immeasurable challenge to maintaining and improving performance levels.

These facts have been validated through many formal and informal exchanges with government managers during the last two years. Inevitably, the dialogue leads to the question of how to build a business case for KM within a government organization. How do you describe its value in ways that decision makers can relate to and understand? This chapter provides a simple, four-step process for handling this important issue. Figure 1 depicts the process.

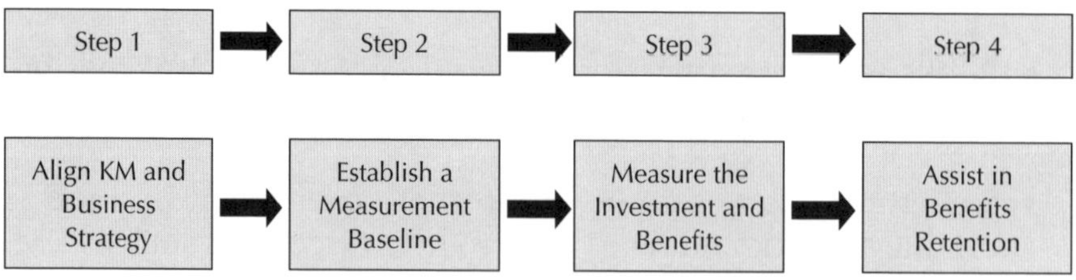

Figure 1. Building the Case for Knowledge Management

This chapter is organized into three key sections:

- ***Building the Business Case for Knowledge Management:*** Discusses the four steps shown in Figure 1.
- ***Case Study:*** Provides an exemplary case study on a mythical government agency to illustrate how this process could be used to develop a KM plan for a federal agency.
- ***Chapter Summary***: Synopsizes the points covered in the chapter and provides some final thoughts on what all of this may mean strategically for government organizations.

BUILDING THE BUSINESS CASE FOR KNOWLEDGE MANAGEMENT

Step 1: Align KM and Business Strategy

> *Knowledge Assets, like money or equipment, are worth cultivating only in the context of strategy.*
>
> Thomas A. Stewart
> *Intellectual Capital: The New Wealth of Organizations*

Assessing business value for KM begins with targeting where value can be obtained. This is an important perspective to take when applying KM disciplines to a business. Too often, we observe clients take an approach where they attempt to apply KM technologies and disciplines because they can help improve collaboration, share best practices, enhance business intelligence . . . the list goes on. Although these are all very valid reasons for implementing KM, we are focusing on the "means" rather than the end result of business impacts. We must invest in KM with a context for how it can provide measurable business results across a set of key business concerns. Having this business imperative is especially important for the government given the intense competition that KM initiatives face for new funding. We suggest that a focus on business strategy and goals is key to pointing a

KM program in the right direction. We have to know where the business unit is going in order to impact its ability to get there using KM.

Figure 2 provides a simple mental framework for linking KM to business strategy and goals. It suggests beginning with a clear understanding of some set of business goals that are important, measurable, and can be assisted through the application of KM. Typically, this means focusing on the activities that the business must do well to achieve its goals. If we know these, opportunities begin to reveal themselves for improved leveraging of employee knowledge and business critical information. Ask yourself the question, "How can KM be used to support these objectives in ways that other capabilities within the organization cannot?"

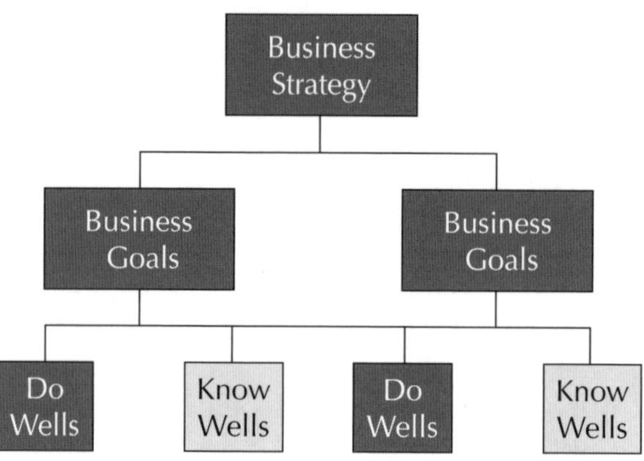

Figure 2. Linking Knowledge Management to Business Strategy

For example, U.S. federal government agencies have undertaken significant "rightsizing" initiatives since the Cold War ended. In many cases, agencies are fighting to maintain their relevance and importance by performing the same mission with reduced human resources or adding new services. These are major business transformations that change the way the federal government carries out daily activities in order to maintain performance levels. Both of these endeavors require building new competencies within the workforce. Both demand an enhanced focus on how rightsizing can be accomplished with a concentration on the critical knowledge and information needed to support the business.

This approach suggests a top-down, leadership-driven approach to determining where KM can be targeted for business impact. The more we concentrate on business outcomes at the beginning of a KM initiative, the greater our chances for a return on our KM investment during implementation. Several key people play a role in clarifying the goals, and the business activities ("do wells") needed to achieve them. With the involvement of such key leaders, we can quickly determine the associated knowledge and information ("know wells") needed to fuel these activities.

Who Is Involved In Strategic Planning For KM?

Any manager who plays a role in the decision-making process for the critical business activities must be involved in the strategic planning process for KM. This includes roles such as the chief knowledge officer (CKO), chief information officer (CIO), chief financial officer (CFO), and middle-level business and technology managers. It is important that these role players be involved because of the significance of their input to the targeting effort. It is also important that we begin to get their support and advocacy for including KM as part of their overall strategy for achieving business goals and objectives.

Remember that to be successful, we must not only pick the right initiatives for KM, but we must also commit to the business changes that must be made to drive business impact. This requires senior leadership and commitment. A grass roots approach alone will not typically drive success for KM projects.

Finally, as we conclude this discussion on targeting, it is important to make the point that value originates from the actions of people, not from the implementation of KM technology. Figure 3 illustrates this point. As we define the business areas where KM can add value, candidate business activities and outcomes must first be identified. Once this is done, information and content needed to support the selected business activities can be determined. However, the actions of managers and others will eventually drive the achievement of outcomes that are identified. Therefore, one of the most crucial aspects of targeting is obtaining commitment from managers and others to use the new KM capabilities in ways that will deliver the identified business impacts. Managers must commit to implementing the KM system(s), taking the actions that will lead to goal realization, and monitoring progress towards goals. These are issues of advocacy and commitment. They must be dealt with early in the stages of any KM project if lasting benefits are to be achieved.

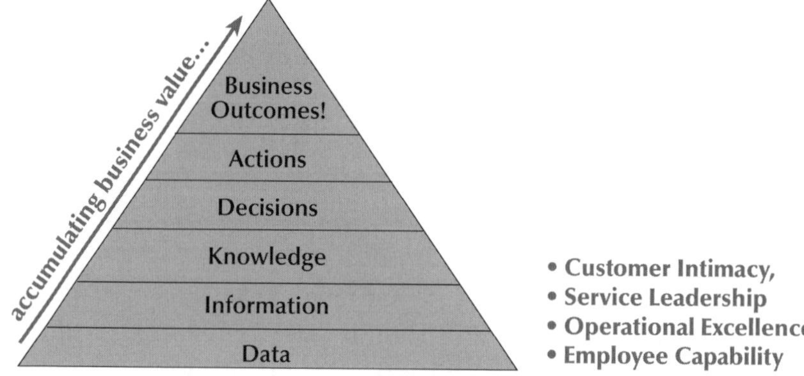

Figure 3. The Value Pyramid

Table 1 represents an example of summary results that could be obtained from a targeting process for KM. Note: some degree of prioritization may be needed in cases where many opportunities were identified.

Table 1. Targeting Summary for KM

Organizational Critical Success Factors (Prioritized)	*Performance Goals*	*Knowledge Management Opportunities to Add Value*
1. Be viewed by customers as a supplier that is flexible to do business with	Improve customer satisfaction rating from 9.5 to 10.0	• Implement an Intranet-based product tracking application for customers
2. Maintain current position as market leader in competitive pricing	80% of products will be lower than all suppliers	• Provide data warehouse competitor pricing comparison data
3. Offer customers Just In Time delivery to minimize inventory	Maintain inventory levels at 70% of prior year inventory level	• Implement a data mart to measure the % of inventory decreases
4. Reduce number of personnel in the administrative support function by 20% over the next 24 months	Maintain current workload and customer support capabilities through better leveraging of existing competencies and staff.	• Implement an administrative knowledge sharing and collaboration system that enables the sharing of administrative best practices and virtual mentoring

Step 2: Establish a Measurement Baseline

Once a list of pertinent KM initiatives for the organization is identified and prioritized, preparation is made for implementing them. One key step is to ensure that the current business processes are baselined. This will ensure a solid understanding of the extent to which the business will improve with KM disciplines in place. This step is analogous to performing a diagnostic of the business to measure its health prior to an intervention with KM and/or other transformation techniques. This tells us where the "starting line" is before we attempt to take on the challenges of improving the business. Without this step, we run the risk during implementation of not being able to successfully measure the extent to which we have impacted the business with KM. In determining the baseline, the following activities are executed:

1. Conduct a business opportunities analysis.
2. Develop concrete, measurable business goals.
3. Develop a set of performance metrics to gauge the achievement of outcomes.

Baselining Activity 1: Conduct a Business Opportunities Analysis

The goal during this activity is to drill down on each priority business goal identified during the targeting step. This is by no means a detailed business process analysis. It is meant to be a pragmatic uncovering of the "pain points" that can be relieved within specific business activities by implementing KM. If we use the value pyramid (Figure 3) as a guide, the targeting step focuses on the business outcomes and critical success factors within the business. Baselining focuses our analysis on the actions, decisions, and knowledge that drive these outcomes. We are looking for impediments to performance, such as lack of information, inability to leverage best practices, inefficient collaboration, or inability to make timely, sound, and credible decisions because of unreliable or untimely information.

The information gathered in this process helps identify two critical items. First, we obtain an understanding of the current performance of the business, based on information and knowledge "pain points." Organized effectively, this provides the needed baseline data that will be used during implementation to determine the amount of impact we can make by implementing specific KM solutions. Second, this information helps identify the types of solutions that may be appropriate for the challenges that are discovered.

There are several ways to effectively collect and organize this information. Table 2 depicts a form that may be used to organize and display some of the key information that is gathered from an opportunities analysis session.

Table 2. Activity versus Role Matrix

Activity versus Matrix for Business Area _______

	Role A	*Role B*	*Role C*	*Role D*	*Role E*
Business Activity A	Knowledge Elements				
Business Activity B			Knowledge Elements		
Business Activity C					
Business Activity D					
Business Activity E					
Business Activity F					

Note: The intent is to focus on capturing the critical information and knowledge that is needed by individual role players within a business activity. The activities within this matrix map directly to critical success factors identified during the targeting phase. Typically, these data are collected from business process owners, managers, and decision makers, who represent the best subject matter experts within the targeted business areas. Remember, this analysis is conducted to help baseline business activities and their information "pain points." This is done for each priority established during targeting. Once the information pain points are known, knowledge solutions and associated sources of content to enable these activities can be determined.

Baselining Activity 2: Set Measurable Business Goals

The purpose in setting goals is to describe a set of results in ways that are measurable and identifiable once they are achieved. The bar is set for how much impact is wanted on the business. The important thing to remember here is that in setting goals, we are describing quantifiable (if possible) business impacts. We are not just describing KM implementation goals. For example, let's look at the following goal statement:

> ***Install a web-based procurement information system for the procurement department by March 30, 2001.***

This goal describes an event that, when reached, adds KM *capability* to the organization. This capability is a prerequisite to realizing the business impact goal cited above. However, as costs and investments are discussed, adding capability and impacting business performance must be differentiated. The goal statement above describes an investment proposition; however, it does not describe a business impact. For success, the ultimate aim in KM is to contribute to achieving meaningful business impacts, which have significance in helping the business do something better. Instead, a better statement of the goal would be:

> ***By March 30, 2001, decrease cycle time for small procurements processing from sixteen hours to four by implementing a web-based procurement information system for chief procurement officers and their assistants.***

This goal provides measurable, verifiable insight on:

1. The activity that is being measured (small procurements processing)

2. The specific role players (chief procurement officers and their assistants) whose actions will be measured after arming them with the new capability

3. The degree of business impact that will be achieved (decrease cycle time for small procurements processing from sixteen hours to four)

4. Time frame for achieving the goal (March 30, 2001).

Baselining Activity 3: Develop Performance Metrics

In determining performance metrics for KM projects, we must consider metrics and performance in two distinct arenas.

- What are our measures for gauging business impacts?

- What are our metrics for gauging and controlling investment?

Business Measures

One challenge faced in determining measures for KM projects is that tangible, quantifiable results cannot always be identified. For example, collaborative technologies can significantly improve the efficiency of interaction and knowledge sharing among colleagues. How do you measure the business impacts of these new efficiencies? Often, with KM projects, measures that are best described with words rather than numbers may need to be defined. When setting business goals, setting goals for two areas that require measurement should be considered. First, some goals must be set for measuring end-user participation in the KM initiative. A prerequisite for success of any KM project is getting the business users to use the new technologies and participate in the business changes that are enabled by KM. If enough momentum is gained in driving usage and participation up, we then have a foundation for measuring impacts on bottom line business performance. By ensuring that people participate in a KM initiative, in effect, we are building knowledge capacity for the affected business unit(s). If an analogy to driving a car is drawn, this can be likened to putting fuel in a gas tank. Putting fuel in a car provides the capacity to get the value sought when we bought the car. Fuel levels are monitored to ensure the capability to get to a destination. The same principle applies to improving participation levels on a KM project.

Business value is the second, and most important, area for which business measures must be developed. We are what we measure. We must develop measures for bottom line business impacts to set a bar for measuring the achievement of these goals during implementation. Generally, business performance improvement measures can be lumped into four major categories:

- *Measures to gauge improved operational excellence*—delivering solid products and services at the best price and with the least inconvenience

- *Measures to gauge increased product leadership*—delivering the best products and services—offerings that push performance boundaries

- *Measure to gauge increased customer intimacy*—cultivating relationships to gain customer knowledge—delivering what specific stakeholders want

- *Measures to gauge improved employee capability*—leveraging human intellectual capital in service design and delivery.

These are cited because it is important to understand not only how each will be measured, but also how KM disciplines and technologies can contribute to their achievement. There are arenas where injecting KM technology may not be the best strategy for obtaining a business result. For example, if the objective is to improve employee capability by increasing the rate at which employees learn new competencies, a mentor-protégé program may have more impact than implementing a best practices knowledge-sharing system.

Finally, as business goals for KM, we must appreciate the fact that not all goals will have quantifiable, measurable results. Some deep thought must be given to the intangible value that can be obtained from these initiatives. For example, imagine a Web-enabled KM system that e-mails a reminder to Department of State customers to renew their passports three months before the passport expires. Does this system affect the impression of the customer on the value of State Department operations? How would you measure that? How do you measure the impact of State Department employees feeling that they are servicing the customer better? Surely, a questionnaire or survey could be designed to measure these qualitative trends in customer or employee satisfaction over time. However, we would have to think of these value propositions early in the project and plan for their measurement. Furthermore, we must get better at articulating the value of intangibles. This is particularly important in the federal government where the Clinger Cohen Act demands such rigor in upfront, cost-benefit analysis for large information technology projects.

We recommend that when describing benefits, both tangible and intangible, focus on developing a measurement plan that clearly shows the metrics that will be used to gauge performance improvement. Managers typically understand the significance of a change in a qualitative measure, such as customer satisfaction. The key is to develop pragmatic, relevant measures and articulate them in our business case for the KM project.

Because we know that business outcomes are driven by the actions of people, we must include in our plans a commitment by employees and managers to act in ways that will achieve the outcomes that we seek. Let us use the passport example. If by better managing information and knowledge, we seek to decrease the effort involved in processing passports, we should expect managers to shift labor from this activity to another within the Department of State. The measurement plan should then monitor the reduced costs related to this activity.

Common pitfalls in choosing metrics include:

- Using too many metrics
- Using delayed and risky reward ties
- Choosing metrics that are hard to control
- Choosing metrics that are hard to focus on
- Choosing metrics that measure the hard results and neglect the "soft stuff"
- Choosing metrics that are too rear-view oriented
- Measuring the wrong things.

Investment Measures

The objective when developing investment measures is to shorten the time it takes for the cumulative benefits of a KM initiative to exceed the cumulative costs needed to develop and implement the solution. The Federal Information Technology Management Reform Act (ITMRA) now requires that federal agencies implement a rigorous approach to selecting and prioritizing information technology projects based on relative benefits and costs. This requires CIOs and other executives to scrutinize these investments using traditional cost-benefit analysis techniques.

Step 3: Measure the Investment and Benefits

We must note one very important principle about measurement. The purpose of measurement is to get results. Measurement is a means to the end result of improving performance.

Implementing KM requires using common sense in determining the amount of rigor used in measuring results. As mentioned earlier, we must measure in two domains:

- The extent to which we are controlling investment
- Business impact, quantitatively and qualitatively.

Measuring Investment

Measuring the extent of your investment in knowledge management is rather straightforward and does not differ much from the typical measurement that is done on technology projects. We must measure the amount of labor and technology purchases that must be managed in order to develop the KM system and any new associated business processes. However, we have to keep a proper perspective on the management objective with the investment component of measurement. The managerial objective with investments is to control them and to keep cumulative investments within a reasonable range of business benefits. The key to this is having a strategic plan and vision for what must be accomplished and to develop the capabilities in small, manageable chunks of investment. This is why we must prioritize KM implementation projects based on business impact and feasibility as described earlier in the chapter.

Finally, it is very important that in keeping investments in proper perspective we do not confuse technology's role in obtaining business impacts for KM. Technology is an investment proposition. When viewed as a business enabler, we must not see a successful roll out of new technologies as the key driver of value. People drive value in knowledge management. The insight and action that are enabled from the use of collaborative, business intelligence and other KM tools is the true value proposition. All that we do in building these capabilities are investments towards business outcomes that were targeted in earlier phases of the knowledge management implementation process.

Measuring Business Impact

In measuring business impacts, two areas stand out as key focal points for measurement. We must measure the extent of participation by the employees, and we must measure business impacts. Figure 4 illustrates this point.

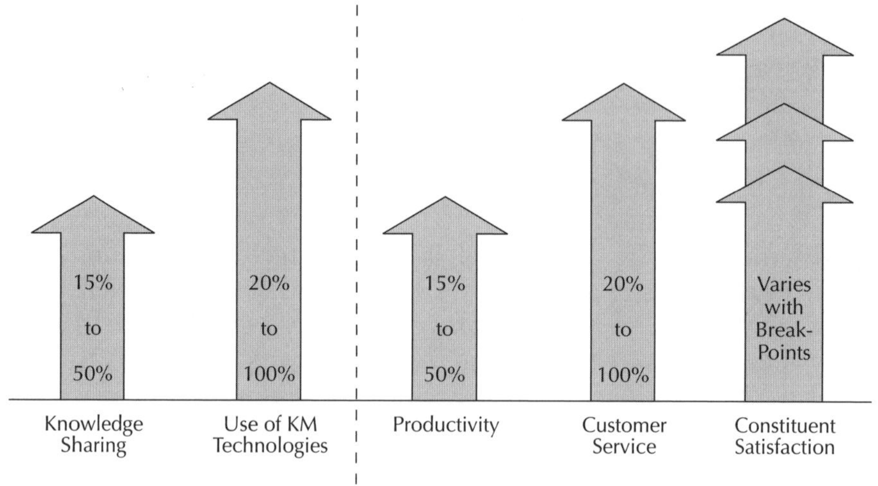

Figure 4. Measuring the Impact of KM

One technique found to be quite successful is that of "value assessments." The value assessment consists of two activities designed to gauge success in the participation and impact domains.

In the first activity, soon after the deployment of a KM system, conversations are aggressively conducted with end users to determine whether they are using the new system. These conversations are designed to uncover any issues that end users may have with using the system to support their daily business activity. If we discover that a particular user is not taking advantage of the system, the conversation would then focus on developing a plan to help users get to a point where they are using the system. Often, the reasons users give for not using a new system are very simple and can be overcome by additional training or personal assistance by the KM project team. Once we get the particular end user to use the system on a consistent basis, we can then move to the second step and begin to measure the value of the system based on predetermined measurement criteria. The important point here is that the second step cannot happen until it is known that end users are consistently using the KM system.

Step 4: Assist in Benefits Retention

This final step in justifying KM implementation within the government is the step that is most important to the long-term success of knowledge management. This step ensures that after we successfully deploy the first increment of KM capability we begin to focus on ensuring that the forecasted benefits continue to be achieved. This step is a logical segue from the measurement step but is more strategically focused. In benefits retention we suggest a focus on the following:

- Working with key executive and middle managers to ensure that their actions are helping to drive rather than hinder the achievement of business outcomes targeted for the KM implementation.

- Assisting executives to ensure that strategic planning processes for the organization include an appropriate focus on the role for knowledge management in achieving the organization's objectives. In other words, we periodically (annually) refine our use of KM technologies and techniques based on refinements in organizational strategy and business objectives.

- Ensuring that the infrastructure of KM people, processes, and technology is robust enough to support and continually drive KM throughout the organization.

We know that these activities may not be easy to implement in some organizations. Indeed they may be more important, from a strategic perspective for some government organizations than others. For example, any government organization that is in the business of producing knowledge may find that maintaining a strategic focus on KM is extremely important to its survival. Research and development organizations, intelligence organizations, and training institutions are good examples of this. Nonetheless, a focus on continually harvesting the benefits of KM is one that is often overlooked in large and small implementations. Our experience has shown that a proper focus here helps to drive both tactical and strategic momentum for KM within organizations.

In this chapter, we have described a process for planning and justifying KM projects by using a top-down, strategy-driven focus. However, experience has shown that one of the best ways to create a clear picture of how this all works is through a story. Therefore, the final pages of this chapter are devoted to a case study that illustrates some of the issues and considerations faced in building a business case and plan for KM initiatives.

The next section presents a case study about a mythical government organization, the U.S. Department of Knowledge (DOK). It is based on an actual KM planning project performed on a federal agency. The case study summarizes many of the processes and techniques discussed in this chapter and culminates with a description of how the up-front KM planning results in an implementation that is measured and focused on business impact.

CASE STUDY

Implementing Knowledge Management at the U.S. Department of Knowledge

The DOK is the United States' premiere government agency for creating and disseminating information about the services and capabilities of all federal agencies. DOK's mission is to create, collate, and disseminate information to the taxpayer about the services and performance history of all federal government organizations. During the past few years, DOK's mission has come under increased scrutiny. Taxpayers and Congress are questioning the relevance and value of performing the services that DOK offers. As a result, DOK has been asked to reduce its staffing by 30 percent over the next five years and to improve its ability to more effectively disseminate information to the public. Beginning next fiscal year, DOK will start to see the effects of downsizing on its budget ceilings.

In preparation for these sweeping changes, the CIO, CFO, and CKO have been tasked to form a rightsizing task force whose charter is to design a plan that will help DOK achieve these goals. Furthermore, the task force will analyze and recommend to the secretary of DOK regarding ways in which DOK can improve its public image so that it will be seen by Congress and taxpayers as a more viable and operationally effective entity. The task force must consider the perspectives and guidance provided by each of its founders, the CFO, CIO, and CKO. Chaired by the Chief Operations Officer (COO), the following guidance was provided to the task force:

- **From the CFO:** *We must learn how to do more with less. Any initiatives must show a positive return on investment within twelve months and must directly help us reach our rightsizing goals.*

- **From the CIO:** *In order to achieve these goals, we must do a far better job of leveraging our technology as an enabler. We could be 50 percent more productive just by automating workflow and minimizing the flow of paper. Technology has to be a part of the DOK right-sizing plan.*

- **From the CKO:** *Knowledge and our people are the key here. If we lose 30 percent of our knowledge workers over the next few years with no plan on how we will retain business-critical knowledge, we cannot succeed. We are past the days where headcount is the most critical measure of our capacity for work. This task force must make knowledge management the cornerstone of its charter and recommendations.*

As the task force chair, the COO, Ken Caller, knew that he must maintain the support from the three key leaders and the Secretary of Knowledge. The guidance that he had received from leadership intuitively made sense to him, but he needed to convert the guidance to an actionable plan for the task force. He devised the following four-step plan for the task force:

- *Step 1:* Determine business goals for DOK over the next five years.
- *Step 2:* Develop a list of initiatives to help DOK achieve these objectives. The initiatives must focus on measurable business benefits that support the business goals, balanced with their feasibility for success.
- *Step 3:* Consolidate the initiatives into a strategic plan to lead DOK to success in small measurable increments over the next two years.
- *Step 4:* Implement the plan and measure results.

Step 1: Determine Business Goals for DOK over the Next Five Years

The COO organized the task force, as shown in Figure 5. A business subcommittee was formed to analyze DOK's options for achieving the rightsizing objectives mandated by Congress. The business subcommittee was also responsible for addressing alternatives for improving DOK's image and significantly improving operational excellence in creating and disseminating information for public use. The technology subcommittee was formed to address information technology needed to support the recommendations coming from the business subcommittee. This committee worked directly with the CIO's office to understand gaps between current IT capabilities and future needs. Finally, an outcomes committee was formed to analyze business benefits of the initiatives brought forth by the task force. This committee was primarily responsible for facilitating the prioritization of efforts based on inputs from both the business and technology subcommittees. Value assessments and return on investments analyses that would be key components of the strategic plan were the responsibility of this subcommittee.

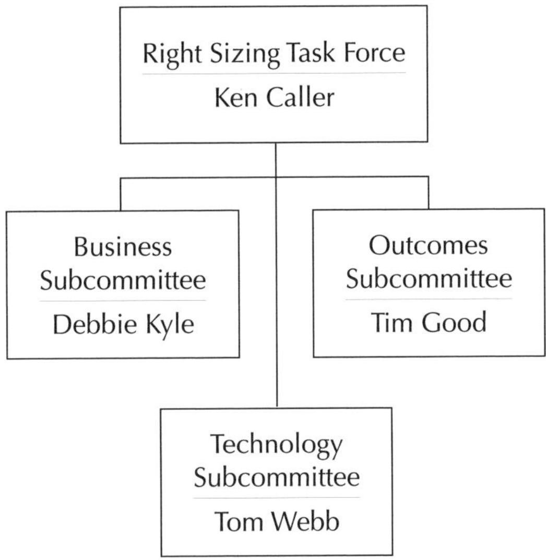

Figure 5. DOK's Rightsizing Task Force Organization

Ken, the COO, began work with the business subcommittee first. He first gave Debbie, the chairperson, the guidance he had been given by the CIO, CFO, and CKO. Next, both he and Debbie developed specific strategic objectives for DOK that would be used to guide the analysis of the business subcommittee. Their aim was to complete a vision for DOK's future that would accomplish the mandates set forth by Congress and their Secretary. Table 3 details the results of their work.

Using this information as a foundation, Debbie met with her committee to move forward with the second step of Ken's plan.

Step 2: Develop a List of Initiatives to Help DOK Achieve These Objectives

Armed with knowledge of the major business outcomes as a focus, Debbie held a brainstorming session with her subcommittee to discuss how each business outcome could be achieved. Given the magnitude of each outcome, she decided to hold at

Table 3. DOK's Business Outcomes and "Do Wells"

Business Drivers (Why?)	*Business Outcomes (What?)*	*"Do Wells" (Actions/How?)*
Rightsize DOK workforce in accordance with congressional and public mandate.	Reduce headcount by 6 percent over the next 12 months, enroute to five-year goal of 30 percent.	TBD by the business subcommittee.
Overcome current congressional and public scrutiny of DOK's mission and relevance to the needs of the taxpayer.	Increase DOK's relevance to the public by improving image and becoming more customer-intimate.	TBD by the business subcommittee.
Increase operational efficiency in disseminating information to the taxpayer.	Improve DOK workforce productivity by X % over the next 12 months and by X % per fiscal year through FY 2005.	TBD by the business subcommittee.

least two brainstorming sessions for each outcome area. The first session would focus on identifying initiatives that could achieve the outcome. This would include identifying business processes that would need to be transformed and the resulting information and knowledge that would be needed to support the change. The second session would then refine the analysis and identify technology needs to support the initiatives. The latter information would be passed to the technology subcommittee for further analysis and insight into the feasibility of each initiative.

Picking up from where she and Ken left off, Debbie used Table 4 to facilitate the first brainstorming session for each outcome.

In the first session, on outcome #1, Debbie's subcommittee needed clarification on the term "do well." One person asked,

Table 4. DOK's KM Candidate Initiatives

	Initiatives	
Business Outcome (What?)	*"Do Wells" (Actions/How?)*	*"Know Wells" (Information and Knowledge Needs)*
1. Reduce headcount by 6 percent over the next 12 months, enroute to the five-year goal of 30 percent.	1. Manage and forecast knowledge skills and abilities (KSA) needs by critical business function. 2. Transfer mission-critical knowledge from exiting personnel to remaining employees. 3. Reduce headcount through: • Natural turnover and retirement • Targeted release and career transfers of nonmission critical workers.	1. Need to know: • Critical business functions • Critical knowledge and skills by function • People who possess these skills • Projected retirement dates for these people. 2. Need to know: • Who is forecasted to leave in the next three years and when • Candidates for protégés • Knowledge that must be transferred • Progress on the knowledge transfer. 3. Need to know: • When employees are retiring • Where opportunities exist for employees targeted for release • Career aspirations of targeted employees • Public perceptions of DOK rightsizing initiative.

"Are we trying to determine the things we must do well as a business entity going forward or are we describing what the initiative must do well to be considered successful?" To this question, Debbie answered that we are discussing *both*. She explained that each initiative that the group identifies will become an integral part of how business is conducted at DOK and, therefore, is inseparable from the "do wells" of the business. In some cases, the initiative may change how business is done in a significant way. Debbie also clarified that because DOK's success is highly dependent on the knowledge of its people, the information and knowledge needs of the people must be understood as they discuss these new initiatives. For example, how can decisions on rightsizing be made unless they have the ability to know where they may suffer knowledge losses, particularly knowledge losses in critical business functions? Table 4 documents some ideas that the committee chose to achieve the outcome of reducing headcount. This thought process was repeated for the other two sessions.

During the final session, the business subcommittee focused on determining the specific solutions needed to enable the actions listed from the first session. Clearly, current business processes at DOK were going to require transformation if the department was to be successful in reaching its performance goals. Several daunting challenges stood in the way, including information technology shortfalls and some organizational culture concerns. For example, the department did not have an information system that could provide reliable workforce statistics to support workforce planning. They needed this to enable managers to perform the actions discussed earlier. More challenging was the fact that the culture of DOK would make it very difficult for managers to act on workforce reduction decisions even if they did have the proper management information. Many DOK managers and staff had worked together for more than 15 years. Managers were already complaining of the possibility of having to transfer or "lay off" valuable friends and co-workers.

Debbie invited Tom Webb, head of the technology subcommittee, to each of her final sessions. Tom could help the business subcommittee with ideas on how technology could be used as an enabler to some of the initiatives. Tom was also very aware of some of the latest KM technologies that could support DOK's needs because he worked directly for the CKO. After just a few minutes of listening to the business subcommittee's discussions,

Tom came up with a few key technology solutions. His recommendations for outcome number 1 are shown in Table 5:

Table 5. DOK's KM Alternative Solutions

	Initiatives		
		Alternative Solutions	
Business Outcome (What)	*"Do Wells" (Actions/How?)*	*Solution*	*Major Features & Functions*
1. Reduce headcount by 6 percent over the next 12 months, enroute to five-year goal of 30 percent.	1. Manage and forecast knowledge, skills, and abilities (KSAs) needs by critical business function.	1. A workforce planning and forecasting system that extracts information from the human resources system and forecasts KSAs at the business function level.	• Allow KSA forecasting • Are Web-enabled • Enable entry and changing of KSAs for each employee • Provide aggregate reporting of KSA gaps and shortfalls • Supports entry and management of mentor-protégé relationships to support Outcome #2.
	2. Transfer mission-critical knowledge from exiting personnel to remaining employees.	2. A knowledge-sharing and collaboration system that enables the electronic storing of best practices and mission-critical knowledge. This system would enable employees involved in mentor-protégé programs to share experiences across geography and time.	• Allow Web-enabled network collaboration • Provide for virtual meeting and whiteboard • Store audio and video files for search and retrieval • Provide expertise secretary and search • Enable mentor-protégé reporting and tracking.

Business Outcome (What)	*Initiatives*		
		Alternative Solutions	
	"Do Wells" (Actions/How?)	*Solution*	*Major Features & Functions*
	3. Reduces headcount through: natural turnover and retirement; and targeted release and career transfers of nonmission-critical workers.	3. See solution # 1.	• Add functionality for tracking job openings and opportunities across federal government; • Provide web-enabled access to employees to access career opportunity information; and • Enable employees to apply for opportunities via the Web.

Tom recommended two technology solutions to support this business outcome. He also concluded that his technology subcommittee had their work cut out for them because he knew the department did not have the technology in place to support some of the needs described in Table 5. He could already envision some near-term and longer term projects that he and his committee would discuss to quickly enable the department with the needed capabilities. As he left the last session, Tom recommended that Debbie and her business subcommittee think about how DOK would overcome cultural barriers to get managers to use the new solutions to achieve stated business goals. In his mind, that was a far greater challenge than the technology solutions he would now tackle.

Step 3: Consolidate the Priorities into a Strategic Plan to Lead DOK to Success in Small Measurable Increments over the Next Two Years

Let's review quickly the organization of Ken's rightsizing task force. If you remember, Ken established an outcomes subcommittee, led by Tim Good, to ensure that a measurable plan was developed to ensure that DOK's investments in rightsizing initiatives bore fruit for the enterprise (see Figure 5).

To that end, Tim's subcommittee had to accomplish the following:

- Assess value of the proposed solutions
- Prioritize them based on technology, organizational, and financial risks
- Develop a measurement plan.

In effect, Tim saw his charter as ensuring that the recommendations from the rightsizing task force would add value in the near term (under 12 months) and that there was a clear way to measure business outcomes. Working with his team and armed with the results of the business subcommittee's analysis, Tim focused on how he would help the rightsizing task force prioritize work and measure results. Debbie's group had done a great job in describing high-level value propositions across the three business outcome focal points. Tom was busy with his technology subcommittee planning the technology solutions and initial budget estimates for each. Tim began preparing for how he would use these inputs to set priorities and measure results.

Tim wanted to keep the process simple and intuitive. He directed his committee to produce an output that was appropriate for executive-level consumption. The tool used to evaluate and prioritize alternatives is depicted in Table 6:

Table 6. DOK's KM Project Prioritization Scoring
U.S. Department of Knowledge Rightsizing Initiative
Date: February 1, 2001

Project	*Priority Score*[1]	*Business Value Ranking*[2]	*Feasibility and Risks Ranking*
1. Workforce planning and forecasting system	3	1	2
2. Knowledge sharing and collaboration system	4	2	2

Legend:

Priority score was derived by totaling business and feasibility rankings. Lower score means higher priority.

Business value ranking based on the following criteria: scoring: 1 = high 2 = medium 3 = low

Feasibility and risks ranking based on the following criteria: Scoring: 1 = high 2 = medium 3 = low

Scoring: 1 = high 2 = medium 3 = low

Table 6 contains a small sample of the projects that were ranked. To obtain this ranking, Tim first led his team through a process of selecting the criteria that would be used to compare projects. The criteria were selected based on their relevance to the department's goals and internal challenges. For example, the risks and feasibility criteria included the extent to which the project could enable the achievement of the targeted business outcome while overcoming managers' reluctance to lay off employees.

Once criteria had been identified and defined, a simple scoring scheme of one to three points was used to determine the rankings. Tim's group gave great thought to ensuring that the scoring scheme left little to no ambiguity as to how a project would be scored. Once complete, Tim used the scoring matrix as a tool to verify the rankings with the rest of the rightsizing task force. Generally, the business subcommittee reviewed and verified the business value scores, and the technology subcommittee focused on the feasibility and risks. With only a few minor exceptions, the matrix was approved for inclusion in the strategic plan.

The final task that Tim's outcomes subcommittee performed was to prepare a measurement plan. The intent of this plan was twofold:

- Complete an in-depth, cost-benefit analysis for the top priority projects
- Prepare a straightforward plan for measuring the business benefits and costs of the projects as a prerequisite to proceeding with implementation.

The cost-benefit analysis was straightforward. By the time Tim was ready to conduct this work, Tom Webb, the technology subcommittee leader, had completed his analysis of needed technologies and provided Tim with associated costs for the priority projects. However, as Tim's group discussed benefits, they discovered some ancillary, intangible benefits that did not lend themselves to traditional return on investment (ROI) analysis. The KM collaboration project, for example, would help the organization collect knowledge from retiring experts, which would indirectly make it easier for DOK to manage the mandated attrition of some knowledge workers. This could be measured, to some degree, by the extent to which cost savings with rightsizing began to accrue with no appreciable productivity losses. However, how would DOK account for the anticipated increases in employee satisfaction due to the improved ability to find expertise using the expertise database and locator? This was a tremendous benefit but could only be described qualitatively in the cost-benefit analysis.

Tim chose to design and include in his measurement plan a survey that would be used to query employees on the utility and value of the collaboration technology project. He would use the survey to baseline the current level of satisfaction in workers' ability to find and collaborate with department experts. During implementation, he would follow through to determine the degree to which these scores changed as a result of managers' using the new technology.

The resulting measurement plan included a table like Table 7. The outcomes subcommittee wanted to ensure that the summary included both tangible and intangible measures of business impact. Intangibles were described in prose and typically presented after all the tangible benefits and measures were described.

Table 7. DOK's Performance Measurement Plan
U.S. Department of Knowledge Rightsizing Initiative Performance Measurement Plan Date: February 1, 2001

Project	*Key Performance Indicator(s)*	*Baseline Performance Level*	*Targeted Performance Level*	*Business Benefits*
1. Workforce planning and forecasting system				
2. Knowledge sharing and collaboration system				

Legend:

Tim presented the Performance Measurement Plan to Ken Caller, head of the rightsizing task force. Ken gave the plan high marks. He used the plan and all the previous subcommittee deliverables as the foundation for the rightsizing strategic plan. After review by the CFO, CIO and CKO, the strategic plan was approved, and Ken was given the task to lead the implementation of the priority projects.

Step 4: Implement the Plan and Measure Results

As planned, Ken Caller established a team of information technology and human resources practitioners to develop and implement the KM systems. The human resources department was brought in to advise managers on issues related to managing performance expectations. This was a very important facet of each project because DOK employees had never been challenged or evaluated in knowledge sharing and collaboration. The human resources department decided to redesign performance evaluations to encourage workers to collaborate and share ideas and best practices.

As each project evolved from pilot phase to enterprise-wide usage, Ken directed a project member to interview the affected managers. The interviews focused first on ensuring the manager was using the system. Managers were then asked to assess the extent to which the system enabled them to perform their roles better. These questions focused on intangible value and when compared to the baseline responses obtained at the beginning of the project, helped to assess intangible business impacts. Finally, tangible benefits were measured using the key performance indicators (KPIs) established in the measurement plan.

After the first 12 months, DOK was well on its way to achieving many of its crucial rightsizing mandates, primarily due to the successful use of KM tools and techniques.

CHAPTER SUMMARY

This chapter has described a four-step process aimed at maximizing the value obtained from KM projects. We have also shared some examples of tools and techniques that can be applied in planning KM projects. Finally, we have illustrated how some of the processes and techniques could be used within a case study on a mythical federal government agency.

The ultimate aim of this chapter is to help jump-start your KM projects. As a parting thought, as you pursue KM within your organization, we suggest you view each project as a step in a longer journey toward knowledge-centricity. This journey follows an evolving maturity continuum similar to the one shown in Figure 6.

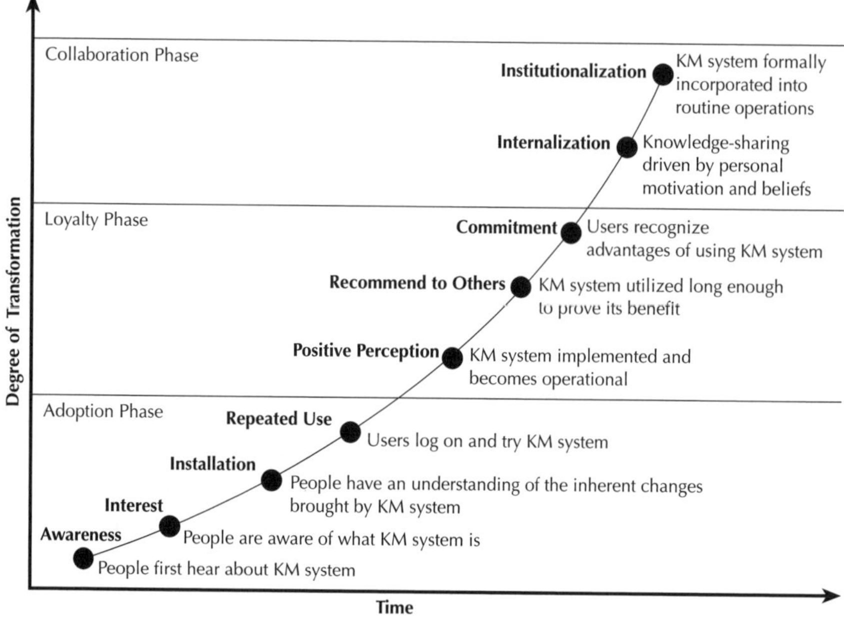

Figure 6. The KM Journey

We need a focus on discipline and the tactical project-level successes to catalyze this evolution toward knowledge-centricity. Focus on people. Measure for results. Use technology to enable the transformation.

CHAPTER 16

Creating Knowledge-Based Communities of Practice

Lessons Learned from KM Initiatives at AMS

Cathy Hirsh
Mark Youman
Susan Hanley

American Management Systems, Inc. (AMS) today has a successful and widely recognized knowledge management (KM) program, but it did not happen overnight. Its journey to become an effective knowledge-leveraging organization has been an evolution, with many challenges along the way. This chapter presents a case study of how AMS established its current KM program and the lessons it learned during the process. It provides a brief background on the drivers that alerted AMS to the need for improving the way knowledge is leveraged across the enterprise and discusses the challenges of implementing the KM program in place today. It continues with a discussion of the AMS KM framework, which outlines how people, process, and technology were integrated to deliver value to client engagement teams. The chapter emphasizes the "people component" of the framework—the AMS knowledge center®—which consists of the virtual communities of practice in AMS's eight core business disciplines. Key lessons that AMS has learned from implementing its KM framework, as well as the results of the KM initiatives for the primary stakeholders in the process, are shared. Finally, the chapter includes a description of how KM initiatives in the federal enterprise can learn from the process AMS followed.

An earlier version of this chapter appeared in *Knowledge Management and Virtual Organizations*, edited by Yogesh Malhotra and published by Idea Group Publishing (2000). Reprinted by permission of the publisher.

THE NEED FOR KM AT AMS

In the early years of AMS's history, knowledge was shared in the coffee rooms and in the hallways. The company, which was started by a small group of U.S. Department of Defense "whiz kids" in 1970, leveraged its relatively small size for flexibility and efficiency. As AMS grew, however, it began to experience some of the pain associated with the way it was growing—rapidly and across many locations often thousands of miles apart, with a mix of cultures and personalities.

In an effort to become a billion-dollar organization, AMS needed to manage its growth and ensure that it would continue to win business by maintaining a competitive advantage and fostering strong relationships with existing clients. In 1992, as part of the management strategy process, senior executives closely examined the way AMS was leveraging its people and their collective knowledge. The company, with thousands of people in offices around the world, was relying on a 20-year-old knowledge-sharing model. This "water cooler" model was sufficient when AMS had 500 employees on only 50 engagements, but not with thousands of employees on 500 engagements around the world. Clearly, changes had to be made. Strategies for pursuing engagements were not easily shared, project teams across the company were individually solving similar technical problems, and there was no way of knowing what knowledge resided where within the company.

IMPLEMENTATION CHALLENGES

As a result of the strategy process in the early 1990s, AMS began implementing a series of KM initiatives. In their book *Working Knowledge: How Organizations Manage What They Know*, Tom Davenport and Larry Prusak suggest that firms should try to use existing management approaches and initiatives to "jump-start" KM programs.[1] This is the approach that AMS used. Values and competencies formed the foundation of AMS's strategy, and a strong company-wide culture of teamwork and knowledge sharing shaped all of its activities. Still, AMS faced a number of challenges during the process of building the KM program it has in place today. First, AMS had to *find* the knowledge that everyone knew already existed both within and outside the company. Next, it had to *capture and organize* this knowledge, and finally, it had to *share* the knowledge globally.

Finding the Knowledge

Meeting the challenge of finding AMS's knowledge started with creating two formal business groups: the AMS Center for Advanced Technologies® (AMSCAT) and the AMS knowledge centers. The two groups, whose charters include identifying and researching innovative technologies that deliver practical business value for AMS clients and the AMS Best Practices Program, make a formal effort to discover, disseminate, and apply the best methodology and management practices from both inside and outside the organization. In addition to a full-time research staff, AMSCAT also includes advanced technology associates from across the company as well as practitioners who commit to advancing the research agenda of the center. At the same time, these individuals time-share their experiences and insights with other members of the community and the company at large.

AMS business unit managers identified the original group of associates. Today, associates "nominate" themselves for membership by describing the contribution they will make. In 1996, AMS established additional communities of associates, each representing an AMS core competency. These associates, like AMSCAT associates, make a formal commitment to contribute to the process of "finding" knowledge within the firm. The communities of associates together form what is now known as the AMS knowledge centers.

Capturing and Organizing the Knowledge

Although KM is not about simply deploying the latest technology, AMS recognized that technology would be the *enabler* to allow it to capture, store, and organize the knowledge it was beginning to collect. The company embraced several enabling technologies that are still integral to making KM work at AMS today: voice mail, e-mail, video teleconferencing, and the most crucial, Lotus Notes. The Lotus Notes databases are expansive, corporate-wide knowledge repositories that are organized as the AMS corporate intranet under the umbrella term, the AMS Knowledge Express®.

The Knowledge Express databases include more than 10 gigabytes of data, with more than three gigabytes accessed every day by AMS staff around the world. These databases are accessible by client teams onsite, who can maintain local copies of the databases they need and view others when necessary using the internal network or the Internet. The range of information captured by the Knowledge Express is vast—best practices, examples of the best of the company's work products with key insights and lessons learned in their creation, and continual research into new technologies and techniques. Nearly all of AMS's intellectual capital is stored in the Knowledge Express, and a core team, which includes professional librarians, monitors the growing content of key databases to ensure that it is accurate, current, and useful.

Sharing the Knowledge

Once AMS found a way to collect and organize corporate knowledge, the third challenge was to ensure that the knowledge could be shared across the company. Today, all employees have access to the AMS Knowledge Express at their desktops. The Knowledge Express includes a growing number of portal interfaces to the content to help ensure that knowledge can be shared effectively.

Even with a robust technological infrastructure, however, it soon became clear that there would be times when AMS staff would be unable to get content electronically—and so a people infrastructure, AMS Know, was developed. AMS Know is a highly efficient information service staffed by professional reference librarians who find vital information for project teams quickly and efficiently. As online resources have grown both inside and outside AMS, the need for this kind of serious research help has became imperative. AMS Know staff handle information requests via phone and e-mail for consultants across the company, ranging from questions such as "Who at AMS knows about C++?" to "What are the call-pattern trends in the U.S. telecommunications market?" If the AMS Know staff person is unable to answer a consultant's question directly, he or she connects that consultant with another AMS employee who can. AMS Know is an increasingly valuable vehicle for sharing AMS's knowledge.

THE AMS KM FRAMEWORK

The three challenges of building a successful KM program led to the framework AMS eventually embraced: a mixture of people, process, and technology. AMSCAT and the Best Practices Program form the process component of the framework—the focus within these programs is on research, discovery, dissemination, and practice. The Knowledge Express is the technology component. The heart of AMS's KM initiative, however, is the people component of the framework—the formal communities of practice, the AMS knowledge centers.

Even before AMS began undertaking a formal KM initiative, it had a model that worked: networks of people who formed informal communities united by common interest or experience. These groups flourished on their own when the company was smaller. However, as the company continued to expand at a rapid rate (with many new, experienced people being hired who had lots of information to share), a formal model needed to be developed to ensure that the "heart" of the knowledge sharing culture continued to beat and that AMS would still be able to deliver successes for its clients. Two types of formal "people networks" are currently established at AMS: communities of interest and communities of practice.

Communities of Interest: Special Interest Groups (SIGs)

AMS's communities of interest are known as special interest groups (SIGs). Membership in a SIG is open to any person with an interest in learning or sharing more about a business or technology topic. SIGs flourish, based on need, and tend to be wrapped around either a particular technology (such as object-oriented programming), a concept (such as leadership), or a problem (such as Y2K).

SIGs are not formally funded. The momentum behind them usually comes from an energetic leader and a core group of people with a passion about the topic. Anyone can be a member of any number of SIGs. There is no expected deliverable from members—the primary goal is to provide a forum for members to share and learn and to apply that knowledge on their engagements. Because there is no commitment, a person can choose to go to meetings or skip them; to participate actively in discussions or "lurk" in the background; or to read group e-mails, yet not respond. These SIGs are not accountable for tangible blocks of reusable knowledge for AMS's collective knowledge base. They do, however, bring together people with knowledge to share and help the company identify who may be most interested or experienced in a topic as a useful starting point when looking for information on that topic.

Communities of Practice: The AMS Knowledge Center

AMS has always had a culture that rewards people for leveraging their knowledge. The company embraces the concept of "one firm," with all employees and clients benefiting from the full range of AMS's experiences and expertise; in fact, it has made that idea part of the corporate business strategy. This knowledge-sharing culture helps define AMS and has been recognized and praised by people both inside and outside the company. AMS facilitates knowledge leverage by connecting people through the AMS knowledge centers.

Unlike the SIGs, where anyone can join and take a very "low-key" role, participating in the knowledge centers requires active involvement. The knowledge centers are virtual communities of practice in AMS's core disciplines, which include:

- Business process renewal
- System development and information technology management
- Organization development and change management
- Advanced technologies
- Engagement and project management
- Customer value management
- KM
- E-commerce.

Taken together, the skills and experience developed within the framework of the knowledge center represent the practical way AMS leverages the collective knowledge of all of its employees to take the best of that collective knowledge and experience to every client engagement.

Because the knowledge centers are virtual communities, they traditionally have been supported by only a very small number of full-time staff. Each knowledge center community is led by a team of coordinators who are recognized as leaders in their respective disciplines. Coordinators are full-time practitioners of that competency. Their leadership role in the knowledge center requires a commitment of about three to four weeks each year.

Knowledge Center Associates

Members of the knowledge center, called associates, are all experienced practitioners in their discipline who agree to make an explicit contribution to AMS's intellectual capital each year. This contribution, the associates program, helps AMS continually grow the knowledge base, with contributions that reflect the direction and strategy of the firm. Associates include not only the company's leading practitioners but its emerging leaders as well. The most important criterion for membership in a knowledge center is the willingness and ability of the member to make a valuable contribution.

What sets members of the knowledge center apart from other employees in the company is that while everyone at AMS is expected to contribute and share knowledge, knowledge center associates are required to do so if they wish to remain part of the community. These are communities of experienced practitioners; therefore, associates' contributions are ones that AMS wants to share across the company.

Reusable Knowledge

Although a commitment to making a knowledge contribution is required, AMS does not simply harvest what its employees know through the knowledge centers. The company does not want disconnected bits of information; it does not want content without the context that experience provides. The knowledge center program emphasizes that its associates must contribute *reusable* knowledge (practical rather than theoretical). The result is that associates' projects have a clear and direct link to practical applications on AMS projects. In the spirit of providing content with context, associates also agree to be willing to solve problems "in the moment," by responding to e-mail directed to their community as appropriate and by being an acknowledged source of information in their area of expertise.

KEY LESSONS LEARNED

AMS's KM initiatives have become imperative as the company continues to grow. These initiatives have been successful thus far, but their success has not come without challenges. Looking to the future of KM at AMS, the company has crystallized five lessons learned from the process of developing the program:

1. Recognize individual achievement.
2. Build group identity.
3. Motivate and reward participation.
4. Celebrate successes.
5. Deliver value.

These lessons have provided guidance for developing many facets of the program that still exist, as well as a framework for new enhancements that AMS has just begun to implement.

Recognizing Individual Achievement

Before becoming a knowledge center associate, a prospective member must first be nominated. For several years, the associates program was structured so that business unit managers nominated only those people who exhibited a superior knowledge of a specific discipline. This model led to the development of small groups of highly skilled practitioners who generally had to gain several years of experience before being considered for inclusion. To be selected was in itself a recognition of the skill that person had attained.

Today the nomination process has expanded to include not just current experts, but also those emerging or "next generation" experts whom AMS wants to develop to be its future experts. To help identify these emerging experts, AMS instituted a self-nomination process so that any person with a sincere interest in a discipline and a meaningful contribution to make could be considered for inclusion. Opening the nomination process stemmed concerns that the program was elitist, yet the selection process remains rigorous. Knowledge center coordinators review all proposed projects to make sure that the proposal has value to AMS and that the nominee meets the basic qualification criteria for each knowledge center. Business unit managers must still provide approval and funding for all associates' projects. They also have the opportunity to nominate other candidates for the program who they feel would make an excellent contribution but who may require an extra incentive—formal recognition of their ability to make a contribution—to encourage their participation. To be an associate is still recognition that the employee has valuable knowledge to contribute to the company as a whole. Being recognized for membership in a knowledge center comes not just at a corporate level but also at the level in the organization where there is a person who has direct responsibility for performance evaluations and promotion.

AMS recognizes individual contributions in many other ways as well. Aside from special awards for outstanding contributions by individual associates, AMS has implemented "Knowledge in Action" awards as a method of recognizing individuals who have successfully leveraged the AMS knowledge base. The winners of the Knowledge in Action award embody the essence of AMS's knowledge-sharing culture. These financial-equivalent awards are distributed at the annual associates conference.

Building Group Identity

As AMS has tried to replicate the success of the "coffee room" environment on a global scale, the value of building a group identity has become apparent. Building group identity within the knowledge center starts early with all associates receiving identifiable business cards. The process continues with an infrastructure that includes e-mail and voice mail distribution lists and collaborative databases to facilitate communications among the members of each knowledge center community.

Every AMS employee has access to the repository of knowledge available on the Knowledge Express, but the knowledge centers are also set apart by developing a "home page" database for each community, dedicated to the interests of that community. These databases provide places where people can request help, post lessons learned and useful information, and engage in discipline-specific discussions. All employees have "read" access to these databases; only associates have "write" access.

Until recently, each knowledge center was largely responsible for building its own community using the "home page" databases and the energy of the community coordinators. Inevitably, some communities were more engaged than others. AMS realized that to truly leverage the many associate "volunteers," it would have to reach out to them proactively. From the beginning, frequent communications (through e-mail, newsletters, etc.) have played a key role. Recently, AMS also began to address this challenge by developing a role of knowledge manager for most of the knowledge centers.

The primary mission of the knowledge manager is to increase the value delivered by the knowledge center by increasing awareness and use of the assets in each discipline and building and leveraging AMS intellectual capital. The knowledge manager is a subject matter expert in each discipline who proactively contributes content, as well as synthesizes knowledge from other sources. The knowledge manager is a key factor in building a group identity because he or she will plan events, work closely with the knowledge center coordinators to encourage active associate participation, and continuously monitor the "home page" database, looking for ways to stimulate discussion in the database and advertise content. AMS's success with the knowledge manager role has been promising so far, and the vision is to have one full-time knowledge manager dedicated to each of AMS's core disciplines.

Motivating and Rewarding Participation

Many organizations have found that when undertaking any KM initiative, motivation and reward are among the two biggest issues related to success. These factors are especially important when the knowledge to be shared is being leveraged with technology, which today requires intellectual capital in written form. After all, the people who are expected to contribute content already have full-time jobs. How do you get people who are already working ten- to twelve-hour days to spend "just a little more time" to write something down so that it may help someone else (someone else they may not know and who may not even thank them)? Even the most altruistic of people will be forced to prioritize tasks and may not carry through on a good intention. Undoubtedly, motivation is a big challenge.

At AMS, it has helped that the culture historically has tied success (promotions) to how well an individual leverages knowledge. The company has also formally motivated people by making the associates program (and a tangible associates project) a requirement for inclusion in a knowledge center community. AMS learned the value of this requirement through experience. In the first year of the program, when no contribution was required for membership, approximately one-half of the 1,100 associates committed to completing an associates project. Of those who made a commitment, only 70 percent (or approximately 400 people) actually completed their proposed projects.

In contrast, the following year AMS required that 100 percent of associates make a commitment. As a result, the pool of associates became much smaller—only 800 people were willing to become involved and make the commitment. Again, there was a completion rate of approximately 70 percent. However, that 70 percent amounted to approximately 560 completed projects in the second year. So, although the community was nearly 30 percent smaller, the actual contribution was more than 40 percent larger than in the first year.

Since that time, AMS has continued to make the formal commitment to complete an associates project a prerequisite to membership in a knowledge center. Many employees have the completion of an associates project written into their formal performance objectives for the year and thus have tied their participation to financial incentives external to the program.

Beyond the formal commitment, AMS has developed a number of other highly successful techniques for motivating and rewarding knowledge-sharing commitments. Every member of a knowledge center community is listed on the "Board of Associates" at headquarters. Every client visiting the building stops at the board; most spend time looking for the names of key people on their project. AMS employees realize that inclusion on the board sends a powerful message to clients, and most people do not want to be left out. The most highly leveraged associate contributions are publicized in an online collection and acknowledge both the author and the contributor (if not the same person). Providing visibility is an excellent motivator for participation.

Aside from recognizing associates by name, AMS also rewards participation in more tangible ways. Last year, AMS implemented a cash award to the employee whose submission to the "examples library" was reused the most times. Shirts, embroidered with the knowledge center name, were given to every associate who completed a project. These relatively inexpensive gestures are greatly valued by the associates who receive them.

Finally, the annual associates conference has come to be one of the most powerful motivation and reward mechanisms of the entire AMS KM initiative. The conference is an invitation-only, face-to-face event featuring a wide variety of workshops for networking and learning that are planned and organized by associates across all eight of AMS's disciplines. The conference always features a keynote address by a well-known thought leader in the KM arena. Each year the conference generates more excitement and enthusiasm among the associates' communities.

Celebrating Successes

The annual conference has also become a vehicle for celebrating the successes of the associates, with a number of associates' awards being distributed at the event. At another AMS conference, for senior AMS staff, awards are given for both the creation and reuse of knowledge assets. On a more day-to-day basis, AMS publishes online links to associate papers and stories about individuals or project teams who have reused knowledge successfully in both the associates newsletter and other corporate-wide publications.

Celebrating the successes of individuals has translated into recognition for the program as a whole. AMS has received numerous awards for its knowledge-sharing culture[2] and proudly publicizes these awards to the AMS community. Associates take pride in these external recognitions of a program that they have worked so hard to nurture. AMS creates its own self-fulfilling, continually renewing prophecy: the company shows associates that it is doing things right and that AMS has been recognized externally for its successes. Employees take that knowledge to heart and extend an extraordinary effort to make the program a success, external organizations applaud the program's success, and so on. Unabashedly celebrating the things AMS does right goes a long way toward ensuring that things continue to go right in the future.

Delivering Value

AMS's commitment to both sharing and advancing knowledge as a company enables it to deliver superior value and to increase its effectiveness in serving three primary stakeholders: the clients, the employees, and the company. Ultimately, the benefit to these stakeholders is the driver behind every new plan implemented.

All AMS employees, not just associates, benefit from the lessons and insights that are shared by associates through the completion of their projects. AMS as a whole benefits from the infrastructure that enables each employee to leverage the entire explicit intellectual capital of the organization. In addition, the company is able to leverage the tacit knowledge of the employees through the directed e-mail messages that are sent to the specific community of experts most likely to be able to provide solutions. The typical "solution time" for an e-mail question sent to a knowledge center community is 12 to 24 hours. In 1998, the knowledge centers' resources enabled AMS to save more than $5.5 million through the ability to provide rapid solutions to critical problems. This efficiency allows AMS to deliver rapid, high-quality solutions to the most challenging problems on client engagements. Clients, in turn, can leverage the entire knowledge and expertise of AMS on each and every engagement.

RESULTS OF THE PROGRAM

Measuring the value of KM initiatives is almost as challenging as implementing them. AMS works continually to improve the way this value is measured. The measurement approach includes tracking key metrics as well as collecting "serious anecdotes" from clients and employees documenting the value of the initiatives.

Clearly, AMS's KM initiatives have had a positive effect on the overall working atmosphere at the company. However, the success of the overall program cannot truly be measured without looking at the results of the program from a number of different perspectives: financial, customer, internal business, and innovation and learning.

Financial Perspective

From the financial perspective, AMS has saved significant labor costs in terms of how it has helped consultants avoid "spinning their wheels" by providing easy-to-use, fast, and effective mechanisms for getting at the knowledge that exists within the company. For example, AMS Know resolved more than 8,000 knowledge requests in 1998. Funding a team of four highly skilled reference librarians who know where and how to search for information has saved significant labor dollars. The librarian staff's speed and efficiency at performing research resulted in an estimated $500,000 saved in 1998 alone. This financial figure does not take into account the quality of the information they were able to deliver to project teams, which is of inestimable value.

AMS has profited from other components of its KM program as well. A recent survey of users of AMS's corporate Intranet indicated that the time saved by AMS consultants through the use of the Knowledge Express databases amounted to a savings of more than $5 million a year.

Customer Perspective

From the customer perspective, AMS has gained positive results from the KM initiatives as well. AMS is focused on delivering business benefits to clients. As expertise has grown in core disciplines, the company has also refined the way it works—organizing collective knowledge, developing effective delivery channels to share and apply this knowledge, and informing and training consultants in its use. As a result, AMS employees in all industry practices know where to find and how to use the rich repository of practical skills and experience that spans the company—across industries, across borders, across time zones, and across specialized competencies.

These KM initiatives are more than a way for clients to receive increased information, however. Through its KM initiatives, AMS is able to make its best practices available to every client engagement. Clients benefit because they receive *leveraged* knowledge—information of high value to them, based on the best of AMS's global experience, delivered by a team that can apply it.

Clients are able to see tangible evidence of AMS's commitment to KM, which is a critical way to provide assurance that AMS pays more than "lip service" to the idea of leveraging knowledge across the company. More than 300 clients visited AMSCAT and the AMS knowledge center facility in 1998. Visits such as these allow clients to see how it works, and most clients form a very favorable impression. According to Karla Pierce, Director of Transition for the Kansas Department of Revenue:

> *Because the challenges we faced impacted many parts of our operation, AMS's multi-disciplinary approach and the resources of their Knowledge Centers helped us achieve the integrated solutions we were seeking.*

AMS captures feedback from clients and shares it with people across the company to reinforce the importance of AMS's KM program to the company's bottom line.

Internal Business Perspective

AMS's groupware infrastructure enables it to respond rapidly to the needs of clients and employees, both for client work and for business development. Employees electronically shared more than 8,000 deliverable examples in 1998 and exchanged more than 70,000 e-mail messages every day.

How do these statistics translate into true internal business value? Again, testimonials make the picture clear. One AMS employee, a newly hired consultant, wrote about his experience when he sent out a directed e-mail to one of the knowledge center communities, looking for help preparing a requirements traceability matrix for one of his clients:

> *I was able to look at the way other projects have done it and, in fact, I am currently working to implement an approach that I hadn't originally considered. In the end, I not only received different ideas and considerations, but after deciding what my best approach was, I had* a finished, documented *product to work with. This saved a week of work—but it isn't a minimal product—it's professionally developed and ready for 100 percent reuse.*

AMS's emphasis on reusing knowledge saves project teams significant time and allows all employees to "bring the rest of AMS in their briefcase for every client engagement."

Innovation and Learning Perspective

Through its KM program, AMS offers a number of learning opportunities to the company as a whole. These learning tools include SIGs, databases, AMS Know, and KM and technical seminars. Some of the most valuable learning components, however, are the conferences and other events that bring together the core group of knowledge-sharing champions—the associates—to network and share ideas. In the words of one associate:

> *The opportunity to interact with people across AMS who have similar interests as mine, struggling with (or having solved!) the same*

> *issues, is absolutely invaluable to me. I also like the feeling of belonging to something that is broader than just my business unit and contributing in a way that helps others at AMS. I really get a better feel for what the whole of AMS is, not just my slice.*

KM initiatives have nurtured the corporate culture within AMS, a culture that values the sharing of knowledge and experience. Similarly, AMS values staff training that goes beyond simple training courses. In 1998, nearly all of the 800 associates participated in at least one workshop or conference. Sharing information creates a sense of belonging and camaraderie and reduces apathy, ultimately contributing to retention of employees.

APPLICATIONS IN THE FEDERAL GOVERNMENT

The need for KM in the federal sector has never been more critical. First, as the current generation of government workers retires, an urgent need arises to capture the knowledge that they have. Second, there is a unique driver in the government because knowledge exchange is not simply a support function but part of the core business of government.

Setting up Communities of Practice

The government can use communities of practice much like those represented by AMS's knowledge centers to capture knowledge. Communities of practice are not new to government. Government employees have long maintained informal networks of experts that they could leverage. These informal networks can prove highly valuable, but they can break down, leaving knowledge gaps that make the government enterprise less effective. High turnover and retirement threaten networks of expertise, and it can take years for new staff to develop networks of their own. Communities of practice can provide structure and consistency to these networks and can be based on cross-organizational expertise areas, common job functions, core business processes, or user groups of critical information systems.

Many federal organizations can only achieve their goals by working in close partnership with other government and private-sector organizations. Communities of practice provide a mechanism to improve the effectiveness of this extended government enterprise, allowing knowledge exchange on key topics while building new networks of people that can help achieve government's mission. These networks can provide federal organizations with information from key individuals with hands-on experience that they can share with others who are implementing, operating, or applying government policies, regulations, and programs. Federal organizations are uniquely positioned to play this facilitator role in establishing communities among multiple federal, state and local, academic, private sector, and citizen organizations.

The Federal Highway Administration (FHWA) uses online communities of practice to reach out to its partners in state and local government, as well as those in private organizations. These communities are designed to streamline inter-organizational processes, move innovative highway technologies into practice, gather lessons learned, and reach out to customers on key safety and environmental issues. *Rumble Strips*, the first of these communities, receives over 1,200 visits per month, most of them from the primary audience, state transportation organizations (http://safety.fhwa.dot.gov/rumblestrips). FHWA has designed a new, more interactive online community known as *Re:NEPA* that will be replicated for multiple internal and external communities (http://nepa.fhwa.dot.gov). These communities help achieve FHWA's strategic goals by enabling multidirectional knowledge exchange among experts, research and development professionals, practitioners, and citizen groups.

Knowledge for Serving the Citizen

This aspect of KM was definitely not a part of the AMS KM environment and is an important difference between the public and private sectors. KM can radically alter information/knowledge flow between the citizen and the government, and any KM system within the government has to take that interaction into account. While the tools and practices of KM have typically been applied to improving knowledge flow inside organizations, the application of KM to the customer interface (as well to interactions with suppliers and partners) directly improves customer service and program delivery. As part of its core business of serving the citizen, knowledge-sharing initiatives should not be pursued as a separate activity but as a direct part of delivering government programs and services.

When pursuing knowledge-sharing initiatives, government organizations need to do things very differently than when pursuing internal KM initiatives. An organization should start at the citizen/partner/supplier interface and work backward, first finding out what knowledge is needed and how it can be made available consistently across multiple access channels (Web, Interactive Voice Response, phone, face-to-face) and multiple contact points (headquarters, field, etc.). A mechanism must be in place to monitor needs, wants, and interactions so that appropriate tools and knowledge are made available to those who have direct contact with those citizens/partners/suppliers to provide high-quality, consistent service.

KM takes a very different shape when external service, rather than just internal knowledge sharing, is a requirement. KM can support a whole range of outward-facing initiatives; however, as stated earlier, the knowledge-sharing systems should be designed to implement these initiatives from the start, rather than adding them later. The sorts of knowledge-based external services that government has to consider include: running the business of government over the Web using direct self-service and access for government information and services; community-based portals for government partners to collaborate on key issues and projects; and customer relationship management engines that are integrated into the knowledge base to provide the tools for consistent information delivery.

An example of a customer-focused knowledge initiative is the Illinois Office of the Comptroller's *linc.net* (www.comptroller .state.il.us). The comptroller's office was faced with 60,000 requests per year for information about the state's finances and expenditures. The processes for answering the requests were manual, paper-intensive, and challenged by higher expectations for customer service and the wide range of customer information needs. Based on customer needs, the comptroller's office created a Web-based portal into a statewide financial information warehouse. Customers can browse and drill into the information on a 24-hour, seven-day-per-week basis. The knowledge solution not only provides faster service for less money, but it also provides a new level of service and satisfaction for the customer.

USING KNOWLEDGE

Combining internal knowledge and expertise with a way of working that provides every AMS consultant and engagement team with access to company-wide resources enables AMS to deliver solutions built through experience. It is how AMS delivers value to its stakeholders: to the individual, the company, and the clients. The result of AMS's KM initiatives is highly leveraged engagement teams with AMS's collective knowledge at their fingertips. This *is* KM: people, processes, and technology working together to deliver value. The government enterprise can use many of the same organizational ideas and techniques to create similar value, both for internal innovation and for delivery of government programs and information to the citizen.

NOTES

Davenport, T. and L. Prusak. *Working Knowledge: How Organizations Manage What They Know*. Cambridge, MA: Harvard Business School Press, 1997.

Moore A. An Environment for Innovation: American Management Systems. *KMWorld* [Online]. February 1, 1999. Available: http://www.kmworld.com/magazine/article.cfm?Article ID=325.

CHAPTER 17

Harnessing Customer Knowledge

Merging Customer Relationship Management with Knowledge Management

Timothy L. Cannon, PhD

In June 1999, the Department of the Navy identified a goal of improving decision-making ability through the implementation of strategies that facilitate the creation and sharing of knowledge.[1] The continually escalating amount of data and technology with which to capture and present it have led to increased complexity—not decreased—for making decisions. This increased complexity is driving the need for organizational knowledge management systems.

Nowhere is the proliferation and duplication of data more pronounced than in the gathering of customer information. And never has it been more difficult to understand the relationship between the organization and the customer. Using the paradigm of external and internal customers (or "Big C" and "Little c," as introduced by Treacy and Wiersema[2]), the Navy customers are employees, businesses, citizens, politicians, management, and international bodies. And sometimes the same person or entity can be more than one type of customer at the same time.

Poor decisions can be made without explicit knowledge of the customer's value to the organization or, more importantly, the organization's value to the customer, and the impact of the decisions may not be realized until after the customer has defected. By employing new techniques to harness the customer data and transform it into knowledge, customer defections can be slowed, resulting in increased customer satisfaction, improved quality, and decreased organizational cost.

Popular research today is littered with references to knowledge management (KM) and successful (and unsuccessful) applications of the approach. Most of the research is centered on how knowledge is captured and the cultural approaches for more effective capture. Great attention is paid to the importance of capturing the knowledge worker's product, yet little attention seems to be paid to the distribution of that knowledge to the ultimate recipient—the customer.

Paralleling the research activities in KM, the field of Customer Relationship Management (CRM) is reaching the forefront of research and popular acceptance with an equal amount of hope and promise. However, there has been little correlation of the two domains, each concentrating on its own microcosm. The purpose of this chapter is to draw a parallel between the two fields, identify how the two are truly complementary, and provide some examples of use.

WHAT IS KNOWLEDGE MANAGEMENT?

Many working definitions of KM have been offered over the years. Most center on the concept of creating and sharing the asset known as knowledge. Perhaps one of the most complete is the Gartner Group's.[3]

Before discussing KM, a perspective must be established around the term "knowledge." As shown in Figure 1, knowledge is but a point on the journey from data to wisdom. A distinction must be made between data, information, and knowledge. Data represent just a meaningless point in time when not considered in context. Information is about taking data and putting them into a meaningful pattern. Knowledge is the ability to use that information.

Information consists of data, passed through a person's mind, that becomes meaningful. It is something that happens as a per-

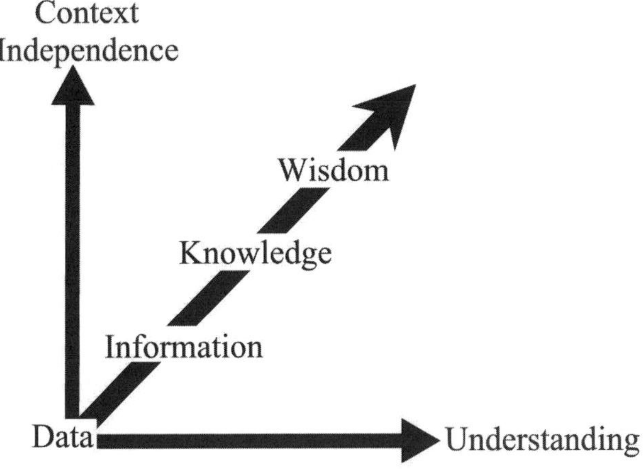

Figure 1. Data/Wisdom Continuum[4]

son mentally "decodes" the data from audible or visible expression. This may happen in the interaction between minds or between mind and objects or other pieces of information. The quality of information rapidly degrades over time and in distance from the source of production. Moreover, its value is highly subjective and conditional. For example, last year's newspapers are quite valuable to the historian; on the other hand, news that occurred more than an hour ago may have lost any relevance to a stockbroker. Therefore, information is experienced, not possessed.

Knowledge is generally divided into two types: explicit and tacit. Explicit knowledge is formal knowledge that can be packaged as information and can be found in the documents of an organization (e.g., reports, articles, manuals, patents, pictures, images, video, sound, software). Tacit knowledge is personal knowledge embedded in individual experience and is shared and exchanged through direct, person-to-person contact. Clearly, tacit knowledge can be communicated in a most direct and effective way. By contrast, acquisition of explicit knowledge is indirect: it must be decoded and recoded into one's mental models, where it is then internalized as tacit knowledge.

In reality, these two types of knowledge are like two sides of the same coin and are equally relevant for the overall knowledge of an organization. Tacit knowledge is practical knowledge that is key to getting things done but has been sadly neglected in the past, often falling victim to the latest management fad. For example, the recent spate of business process re-engineering initiatives, in which cost reduction is generally identified with the laying off of people—the real and only repositories of tacit knowledge—has damaged the tacit knowledge of many organizations. Explicit knowledge defines the identity, the competencies, and the intellectual assets of an organization independently of its employees, but it can grow and sustain itself only through a rich background of tacit knowledge.

Knowledge that does not flow does not grow, eventually aging and becoming obsolete and useless. By contrast, knowledge that flows by being shared, acquired, and exchanged generates new knowledge. Existing tacit knowledge can be expanded through its socialization in communities of interest and practice, and new tacit knowledge can be generated through the internalization of explicit knowledge by learning and training. New explicit knowledge can be generated through the externalization of tacit knowledge. Existing explicit knowledge can be combined to support problem solving and decision making through the application of data mining techniques to identify meaningful data relationships inside corporate databases. These four different phases of the knowledge lifecycle—socialization, internalization, externalization, and combination—have been formalized by Nonaka and Takeuchi in the diagram in Figure 2. Under this view, "knowledge management" can be explained as the management of the environment that makes knowledge flow through all the different phases of its life cycle.

IBM[5] has identified that to be valuable, KM must take on two dimensions. One dimension is knowledge type—from tacit knowledge, through project experiences, to explicit knowledge. The other dimension is knowledge community—from individuals, through teams and groups, to enterprise organizations. Tacit knowledge represents what works, discovered over time and through the experience of an individual or team. It normally resides in the minds of individuals and is a tremendously valuable

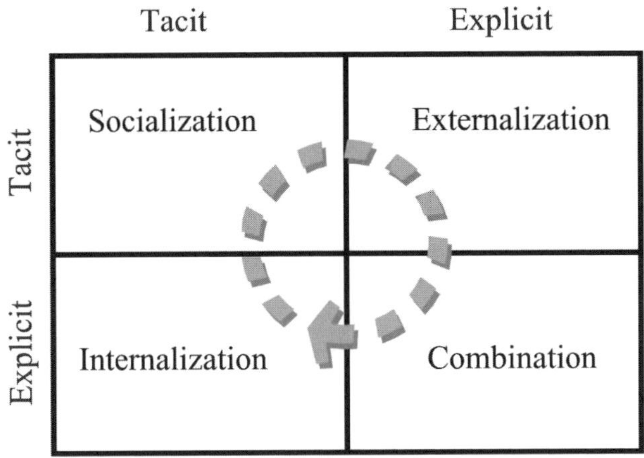

Figure 2. Knowledge Conversion[6]

corporate asset. Explicit knowledge is tacit knowledge that is documented and externally visible.

WHAT IS CUSTOMER RELATIONSHIP MANAGEMENT?

Customer Relationship Management (CRM) focuses on automating and improving the business processes associated with managing customer relationships in the areas of sales, marketing, customer service, and support. CRM software applications embody best practices and employ advanced technologies to help organizations achieve these goals. The primary benefit of CRM solutions is improved service, improved quality, and reduced cost.

CRM takes a very customer-oriented view of the entire customer life cycle, which means that CRM applications place the customer at the center of the organization's universe. CRM applications facilitate the coordination of multiple business functions (sales, marketing, and service) and focus them on satisfying the needs of the customer. CRM applications also coordinate multiple channels of communication with the customer—face-to-face, the call center, and the Web—so that organizations can accommodate their customers' preferred channels of interaction.

CRM applications provide the potential for a wide range of benefits to customers and companies, including, from the customer's perspective, enhanced, increasingly personalized, and instantaneous support; and from the company's perspective, additional sales and marketing opportunities resulting from the new channel's ability to capture customer information on an ongoing basis.

Sales, marketing, and customer service/support organizations work as separate entities in many organizations today. Faced with divisional boundaries, it is often very difficult for these different business functions to focus on their customers in a coordinated fashion. Take the example of a sales person going on a sales call, only to be blindsided by the fact that the customer has several unresolved service issues. By providing a common platform for customer communication and interaction, CRM solutions aim to eliminate the organizational stovepipes that allow problems like this to exist.

CRM applications are also designed to increase the effectiveness of employees who interact with customers. The use of CRM applications can lead to improved customer responsiveness and a more comprehensive view of the entire customer life cycle. CRM solutions that tie directly into back-office systems are particularly enticing because companies can take prospects and existing customers through a closed-looped set of well-defined steps and processes to satisfy their needs. While CRM applications provide the framework for embodying, promoting, and executing best practices in customer-facing activities, back-office provides the backbone, resources, and operational applications to make organizations more efficient in achieving these goals.

CRM FUNCTIONAL CLASSIFICATIONS

CRM solutions typically fall into one of three basic groups: marketing, sales, or service. The applications aim at understanding, anticipating, and servicing the needs of an enterprise's current and potential customers. From a technological perspective,

CRM involves capturing customer data from across the enterprise, analyzing consolidated data, and then distributing the results of that analysis to the various customer contact points around the enterprise.

Leading CRM solutions combine the basic groups of functionality with user-defined methods of access; there should be no difference in data accessibility from one channel to the next. To provide the data to complementary applications, the applications need to be supported by a common data description and an enterprise-level database. Finally, intelligence tools that can develop trends and enhance the knowledge base should have complete vision into the applications and transaction history. A schematic of this approach is shown in Figure 3.

Marketing Applications

Marketing automation applications, which complement sales applications, provide certain capabilities that are unique to mar-

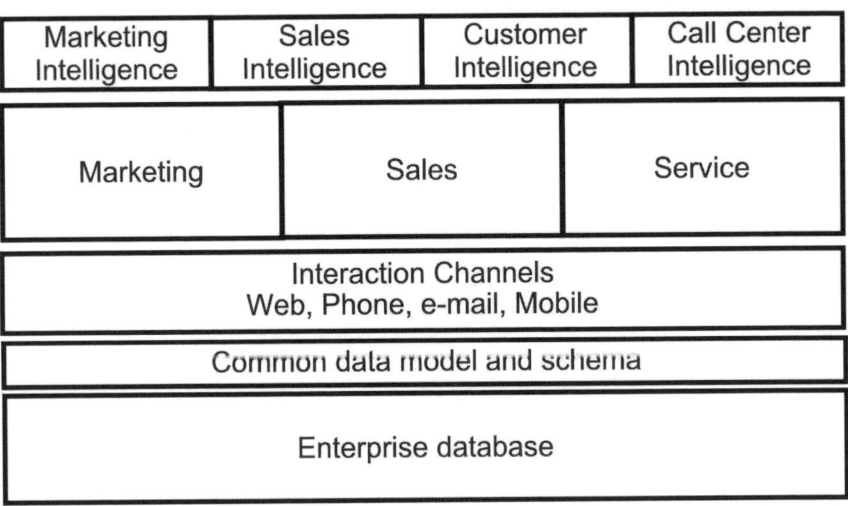

Figure 3. CRM Application Architecture

keting. These can include Web-based and traditional marketing campaign planning, execution, and analysis; list generation and management; budgeting and forecasting; collateral generation and marketing materials management; a "marketing encyclopedia," which is typically a repository of product, pricing, and competitive information; and lead tracking, distribution, and management.

Marketing automation applications differ from sales applications in the services they provide and the targets of those services. Rather than focusing on automating the activities of sales professionals, marketing automation applications aim to empower marketing professionals by providing a comprehensive framework for the design, execution, and evaluation of marketing campaigns and other marketing-related activities. In many cases, marketing automation and sales applications are complementary. For example, a successful marketing campaign typically generates qualified sales leads. Yet for a campaign to be truly effective, the leads need to be distributed immediately to the people who can act on them, which in many cases are sales professionals. The key point is that both types of applications play different, yet often complementary, roles in the customer-fulfillment life cycle.

Sales Applications

Perhaps the most recognized type of CRM solution is the sales force automation (SFA) application. SFA was a launch point for early customer-facing applications but has broadened significantly since the mid-1990s to include a more integrated, holistic approach to managing customer interactions and accessing critical management information. As the name suggests, the thrust of SFA is automating the fundamental activities of sales professionals, both in the field and internally. Today, SFA solutions encompass a wide variety of functionality to automate sales processes and empower sales managers and professionals with productivity-enhancing tools. Common applications include calendar and scheduling, contact and account management, compensation, opportunity and pipeline management, sales forecasting, proposal generation and management, pricing, territory assignment and management, and expense reporting.

Unassisted Web sales capabilities, which enable customers to select and purchase products or services via the Web, round out the sales portion of a CRM solution. In conjunction with a sales configurator, unassisted Web-sales solutions give organizations a powerful means of conducting cost-effective, Web-based e-commerce directly with their customers.

Service Applications

Rounding out the functional components of a CRM solution are customer service and support applications. These applications, which are typically deployed through a call center environment or over the Web, allow organizations to support the unique requirements of their customers with greater speed, accuracy, and efficiency. Customer service and support have become critical for many organizations because customer retention and profitability depend in many cases on delivering superior service.

Typical service applications include customer care; incident, defect, and order tracking; field service; problem and solution database; repair scheduling and dispatching; service agreements and contracts; and service request management.

CRM IN THE PUBLIC SECTOR

In virtually every part of the public sector—federal, state, and local—a major emphasis is being placed on e-governance. With increasing pressure because of successes in the private sector, public agencies are finding themselves being thrust into delivering their work product in an entirely different paradigm. When transformed to an e-government, the agency will generally find that it has three key components in conducting the business of government: suppliers, employees, and citizens (see Figure 4).

It is easy to see how a citizen can be considered a customer of an agency, and most CRM public sector solutions are being focused in that area. But in many cases, and particularly in the armed forces, employees are increasingly being placed in the

Figure 4. The Facets of an E-Government

"customer" category. Indeed, when considering the typical CRM promise of increased customer retention and decreased cost, the employee as a customer takes on a new imperative.

Public sector customers are demanding more from the government than ever before (see Figure 5), insisting on a responsive, efficient, personalized government for their tax dollars. In return, the government is providing more innovative methods of delivering value to their customers.

The relationship between the functional areas of CRM and the public sector are best demonstrated in the following examples.

Marketing	*Sales*	*Service*
• Identifying new recruits for the Armed Forces	• Navy exchange online store purchases	• Social Security Administration earning statements
• Notifying on-base personnel about new parenting courses	• Defense Reutilization & Marketing Service purchases	• Enlisted benefits information

Marketing	*Sales*	*Service*
• Advertising anthrax vaccination programs • Advertising new civilian employment opportunities	• Selling visual information products • Naval Supply System documentation from the Navy Logistics Library	• Bureau of Personnel service requests • Reserve family member benefits

By combining the functional areas of marketing, sales and service, an organization is readily equipped to add value to their relationships with their customers: employees, citizens, and businesses.

MOVING TO A 24/7 OPERATION

Providing more customer-centric government services is only half the solution; providing them when and how the customer wants those services is the other half. In the past, it was an acceptable business practice to provide customer service during limited hours. Today, because of the impact of e-business in the private sector, government customers have come to expect an improved

Citizen Demands

- Economical and practical customer service solutions
- High availability, high accessibility, hassle-free service
- "We remember you" service and "one call does all" processing

Government Response

- Developing "competitive government" initiatives to target core responsibilities and to allocate and manage resources more responsibly
- Creating infrastructures that support increased customer demand and communications innovation
- Examining customer service applications, which improve constituency service and allow citizens to become more self-sufficient

Figure 5. Citizen Demands and Government Responses[7]

level of service. To meet that demand, enterprises must adopt a multi-channel communication approach as depicted in Figure 3.

The impact of the Internet is evident in call centers around the world as enterprises change how they staff and operate these centers. The distinct boundaries between the Web, call centers, and mobile devices continue to blur. The call center no longer serves as simply a "silo" of incoming and outgoing telephone calls, nor is the individual call center focused only on a single business application, such as sales or service. The Internet is accelerating the integration of sales, service, and marketing into overall corporate customer-facing strategies by providing additional venues for customers to contact their vendors. In response, call center solutions must adapt to the changing ways that companies use the Internet.

Call centers have been gradually evolving over the past several years from the simplest ACD/PBX switch-only solutions to those incorporating detailed computer telephony integration (CTI) and functionality. A few years ago, a company had a predictive dialer in one department for outbound calls; a separate department would handle inbound calls. Inbound agents would have to ask customers for account or telephone information. Later, "screen pops" dramatically improved the operation of departments handling inbound calls by automatically locating customer information as "live" calls were transferred to agents. Customers spent less time waiting, and companies experienced higher levels of customer satisfaction as agents handled calls more efficiently. More recently, companies deployed technology to blend inbound and outbound telephone calls to the same agent pool. The benefits of CTI have been dramatic. Call center managers have reported a 40 percent increase in agent productivity, a substantial decrease in training time, and decreased agent turnover.

The next challenge for the call center was simple integration to the Internet. Companies added "call me" buttons on their home pages or fulfillment literature requests, which required "light" integration between the Web and their call centers. Some companies utilized Web "chat" and "push" technologies to improve customer communication; however, the adoption of this technology has been slow.

More recently, two technologies have had a major impact on the way companies are initially contacted—e-mail and e-tail. These Internet capabilities have fully saturated the operational environment of today's call centers. E-mail use has become commonplace, and e-mail messages have begun flooding companies—all sent by customers who are expecting timely responses. Additionally, the popularity of e-tail continues to increase rapidly as consumers turn to e-commerce and online shopping. Online customers expect superior sales and service from their vendors via either the Internet or their call centers. The floodgates into the call center and through the Internet have truly opened. Call centers must accommodate this new flood of contacts—and evolve into interaction centers.

As the communication between consumers, their vendors, the Internet, and interaction centers accelerates, immediate and real-time communication becomes a necessity. This drives new communication media, such as Web collaboration and online chat, to become required tools in the very near future. Internet Protocol (IP) telephony will become another technology that allows interaction centers to provide real-time, cost-effective customer communication. Consumers will be able to leverage their data connections from the Internet and have voice communications with their vendors. Voice-over Internet Protocol (VoIP) will become a commonplace interaction center tool.

Figure 6 shows the technology evolution that is transforming the call center into an interaction center. From the simple beginnings of predictive dialing, call centers have evolved through inbound screen pops and e-mail to a futuristic, virtual interaction center—a highly effective solution that must adapt to the capabilities continuously introduced by the Internet.[7]

HOW DO CRM AND KM RELATE?

In a typical enterprise, each department or function establishes a view of its customer according to that department's business processes. When more than one department deals with the same customer, some data are duplicated. The two departments rarely

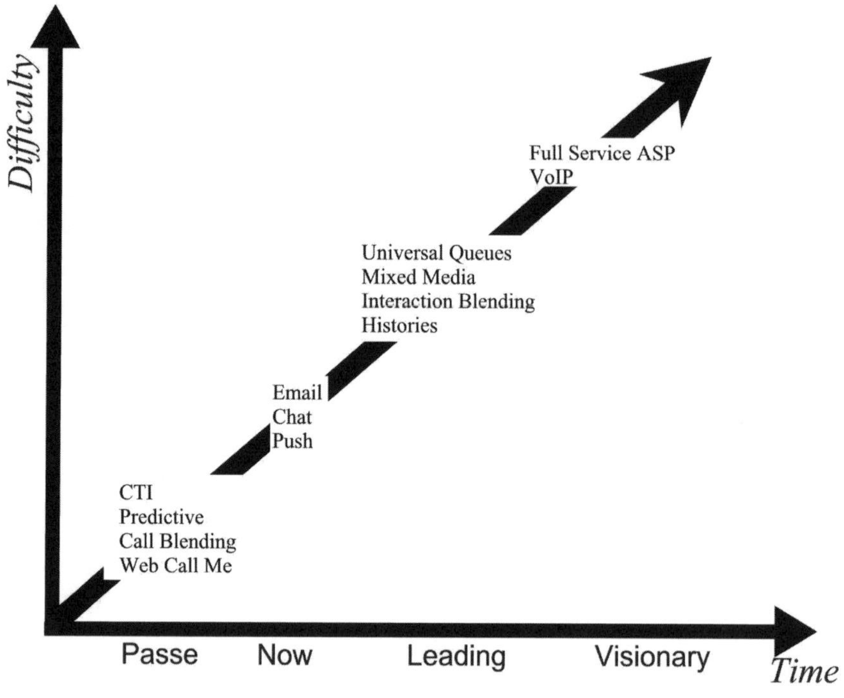

Figure 6. The transformation of call centers

know about the data stored in the other systems; even if they are aware of them, they rarely are empowered to access them.

When a customer transacts business with those different departments, she must establish a new relationship that is totally independent of her other transactions with the enterprise. Certainly inefficiencies exist, but more important, the customer experience is insufficient to retain that customer. One only needs to consider the impact of poor service on each of our lives to understand the contributory nature of each successive encounter with the same enterprise.

The data that can be stored for each customer encounter can include items such as the reason for the call, time of day, call resolution, customer account number, contact numbers, household information, demographic information, and other personal attributes. Effective CRM solutions have virtually unlimited data that can be collected, stored, and analyzed. The collection of these data is costly for the organization to obtain and often a nuisance for the customer to provide. With repeated queries for the same information, human behavior studies suggest that the customer is successively less willing to share the information.

When put in context and applied for the benefit of the customer, those data become knowledge. Likewise, as knowledge is built in each successive encounter between the customer and each department, the departments do not have the benefit of other information from which to create new knowledge.

The analysis of the data (hence creating customer knowledge) can lead to the discerning of customer traits. Knowing when the customer is most likely to be at home (based on the knowledge of the history of contacts made) will allow the organization to have a higher "hit rate" on calls. Likewise, if the analysis of calls for a customer identifies a particular area of concern, the organization can take steps to predict the needs of the customer and basically solve the problem before it occurs.

The imperative to capture that knowledge has never been as great as it is today. The Navy, for example, must be concerned not only with customer (personnel) retention but also with the aging internal workforce, as much institutional knowledge is departing with retiring service personnel.

Aside from the structural impediments to combining data in existing systems, today's business paradigms do not lend themselves to transforming customer data into institutional knowledge. The reason is quite clear: Each department considers the impact of the customer on the department, not the other way around. A graphical representation of this approach is shown in Figure 7.

An improved organization is one in which the customer is placed in the center of the enterprise. Each functional unit de-

Figure 7. Ineffective CRM/KM Organization

signs business processes with an understanding of that unit's impact on the customer. Through this process, the customer experience is maximized, organizational efficiencies are achieved, and the stage is set for improved knowledge management.

As shown in Figure 8, it is possible to create an environment in which organizational integrity is maintained while centralizing (at least virtually) the data surrounding the customer. All other business processes and procedures stay within the province of the department. Only the meaningful customer data are captured and transformed into knowledge in each successive contact with the customer.

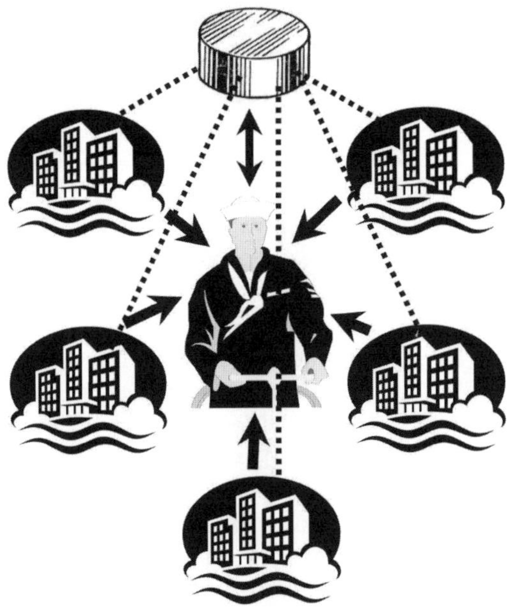

Figure 8. Improved CRM/KM Organization

CREATING KNOWLEDGE FROM DATA

To create knowledge effectively, the data must be stored in a manner that provides flexibility for differing business processes yet is robust enough to model changing relationships between functional units and the customer. Simple hierarchies of data elements are not nearly enough.

Provision must be made to extend the data elements in any schema. The value of customer knowledge management is to model uniquely the behavior and relationships of each customer. Care should be exercised to ensure that future choice is not constrained by the data limitations of some solutions that are commercially available today.

Figure 9 lists some of the basic required elements of a data model that must be implemented to manage the data properly.

Customer Registry	
	The customer master should act as a global registry of information about the businesses and people with whom you do business.
Separate customer relationship from party entering into relationship	• You should be able to record information about a particular customer relationship separate from the information about the party (person, business unit, or group of people or business units) entering into the customer relationship.
Business unit registry	• You should be able to record information about customers who are businesses and then share that information across operating units. • You should be able to validate this information using a third-party credit rating database, such as Dun & Bradstreet.
Person customer registry	• You should be able to record information about customers who are people and then share that information across operating units. • You should be able to validate this information using a third-party credit rating database, such as TRW.
Common location registry	• You should be able to share common location entities across operating units. • You should be able to record location hierarchies.
Date tracking and source tracking	• You should be able to store a history of a person or organization's attribute changes. • You should be able to store information from multiple sources and track the source of the information.
Customer terms	• You should be able to store multiple customer terms for each party with whom you do business. Each negotiated customer relationship is known as an "account." • You should be able to override negotiated terms at operating unit level. • You should be able to store credit profile information by account. • You should be able to store tax exemption information by account. • You should be able to record collection activity for each account.

Figure 9 *continues*

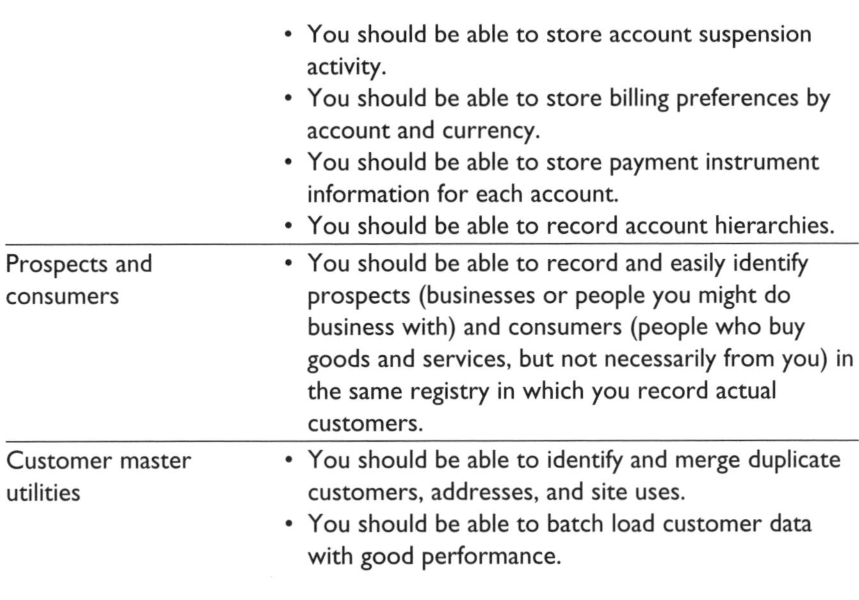

	• You should be able to store account suspension activity. • You should be able to store billing preferences by account and currency. • You should be able to store payment instrument information for each account. • You should be able to record account hierarchies.
Prospects and consumers	• You should be able to record and easily identify prospects (businesses or people you might do business with) and consumers (people who buy goods and services, but not necessarily from you) in the same registry in which you record actual customers.
Customer master utilities	• You should be able to identify and merge duplicate customers, addresses, and site uses. • You should be able to batch load customer data with good performance.
Hierarchies, Groups, and Relationships	
Complex hierarchies	• You should be able to record complex hierarchies of businesses and people.
Logical groups	• You should be able to record logical groupings of businesses and people (for example, a set of people might constitute a household). • Groups should be able to participate in any customer relationships that business units and people can participate in.
Party relationships as parties	• A particular party relationship should itself be able to enter into business relationships.

Figure 9. Data Model Requirements

In addition to data elements, the relationships of the elements within a customer record are of extraordinary importance. Many existing CRM solutions support only vertical relationships among elements in a relationship. This is not unexpected, given that early CRM implementations originated from sales management. The data architecture in these early systems is modeled after sales structures: vertical and one-to-one. This relationship is demonstrated in Figure 10.

A more appropriate data model for today's environment is one in which many different types of relationships can be represented. Some examples of important relationships are given below:

- Parent of/subsidiary of
- Headquarters of/division of
- Global ultimate of/global subsidiary of
- Domestic ultimate of/domestic
- Subsidiary of
- Client of/contractor to
- Supplier to/distributor for
- Seller to/customer of
- Reports to/manager of

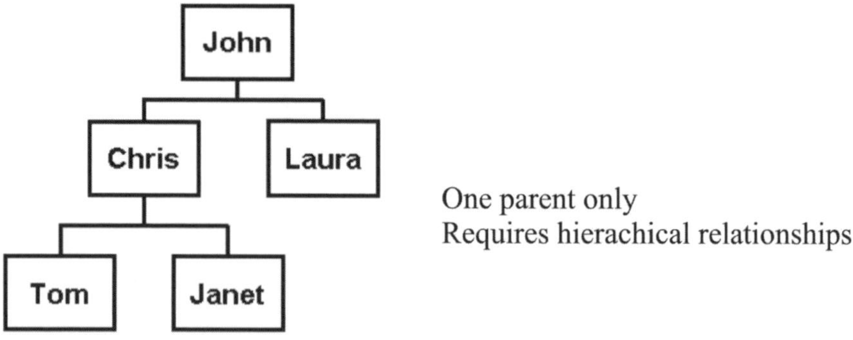

Figure 10. Insufficient Data Model

- Parent of/child of
- Employer of/employee of
- Partner of
- Competitor of
- Spouse of

As noted in Figure 11, a significant difference between the two data models is that the second model allows for multiple "parents" and for modeling of non-related entities. This is an important distinction because so many customer relationships result in a "two-parent" model. To illustrate the point, consider the case of a Navy dependent. Normally the child dependent would be attached to the service person's data record. But what happens if both spouses are in the Navy? Without a data model similar to the one below, the modeling of a dual-parent relationship becomes cumbersome at best.

To be effective, all applications that deal with the customer must access the same data, not copies or replications. To do otherwise would obviate the benefits of the approach described above. For example, if a sailor were to place an order through the Navy Exchange Online Store, he should be validated immedi-

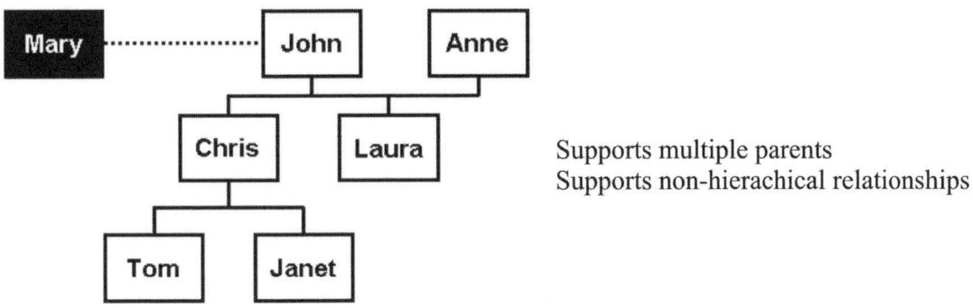

Figure 11. Sufficient Data Model

ately as a "customer" through his attributes. The transaction history of his previous purchases should be quickly analyzed to welcome him back and make some suggestions about new offerings. If it is determined that he has come back a number of times and looked at a particular class of goods without purchasing, a discount could be offered to him if he were to purchase immediately. After completing his order, he should immediately be able to walk into an Exchange and inquire about his order or use the telephone to check on status. The agent should have "perfect vision."

Likewise, if during his store experience he updated his address or telephone number, all other organizations of which he is a customer immediately have access to that information—not because they were notified, but because they all access the exact same data record.

When all customer-facing applications record their transactional history (but not necessarily their work product—medical records, for example, would not be captured), knowledge can be created by analyzing the data. When presented to an interaction center agent, a complete view of the customer can be created. Through the use of scripting (explicit knowledge) and training combined with experience (tacit knowledge), the customer relationship is enhanced.

THREE TOOLS FOR MANAGING CUSTOMER INTERACTION

The cornerstone of data capture and knowledge creation is the customer interaction center. While many tools exist to facilitate this data/knowledge transformation, the interaction center agent must have the tools to enable the total view of the customer. Three tools will be introduced and briefly described: work queues, e-mail engines, and customer intelligence tools.

Work Queues

The traditional ACD/PBX interaction center landscape has dramatically changed with the introduction of e-mail support, Web collaboration, and emerging Internet telephony platforms. The Internet drives the creation and acceptance of new modes of interaction at a fast pace, leaving little time for companies to adapt their business models to respond to these new demands and leverage them. Organizations need new tools to enable interaction center agents to respond effectively to the volume of requests via so many communication vehicles, which include inbound telephone calls, IVR interactions, e-mail contacts, Web collaboration, Web callback requests, and outbound telephone calls. Additionally, knowledge management techniques are used to guide how agents balance these requests with other existing tasks and incoming leads.

An example of a work queue engine is shown in Figure 12. Two important aspects should be noted. First, on the left side of the screen, the agent has a running account of work to be performed. In the frame, he can clearly see that there are:

- Outbound calls to be made
- Inbound calls waiting to be answered
- E-mail to be answered
- Active workflow notifications to be handled
- Service requests to be fulfilled.

The second item to note is that with the active caller, the bottom half of the screen shows a complete interaction history. This history records all contact with the customer without regard to channel of entry (Web, telephone, e-mail, or in person). The

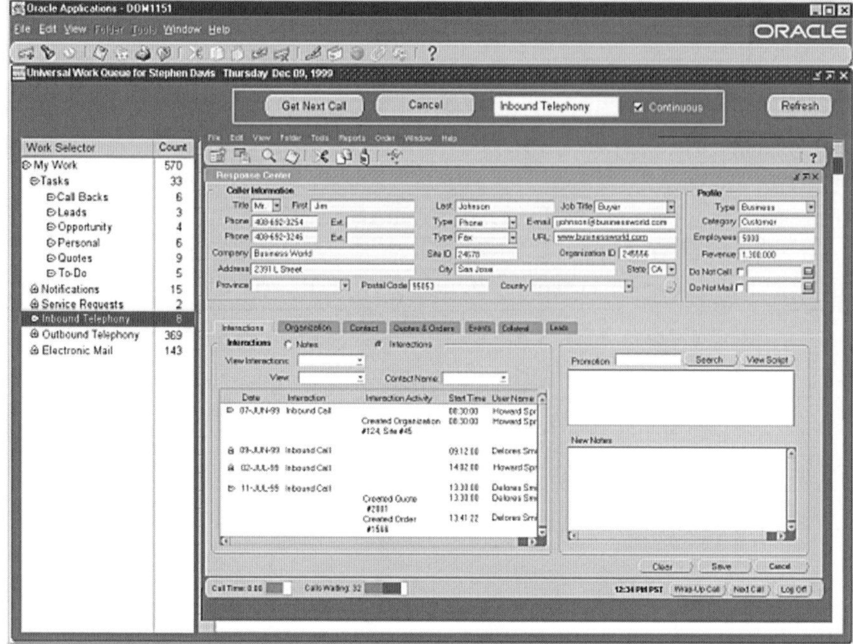

Figure 12. Work Queue Model

agent can then use a combination of training and scripting (both knowledge components) to assist the customer.

E-mail Engines

No discussion of customer interaction techniques is complete without the mention of electronic mail handling. With the exploding use of e-mail and the expectation of quick delivery and even quicker response, the volume has rapidly overwhelmed many organizations. And it is only going to get worse. Even those organizations that are encouraging the use of e-mail are finding that the manual administration and response are cumbersome.

To be effective, the e-mail handling system must be integrated with the other channels of communication (Web, telephone, face-to-face). Without this integration, a complete view of the customer cannot be obtained.

Organizations today should consider intelligent systems to handle not only incoming mail but outbound mail as well. It is important for the inbound processing engine to handle structured e-mail (e.g., Web form, text-based template, survey) as well as unstructured (free-form) e-mail. For structured inbound e-mail, an engine can provide automatic responses without the intervention of a human agent. For unstructured inbound e-mail, the engine can provide an automated response or suggested responses to a human agent, who can then compose a reply by a click of the mouse. On the outbound side, the engine should allow for automated generation of personalized single and bulk mailings, with closed loop processing of the responses to those mailings.

For interactions that cannot be fully automated (or in cases where automated responses are not preferred), the engine should automate as much of the processing as possible—classification, routing, queuing, response selection, and delivery—to minimize the amount of required manual processing. For interactions that need manual processing, the engine should provide a high-performance client designed to maximize agent productivity by suggesting responses, point-and-click access to customer data knowledge base information, and business applications.

The e-mail engine can determine the intent of unstructured (free-form) e-mail, through the application of either user-defined rules or the automated classification functionality. User-defined rules can be based on values of e-mail header information, e-mail contents, customer specific data, and "environmental" variables such as time of day. The engine should also process not just the body of the e-mail but also any readable attachments (Word, text, and other files) associated with the e-mail. An example of an e-mail engine can be found in Figure 13.

Customer Intelligence

As related by Bellinger,[8] the value of knowledge management relates directly to the effectiveness with which the managed knowledge enables the members of the organization to deal with today's situations and effectively envision and create their future. Without on-demand access to managed knowledge, every situa-

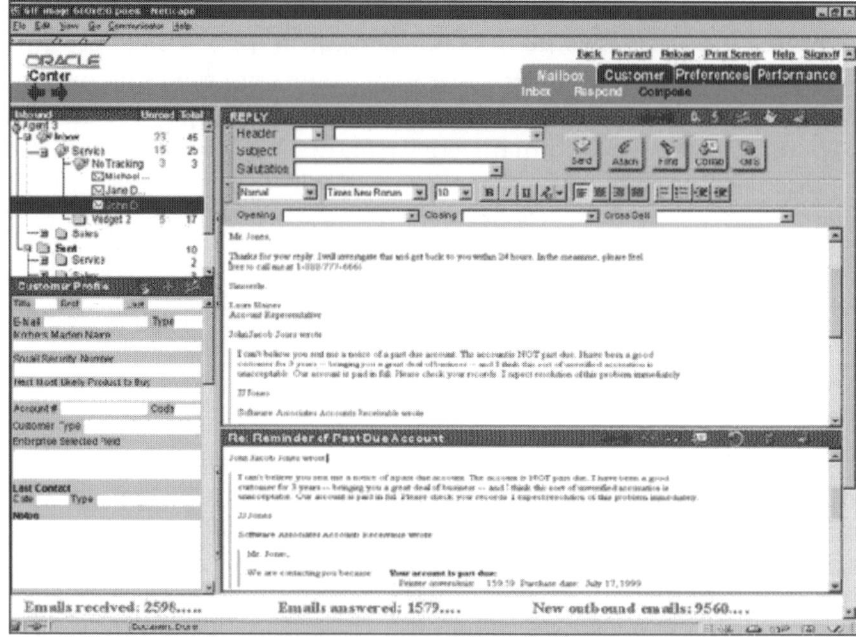

Figure 13. Sample E-Mail Processing Engine

tion is addressed based on what the individual or group brings to the situation. With on-demand access to managed knowledge, every situation is addressed with the sum total of everything anyone in the organization has ever learned about a situation of a similar nature.

The transformation of customer contact data into meaningful knowledge is accomplished with the use of customer intelligence tools. An organization can better manage customer portfolios through analyzing customer acquisition, retention, profitability, satisfaction, loyalty, and lifecycle. Through comprehensive customer portfolio analysis and understanding the impact of different factors on customer retention, the analysis tool enables companies to increase customer retention.

The intelligence tool should use a graphical representation of analytics to provide a high-level view of corporate performance.

(An example of a user interface is presented in Figure 14.) Users should be able to drill down further to view detailed information and investigate the cause-and-effect relationships among analytics to help them design the best customer acquisition and retention strategies, promote customer loyalty and satisfaction, leverage cross-service opportunities, and effectively allocate company resources to valuable customers.

An effective customer intelligence tool should target different levels of users for different purposes. Senior executives, for example, need to view the performance of the entire enterprise in terms of customer acquisition, retention, profitability, satisfaction, loyalty, and lifecycle, and to search for any customer to gain insight about the customer's profile for strategic decision making. Middle managers should be able to get the information they need to monitor the performance of their customer categories, market segments, geographies, or operating units, and to monitor performance measures so they can identify areas of improvement. And business analysts should receive the data they need to perform high-level trends analysis and customer portfolio analysis to understand cause-and-effect relationships between measures.

THE CRM/KM CHALLENGE

All organizations have customers—internal, external, or both—on whom their existence depends. With the imperatives never more clear, each organization must aggressively adopt a new business model. That means:

- Making the organization available to a customer or potential customer through multiple channels, including the Internet, telephone, and e-mail
- Providing a single view of the customer that is accessible by any channel, thereby ensuring that the customer has the same experience regardless of the channel chosen
- Empowering customers to choose the level of interaction and type of interaction they have with the company. This may mean self-service, minimal help or intensive help.

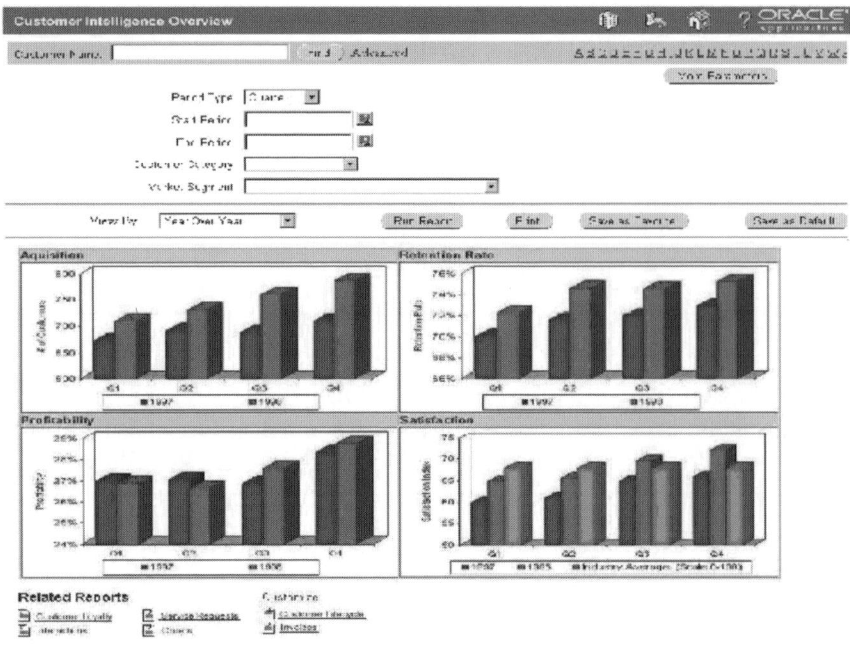

Figure 14. Sample Customer Intelligence Output

The backbone of the solution is the creation and availability of a knowledge base that is accessible by customers for self-service or agents that have varying experience.

Within the customer support arena, companies face additional challenges. The escalating cost of acquiring new customers is forcing companies to review internal policies around customer interactions and to focus on retaining existing customers. The new paradigm has made it easier for customers to switch between companies as the dependency on internal, closely held knowledge has lessened. Customer loyalty is not enough, and customer retention has assumed the highest priority in today's high technology service industry. Customers will continue to work with an organization that provides them with the service levels they expect. Given that customers have different expectations, the expected service level has many facets. Some customers do not want to have to wait on support phone lines to have an issue answered but prefer a self-service approach. Others prefer to interact with a support analyst and expect the organization to have employees who have the appropriate skills to solve their problem in a timely fashion.

Support organizations must adapt quickly to an intensified rate of change to meet customer, employee, and business demands and expectations. The key to success is the acquisition, training, and retention of adequately trained support analysts. This has become increasingly difficult for a variety of reasons. In some companies the support analyst role is not valued sufficiently and is an entry-level job, requiring the vendor to train new people constantly. In other companies there is a constant struggle to provide adequate growth opportunities to retain knowledgeable analysts. In other areas employees with the appropriate knowledge are simply not available. Add to this the complexity of global companies, language difficulties, and diverse business practices worldwide, and the support organizations' difficulties become clearer. Companies can gain a competitive edge if they can deliver cost-effective, superior support services that satisfy their customers.

OUTLINE FOR AN EFFECTIVE CRM/KM ENVIRONMENT

An effective CRM/KM environment can be created when the following foundation is established: unified channels, self-service opportunities, 360-degree view, managing complexity, and improved quality. Each of these foundation elements will be briefly described.

Unified Channels

In today's technology-driven world, businesses and individuals must be able to connect to the support organization easily, using any of the channels of communication available. An effective solution must leverage input through multiple channels including:

- Call centers
- E-mail
- Web.

These channels of communication allow the customer to choose the communication means that best suit their unique business operation while allowing the organization to offer support specifically priced and packaged to suit that need.

Self-Service Opportunities

The shift to self-service should be viewed from two perspectives: the customer of the support organization and the organization itself. Customers are frustrated when their requests for assistance are not dealt with expeditiously. The higher level of expectation by customers is challenging organizations to find a way to reduce the ever-escalating cost of maintaining support service.

The way to solve the problem to the satisfaction of both groups is to empower customers and employees to resolve problems proactively through embedded knowledge management approaches. The use of KM minimizes rediscovery of problems previously resolved by making information readily available once it has been tested, validated, and approved. This lowers the number of unnecessary service requests and reduces cost by requiring a smaller number of highly trained staff.

Self-service can be achieved through seamless integration with a powerful knowledge management system. When combined with the use of scripting, KM facilitates the collection and publication of solutions that are used proactively to solve problems before they are logged. Customers can search the knowledge base through a web portal and can often resolve their problems without logging a service request. Customers have access to much of the same information as an analyst within the organization. In many cases the customer is able to solve the problem by using the solution provided in the knowledge base.

360-Degree View

Integration of enterprise applications provides a single integrated view of the customer and his or her interaction with the entire company, allowing a more proactive, responsive relationship.

Within the application every interaction with the customer (opportunities, sales orders, invoices, shipments, payments, education, service requests, depot repair, and field service) is maintained in a repository. The benefit is that by analyzing the customer interaction history, an organization can monitor the health of customers and improve its business process. The organization can get a complete analysis of the customer through the customer profile. The information makes it easier to know the customer and understand his or her importance to the organization.

Managing Complexity

Complexity is increasing in the Internet age. As support organizations try to deal with diminishing margins and rising costs, there are increasing challenges. These include:

- Rapid introduction of products with shorter lifecycles
- The need to understand complex environments with a multitude of products that a customer has installed in its business
- Increasing demand for quality value-added service
- A greatly increased need for knowledge to be effective at their jobs.

The increase in complexity is putting organizations under increasing pressure to have adequate trained, knowledgeable staff on hand to deal directly with customer issues. Increasing workloads and more demanding customers are adding to the strain. A problem in support organizations is the high attrition of knowledgeable analysts. It is difficult to measure the value of the individual analyst, as statistics normally collected are based on call statistics and generic customer satisfaction surveys. From the customer's perspective, reaching an agent who is not able to answer the questions adequately is a major cause of dissatisfaction. Delays and increased costs occur when insufficient or incorrect data are collected.

A key approach to mitigating these factors is to ensure that the right information is collected once and is then made available to customers and analysts in the knowledge base. The importance of the knowledge base in the self-service approach is discussed above, but there are additional benefits when a well-populated knowledge base is available. Analysts who are not as experienced in a particular area are then able to deal with customer issues more easily, and knowledge transfer is a much simpler process.

Two other key processes are:

- *Assigning the customer to the right support analyst at the time the interaction is initiated.* Intelligent routing will allow a support organization to direct the request to the most appropriate support agent, analyst, or engineer. The routing can be based on territory, skill level, availability, or other business methods.

- *Collecting the right information in a standard way so that even inexperienced analysts can be productive quickly.* To facilitate the entry of accurate and complete data, an organization can use the scripting functionality within the service request flow to enable new analysts to be productive immediately and experienced analysts to handle service requests outside their immediate area of expertise. This can assist a support organization in deploying its resources to meet incoming demand while controlling costs.

Scripts also assist an organization in capturing a consistent set of information during the service request logging process. This not only assists the knowledge creation process but also provides an organization the ability to understand the types of service requests its products generate. Leveraging this important source of product feedback can improve product quality, increasing customer satisfaction and loyalty.

Improved Quality

Organizations need to enhance the product improvement process by tracking product quality issues, defects, and requests for enhancements. The support organization is the main source of this information. A large number of service requests and escalations logged against a product can be indicative of poor quality in the product, product documentation, implementation, or customer training. Whatever the cause, there needs to be a way to complete the process by creating a defect if the problem a customer faces is not resolved within the support organization.

The seamless integration of a defect management module allows the analyst a total view of existing defects and known solutions. All relevant data captured through the service request may be transferred automatically to create a defect for the development organization with minimal additional entry. Notification to contacts regarding the progress and status of the defects and enhancements is automated. Open service requests, linked to the product defect or enhancement request, are automatically notified of selected status changes.

THE BOTTOM LINE

Managing customer knowledge is a critical concern for all organizations. The impact of effective knowledge management techniques on employees and customers is profound. Employees exhibit a higher degree of satisfaction in their work environment, the quality of their work improves, and retention is enhanced. Customers find that they receive better service, they can interact with the organization on their own terms, and they have a higher degree of confidence in the organization.

Underpinning customer knowledge management is a collection of tools, best practices, and data management solutions. When matched with the organization's needs, appropriate tools can significantly enhance the customer experience while increasing revenue and decreasing cost. Effective data management provides for the ability to model business processes and to adapt quickly to changing environments.

Finally, the mere collection of customer data is nothing more than a technology exercise. The analysis of the data in conjunction with the corporate mission creates knowledge that can be used for the benefit of both the customer and the organization. The challenge for the organization is to then use that knowledge to create new value for the customer while continuously decreasing the cost of providing that value.

NOTES

1. Bennet, Alex. "Knowledge Management: Unlocking the potential of our intellectual capital." *Chips,* Winter 2000. http://www.norfolk.navy.mil/chips/archives/00_jan/km.htm.
2. Treacy and Wiersema. *The discipline of market leaders: Choose your customers, narrow your focus, dominate your market.* Perseus Press, 1997.
3. Harris, Fleming, Hunter, Rossner, and Cushman. *The Knowledge Management Scenario: Trends and Directions for 1998–2003.* Gartner Group, 1999.
4. Bellinger, Castro, and Mills. "Data, Information, Knowledge and Wisdom." *Outsights.* http://www.outsights.com/systems/dikw/dikw.htm, September 2000.
5. Huang. "Capitalizing on intellectual assets." *IBM Systems Journal* 37(4), 1998.

6. Borghoff and Pareschi. "Information technology for knowledge management." *Journal of Universal Computer Science* 3(8), 1997.

7. PricewaterhouseCoopers. IPIC Conference, Orlando, FL. April 2000.

8. Bellinger. "Knowledge management—Emerging perspectives." *Outsights.* http://www.outsights.com/systems/kmgmt/kmgmt.htm, September 2000.

PART IV

Case Studies in Knowledge Management

The first three parts of this book concentrated on theory, policy, management, methodologies, approaches, tools, and techniques of knowledge management. These are all building blocks necessary to impart an understanding of knowledge management. But this part, *Case Studies in Knowledge Management,* strikes at the heart of the practitioner. This is where some of the organizations that have been pioneering knowledge management in the public sector present their cases. Here the practitioner searches for answers to the really hard questions: What worked? What should be avoided at all costs? Can we do this ourselves, or must we hire consultants? How much does it cost? How can we justify it to our management? Not all the answers are in the case studies, but a good number of them are.

The anchor case study is provided by Shereen Remez, former CKO of the U.S. General Services Administration, and the first CKO in the U.S. federal government. In "The GSA Story: Swimming with the Dolphins," she explains how that organization, the principal supplier of office space, goods, and services for the U.S. federal workforce, is implementing its knowledge management initiatives.

The World Bank is in the process of reinventing itself to be relevant in today's environment. To do so, it launched a major knowledge management initiative to empower its network of professionals to share what they know about their work with others in the same line of business. The premise, as in all knowledge management efforts, is that from this sharing emerges an improved approach to tackling the communities' problems. The effort has been very successful in many ways, and has also garnered for the bank admission into the select group of the top ten knowledge management initiatives worldwide. Steve Denning heads that effort, and he tells the story in, "Knowledge Sharing at the World Bank."

CHAPTER 18

The GSA Story
Swimming with the Dolphins

Shereen G. Remez, PhD

The General Services Administration (GSA) strives to be an innovator in the federal government. Back in June 1996, on Flag Day, GSA debuted its first intranet, InSite, and gave Internet access to every employee, from maintenance worker to senior executive. So it came as no surprise to anyone that GSA's entrance into the knowledge era was marked with the appointment of the federal government's first chief knowledge officer (CKO). Although the majority of private sector firms had already launched knowledge management efforts, and about one-fourth of them had chief knowledge officers, the federal CKO position was still shrouded in confusion and the source of some curiosity. What would a government chief knowledge officer do? How could a CKO change GSA and the government?

Since I was the lucky first choice for GSA's foray into knowledge management (KM), I suppose I am the most likely candidate for telling the "GSA Story." And this is what I hope to convey in this chapter. You will not find here a blueprint for starting a knowledge management program; rather, this is my own recollection of how GSA dipped its toe into the knowledge management pool, and began the sometimes wonderful and sometimes discouraging task of learning how to swim—because that is precisely what knowledge management is all about—swimming with the dolphins, not building the swimming pool.

I could never have predicted that one day I would call myself a chief knowledge officer. Just as I often talk now about the migration from data to information, and from information to knowledge and eventually (hopefully!) to wisdom, my jagged career path has managed to follow this same paradigm.

In the mid-1980s, I was getting the word out as GSA's Director of Communications. This was a public affairs job in which I worked hard to tell the good stories and "spin" the bad ones. Then times changed; Peg Neustadt, the chief financial officer of our Information Technology Service, invited me to join the IT department, presumably to help an acronym-laden, back office shop move toward the mainstream. Well, history helped me on that one, and with personal computers and e-mail exploding on every desk and in every job, I gradually moved toward broader assignments, culminating in the position of chief information officer (CIO) in 1998. Here my prime concerns were keeping the networks running 24x7, investing in the right technology, getting over the hump of Y2K, outsourcing our infrastructure, and putting GSA on the map as a "cyber" agency. Remember that the middle word in "CIO" is *information*, and keeping it moving in a large agency is no small task.

In June 1999, Dave Barram, GSA's administrator, asked me to be the government's first chief knowledge officer. Neither of us knew exactly what that meant or how I would bring GSA to the next level, but I was given the gift of freedom to explore and experiment with this new idea called *knowledge* and the responsibility to help craft GSA's future.

GSA is not the same place it was when I first started at the agency back in 1977. First of all, it's a lot thinner. Just since 1992 we have shed some 25 percent of our staff, down now to 14,200 from just over 21,000. Along with the bloat, we also shed our status as a monopoly provider of goods and services. By the mid-1990s, our customers could "vote with their feet" and buy a desk, computer, or telephone services directly from Walmart, Office Depot, MCI, or any other vendor. To keep and grow customers in this free market, we needed to become more customer-centric and operate more like a business. Marketing, sales, knowledge-sharing, "thrilling customers"—this was foreign and "ungovernment"-sounding language. And yet if we intended to survive, if we wanted to bring real value to our federal customers, a transformation was in order.

So we leveraged new technology, business process reengineering (BPR), and reinvention to transform our processes, our measurement systems, and our business models in an effort to reduce prices, telescope delivery times, and reach out to customers. We drove long-distance telephone costs down to less than 4 cents a minute; we launched a 24x7 Website, GSA Advantage, with goods and services available anywhere, anytime, at least 20 percent below retail; made airline travel available at 70 percent below below individual rates; and arranged for cars to be leased at less than $136 per month. Our customers began to notice the changes—our revenues began to leap upward, and we began to earn kudos from the likes of *Fast Company, Federal Computer Week*, and *Government Computer News*.

The internal atmosphere was ripe for transformation. Dave Barram had come to us from his job as Deputy Secretary of Commerce. But for 24 years before that he had lived and worked in Silicon Valley, at Hewlett Packard, Apple Computer, and Silicon Graphics. He was no stranger to change and thought that "learning to be nimble" was a worthy goal, even for a large legacy agency like GSA.

For myself, this trip to CKO was like an adventure in extreme learning. Having spent the better part of the last two years as the chief information officer of GSA, overseeing all of our capital investment in technology, infrastructure, IT architecture, outsourcing, Y2K, and the move to a cyber GSA, my only brush with knowledge management had come in the spring of 1999. At the Federal CIO Council Strategic Planning meeting, Marv Langston, then Deputy CIO of the Department of Defense, led a small group that explored the possibility of KM becoming one of the CIO Council's priorities for the coming year. Unfortunately KM didn't make it out of committee, but at least the concept was proposed and considered. A few thought KM should be at the top of the priority list for the IT community, but others could not fathom what knowledge management was or how it might be different from information management. Corroborating this view, the 1999 American Federation of Information Resources Management survey of federal CIOs did not even mention knowledge management in its top ten issues.

The same was true for GSA. Most people had never even heard of knowledge management, and those who had thought it was a buzz word, the next fad, like total quality management (TQM) or business process reengineering (BPR). My own father, when I told him about my new job, thought that I was moving back into public affairs. Even today, many people still greet me with a friendly jibe, "Hey Doc, how's the knowledge business?" or "Good morning, Dr. Know." So what is the knowledge business, anyhow?

In GSA, we have started thinking about the power that knowledge can bring, the advantage of sharing knowledge across the enterprise, and the critical value of our own workforce and what it knows. In the past, GSA has been known as a "leveraged reseller," a huge buyer of goods and services who then passes along the discounts to its customers, the other federal agencies. Our customers save not only because of the great prices, but also through the time and resources saved by avoiding their own procurement process.

But as our margins shrink with increased competition, we have to sell more and more "things" and services just to stay even. And as the world of work becomes increasingly complex, with telework, security, and Internet time literally transforming how we work, our customers look to GSA not only for goods and services, but for our expertise and knowledge about the working environment. We are now selling what we know as much as what we have, as customers look to GSA for "solutions," not just commodities. Customers are looking for a "total buying experience," which requires knowledge about our wide array of products and services.

In addition, GSA is rapidly becoming a focal point, not just for commodities and real property, but for knowledge about the federal government as well. With the debut of the "FirstGov" web portal, an initiative of the President's Management Council implemented by GSA, we are beginning to see opportunities for leverage and economies of scale on the intellectual property side of the government. GSA's Consumer Information Center, a vast storehouse of valuable government consumer information, is another example of this new role.

To fill this new role, we need to share our knowledge and our best practices more rapidly. We cannot afford to make the same mistakes twice, even if they happen in different parts of the country. We also must be sure that everyone has access to the information they need to do their jobs. Finally, we need to become a learning environment, encouraging people to value—and increase—the knowledge they have and to share it with others.

PILOTS

When we started thinking about how to introduce KM into GSA's culture, I could not help but remember how ideas that had been forced into the culture fared so poorly. Although TQM and business process reengineering had their moments, by and large, most folks ended up shaking their heads in confusion or discouragement.

So when folks asked my how large the KM empire would be (both in people and resources), I also shook my head vigorously and thought about what John Koskinen, the President's Y2K Czar, would tell people when they asked him a similar question.

He would say, "I can't solve the Y2K problem by myself—others have to." And that is exactly the beauty in what happened. Koskinen mobilized others, causing communities of interested professionals to leverage what they knew and what they could do—everyone from the Federal Emergency Management Agency (FEMA) emergency community to GSA and Building Owners and

Managers Association buildings communities. People are attracted to an idea or a concept if it makes sense. My feeling was that knowledge management made sense for GSA. So I began to ignite fireworks—little sparklers—among interest groups and across GSA's geography that would hopefully become multicolored and elaborate displays in the night sky and elicit a few "ooh's and ah's" from management.

The only requirements we insisted on from the pilots were that they began with a business purpose and ended with a measurable result of performance. That way we would be sure to have a good story to tell as they moved toward success.

Best Practices Pilot

In the Public Buildings Service (PBS), Commissioner Bob Peck had instituted ten performance measures, such as customer satisfaction, occupancy, and maintenance costs. They were tied to individual and group performance and resulted in significant bonuses of $5,000 to $15,000 to GSA employees. Our regional structure of offices located in eleven different cities from New York to San Francisco encouraged many different approaches to achieving these performance goals; it also fed a "not invented here" attitude that put a damper on sharing best practices across geography. The "good practices" pilot was the first knowledge sharing that PBS tried. Paul Lynch, Henry Singer, and Steve Hochman deserve credit for taking the risk of changing the culture.

They brought together staffers from all over; sponsored a rally-type conference where "good practices" (they didn't want to call them "best") were shared and bragged about; and made a video of the conference and sent it around as VHS and posted it to our intranet Website, InSite, as streaming real video. They published a handbook with documented results of the good practices. But they didn't offer big extrinsic rewards for feeding the database on the Website. Instead, they gave everyone who contributed a good practice a symbol, a $20 GSA desk clock—very nice, but no Waterford. People responded favorably to this, perhaps an indication that the intrinsic rewards of sharing are more important than the extrinsic. But here is the most astounding finding: after six months of work, response to GSA's customer satisfaction survey nationwide has risen from 32 to 53 percent, and independently verified customer satisfaction has risen 4 percent. In Kansas City, it has been as high as 14 percent, and some individual buildings have seen customer satisfaction more than double!

A survey of more than 7,000 employees found that 40 percent of them had tried one of the good practices and found it useful. Only 1 percent had tried a practice that did not work.

Communities of Practice Pilot

Folks who work in our Real Property Disposal office are located, of course, where the property is, which means they are spread throughout the country. They traditionally have worked locally, and many of the rules and procedures that govern GSA's disposal of federal buildings and land that is no longer needed have been captured on forms and in printed manuals. Until the community of practice pilot, it would not be unusual to keep these forms in a bottom left-hand drawer, right next to the dog-eared, marked-up copy of the regulations. But what happens when the one guy who knows about the disposal of an historic building leaves? What happens if the one woman who tracked ex-courthouses gets a job with the courts and leaves GSA? How could we capture and share lessons learned, procedures that have to be followed, and most important, the knowledge gained by people over years of practice with real property disposal?

Brian Polly, Assistant Commissioner for Real Property Disposal, felt strongly that building his "virtual" community was the right thing to do. So with the help of a contractor, he established a Web presence where he could bring together the people, places, and things to do the work electronically. Culture was his biggest challenge.

There is a sense of security in paper and in those old dog-eared manuals, and few people with 15 or 20 years of practice in paper will give up the old ways easily. Getting his employees to feed and use the system was the great barrier to overcome. According to Brian, that those that think you can just put up an electronic community and they will come are fooling themselves. I agree. Start with the people and the business purpose, not the technology. Technology is necessary but not sufficient to build a robust and active community.

Today, almost a year after the Real Property Disposal community began, many are beginning to reap the benefits. The forms and templates are all online at the site, and they can be downloaded, completed, and sent electronically—saving time, mistakes, and codifying a more standard process across geography. There's a listing of experts (colleagues) that folks can turn to for advice, which not only helps build community spirit and reduce isolation, but also spread lessons learned and knowledge faster. And, most surprisingly, Brian's group scored the highest within the Public Buildings Service in our Gallup Q12 Employee Satisfaction survey. I can't help but wonder if the community of practice pilot may have contributed significantly to their achievement on this survey.

Another community of practice demonstration can be found in GSA's recent support of the Bureau of the Census in the largest peacetime mobilization of personnel and facilities ever conducted anywhere in the world. In this project, an online system, open to both GSA and Census staff, tracked and monitored the progress of more than 1,000 office installations, cost information by square foot, design and alteration data, and points of contact. The success of this $300 million logistics project is due in large part to the community of GSA and Census employees who were committed to sharing what they needed to know and to getting the job done on time.

Expert Locator

Ever wonder if someone in your firm or agency knows exactly what you need to know? Matching knowledge seekers with knowledge sources is the real goal of expert locators. Methodology and technology vary, but the aim is the same. In some companies, dynamic profiles are derived from the clicking behavior of knowledge workers. These profiles "see" that you are an "expert" in IT or telecommunications or knowledge management from what you read in e-mail, on Web pages, or in documents. These profiles then are made available to others. For example, if I write an e-mail about knowledge management, a listing of those in my firm who might benefit from a copy of this e-mail appears on my PC screen. I can just click to copy or contact them if I think I need more information. Conversely, if my profile shows that I am an expert in microbiology and either I am not or do not want to be listed, I can edit my profile or keep my expertise private.

At GSA, we decided for our first "Info-Center" just to encourage all of our San Francisco regional employees to develop Web pages, many with photos, listing their areas of expertise and competencies and contacts with particular customers. A robust search engine then allows the user to find the help they need. Soon, this effort will extend to other geographical areas and, we hope, across our entire agency.

Customer Relationship Management

Sharing knowledge about our customers, the other federal agencies, is becoming a critical competency for GSA. When we were a mandatory source of supply to the government, this was not as important. Today, as a highly competitive provider of choice, GSA values its customers above all else and is slowly amassing and sharing customer data across business lines. Our Federal Technology Service (FTS) is reorganizing its sales force and its project teams around customers. FTS is stepping up to automation of customer information. It is building a project database, a database of products and services offered, and a customer contact database. All of these will feed the customer data warehouse. Our customer action teams, or CAT teams, will use this data to serve customers more intelligently. Even before the automation project is operational, the teams show sales increases over last year of up to 30 percent, just by sharing information and working as a team for a particular agency, such as EPA or Navy. We are becoming customer-centric, and as a result, our employees need new types of knowledge to function well.

Knowledge Management Portal

Like many agencies, our Web presence more closely resembles an attic than a library. It is difficult to find the information you need unless you understand our plumbing. I once spent 15 minutes looking for the number to our Federal Information Centers for an outside caller until I finally remembered that they had recently been transferred from FTS to Public Affairs.

We are working hard to clean up our act when it comes to both our Web site for the public and our internal intranet, InSite. What we are moving toward is a knowledge portal, sometimes called an enterprise information portal. The goal is to dynamically feed data, news, and important information to the site, linking the portal to applications, data marts, and warehouses to other Web sites, such as newspapers and magazines. The user or employee should be able to customize the data any way that makes sense. Graphics are kept to a minimum; it is the information that is important. There are different "views," depending on your role in the organization. In other words, a financial analyst might not want to see exactly the same view as a personnel specialist. Visitors to our Website from other agencies or outside the government may not be interested in our organization chart—they may just want to buy a computer from us or contact the Consumer Information Center for a free booklet. Putting the action up front is key.

In this project, a consortium from GSA's Chief Financial Office, Chief Information Office, and Office of Public Affairs is looking to demonstrate how a knowledge portal can help our own employees find what they need when they need it. A parallel project, led by our deputy administrator, is planning to radically improve our gsa.gov site for the public.

In addition to these pilot projects, we are emphasizing knowledge on the enterprise level as well. Making "Knowledge Advantage" our theme, GSA is putting the enhancement of the enterprise IQ as one of its five major goals. Knowledge Advantage will give GSA a competitive advantage in the federal marketplace, will help advance our world class workforce, and will encourage each employee of GSA to create and share knowledge and to foster their own personal growth and develop their skills. To support this goal, we are growing a number of knowledge communities (communities of practice) in our core competency areas: procurement, IT, marketing and customers, HR (world class workforce), and, of course, knowledge management.

LESSONS LEARNED

Knowledge management is not a science, and it's not an art. It is a growing body of theory, practice, and lessons learned that we try to share. Many of these lessons are not learned from mistakes we have made here at GSA, but, rather, gathered from other KM practitioners who have shared them with us. Here are six important things to remember as you begin your own journey into knowledge management:

1. *Technology is necessary but not sufficient.* Technology is great. As a former CIO I am as hypnotized by the latest wonder as anyone. But it is a grave mistake to start with technology, even though 90 percent of all vendors will be glad to sell you some right off the bat. Granted, technology is driving the knowledge revolution. Technology reduces the barriers of geography and time to mere annoyances, and broadband will probably take care of that. But knowledge management has to be about people and what they know. Start with a business problem and people, and you are a lot more likely to see success than if you start with a fancy technology build-out and a "they shall come" attitude. That is because they won't come, and they may even resist the very technology that could help them the most.

2. *Demonstrate leadership from the top.* You can't order an organization to become smart and share knowledge, but you also are courting failure if your top people don't get it. In some companies, it is the Chief Executive Officer (CEO) who personally appoints the expert who will become the leader of a community of practice. In some companies, it is the CEO who signs up himself to teach a new skill. The leadership must set an example by valuing knowledge in people and by sharing it as well. In one company, no one is promoted unless they can demonstrate not just what they know, but who else knows what they know. Mentoring, brown bag lunches, community participation, teaching—these are just some of the ways more senior people can share their knowledge.

3. *Light fires, sparklers, and spread the word—don't mandate.* Too many movements like TQM, BPR, and others have failed because they followed a top down, mandated, enterprisewide approach from the start. In GSA, we thought it better to experiment with some ideas, getting a feel for knowledge management before committing to any enterprisewide implementation. Investing in a KM architecture before thinking through the value proposition for the agency is a mistake that could result in wasted resources. Of course GSA was fortunate to have a good IT infrastructure, one e-mail system, good hardware, and an enterprisewide system in Lotus Notes.

4. *Start with a business purpose.* "Knowledge for knowledge's sake" belongs in the ivory tower—not the business world. I can remember back in kindergarten how the teacher would patiently admonish us, "Share. Share your toys—play nice." Well, in GSA that balloon holds no air: there has to be a business reason to share, and it helps immensely if you can measure the benefits of sharing. The most common reason that knowledge management projects fail may well be lack of a defined business purpose. The old saying reads: "If you don't know where you are going, any road will do." I would add that you can't get there without some idea of your

destination. What is important is to first define, articulate, and agree on a business idea, problem, or innovation, and then think about how sharing knowledge across traditional boundaries will help or enhance that result. Conversely, entertain thoughts of knowledge nirvana and then return to the real world to define some measurable outcomes of success.

Common measurements include sales or market share, customer satisfaction, and employee satisfaction. Knowledge management can save resources by avoiding the reinvention and the same practices in different parts of a large organization. It can fuel the creation of new ideas and innovations, and extend the ability of an agency to accomplish its mission. Like technology, knowledge management is there for a reason—and the reason is to accomplish the job or mission more effectively.

5. *Think globally—but act locally.* If knowledge management came in packages—even in a big one—we could reliably invest in a system to store all our corporate knowledge. Then we would give all our employees laptops to "plug in" and, *voila,* the employees would be instantly smarter. Unfortunately, change on the enterprise scale is never so easy. There is no switch, program, or pronouncement that will get you there. But it is the job of the CKO to set the vision—something that is always just a bit out of reach and global—then look for opportunities that emerge from the vast octopus that is the organization. Feed and grow those smaller experiments, and, by all means, scale up the promising idea that works *with* rather than against the prevailing culture—that could be communities or knowledge repositioning or portals or sharing best practices.

   What is important is that a particular brand of knowledge sharing grows naturally out of the business culture. It is essential to involve the IT community in knowledge management, since IT architecture will enable or limit an agency's ability to share knowledge across programs and around the nation.

6. *Remember the culture.* This is the United States of America. Most of us have been taught to compete, to do our own work, and to be proud of our own achievements and expertise. After all, knowledge is power, and we have gotten to where we are not by sharing knowledge, but by hoarding it. What we have *not* traditionally been taught is an ability to work together, to share knowledge, to trust our colleagues, and to get over the fear that, once given away, our knowledge, and therefore our sense of self-worth, is gone.

There is a lot of fear about and resistance to sharing what we know. We make all sorts of feeble excuses—no time, not a high priority, can't see what's in it for me, and so on. The aspiring knowledge manager would be wise to address seriously the feelings underlying those excuses. They hold the subterranean dangers that can undermine the best intentions of any leader in this field.

I have been asked nearly everywhere I go how to deal with a culture of resistance. I fumble for an answer that will satisfy, knowing there isn't one. Cultural change moves like mass hysteria—no one thing starts it, but once it gets going you can certainly see it. Knowing the "tipping point" or seeing when you have reached that critical mass is about as close as you will get.

There are, however, some carrots and sticks that at least can help the organization lead the ponies to the lake. By using rewards, everything from large monetary awards to fast, small, even symbolic recognition, you can show how an agency values people and their contributions to knowledge. Reward not just smart people, but smart people who share their knowledge. *It's not just what you know but who else knows what you know* that should become a cultural mantra.

Knowledge values can be embedded into practices for hiring, promotion, and recognition. Make knowledge sharing part of strategic plans and the Government Performance and Results Act (GPRA) reports. Most of all, note that culture does not change in the blink of an eye, but, rather, over several years.

THE FUTURE: CONNECTING THE DOTS

Looking ahead, I see GSA developing a robust knowledge-sharing architecture. This will look like a seamless, connected network. At its base a large enterprise data warehouse (or connected data marts) will hold data about our customers, as well as financial, personnel, and procurement data. External data will also play a role by providing information such as marketing trends, federal employment and housing projections, credit card data for purchases made from sources other than GSA, and, of course, best practices from both inside and outside of GSA.

The window to this huge resource will be a knowledge portal. Connecting the dots between the seeker and the gold will be a number of applications and tools that will help our employees share, collaborate, learn, work, and create.

Our culture will reflect the values of a world-class workforce. GSA will be one of the top 100 places to work. Why? Because we will exemplify the best in public service grafted to the best in business practice. GSA employees will know that knowledge *is* their business. Part of their contract will be a commitment that they continue learning throughout their careers, contribute new ideas and innovations to the agency, and share what they know with their fellow colleagues.

My hope is that all our employees become "self managed" and that supervisors become coaches to teams rather than authority figures. This will be a real change in the contract between GSA and the people who work here, it will help GSA attract world-class employees, and, even more important, it will help keep them.

In the future, position on the organization chart will matter less and less—it's what you know, who you know, and who you share it with that will matter most. You cannot change a culture overnight, but you have to behave as if you can. You need strength, passion, and persistence to move the immovable. You are not pushing a large rock up a hill. You are lassoing the future and pulling yourself and your colleagues toward it. Attack the scratchiest but most workable problems first. Look for the low-hanging fruit that means the most to the most influential people in your environment, but that also offers the greatest opportunity for knowledge sharing.

If knowledge management can solve a nagging management problem or add new values to the business, you will have earned the credibility and trust of those who can lead us to a different future.

In GSA we like to see ourselves as innovators—first to Internet, first to telework in a big way, first to seat management, first chief knowledge officer in the federal government, to name a few. Well, I'd like to see GSA become the first government agency to realize "knowledge as power"—the power of sharing, the power of people to imagine the future and "swim with the dolphins."

CHAPTER 19

Knowledge Sharing at the World Bank

Stephen Denning

Bruno Bettelheim pointed out that "contrary to the ancient myth, wisdom does not burst forth fully developed like Athena out of Zeus's head; it is built up, small step by small step." Clearly, the World Bank had been a knowledge organization for many years before it explicitly declared itself to be one. The bank was set up after the Second World War to help finance the reconstruction of Europe and the economic development of other counties. It was a public lending organization, an international organization owned by the governments of the world that also generated much useful information and knowledge about the countries in which it operated.

The bank's first economic missions, to Spain in the 1950s and to China several decades later, produced the first modern, comprehensive analyses of the economies of those countries. The reports that emerged had—for economists—something of the aura and wonder of Marco Polo's account of his first visit to China in the 13th century. The economies of these countries, which had been *terra incognita* in the economic landscape, suddenly became visible and brought into focus. The economies had of course existed before the World Bank's reports, but little was known about them. Even when the World Bank's reports became merely one among the large number produced by many different organizations, the authority that had come from being first still lingered.

THE INFORMATION EXPLOSION

Over the succeeding decades, more information—much more information—became available. With the advent of the World Wide Web, information became very abundant. The proliferation of data made it appear less solid, and liquid images were widely used to depict the situation. The "drought" of data and information had become a "flood." People found themselves "drowning in information." They described themselves as "drinking from a fire hose." In this "ocean of information," it was becoming very difficult to find the specific piece of information one needed.

As the information proliferated, so also did inconsistencies. When there was only one source of information, it was easy to agree on basic data by going to the one and only source, even if—in retrospect—it turned out, like Marco Polo's account of his travels, to be less than entirely reliable. Once multiple sources of data appeared, judgments had to be made about the sources to resolve discrepancies. As multiple sources of data emerged even *within* organizations, internal questions about data started to have many answers. The answers to apparently simple factual questions began to resemble a tangle of contradictions.

Efforts were needed to establish order in the multiple conflicting information systems. Data repositories or warehouses needed to be constructed with the accurate information. Logical data taxonomies needed to be set up. Clear procedures for inputting information had to be established. Hierarchical responsibilities were required for establishing and maintaining order in the luxuriant overgrown data jungle. Scientific principles were aggressively applied to data storage. The categories of information were known, or at least knowable. In these efforts, it was usually believed that given sufficient willpower and resources, a system could be engineered—and built. Progress in its construction and maintenance could be readily measured.

These plans rested on the assumption that information is a thing. It is something that can be managed and measured. It is a resource that can be extracted from stores of information, like a precious mineral is extracted from rock. It is something that can be traded for a certain value, an asset that can be put on the balance sheet and tracked from quarter to quarter. As a thing or an object, information is something that can be controlled.

THE KNOWLEDGE QUANDARY

When it came to knowledge, the situation was less clear cut. Sorting out differences among different data sets involves asking an expert—someone who knows—what the right answer is. When there is more than one expert, one encounters the dilemma that the experts may not agree. The disagreements often concern not so much questions of fact, but questions of interpretation of those facts, or even disagreements over the right questions to ask.

In its mission of reducing poverty in the poorest countries in the world, the problems that the World Bank grapples with are what are known as *wicked problems*. In these the problem is not so much what is the answer to a given question, but rather what is the right question to ask (see Attachment 1). Thus when it comes to questions of helping poor farmers improve productivity, getting and keeping girls in school, or improving health conditions in poor villages, is one dealing with an economic problem, a social problem, an environmental problem, or a gender problem? If one could be sure of what sort of problem it was, finding the answer would be much easier.

More fundamentally, questions start emerging as to who is the real "expert." Who is the person who *really* knows how to resolve such problems? The post-modernist critique of knowledge began to seep, at least implicitly, into debates about development, as independent voices, reflecting third-world, environmental, or gender concerns, began to question not only whether traditional expert organizations, such as the World Bank, had any monopoly on knowledge, but also whether there was any basis at all for the underlying concept of truth. There was a growing sensitivity to the political dimensions of the claim to possess knowledge, with the suggestion that what you knew depended on who you were, what you did, and where you sat.

Amid such debates, it became steadily more important to know what expertise an organization like the World Bank was relying on. Managers needed to know the organization's view on issues for decision making and representing the organization. Staff—particularly new staff—needed to know what the bank knew so that they could implement the World Bank's knowledge. And because all development projects were not successful, the organization needed to understand whether the best know-how was being used in the organization's work. As staff members retired, what knowledge they were taking with them was becoming an issue. Outsiders also needed to know what the bank knew so that they could understand the organization and scrutinize its policies and accompanying actions and rationale.

As preliminary efforts to establish what the organization knew were launched, it started becoming apparent—to the surprise of many—that the organization did not know what it knew. Thus in the Africa region, an effort in 1995 to establish a "best practice system" had encountered great difficulty in getting experts to record best, or even good, practices. Inquiries as to the cause of the hesitancy revealed that even the experts were not sure of what they knew. The experts even contested whether they were responsible for sharing their knowledge. They often contended that their job was to meet with their clients and deal with their needs, not sit in an office in headquarters and assemble best practice manuals.

If the World Bank's knowledge was difficult for managers and staff to access, the situation was even more difficult for those outside the organization. It was common ground that the World Bank was a treasure house of expertise on what worked, as well as what didn't work, in development. A succession of world development reports on central development issues, published annually, repeatedly demonstrated this capability. But how did one get access to such expertise outside of a formal report? The reality was that in the mid-1990s, one couldn't. Most of the organization's knowledge remained locked away in the minds of staff or in the organization's filing cabinets. Yet the emergence of the World Wide Web showed that there was no reason in principle why large-scale access both inside and outside the organization could not be accomplished if the necessary decisions were taken and strenuously implemented.

THE STRATEGIC COMPACT OF 1997

By the mid-1990s, the World Bank faced a twin set of challenges that the new president, James D. Wolfensohn, set about meeting in the context of a comprehensive *strategic compact,* unanimously approved by the World Bank's Board of Executives in March 1997.

Thus *information* needed to be managed in a structured and disciplined fashion through *information system renewal,* and a comprehensive plan was developed and funded for consolidating over 60 different information systems into a single, integrated, comprehensive system.

At the same time, *knowledge* needed to be shared not only internally with staff but also externally with clients, partners, and stakeholders around the world so the millions of people making decisions related to poverty reduction could access the know-how they needed to make the best decisions. A bold plan was also put in place as part of the strategic compact to make knowledge sharing a reality (see Attachment 2).

It is clearer in the wisdom of hindsight than it was in 1997 that the twin tasks of managing information and knowledge were related but fundamentally different in nature. Information management reflected an engineering perspective. The building of information systems was something that many organizations had done before the World Bank. There were known procedures and systems. There were established good practices. There were known pitfalls. It was a matter of implementing structures and systems that had been successfully built many times previously in other organizations.

Knowledge management (KM), by contrast, was a relatively new idea that had only recently emerged in a few pioneer organizations, notably the consulting firms and some oil companies. It appeared to be less one of building structures and more one of handling flow and managing people. The skills needed were less those of building simple predictable structures than of coping with multiple variables undergoing frequent, unexpected phase changes. Knowledge seemed to involve a set of interacting patterns that were inseparable from the whole. It seemed less possible to extract knowledge than it was to nurture it. Knowledge emerged out of people interacting with people, with their environment, with ideas. It involved less an engineering perspective than an ecological approach (see Attachment 3).

Ambiguities of language contributed to the confusion between managing information and knowledge. The very term *knowledge management* seemed to reflect both engineering and ecological approaches. Some saw KM as merely "a database with a fancy name," which could be engineered and implemented, rather than as an ecological task involving flow and community. The confusion was further compounded by the use of the phrase *knowledge management system*, which was frequent in the early years of the program, both inside and outside the organization. Eventually, the term *knowledge management* was dropped in favor of a more intuitively comprehensible term, *knowledge sharing*, which reflected more explicitly the ecological perspective. Since then, efforts have been to use *knowledge sharing* throughout the organization. However, the continuing widespread use of *knowledge management* outside the World Bank, as well as the fact that knowledge management terminology is embedded in work programs, budgets, and job titles, means that this term also continues to be widely used.

During the three years following the adoption of the strategic compact in 1997, a set of arrangements were put in place—strategy, organization, budget, community, technology, incentives, and measurement—to implement the enterprise-wide knowledge sharing program.

The following is a short account of these arrangements. At the outset, the bank's management faced a daunting array of possible actions, involving culture, structure, processes, organization, and personnel. Because these actions engaged every facet of the organization, it was hard to know where to begin or in which order to attack problems. The sequence of actions that occurred came as much from the specific institutional issues and context of the World Bank at the time as it did from any grand plan or underlying imperative. Recounting the history of this implementation is not intended to portray a model of implementation for other organizations. Other organizations will undoubtedly find that different patterns and sequences are a better fit for their needs. It is presented here so that readers may choose those parts of the implementation that may be useful to them.

Strategy

The bank's knowledge-sharing program benefited from a relatively clear articulation from the outset as to the strategy being pursued in the *strategic compact* of March 1997 (see Attachment 2). The preparation of the strategic compact document provided a vehicle for developing consensus among the management and staff as to the elements of the KM program. It covered:

- **What knowledge to share?** The World Bank's program focused sharply on sharing know-how (i.e., what works and what doesn't work) in the implementation of development programs. This focus made clear by implication that other areas of knowledge (i.e., knowledge of clients, competitive intelligence) or knowledge of processes were not the principal focus of KM.

- **With whom to share knowledge?** Unlike many private-sector programs, the World Bank's knowledge-sharing program was explicitly focused from the outset on *external* knowledge sharing, as well as internal knowledge sharing among staff. The program aimed at making it easier for staff to get access to higher quality, up-to-date, and easily accessible tools and inputs to do their jobs. But it also aimed at sharing this knowledge with clients, partners, and stakeholders around the world. In a public-sector organization, no issues of proprietary know-how were involved, so making the bank's know-how externally accessible was an obvious step.

- **How will knowledge be shared?** It was envisaged that knowledge would be shared through multiple channels (i.e., face-to-face, or by help desks, telephone, fax, e-mail, collaborative tools, the Web, or some combination of these).

- **Why will knowledge be shared?** Explicit agreement was reached on the reasons for sharing knowledge. They included *increasing speed, sharing of best practice, furthering decentralization, stronger capacity building, better incentives for excellence, and greater development impact* (see Attachment 2, paragraph 38.) It should be noted that the strategic compact did not claim that knowledge sharing would lower operating costs for the World Bank. Although individual operations might move faster, it was also expected that the business would expand and change as a result of widespread knowledge sharing. The experience of other organizations seemed to indicate that net cost savings were unlikely unless that was established as the central objective of knowledge sharing. Hence, no promises of net cost reductions were made.

- **Will knowledge be shared?** In large organizations, discussions of strategy can go on for long periods, sometimes years, without ever coming to closure on the components. In some organizations, it is difficult to find an appropriate occasion or modality for expressing the organizational will. In the World Bank, the strategic compact was being put forward at the time to explain a wide range of changes, and it provided the obvious instrument to record the commitment to knowledge sharing. The World Bank's strategic compact was endorsed by top management and formally approved by the board of executive directors. This clearly demonstrated that

> the organization had taken a decision to implement knowledge management, and the general lines of approach were laid out. The Rubicon had been crossed.

At each stage of the program, storytelling was used to communicate the overall nature and significance of knowledge sharing. One particularly effective story involved a team working on highways in Pakistan, which was used in 1998 to explain meaning of knowledge sharing. (See other stories in Attachment 4 and also Stephen Denning, *The Springboard: How Storytelling Ignites Action in Knowledge-Era Organizations*, Boston: Butterworth-Heinemann, 2000.)

In August 1998, the government of Pakistan asked the field office of the World Bank for help with widespread pavement failure. They wanted to try a technology that the bank had not supported or recommended. A staff member contacted a community of highway experts inside and outside the bank via an electronic network and asked for help within two days. Almost immediately the task manager for bank activities in the highway sector in Jordan replied that Jordan was using the technology with interesting results. Later that day, an expert from the Argentina office reported that he was writing a book on the subject and was able to give the genealogy of the technology over several decades and continents. Then the head of the highway authority in South Africa reported on his experience with a similar technology. Next, New Zealand reported on the standards it used for implementing the technology. Within 48 hours, the task manager in Pakistan was able to start a dialogue with the Pakistani government on how to adapt the bank's experiences to their situation.

Organization

To launch enterprise-wide knowledge sharing, some kind of organizational arrangements need to be put in place. Different organizations are experimenting with the various ways to organize. The World Bank adopted a pattern of arrangements becoming increasingly common:

- A very small central unit is given responsibility for coordination.

- Implementation responsibility rests with line managers of the existing business.

- Communities of practice or help desks are the key instruments for sharing.

- Some capacity is established for organization-wide policy making.

Thus, a KM board was created with ostensible authority to make decisions related to knowledge management across the organization under the guidance of a higher-level Knowledge and Learning Council.

As to where the coordinating unit should be put, the initial decision in 1996 was to place it in the computing group, where it resided through mid-1999. By 1999, it had become clear that knowledge sharing was not a computer system, but rather a different and better way of doing the business of the organization. Hence, the coordinating unit was moved in mid-1999 to one of the operating networks—the Operational Core Services Network, which provides services in those aspects of the work that have enterprisewide implications.

Budget

The provision of financial resources for sharing knowledge is often an unambiguous signal to staff that the organization has decided to incorporate knowledge sharing into the way the organization functions. In the case of the World Bank, a budget allocation for the central coordinating group and the information technology resources, foreshadowed in the strategic compact, was supplemented by a decision in mid-1997 to earmark "two staff weeks of everyone in operations" for knowledge sharing. The effect of these decisions was to allocate some 3 percent of the entire administrative budget to knowledge sharing, with more than 90 percent of that residing in operational budgets and less than 10 percent in information technology. Considerable practical difficulties were, however, experienced in implementing the two staff-week decision, and resources were not initially available to the communities of practice that needed resources. To solve this problem, in mid-1998 one-third of the knowledge-sharing budget was given to the network sector boards to distribute directly among the communities of practice (known in the World Bank as "thematic groups"). The main focus of the financial provisioning was supporting bank operations.

Community

The strategic compact of 1997 refers to communities of practice, but without clearly indicating the central role that they would come to play in knowledge sharing in later years (see Attachment 2, paragraph 36). It was only in the context of implementing knowledge sharing that the World Bank—like other organizations—learned that nurturing knowledge-based communities of practice is a *sine qua non* to enable significant knowledge sharing. In early 1997, there were only a handful of enterprise-wide communities of practice; however, more communities emerged as staff explored how to go about implementing the institutional mandate to share knowledge. By late 1997, it was becoming apparent that knowledge sharing was only taking place effectively where communities had formed, and the central coordinating unit for knowledge sharing started to count the communities (known as "thematic groups"). At this time, there were around 25 thematic groups. In January 1998 the bank's management decided to support the communities with about one-third of the overall knowledge-sharing budget. This decision was implemented by mid-1998 and helped accelerate the growth of the number of communities to over 100, covering almost every aspect of the World Bank's operations. Funding for communities was administered by sector boards, which selected which communities should receive funding and approved broad work plans that covered such matters as building knowledge collections, strengthening the community itself, and providing ad hoc advice to community members.

Technology

The bank's knowledge-sharing program aimed at exploiting multiple technologies, including face-to-face meetings, telephone, fax, e-mail, Lotus Notes, and the World Wide Web, both intranet and external Web. While the evolution of technology created the possibility of extending the scale of knowledge sharing in ways that were almost unthinkable just a decade ago, the thematic groups tended to remain grounded in simpler technologies. Face-to-face meetings were central because without such meetings, it was found impossible to form communities. Brown-bag lunches and informal clinics were ubiquitous features of the work of the thematic groups at headquarters. Thus while technology extended the reach of knowledge far beyond the immediate confines of its creators, the direct human connection remained important.

The World Wide Web provided a means of sharing knowledge across the organization and beyond. In practice, however, it proved more difficult than expected to design the Websites in ways that met staff needs, and much trial and error were involved in finding formats that met with broad acceptance. Thus although it had been suggested by outsiders that technology would be the easy part of KM, developing user-friendly information technology (IT) tools that people actually used proved to be more than a trivial task. The potential of the technology was evident. However, reaching agreement across many units on how to design and use the tools became a major challenge, eventually requiring several years of effort.

Incentives

Because knowledge sharing entailed a change in the way the business of an organization was conducted—with a shift from vertical hierarchical modes of behavior to horizontal knowledge-sharing behaviors—a decision was made in early 1998 to change the personnel evaluation system of the bank so that knowledge sharing would be reflected in the annual performance review of every manager and staff member. It took more than a year to implement the decision, but eventually the personnel evaluation was changed so that only four core behaviors were tracked and rewarded in the annual evaluation, one of which was knowledge sharing and learning. Each manager and staff member was assessed annually according the following criteria:

Knowledge sharing and learning:

- Open to new ideas and continuous learning
- Shares own knowledge, learns from others, and applies knowledge in daily work
- Builds partnerships for learning and knowledge sharing.

The modification of the personnel system did not solely drive change in the organization. In the first year of implementation, there was some cynicism and posturing; however, over time the change effectively sent an unmistakable signal throughout the organization that knowledge sharing is here to stay, as a permanent part of the organization for years to come, not just a passing fad.

Measurement

As the bank's knowledge-sharing program unfolded over a period of years, an underground current of management gossip and water-cooler conversations provided a running commentary of the progress of implementing the initiative. This flow of anecdotal information did not, however, provide anyone with a precise understanding of what was happening, given the large scale and diversity of activity. Systematic efforts were undertaken to count what could be counted—dollars budgeted and dollars spent, numbers of communities, numbers of entries in the knowledge base, numbers of queries responded to, and numbers of Web hits. Surveys were undertaken of staff generally, and of members of thematic groups. These surveys provided valuable insights about differentials in performance. Ideally, one would have measured the impact of knowledge sharing, but in the organizational context, clear causal links between inputs and outcomes could not be determined with any certainty. Clearly, no rate of return calculations were feasible.

While the measures undertaken showed the relative progress of the initiative over time, management wanted more. It wanted a clearer sense as to whether the program was succeeding. As a result, the management commissioned an external evaluation—a quick action review—to help determine whether the program was on track and to identify the most important actions to strengthen performance.

The review concluded that much had been accomplished in a short time without spending a great deal of money and that the program was broadly on track. In particular, the review gave more importance to the bank's thematic groups than had been expected. The review said that they were "the heart and soul of knowledge management in the bank" and that an extraordinarily good start has been made in launching more than a hundred of these groups, which were adding considerable value to bank work. The review's recommendations included issuing a short update on the knowledge-sharing strategy, cleaning up some of the disorder on the bank's intranet, providing more support to thematic groups, and integrating knowledge sharing more closely with the rest of the operational work (see Attachment 5). These recommendations were accepted and implemented over the succeeding months.

At the senior management's strategic forum in January 2000, knowledge sharing was endorsed as a key strategic dimension for the coming years, and thematic groups in particular were endorsed as the agreed vehicle for nurturing knowledge sharing. This key decision was based less on the available quantitative metrics than on a broad business judgment that knowledge sharing and communities of practice were essential for the very survival of the organization, both in its traditional business of lending and in its new mission of global poverty reduction.

External recognition of progress made also followed. In early 2000, the American Productivity and Quality Center (APQC) selected the World Bank as one of five "best practice partners" in its global benchmarking of "successfully implementing knowledge management." In June 2000, the World Bank was nominated in the top ten of the world's Most Admired Knowledge Enterprises (MAKE 2000), the first public-sector organization to be so honored. This external recognition facilitated management decisions in favor of pressing ahead with the knowledge-sharing agenda.

Second-Generation Issues

By the year 2000, the basics for launching an enterprise-wide knowledge-sharing program had been put in place: strategy, organization, budget, community, technology, incentives, and measurement. Much remained to be done to complete the implementation and to integrate knowledge sharing fully into the work of the organization.

But attention also was also being given to second-generation issues, including measuring and accelerating the culture shift; integrating knowledge sharing with learning, evaluation, and research; streamlining the structures needed to launch the knowledge-sharing program; strengthening the communities of practice; and further improving the technology tools.

It was also coming to be recognized that the same logic that drove the World Bank to manage its knowledge applied with equal force to its partners and clients (i.e., other development organizations and the developing countries themselves). This was reflected in the fact that the focus of the Economic and Social Council of the United Nations (ECOSOC) in 2000 was information and knowledge. There is a growing recognition in these discussions that all organizations and economies will need to nurture their own communities of practice, establish their own knowledge bases, authenticate them from their own experience, interpret what is meaningful from their own perspectives, and create a future that meets their own needs. As international institutions themselves learn how to share knowledge more effectively, they increasingly recognize a responsibility to help developing countries to understand what is at stake in terms of sharing and managing knowledge and to nurture similar capacities there. This is seen to be a large-scale and long-term undertaking, on which the international institutions and developing countries are making a start by discussing the appropriate arrangements to catalyze the process.

Overall, the emergence of the global knowledge-based economy means that the process of development is increasingly viewed not so much as a transfer of financial resources and advice from the north to the south, but as a process of groups, communities, and networks learning to learn faster, facilitated by financial flows where appropriate. Knowledge is increasingly recognized as being located in both the north and the south. Development knowledge needs to flow in all directions, north-south, south-north, south-south, and north-north. In this world view, the process of development is becoming seen as one of building networks of knowledge communities that can share know-how more agilely than in the past.

Knowledge sharing thus has come to be seen as considerably more than a managerial improvement initiative, separate from the rest of the organization. There is an emerging consensus that knowledge sharing is being woven into the fabric of operations not only to enhance and transform the overall enterprise but also to transform the very process of development itself into a knowledge-sharing activity.

ATTACHMENT I

World Bank's Mission Statement (issued January 1999)

Our dream is a world free of poverty

Our Mission

To fight poverty with passion and professionalism for lasting results.

To help people help themselves and their environment by providing resources, sharing knowledge, building capacity, and forging partnerships in the public and private sectors.

To be an excellent institution that is able to attract, excite, and nurture committed staff with exceptional skills who know how to listen and learn.

Our Principles

Client centered, working in partnership, accountable for quality results, dedicated to financial integrity and cost-effectiveness, inspired and innovative.

Our Values

Personal honesty, integrity, commitment to working together in teams—with openness and trust empowering others and respecting differences, encouraging risk-taking and responsibility, enjoying our work and our families.

The World Bank's mission is to fight poverty and improve the quality of life through sustainable growth and investment in people. It does this through five goals:

Pursuing economic reforms that promote broad-based growth and reduce poverty. The Bank will help countries to accelerate and deepen policy and institutional reforms to embrace growth, improve living standards, and reduce poverty.

Investing in people through expanded, more effective programs in education, health, nutrition, and family planning. This implies striving to reach the point where human capital limitations no longer restrain growth or keep people in absolute poverty.

Protecting the environment so that growth and poverty reduction can be lasting. The Bank will help countries reconcile the needs and aspirations of growing populations with the needs of the environment.

Stimulating the private sector so that countries can become more productive and create jobs. The Bank will help countries realize the potential of the private sector to promote investment, stimulate growth, and create jobs.

Reorienting government so that the public sector can efficiently undertake essential tasks, such as human resource development, environmental protection, provision of social safety nets, and legal and regulatory frameworks.

ATTACHMENT 2

The World Bank
The Strategic Compact: Renewing the Bank's Effectiveness to Fight Poverty February 13, 1997

(approved unanimously by the Executive Directors on March 31, 1997)

(The Strategic Compact is a document of 34 pages, accompanied by a separate volume of more detailed annexes. It proposes a comprehensive program of renewal for the Bank, of which a part is knowledge management. The following excerpt is the section of the main report of the Strategic Compact dealing with knowledge management.)

"III. KEY ELEMENTS OF THE COMPACT

An Integrated Package

(1) Refueling Current Business Activity

.....

(2) Refocusing the Development Agenda

.....

(3) Retooling the Bank's Knowledge Base

29. Access to lessons learned and best practice is key to development effectiveness. Yet the Bank Group's knowledge is not always easily available to those who need it—inside or outside—when they need it, or in formats they find useful and accessible. As a result, the effectiveness of all our services suffers. To address

this problem, the Bank needs to make a substantial effort to rebuild its knowledge management base—and utilize more fully its institutional comparative advantage in this area. In short, the Bank needs to capture and organize its knowledge; make it more readily accessible to staff, clients and partners; strengthen its dissemination and capacity-building efforts; and ultimately, enhance the effectiveness of all its products and services. In this respect, a knowledge management system is the key to a more effective Bank—and investment is required to build that system.

30. While the preliminary focus of the system will be on improving the effectiveness of Bank staff, its eventual goal is to meet the needs of both *internal* and *external* users. An effective knowledge management system holds the potential to change the way in which the Bank operates internally and transform the organization's relationships with clients, partners and stakeholders—to become, in effect, a key strategic thrust for the 21st century.

31. In moving in this direction, we must first build on our assets: principally, our own human resources: Research, knowledge generation, and dissemination have long been a function of DEC, for instance. Other knowledge-oriented units in the Bank include EDI, helping to build capacity and consensus for reform in countries; Finance and Private Sector Development, working with corporations through *infoDEV* to finance and learn from pilot projects in information technology; the Human Development Network, making knowledge available electronically; the Corporate Relationship Information System of the PSD Group, designed to link internal corporate relationship information for Bank Group management and staff; and the Legal Department, which maintains a legal database with records on performance under legal covenants and other relevant legal matters. In the Regions, too, of course, there are substantial knowledge bases founded on long-standing relationships with our clients. The effort to create a much stronger knowledge management system must build on those assets.

32. Building a better knowledge management system involves generating new knowledge both through formal research and

through learning via the Networks; pulling, reviewing, analyzing, and systematically assembling information from existing internal and external sources; drawing from electronic discussion tools and on-line communities, and synthesizing key findings. A substantial effort will be required to maintain the *quality* of the knowledge—updating existing material and architecture and weeding out obsolete material.

33. The content of the system will depend on user interest and demand. To stimulate demand will require the establishment of: *help-desks*, with the capacity to answer queries and provide resource maps and information packets; *databases*, including terms of reference, consultants, lessons learned and key technical papers and reports; and *knowledge bases*, including sector strategies, tool kits, best practices, and think pieces. The system will aim at improving product quality and impact through being demand-driven, user-friendly, and authoritative—and it will be periodically benchmarked against other world-class knowledge management systems.

34. It is important to emphasize that while knowledge management can be greatly facilitated by technology, the system is principally about people. The challenge is to harness the technology to link people together and to leverage its impact for development. That means both accumulating the right kind of knowledge—and also helping our clients build the capacity to use it.

35. In that sense, acquiring the right technology is the relatively easy part of the new investment required. The more difficult part is the organizational culture shift which must take place in parallel: from an individualistic mode of working and storing knowledge, towards a team-based, sharing mode. A sustained effort will be needed for this culture shift to succeed and much work needs to be done to develop the right kind of behavior. In the end, people will be the key determinant of success of the knowledge management system.

36. Various units will be involved in building this new system:

- The *Networks* will generally take the lead in developing the requisite knowledge bases, i.e. organizing operational staff so that the flow of global knowledge is facilitated. Each knowledge area will be led by a full-time knowledge manager and supported by subject-specialists and other operational staff who will spend part of their time building and maintaining the knowledge base—constituting "knowledge communities" in their fields of expertise. They will be assisted by help desk personnel.

- Since the Networks also must do the Bank's day-to-day business, there will also be a small central *knowledge management group*—with operational staff dedicated to overseeing the knowledge management system. This will include establishing an integrated framework; designing an institutional classification system; setting priorities among multiple activities; managing issues of quality; managing external access to the system and consolidating external partnerships; facilitating the required organizational culture shift; and in general, championing the knowledge management effort.

- The *Economic Development Institute's* expanded program will be geared towards the increasing use of new technology to improve training programs and reach a broader audience. This includes the Global Link series of commercial quality television programs, school-to-school links between primary and secondary schools in part I and part II countries, and media and communications training programs to equip journalists and broadcasters with the necessary skills to help citizens better understand the economic and social changes taking place.

- The *Information and Technology Services Department* will support the overall effort with the necessary technology, as well as by ensuring that the knowledge management system is fully integrated with other information systems across the Bank Group.

37. Implementation of the system will be phased. Work is already under way within the HD network, with knowledge bases under construction and help desks in place. In light of progress

with HD, and depending on resource availability, two other sector families (Environment, Infrastructure) will get started in the remainder of FY97. By the end of FY98, it is expected that half of all sectors will be active in knowledge management. The pace of further expansion of the knowledge management system will be decided on the basis of experience and demand from clients. It is anticipated, however, that knowledge management in *all* sector groups will be under way by FY99.

38. With the strengthened knowledge management system, the Bank will be able not only to provide new services, but also *higher quality services*. Lending will have a firmer foundation, which will lead to better development outcomes; and the advice offered by the Bank will be taken to a higher level. The knowledge management system will also result in:

- *Faster speed:* client access to the Bank Group's knowledge will be accelerated and transaction costs lowered;

- *Best practice:* the Bank's comparative advantage in providing international best practice will be consolidated;

- *Further decentralization:* a better knowledge management system is critical for facilitating geographical dispersion—and thus constitutes a prerequisite for more effective decentralization and closeness to the client;

- *Stronger capacity building:* genuine partnership can be facilitated through sharing of knowledge with clients and stakeholders, particularly in the poorest countries;

- *Better incentives for excellence:* with knowledge generation and dissemination at the center of our development role, incentives for staff and managers to maintain their skills at the cutting edge and share their know-how will be stronger; and

- *Greater development impact:* all of the Bank's products and services will benefit in terms of better information and analysis, design, implementation and feedback.

39. The development of the knowledge management system will be complemented by the following initiatives:

- *On-line communities:* building on the successful IPA*net* experience, the Bank will develop electronic communities, with an environment for diverse individuals and groups concerned with economic development to exist side by side. Expert as well as non-expert users will be able to take advantage of the system—anyone with access to the World Wide Web is a potential participant.

- *World Development Report (WDR) on knowledge:* the implications of knowledge in the world's economy are becoming increasingly important. Thus the 1998 WDR will focus on the role of knowledge in development which should, in turn, contribute to the strengthening of the Bank's efforts in this critical area.

(4) Revamping Institutional Capabilities

……"

ATTACHMENT 3

The World Bank's Knowledge Management Strategy (issued September 1999)

Sharing knowledge to fight poverty

Fighting poverty requires a global strategy to share knowledge systematically and energetically and to ensure that people who need that knowledge get it on time, whether from us or others. From a fairly closed organization a few years ago, the Bank has become a global development partner making it easier for people to find out who knows what and where the best expertise can be drawn upon, wherever it resides. Continuously sharing this global and local know-how with client countries, public and private partners, and civil society will better equip the development community to fight poverty.

The benefits of knowledge sharing

Speed—responding faster to client needs.

Quality—delivering to clients the experience of many countries, adapted to local conditions.

Innovation—not just doing what we've been doing better, but bringing new services, finding and testing the never-before-thought-of.

Putting knowledge on a par with money

Because sharing knowledge is an essential ingredient of our comprehensive development strategy, we are giving high priority to:

— Supporting more than a hundred thematic communities of practice in all our areas of expertise so that we can share experience across internal and external boundaries.

— Making reliable statistics on development much more broadly available, including live databases of country economic data and key sector statistics needed to help clients.

— Enhancing our directory of expertise and the ability of staff and outside practitioners to connect with each other.

— Strengthening our advisory services so that staff and clients can find solutions quickly.

Learning from our clients and partners

Our clients need access not just to the expertise of the individuals in a team assigned to them, but to the entire range of global experience on development issues—and they demand nothing less. That is why we are:

— Adding to our wealth of cross-country know how and expertise by systematically capturing new country-specific experiences and indigenous knowledge.

— Enlisting our clients, partners, and stakeholders in sharing knowledge for development by having them join thematic communities and inviting them to participate in global dialogues on development.

— Using our ability to bring together the world's leading practitioners with our many external partners to exchange experiences and innovations.

Reinforcing continuous learning

Bank staff are sharing their knowledge across organizational boundaries in communities of practice (thematic groups) to find the best know-how in or outside the organization. To get our clients better answers faster—and to improve the quality of their operations through continuous learning—we are:

- Making the Bank more open and transparent so that knowledge flows swiftly across internal and external organizational boundaries.

- Linking our internal and external learning programs with knowledge sharing, taking them out of the classroom and into the world.

- Putting budgets and personnel incentives in place to manage the full array of knowledge services.

Building client capacity and widening client partnerships

By reaching out to those who previously did not have access to World Bank services and know-how, we are providing the information clients and stakeholders need to do things themselves. We are:

— Building the capacity of countries to tap into global resources online.

— Developing the skills of clients to adapt the best global practices in knowledge sharing and management.

— Making our knowledge much more widely available through direct external access to our knowledge bases.

— Putting electronic collections of relevant information and knowledge about particular areas of activity—previously available only internally—on the Internet for all those interested in fighting global poverty.

ATTACHMENT 4

Examples of Widely Told Stories about Knowledge Sharing

In June 1998, a World Bank economist in Saudi Arabia requested information on training related to an upcoming operation of a set of air quality monitoring stations from the Bank's Environmental and Socially Sustainable Development (ESSD) help desk. Although the economist was a member of another network, he knew that the request could be investigated by ESSD. The help desk immediately contacted a bank employee in Pollution Management, who referred the help desk to someone in the South Asia region. This person, after conferring with the Bank's training department, was able to inform the help desk that although the Bank did not offer such courses, the U.S. Environmental Protection Agency did have such classes, and catalogs were sent to Saudi Arabia.

* * * * *

In November 1998, the World Bank was conducting a public expenditure review in Madagascar with the government, the IMF, and other development partners. The program included a simplification of the tax system, including the introduction of a Value Added Tax (VAT). A controversy emerged as to whether the VAT should be applied to medicines. Some participants in the review argued strongly for exempting medicines to avoid a negative poverty impact. Others argued that once exemptions were allowed, implementation became so complicated that many of the intended benefits were lost. The mission was inclined to allow no exemptions but contacted the thematic group on tax administration and asked for help within 72 hours. Within that time frame, the mission received advice from Indonesia, Moscow, the Middle East, North Africa, the research complex of the World Bank, a retired staff member in Canada, and an external partner at the University of Toronto. The mission concluded that the sounder course of action was to exempt medicines from VAT and advised the government and its partners accordingly. As a result, medicines were exempted from the VAT that was implemented in Madagascar.

* * * * *

In September 1999, the Bank's country director for Bangladesh was holding a workshop on urban renewal and discovered that political opposition to slum upgrading was mounting, owing to a series of newspaper articles suggesting that low-income housing bred criminals and that slums ought to be bulldozed, not upgraded. The country director and the urban specialist on the scene shared their knowledge of what had happened in other countries with slum clearance. The government came back with a detailed set of questions to which the country director was able to get answers from a large group of Urban Services members in a matter of days. He was able to show that upgrading was a far superior response than slum clearance, thereby providing a successful first step in turning the tide of the political opposition and permitting discussions of an upgrading program to proceed.

ATTACHMENT 5

From the Lotus Institute
Knowledge by Design/Knowledge by Emergence

Knowledge by design is everything that engineers have learned about innovation in the past century. It is the aggressive application of scientific discovery to practical invention. It is rationally optimistic. It asks: How do we get from here to there? And it believes that there's a logical path—a more or less straight line to the goal—if not now, then next year or the year after.

From this point of view, knowledge is something you can measure (even if not absolutely). It's something you can trade for a certain value, an asset you can put on the balance sheet and track from quarter to quarter. It's a resource, too, something you can extract from stores of information, the way you extract a precious mineral from rock. Or you can create it from scratch, the way chemists invent original molecules. It is, in fact, an object.

The pursuit of intellectual capital is well within this camp. So are many of the guidebooks on creativity and innovation, which share the designer's love of posing problems and finding unique solutions. The artificial intelligence of the 1970s, which attempted to capture human expertise in a machine, starts from this point of view. So do more modern taxonomical approaches to organizational knowledge, from structured databases to structured Web sites to structured conversations.

Knowledge by design focuses on figure and foreground. Its great appeal is the sense of control—of making sense out of nonsense, of making something out of nothing. Its great vulnerability is that it creates knowledge by exclusion, by drawing boundaries. Sometimes the boundaries are mis-drawn. Sometimes what's outside the boundaries is actually more important than what's inside. Ultimately, the boundaries may inhibit innovation—and exclude novel points of view.

Economically, knowledge by design may produce diminishing returns. The overhead to design knowledge, to capture it intentionally, and to impose structures on complex processes reduces the profit margin on knowledge—as well as other products and services. Also, knowledge by design may simply fail. As much as humans like to create novel structures, they resist submitting to them.

Knowledge by emergence begins with both faith and humility. It sees humanity as a limitless source of novelty and invention that suffers when constrained by too many limits. It invokes higher processes—complexities beyond the scope of human minds. It champions freedom, interaction, organic growth in a multitude of directions. It's as interested in the unknown as it is in the known—maybe more.

Analogies: knowledge is a wave, a flow, a process. It's an ecology, a whole system of interacting patterns. The patterns are inseparable from the whole. It's impossible to extract knowledge from anything. Instead, one gardens. Knowledge grows. It emerges out of a fertile field, tended by people interacting with people, with their environment, with ideas. Even when technology enters the picture, this point of view is human-centered. It wants the technology to adapt to people and not the other way around.

Those who see knowledge as an ecology also tend to see organizations as living systems. They are interested in questions of evolution, of the deep, enduring patterns that drive change and provide continuity. One of their primary tenets is that organisms at all levels are self-organizing. Here is the faith—that order emerges spontaneously out of chaos.

Knowledge by emergence honors background—the tacit, the mysterious, the unformed. Its best trick is to sense what isn't obvious, to gather insights in the periphery and let these insights feed clear vision. This can be a transformational insight, a leap to a new level of intelligence. Knowledge by emergence is vulnerable, however, to the chaos it respects. It's difficult to direct, and it may not deliver on a deadline.

This uncertainty doesn't bother the faithful. They have a longer view and are frustrated by those who want to control.

NOTES

1. Stephen Denning is Program Director, Knowledge Management, World Bank, Washington, D.C. The views expressed in this paper are his own and do not necessarily reflect those of the World Bank. The views expressed in this book are the views of the author and do not necessarily represent the views of any other person or organization.
2. Bruno Bettelheim. *The Uses of Enchantment: The Meaning and Importance of Fairy Tales*. New York: Knopf, 1976.
3. O'Dell, Carla S. and C. Jackson Grayson with Nilly Essaides. *If Only We Knew What We Know: The Transfer of Internal Knowledge and Best Practice*. New York: Free Press, 1998.
4. As in the case of CIGNA Property and Casualty's knowledge-sharing approach, which the World Bank visited in early 1997 as part of the APQC benchmarking of knowledge management in 1997.
5. Sector boards are committees of managers in the relevant sector. Thus the education sector board comprises the director for education, as well as the six regional managers responsible for education and a few other key managerial staff.
6. The review was led by Larry Prusak, Director, IBM Institute for KM. He was assisted by an advisory panel comprising Bob Buckman (Buckman Labs), Wendy Coles (General Motors), Carlos Cruz (Monterey Tech Virtual University), Tom Davenport (Andersen Consulting), Eric Darr (Ernst &Young), Kent Greenes (BP), and Brook Manville (McKinsey).

BIBLIOGRAPHY

Amidon, Debra M. *Innovation Strategy for the Knowledge Economy: The Ken Awakening*. Boston: Butterworth-Heinemann.

Davenport, Thomas H. and Laurence Prusak. *Working Knowledge: How Organizations Manage What They Know*. Boston: Harvard Business School Press, 1997.

Denning, Stephen. "Building Communities of Practice" in *Knowledge Management: Lessons from the Leading Edge*. Houston: American Productivity and Quality Center, 1998.

Denning, Stephen. "The Seven Basics of Knowledge Management," in *Communication Technology Decisions*. London, World Trade Group Ltd., Winter 1999/2000.

Denning, Stephen. *The Springboard: How Storytelling Ignites Action in Knowledge Era-Organizations*. Boston: Butterworth-Heinemann, 2000.

Denning, Stephen, et al: *What Is Knowledge Management?* Washington D.C.: World Bank, 1998.

Fulmer, William. *The World Bank and Knowledge Management: The Case of the Urban Services Thematic Group*. Boston: Harvard Business School Case Studies, 2000.

Holtshouse, D. and R. Ruggles (eds.), Christopher Meyer. *The Knowledge Advantage: 14 Visionaries Define Marketplace Success in the New Economy*. Dover, N.H.: Capstone, 1999.

O'Dell, Carla.S. and C. Jackson Grayson, with Nilly Essaides. *If Only We Knew What We Know: The Transfer of Internal Knowledge and Best Practice*. New York: Free Press, 1998.

Conclusion

Knowledge management, both as a concept and as an approach to electronic government, is rapidly becoming central to government performance and productivity. Collectively, the subjects explored throughout this book present an overview of the field and some of the latest thinking about where knowledge management is going.

But we've only just begun. Although knowledge has been around as long as mankind, it is only recently that we've begun to value knowledge over tangible assets, and to build a discipline called knowledge management. This growth of the importance of knowledge—a natural response to the advances in learning and technology—will continue as we move through the first decade of the 21st century. Our job will be to find new and better ways to create, store, transfer, and leverage knowledge to build a government that can meet the coming challenges. These challenges will certainly include increasing demands of citizens for 7 by 24 access to government; the integration of federal, state, and local services; and the flexibility and agility to meet emerging needs.

Leading the charge is a growing cadre of senior-level chief knowledge officers, who are tasked with leveraging the intellectual capital of their organizations. These CKOs are integrators in a hybrid world, evangelists in a shifting climate, and change masters in a government organized for quieter times. They are a new breed of government executive, passionate about knowledge and learning, and savvy about technology without being held captive by it. Where will these leaders come from? Many will be the people who are embracing the principles explored in this book, both inside and outside government.

A significant change from the traditional hierarchal approach of government is the value and power of community. Communities of interest and practice are rapidly becoming the moving forces behind government. For example, the Federal Chief Information Officer Council, made up of CIOs and Deputy CIOs from the 28 largest federal government agencies, has been a leader in bringing electronic commerce and electronic business into the government.

Built on a foundation of trust, communities are enabling cross-fertilization of ideas and sharing of best practices and lessons learned throughout the government. Communities are also streamlining government processes, and ultimately the citizen is the beneficiary of these efficiencies.

But the full potential of knowledge management is yet to be realized. Three of the challenges for government appearing on the horizon are in the areas of people, systems, and flow.

First, we must build a common understanding of the competencies and skills that CKOs and knowledge managers need to lead the transformation. Partnering with academia and the private sector, we need to craft certification programs that address these competencies.

Second, we need to begin looking at the government as a whole entity and build taxonomies and systems that are interoperable across agencies. We're not just talking about information technology here, but about good information management and great knowledge management, taking into account all the areas touched on in the preceding chapters.

Third, we need to create a workforce that freely and naturally shares knowledge horizontally across government, including federal, state, and local governments. This flow of data, information, and knowledge should be as transparent as the flow of water to a faucet—there when you need it.

Given all these factors, we believed it was important to capture the early experiences of the men and women who are in the trenches making knowledge management happen, especially in the public sector. By collecting, organizing, and presenting their combined praxis and presenting it in a rigorous, coherent, and integrated structure, we hope to encourage and facilitate the work of other practitioners.

Greater challenges lie ahead. More change is predicted for the next decade than has occurred over the last 200 years. Peter Drucker has already warned us that "Government rather than business is going to be the greatest area of innovation in the next 25 years."

We hope that the contents shared in this book will propel us to some measure of wisdom and help us in managing that change and channeling it in the public service.

Glossary

A

Action Learning — A process in which participants plan an action, carry it out, reflect upon it, and share that reflection in a group session as they plan to carry out the action again and improve it.

Agents (Agent Technology) — Software programs that transparently execute procedures to support gathering, delivering, categorizing, profiling information, or notifying the knowledge seeker about the existence of or changes in an area of interest.

B

Benchmarking — The process whereby one action, product, or service becomes the reference point from which similar actions, products, or services are measured.

Best Practices — Practices that are considered to be superior in approach and results. This information can take the form of processes, studies, surveys, benchmarking, and research. They represent the experiences of subject matter experts, research, and industry knowledge. Best practices often apply to multiple industries.

Brokering	The transferring of either tacit or explicit knowledge from provider(s) to those with a specific need.
Browser	Short for Web browser, a software application used to locate and display Web pages. The two most popular browsers are Netscape Navigator and Microsoft Internet Explorer.
Business Intelligence	Any information that pertains to the history, current status, or future projections of an organization.
Business-to-Business (B2B)	This term is often used to describe Web sites that sell services to other businesses. Thus, businesses are serving other businesses as opposed to consumers.

C

Change Management	Managing the human dimensions of technological, strategic, workforce, and marketplace change.
Chief Knowledge Officer (CKO)	The person responsible for leading and coordinating knowledge management efforts within the organization. The CKO is responsible for the organization's knowledge-sharing strategy. The CKO champions cross-organizational communities of practice; establishes incentive programs for knowledge sharing; and fosters cultural change.
Clumping	Organizing information and data around decision points to promote efficient and effective decision-making. Clumping is driven by decision-making. When you need to make decisions at the top level, you dig out, down, and around to find the authoritative data fields you need from disparate locations, then you link directly to those fields for continuous

	real-time feed to support your emerging decision-making requirements.
Clustering	Process of categorization by similarities when you bring data and information together that are similar or related, i.e. first and second cousin organization. Clustering supports ease of locating specific data and can lead to innovation and insights.
Collaboration	Involves two or more people working together in real-time, or in a "store-and-forward" mode. Applications will enable a group of people to collaborate in real-time over the network using shared screens, shared whiteboards, and video conferencing. Collaboration can range from two people reviewing a slide set on-line to a conference of doctors at different locations sharing patient files and discussing treatment options.
Communication Channels	Formal and informal networks that are used to communicate specific messages.
Communications Plan	Outlines the approach the organization will use to develop and distribute messages to the organization. A communications plan will determine the content and audience for the communications.
Community of Interest	Groups or individuals with a common interest. This interest does not necessarily relate to their day-to-day work or current tasking. Communities of interest may share ideas and communicate or collaborate.
Community of Practice	A group of individuals who share a common working practice over a period of time, though not a part of a formally constituted work team. Communities of practice generally cut across traditional organizational bound-

	aries and enable individuals to acquire new knowledge at a faster rate.
Competency Management	The ability to use knowledge management to consistently facilitate the formation of new ideas, products, and services that support the core competency of the organization.
Concept-based Search	A form of content-based indexing, search, and retrieval in which the search engine possesses a level of intelligence regarding semantics and lexicons. In such a system, internalization and externalization can be achieved at a conceptual level, providing results far beyond that of word-based queries.
Content	The actual knowledge that is created and shared by an organization.
Context	The parts of a discourse that surround a word or passage and can shed light on its meaning; the interrelated condition in which something exists or occurs (e.g., videotaping a decision maker explaining why a decision was made).
Context Sensitivity	The ability of a knowledge management system to provide insight that takes into consideration the contextual nature of a user's request based on history, associations, and subject matter experience.
Contribution	The act of capturing, codifying, and submitting content to the knowledge base system.
Contribution Process	The process of submitting material to the knowledge repository through four important roles: knowledge administrator, subject matter expert (SME), knowledge contributor, and knowledge champion.
Cookie	Electronic tags placed on the hard drive of an individual user's computer by Internet sites

while on the Internet. Cookies can store information about the individual user, such as the user's name, credit card number, Web sites visited, e-mail address, personal preferences, and spending pattern.

Core Competency	The overriding value statement of an organization. Core competency differs from product and market competency in that an organization's core competency outlives (by a significant margin) product lifecycles and market swings. AT&T's core competency, for example, is connecting people, not telecommunications.
Core Strategic Process	The primary process that allows the command to accomplish its mission. Understanding the core strategic process focuses on the knowledge, skills, and information needed to support that process.
Corporate Capital	Includes intellectual property, both formal and informal (e.g., patents, ideas) and corporate functional and organizational processes. It also includes all the data and information captured in corporate databases and all that we can visibly get our hands around and all that has been made explicit. The challenge for an organization is to fully leverage this capital through sharing, collaborating, innovating, and learning. Corporate capital is one of the components of intellectual capital (along with human capital and social capital).
Corporate Yellow Pages	A listing of individuals, their expertise, and contact information.

D

Data	Symbols that serve as input and which, when acted upon by human beings, become infor-

mation. A string of numbers can be "data," but these numbers need additional context before they can become "information."

Data Mining — A technique to extract meaningful knowledge from masses of data. Using artificial intelligence techniques, data mining identifies unanticipated patterns by considering the interaction of many more variables than is achievable by humans.

Data Warehouse — A technological tool used for storing, retrieving, and analyzing large amounts of data in an effort to glean new insights.

Decision Support Systems — Information databases or other software that is accessible to employees and designed to assist them in making quick decisions. The primary objectives of decision support systems are to (1) give employees the tools to make informed decisions, and (2) prevent delays previously caused by routing questions up a defined organizational hierarchy.

Discussion Database — A running log of remarks and opinions about a subject. Users post their comments and the computer maintains them in order of originating message and replies to that message.

Distributed Learning — Structured learning that takes place without requiring the physical presence of an instructor. Distributed learning is synchronous and/or asynchronous learning mediated with technology and may use one or more of the following media: audio/videotapes, CD-ROMs, audio/video-teletraining, correspondence courses, interactive television, and video conferencing. Often referred to as "e-learning."

Document Management — A software system based on an underlying database, in which unstructured objects (e.g., documents) are indexed and tracked. Document management systems monitor security, log access to files, and maintain a history of file content. If used to track paper documents, maintenance of content is not provided. Within a knowledge management system, document management can provide an automated approach to externalization and internalization. In more advanced systems, user profiles can be maintained as an object. In these cases, the owners of tacit knowledge are tracked and made available as a known resource through user queries via electronic Yellow Pages.

E

e-Business (eB, Electronic Business)	The interchange and processing of information via electronic techniques for accomplishing transactions based on the application of commercial standards and practices. An integral part of implementing eB is the application of business process improvement or reengineering to streamline business processes prior to the incorporation of technologies that facilitate the electronic exchange of business information.
e-Commerce	The buying and selling of goods and services on the Internet, especially the World Wide Web. In practice, this term and the term "e-Business" are often used interchangeably. For online retail selling, the term e-Tailing is sometimes used.
e-Government	The access and interchange of government information via the Internet and electronic media. Often related to the combination of knowledge management and e-business.
e-Learning	See Distributed Learning.

e-Marketplace	Communities designed to automate and leverage transactions between organizations (typically businesses that regularly buy and sell similar items). E-marketplaces provide the opportunity to aggregate a large number of trading partners, offering the potential for efficient prices and minimal transaction costs.
EDI	Electronic data interchange. The computer-to-computer exchange of business data in a standardized format between entities.
EIP	Enterprise information portal. An intranet gateway that provides proprietary, enterprise-wide information to company employees, as well as access to selected public Web sites and vertical-market Web sites (e.g., suppliers, vendors). EIP includes a search engine for internal documents, as well as the ability to customize the portal page for different user groups and individuals. It is the internal equivalent of the general-purpose portal on the Web.
Enterprise Knowledge	Enterprise knowledge covers all intellectual capital the enterprise has—both implicit and explicit—and includes three essential components: human capital, social capital, and corporate capital.
Enterprise Resource Planning	Multi-module application software that helps a complex organization manage the important parts of its business (i.e., supply chain management, customer service, finance, and human resources).
Expert System	A computer system design based on rules (e.g., "if-then" statements) to emulate a human expert to help knowledge workers solve problems. A typical expert system has three main parts: a knowledge base (which contains rules), an inference engine (which interprets

the situation against the rules), and a human interface.

Explicit Knowledge — Formal, systematic knowledge that is easily identified, in items such as policy, operation, and procedure manuals, without vagueness or ambiguity.

External Scanning — Using intelligent agent software or individuals to continuously survey available information sources to retrieve certain information that has been deemed important.

Extranet — A private wide area network (WAN) running on public protocols to foster collaboration and information sharing between two or more organizations. Extranets make it possible for organizations to invite selected guests (e.g., customers, corporate colleagues working around the globe) to have access to their internal data through a Web browser rather than proprietary software tools.

F

Filtering — The process of taking contributions/content from the divergent part of the knowledge base system and moving it to the convergent part of the system. Providing the most relevant knowledge for that subject domain.

Flow — The continuous movement of data, information, and knowledge across organizational boundaries to enable effective and agile decision-making.

H

Home Page — A "welcome page"—the first page browsers see of the information posted on their computers

	attached to the World Wide Web. The home page typically contains a table of contents providing information that a visitor (e.g., browser, surfer) will find on the site by clicking onto hypertext links.
Human Capital	The ability of individuals to apply solutions to customers' needs through attributes, competencies, and mindsets. All the expertise, experience, capability, capacity, creativity, adaptability, etc., possessed by the individuals in an organization.
Hyperlink	An electronic path that connects two places in a network, often represented as buttons or pointers on the World Wide Web.
Hypertext	A type of text that allows embedded "links" to other documents. Clicking on or selecting a hypertext link displays another document or section of a document. Most World Wide Web documents contain hypertext. Also, a set of interactive text files in which the individual words link one file to the next.
HTML	The standard way to mark text documents for publishing on the World Wide Web, using codes or tags surrounded by brackets.

I

Information	Data that have been arranged in meaningful patterns; synthesized data.
Information Literacy	Information age skills that enable individuals to recognize when information is and is not needed and how to locate, evaluate, integrate, use, and effectively communicate needed information.
Intangible or Intellectual Assets	Anything of value without physical dimensions that is embedded in people (employees, customers, and suppliers) or derived from pro-

	cesses, systems, and culture associated with an organization.
Intellectual Capital	The value of an organization that is not captured in traditional financial accounts. It represents the intangible assets of an organization and is the difference between market and book value. Intellectual capital includes human capital, social capital, and corporate capital.
Interface	The primary point of contact between a computer system and a human being.
Intermediation	The process of linking disparate knowledge providers with people in need of the knowledge, both inside and outside the organization. People who are involved in this process are called knowledge intermediaries or knowledge brokers in the knowledge marketplace. Intermediaries play roles similar to a stock broker in the stock market. Intermediaries help people assess knowledge needs, capture and disseminate knowledge, and maintain the relevancy of the knowledge base.
Internalization	The process of embodying explicit knowledge into tacit knowledge; closely related to "learning by doing."
Internet	A worldwide system of computer networks in which users at any one computer can get information from any other computer. Today it is a public, cooperative, and self-sustaining facility accessible to hundreds of millions of people worldwide.
Intranet	An Internet-like network that connects individuals within a particular organization. Most intranets have a computer "gateway" to the wider (external) Internet and deploy a "firewall" to prevent unauthorized access to a company's information.

K

KMAT	Knowledge Management Assessment Tool. A tool developed jointly by Arthur Andersen and the American Productivity and Quality Center (APQC) to gain insight into barriers to knowledge-sharing and drivers. It asks members of the organization questions on culture, leadership, technology, measurement, and knowledge-sharing processes.
Knowledge	Information that has value for decision and action.
Knowledge Assets	Intangible assets that consist of the thought or logic behind the product.
Knowledge Audit	A process to determine how information is collected, stored, and reported, and how the reports are used. A knowledge audit looks at what information is available and what is used.
Knowledge Base	Stored knowledge and expertise of individuals within the organization that can be accessed by users.
Knowledge Base Owner	The person responsible for the overall content and quality of the knowledge base. This person is responsible for ensuring that the knowledge base meets the needs of all users, and that the knowledge base content and functionality are regularly updated to reflect changing business needs.
Knowledge Broker	See Intermediation
Knowledge Business	A company (such as a professional services, advertising, or software development firm) whose competitive success relies primarily on knowledge. Many companies (even those that are asset-based) are viewing knowledge as an increasingly important factor of production.

Knowledge-Centric Organization	An organization that connects people to the right information at the right time for decision and action, and learns, collaborates, and innovates continuously. A knowledge-centric organization (KCO) organizes virtually around its critical knowledge needs and then builds useful and relevant information to fill those needs. This virtual organization is an overlay to the existing organizational structure; personnel integrate knowledge sharing into their everyday lives. By providing access to the breadth of organizational knowledge, people have the ability to quickly and accurately draw upon critical lessons learned to make work time more efficient. The bottom line is that knowledge workers will be up and running faster and more effectively than ever before.
Knowledge Champion	The person responsible for the overall knowledge management effort. This person has the authority to enforce rules related to knowledge management and is in a position of leadership within the organization.
Knowledge Contributor	Initiator of the contribution process; provides materials that may eventually be posted to the knowledge base.
Knowledge Ecology	An interdisciplinary field of management theory and practice, focused on the relational and social/behavioral aspects of knowledge creation and utilization. Its primary study and domain of action are the design and support of self-organizing knowledge ecosystems, providing the infrastructure in which information, ideas, and inspiration can travel freely to cross-fertilize and feed on each other.
Knowledge Economy	A recently coined term that refers to the stage of economic evolution in which knowledge, rather than land, labor, and capital, is the key

	factor of production. This major change has significant implications for the strategy, operations, and organizational structure of a business enterprise. The knowledge economy was preceded by the industrial age, which was preceded by the agricultural age.
Knowledge Elicitation	The process of interrogating an expert to codify his or her tacit knowledge. A technique used to create a rule base of an expert system.
Knowledge Fair	A fair held to create awareness of knowledge management and facilitate knowledge sharing. Considered an event-driven knowledge intermediation.
Knowledge Flow	Knowledge moving across networks of systems and people, shared through teams, communities, and events. This flow is facilitated through knowledge repositories and portals enabling knowledge-centricity. An illustrative representation of information flowing in and out of a process, capturing the owners and recipients of the information.
Knowledge Intermediation	See Intermediation
Knowledge Inventory	The systemic identification of an organization's knowledge. Since such knowledge is often tacit, the inventory may often be "pointers to people" rather than knowledge itself.
Knowledge Management	The process for optimizing the effective application of intellectual capital to achieve organizational objectives.
Knowledge Management System	A type of system that facilitates communications and knowledge-sharing within an organization. The system can acquire, store, and deliver knowledge and experience to knowledge workers.

Knowledge Mapping	The visual display of captured information and relationships that enable the communication and learning of knowledge by observers with differing backgrounds at multiple levels of detail. The individual items of intellectual capital included in such a map can be text, stories, graphics, models, or numbers. Maps can also serve as links to more detailed knowledge sources, as well as pointers to implicit knowledge such as experts.
Knowledge Market	An online gathering place where owners of intellectual property can barter, sell, and otherwise exchange their intellectual property for value. Such markets may be undifferentiated (e.g., knowledge bazaars), organized through knowledge brokers, or modulated.
Knowledge Measurement	A framework for quantifying the value of knowledge in an organization.
Knowledge Object	A complete, discrete package of information/content that has stand-alone meaning. Examples include (1) a spreadsheet that is programmed to perform complex financing calculations, and (2) a causal loop diagram that describes a complex industrial process. Knowledge objects enable the user to be more productive and illustrate the thinking of their author.
Knowledge Strategy	A discussion/description of (1) how knowledge will contribute to a company's competitive advantage, (2) important knowledge categories that need to be created and shared, and (3) a plan for acquiring and using knowledge that addresses people, process, and technological issues.
Knowledge Superiority	Shared understanding that allows us to deter, shape, or dominate an adversary. It provides a decisive edge in war fighting, greatly

enhances our business processes, and vastly improves the individual productivity of our people. Knowledge superiority is achieved through a holistic, synergistic, robust, and adaptive system of people, information, and equipment.

Knowledge Worker — A worker whose job depends on the processing and use of information in a continuously changing work environment. The responsibility to make recommendations and provide value-added solutions is what differentiates a knowledge worker from a service worker.

Knowledge-based Systems — Knowledge-based systems embody within them general forms of reasoning and rules (i.e., case-based and rule-based reasoning), which then permit the system to analyze a new situation or process, finding similarities to existing cases or relevance to existing rules.

L

Learning — An enduring change in behavior or in the capacity to behave in a given fashion, which results from practice or other forms of experience. Learning in organizations means the continuous testing of experience and the transformation of that experience into knowledge—accessible to the whole organization and relevant to its core purpose.

Learning History — Retrospective documents, usually based on a series of interviews and told in the participants' own words using quotes from the interview process. Designed to pass along information as a means of surfacing issues and dynamics within groups.

Learning Organization An organization that is committed to continuous learning. This applies to both individuals in their personal development and at the organizational level.

M

Mentoring Training programs or apprenticeship relationships, where new recruits are assigned to a more experienced employee to help them adapt to the new business environment. Mentoring and coaching relationships can help maintain the balance of knowledge transfer modes within an organization, such that learning is not solely expected to happen through explicit training courses, manuals, etc.

Metadata Data that describe other data. Data dictionaries and repositories are examples of metadata. The meta tag that describes the content of a Web page is called metadata. The term may also refer to any file or database that holds information about another database's structure, attributes, processing, or changes.

Meta Tag An HTML tag that identifies the contents of a Web page. Using a <meta name=" " content=" "> format, meta tags contain such items as a general description of the page, keywords for search engines, and copyright information.

N

Navigation The dynamic interaction process concerned with how the worker moves through the different parts of a computer system.

NetMeeting Internet-based, international conferencing standards, multi-user application sharing, and

	data conferencing system. Features application-sharing that enables users to share programs running on their computers with other people in a conference and allows the other people to see the same data or information that users have on their personal computers.
Network-Centric Warfare (NCW)	Focuses on the combat power that can be generated from the effective linking or networking of the war-fighting enterprise. Characterized by the ability of geographically dispersed forces to create a high level of shared battle space awareness that can be exploited via self-synchronization or self-organization to accomplish time-urgent tasks and other network-centric operations to achieve commanders' intent. NCW is not narrowly about technology, but broadly about an emerging military response to the information age.
News Scroll	The ability for a knowledge base to post relevant and timely information in a scrolling banner across the top of the page.

O

OLAP	On-line analytical processing. Decision support software that allows the user to quickly analyze information that has been summarized into multidimensional views and hierarchies. Enables a user to easily and selectively extract and view data from different points of view. For example, a user can request that data be analyzed to display a spreadsheet showing all of a company's beach ball products sold in Florida in the month of July, compare revenue figures with those for the same products in September, and then see a comparison of other product sales in Florida in the same time

	period. To facilitate this kind of analysis, OLAP data is stored in a "multidimensional" database.
Organizational Knowledge	The valuable knowledge that is retained in an organization regardless of changing personnel.
Organizational Learning	The continuous testing of experience and the transformation of that experience into knowledge that is accessible to the whole organization and relevant to its core purpose. See Learning.
Outcome	A measure used to gauge the effectiveness of mission accomplishment.
Output	The tangible or intangible products of a work process that are provided to a customer.

P

Performance Gap	The disparity between optimal or desired knowledge worker performance and actual knowledge worker performance.
Performance-Centered Design	Design of computer systems/software that support the unique needs of each worker and provide support services (e.g, advice, tools, reference, training) at the time of need.
Platform	The servers, databases, and/or development tools and languages that are necessary to run and/or customize the vendor product(s).
Portal	A Web site that is a "doorway" to the World Wide Web, typically offering a search engine, links to useful pages, news, and other services. There are general portals and specialized or niche portals. Some general portals include Yahoo, Excite, Netscape, Lycos, CNET, Microsoft Network, and America Online's

	AOL.com. Examples of niche portals include Garden.com (for gardeners), Fool.com (for investors), and SearchNT.com (for Windows NT administrators).
Process Knowledge	The collection of tacit and explicit knowledge relating to the effective execution of a process.
Presentation	The primary display of data and information within a system interface. Powerful and effective interfaces, such as those found in performance systems, provide an appropriate simulation of the overall picture of the work, represent access to multiple sources of information with a common look and feel, and provide a picture of the system's capabilities.

Q

Qualitative Measures	Measures based on subjective analysis, including, for example, anecdotal evidence and survey feedback. Although qualitative measures are often more difficult to aggregate and report on, they are important to providing analysis of quantitative data.
Quantitative Measures	Measures that are based on collected data; must be checked for accuracy and other influencing factors to ensure their validity.

R

Raw Information	Information that resides in the holding tank and has not been approved by a subject matter expert.
Real Time	In a performance system environment, system functions that occur at the moment of need. Performance feedback within a performance system, for example, is always up-to-date or

"real time," not based upon figures from a previous month's report.

Records Management	The planning, controlling, directing, organizing, training, promoting, and other managerial activities related to records creation, records maintenance, and use. Records include all books, papers, maps, photographs, machine-readable materials, or other documentary materials, regardless of physical form or characteristics.
Relevance	The ability of the system to provide pertinent and applicable data, information, and knowledge during the search and retrieval process.
Relevance Ranking	A search technique used to display search results from the most relevant to the least relevant of the search criteria. In most instances, relevancy is determined based on a set of parameters defined by the knowledge base administrator.
Retrieval	The process of searching for and receiving content found within the knowledge management system.

S

Searching	The process of taking end-user input and finding matching/relevant content within the knowledge management system.
Security	A way of ensuring that data on a network or in a database are protected from unauthorized use. Security can be imposed at the document, individual, group, database, or server levels.
Semantic Analysis (Semiotics)	The analysis of meaning in text. In the context of knowledge management software, a set of analysis programs that identify concepts in

documents and their relative importance to the subject of the document and to each other. These utilities form the basis for accurate search and knowledge discovery.

Smart Card — A credit card-size device, normally for use by personnel, that contains one or more integrated circuits and may also employ one or more of the following technologies: magnetic stripe; bar codes (linear or two-dimensional); non-contact and radio frequency transmitters; biometric information; encryption and authentication; and photo identification.

Social Capital — Includes human and virtual networks, relationships, and interactions across networks built on those relationships. Also takes into account all the aspects of language, including context and culture, formal and informal language, and verbal and non-verbal. Includes an element of patterning that deals with timing and sequencing of exchange as well as the density and diversity of the content (i.e., how much, how often, and how intense).

Social Network Analysis — A node-map translation of a myriad of relationships and ties into maps that show how the informal organization gets things done.

Static Report — A report that is produced on a regular basis and may be generated from transaction-based systems.

Storytelling — The use of stories to communicate to individuals in an organization so that the individuals see themselves and the organization in a different light, and accordingly take decisions and change their behavior in accordance with these new perceptions, insights, and identities.

Structured Data	Raw facts and figures, such as orders and payments, that are processed into information, such as balance due and quantity on hand.
Subject Matter Expert (SME)	A person who is considered by peers or leaders in an organization to be an expert, or someone with the most knowledge on a particular subject or domain.
System Flexibility	The degree to which software or hardware can integrate with other components.
Systems Thinking	An approach for managing complexity by helping decision-makers understand the cause and effect relationships within data and information; identifies archetypes (or patterns) that occur over and over again in decision-making. Systems thinking expands individual thinking skills and improves individual decision-making.

T

Tacit Knowledge	Personal "know-how" that is hard to articulate because it is derived from individual experience and beliefs. Includes what the organization knows and what it knows how to do but cannot express and codify.
Tags	Labels that are associated with data fields on the contribution form in the knowledge base.
Tangible Assets	Anything valued with physical dimensions that is traditionally accounted for in a corporation's balance sheet. Physical things that are generally divided into cash assets and plant assets (i.e., land, buildings, and equipment).
Taxonomy	The science of classification according to a predetermined system, with the resulting catalog

	used to provide a conceptual framework for discussion, analysis, or information retrieval. In theory, the development of a good taxonomy takes into account the importance of separating elements of a group (taxon) into subgroups (taxa) that are mutually exclusive, unambiguous, and, taken together, include all possibilities. In practice, a good taxonomy should be simple, easy to remember, and easy to use.

U

URL	Uniform Resource Locator. The address that defines the route to a file on the World Wide Web or any other Internet facility. URLs are typed into the browser to access Web pages; URLs are embedded within the pages themselves to provide the hypertext links to other pages. The URL contains the protocol prefix, port number, domain name, subdirectory names, and file name. Port addresses are generally defaults and are rarely specified. To access a home page on a Web site, only the protocol and domain name are required.
Usability	The ease with which a worker can interact with a system.
Usage	The level of use made of the knowledge management system by the intended end users.
User Manual	Steps within process flows that require a decision to be made when moving from one step to the next.

V

Value Proposition	The return on investment to stakeholders (i.e., customers, suppliers, communities, governments, stockholders, and employees) from the

	investment in a knowledge management strategy. The value proposition can be defined in terms of hard dollars or process improvements.
Verication	Decision grounding on implicit data, such as "gut" feelings using the process of consulting a trusted ally, to ensure the reasonableness or soundness of a decision.
Verification	Decision grounding with explicit data through evidence, documents, and references to prove truth and accuracy.
Version Control	The ability to track changes and access to a document that is being developed by more than one person.
Virtual Organization	An organization "without walls" and without many permanent employees; it relies on contractual relationships with suppliers, distributors, and a contingent workforce.
Visualization	The ability to visualize a process in intimate detail, capturing parameters about the process that can be used for interpretation, analysis, and discussion. Visualization ideally depicts the process and helps analyze it. It creates a corporate memory of the process, provides data for analyzing the process, and creates a dynamic framework for a collaborative reengineering of the process.

W

Web-enabled	Provision of global access to required authoritative information independent of application and data location with a standard Web browser mechanism.
White Board	A tool that provides the ability for users to collaborate with one another by posting com-

ments through their workstations to a common spot based on a topic of interest.

Workflow — The ability to define through the system a process by which material gets reviewed and approved before it is entered into the knowledge base; a proactive tool set for the analysis, compression, and automation of business activities

Editors and Contributing Authors

EDITORS

Ramon C. Barquin, Ph.D., an authority on data warehousing and knowledge management, is recognized as one of the pioneers in these fields. He is president of Barquin International, which specializes in developing enterprise information systems strategies. He is also co-founder and past president of The Data Warehousing Institute. Among the corporate entities and government agencies Dr. Barquin has assisted are CIGNA, Deloitte & Touche, EMC, First Union, IBM, KPMG, Lockheed Martin, MITRE, NASDAQ, NCR, and PricewaterhouseCoopers; the Departments of Agriculture, Commerce, Defense, Energy, Health and Human Services, Justice, Transportation, and Treasury; and the General Services Administration. He had a long career with IBM and was president of the Washington Consulting Group. Dr. Barquin holds a Ph.D. from MIT and is the author and editor of several books and more than 100 technical and management publications.

Alex Bennet, internationally recognized as an expert in knowledge management and an agent for organizational change, is the Department of the Navy (DON) Deputy Chief Information Officer for Enterprise Integration. Prior to becoming Deputy CIO in fall 1998, Ms. Bennet acted as the DON Acquisition Reform Executive and Standards Improvement Executive. Ms. Bennet has published more than 500 articles worldwide. Among her many awards and honors, Ms. Bennet is the recipient of the Department of the Navy Superior Public Service Award and the National Performance Review Hammer Award from former Vice President Al Gore. She has an M.S. in Management for Organizational Effectiveness, is a member of the Delta Epsilon Sigma and Golden Key National Honor Societies, and is pursuing her Ph.D. in human and organizational systems.

Shereen G. Remez, Ph.D., is the Chief Knowledge Officer (CKO) for AARP. Until February 2001, she served as the CKO of the General Services Administration (GSA), and was the government's first CKO. She formerly served as GSA's Chief Information Officer and directed GSA's capital planning and IT investment program, served as co-chair of the CIO Council's Capital Planning and IT Investment Committee, and was a member of the President's Council on Year 2000 Conversion. Named as one of the "Federal 100" by *Federal Computer Week* in 1999, Dr. Remez has appeared on numerous panels and participated in symposia on a variety of IT issues. She holds a Ph.D. in human development from the University of Maryland, an M.A. in education from American University in Washington, D.C., and a B.A. in Psychology and Communications from American University.

CONTRIBUTING AUTHORS

Michael Alexander is a Special Assistant to the Chief Information Officer at the Department of Agriculture. He has a master's degree in government from Johns Hopkins University and has spent almost two decades working in local politics, Congress, and the executive branch.

Carolyn Baldanza is a Senior Management Analyst of the Strategic Defense and Technology Center, Computer Sciences Corporation. She has held senior-level positions in organizational development and strategic planning, and executive-level positions in marketing/ business development and personnel. She is a doctoral student at the Department of Systems Engineering and Applied Science as well as a Research Fellow at the Cyberspace Policy

Institute at The George Washington University. She is also an adjunct professor at National-Louis University teaching Management Information Systems. Ms. Baldanza holds a B.S. in Management and an M.S. in Human Resource Development.

Tom Beckman is the Division Information Officer, a mini-CIO position, for the Criminal Investigation organization at the Internal Revenue Service. He presented one of the first seminars on knowledge management to academia and industry. Mr. Beckman's recent tutorials include "KM and the Web: State-of-the-Art" at the AI and Soft Computing conference in Banff, Canada, and "Measuring and Valuing KM, Intellectual Capital, and Organizational Learning" at KMWorld 2000. He has expertise in innovative IT, artificial intelligence, business reengineering, management practices, and strategic human resources.

David Bennet is a cofounder, past CEO, and current Chairman of the Board of Dynamic Systems, Inc. His experience spans more than 40 years in the military, civil service, and private industry. Mr. Bennet received former Vice President Al Gore's Hammer Award for working with the Office of the Secretary of Defense and the Armed Services to develop metrics for acquisition reform. He authored a comprehensive guide for the application of integrated product teams. Mr. Bennet holds degrees in mathematics, physics, nuclear physics, and liberal arts, and is currently working on a doctorate in human and organizational systems.

Timothy L. Cannon, Ph.D., is a Director of Marketing for Oracle's CRM suite of products. He has responsibility for seven industries, including the federal government. His primary responsibilities are to map Oracle's solutions to the needs of the government and to champion the development of new solutions to meet emerging needs. Dr. Cannon has earned bachelor's and master's degrees in engineering, an MBA, and a Ph.D. in information technology from George Mason University.

Stephen Denning is the Program Director, Knowledge Management, at the World Bank in Washington, D.C. Mr. Denning also served as Director of the Southern Africa Department and

Director of the Africa Region. He is a Fellow of the Royal Society of Arts (U.K.). Mr. Denning has sparked international interest in storytelling for knowledge management and organizational change and is the author of the book, *The Springboard: How Storytelling Ignites Action in Knowledge-Era Organizations* (Butterworth Heinemann, 2000). Mr. Denning's website may be found at *www.stevedenning.com.*

Jon M. Desenberg is a policy analyst for the first Chief Knowledge Officer appointed in the federal government. Mr. Desenberg speaks on knowledge management to public and private groups ranging from the Bureau of Alcohol, Tobacco, and Firearms to the Department of Education and SAIC Consulting Inc. His writings have appeared in the *Washington Post, IMP Magazine, Government Computer News, PolicyWorks,* the *Congressional Record* and *Federal Computer Week.* He received his B.A from the University of Michigan and his J.D. from American University.

Susan Hanley, a Senior Principal with American Management Systems (AMS), Inc., is the Director of Knowledge Management. Ms. Hanley manages the resources, programs, and technology infrastructure of the AMS Knowledge Centers and provides knowledge management expertise for AMS's external knowledge management consulting engagements. Ms. Hanley is a frequent writer and speaker on building communities of practice and measuring the value of knowledge management.

Cathy Hirsh, AMS Vice President, manages the IT Consulting practice, providing services to clients in both the private and public sectors. Ms. Hirsh's practice provides services in the areas of business transformation, business intelligence, knowledge management, IT advisory services (including technical architecture and security design), and customer relationship management. Ms. Hirsh has held senior management positions in industry user groups and is a frequent conference speaker. She has a B.A. from the University of the Pacific and an M.S. from Ohio State University.

Stuart Kieffer works as Special Assistant to the Chief Information Officer of the Department of Agriculture. Mr. Kieffer has managed application development for private and non-profit organizations, and holds a master's degree in Public Policy from Princeton University.

Moonja P. Kim, Ph.D., is Chief of the Business Processes Branch at the Construction Engineering Research Laboratory of the U.S. Army Engineer Research and Development Center. She manages research programs in knowledge management and change management. She has authored articles in legal expert systems development, technology transfer, and multivariate approach to implicit personality theory. Dr. Kim holds a B.A., M.A., and Ph.D. in psychology from Rutgers University, an M.S. in Accounting from the University of Illinois at Urbana-Champaign, and is a Certified Public Accountant.

Joseph Leo was the Chief Information Officer (CIO) for the U.S. Department of Agriculture (USDA) until February 2001. He is currently a Vice President at SAIC. Prior to being appointed CIO at USDA, Mr. Leo served as the Deputy Administrator for Management of the USDA Food and Nutrition Service. Mr. Leo holds a master's degree from Purdue University and was a postgraduate fellow in science, technology, and public policy at Case Western Reserve University.

Robert E. Neilson, Ph.D., is Chief Knowledge Officer and Professor at the Information Resources Management College of the National Defense University (NDU), Washington, D.C. Through graduate-level academic programs, he prepares senior military leaders to direct the information component of national power by leveraging information and information technology for strategic advantage. His publications include *Collaborative Technologies and Organizational Learning* (Idea Group Publishing), *Sun Tzu and Information Warfare* (NDU Press), and "Strategic Scenario Planning at CA International" in the *Knowledge Management Review*.

Elias Safdie is a Vice President of Development for Interelate, a leading customer intelligence application service provider (ASP), and president and co-founder of the Cordis Group, a Massachusetts-based technology consulting group. Mr. Safdie speaks regularly and has authored white papers on data warehousing, document management, Internet technologies, and knowledge management. He contributes to a weekly column in *KM World*. He also holds patents in workstation design and was cited by the National Security Agency for his contributions to a major process reengineering effort in the early 1990s. Mr. Safdie holds a B.S. in electrical engineering from Brown University and has done graduate work in linear systems analysis at Northeastern University.

Michael Stankosky, Sc.D., is Acting Director of the Cyberspace Policy Institute and Associate Professor of Engineering Management and Systems Engineering at The George Washington University. Dr. Stankosky held command, staff, and diplomatic positions as an officer in the United States Marine Corps and executive positions in business development and strategic planning in high-tech, systems engineering, and integration corporations. He holds a law degree, master's degrees in systems management, education, and international relations, and a doctor of science in engineering management.

Robert G. Turner is the Director, FAA Team Technology Center, a computer-aided planning and decision support center in Washington, D.C. He also serves as the co-chair of the Federal Knowledge Management Learning>Consulting Network. He has more than 30 years of federal government service, including almost 15 years as an organizational development consultant. His education includes a B.S. in Business Administration from the University of Maryland and an M.Ed. from Boston University.

Joseph Williamson, Ph.D., Vice President, Knowledge Services, for EDS Federal Government, is responsible for the strategy and oversight of EDS's Federal Government Knowledge Management Practice. He is an international leader in the alignment of technology with business success. He was previously Chief Information Officer of the EDS Military Systems Division. Dr. Williamson has earned a bachelor of science degree in electrical engineering, a master's of business administration, and a doctorate of philosophy in engineering management and systems engineering.

Kelvin K. Womack is KPMG Consulting's National Solutions leader for Public Services Data Warehousing and Knowledge Management Consulting. He focuses on systems integration and solutions for public sector agencies. Mr. Womack has provided keynote addresses and learning workshops on value proposition and return on investment from data warehousing and knowledge management projects. Prior to joining KPMG he served as an officer in the United States Marine Corps. Mr. Womack has a B.S. in Technology Management from the U.S. Naval Academy and a master's degree in management and human relations from Webster University.

Mark Youman is a Principal at American Management Systems. Mr. Youman's responsibilities include project management, methodology development, and practice management in the areas of e-government, knowledge management, and IT strategy. He is an associate of the AMS Knowledge Management Knowledge Center. His experience covers federal, state, health care, and insurance organizations. He is a frequent speaker and contributing author on Web-based government-to-government interactions. Mr. Youman holds an MBA and a master's of public affairs from the University of Texas at Austin and a B.A. from Vanderbilt University.

Index

A

Abell, Angela, 320
academic disciplines, 266
Accenture, 3
acceptance testing phase, project management, 260
accessibility, of information, 229
acquisition process, paperless, 227
Acquisition Reform Office, U.S. Department of Navy, 355
action, converting values into, 221
actionability, of information, 229
actions, system-generated, 88–90
activity *versus* role matrix, 369
adaptive learning, 309
aging, effect on workforce, 216, 362
AI. *See* artificial intelligence
Altavista, 239
Amazon, 164
America Online (AOL), 217
American Federation of Information Resources Management, 456
American Management Systems (AMS)
  AMS Know, 396–397, 407
  background, 13, 393–394
  Best Practices Program, 395
  Center for Advanced Technologies (AMSCAT), 395
  customer perspective, 408
  customer service, 411–413
  financial perspective, 407
  group identity, building, 402
  implementation challenges, 394–397
  individual achievement, recognizing, 401–402
  internal business perspective, 409
  knowledge centers, 395, 398–400
  Knowledge Express database, 396, 407
  knowledge managers, 403
  learning, 409–410
  participation, motivating and rewarding, 403–405
  special interest groups (SIGs), 398
  success, celebrating, 405–406

technology enablers, 395–396
value, delivering, 406–407
American Productivity & Quality Center (APQC), 127, 132–134, 483
AMOCO, 3
AMS. *See* American Management Systems
AMSCAT. *See* American Management Systems Center for Advanced Technologies
analysis phase, project management, 260
Andersen Consulting, 288, 295. *See also* Arthur Andersen
Apple Computers, 164
applications, evolutionary path for developing, 91–92
Applied MetaComputing, 173
APQC. *See* American Productivity & Quality Center
architecture, document management, 244–245
archiving, 51
Argentina, 477
Argyris, Chris, 307
Arthur Andersen, 139–143, 168. *See also* Andersen Consulting
artificial intelligence (AI), 50, 174, 240
associates program, AMS, 399–400
ATM technology, 228
attention
gaining, 343
spans, 346
audit trails, 279
award systems, 327, 350. *See also* incentives

B

B to G. *See* business to government
backfile conversion, 254
Bangladesh, 497
Barquin, Ramon, 6
Barrales, Allen, 168
baselining, 368
B2B. *See* business to business transactions
Bennet, Alex, 295
Bernard, Chester, 28
Bernard, Claude, 215
Berner, Richard, 162
best practices, 325–327, 395, 457–459, 472
Bettelheim, Bruno, 469
Bezos, Jeff, 164
Boeing, 173
Bonner, Dede, 320
Boorstin, Daniel, 15
Boyd and Kull Model, knowledge-centric organizations, 129–131
BP. *See* British Petroleum
BPR. *See* business process reengineering
brain drain, 216
brainstorming, 194, 337
Brennan, Andrew, 155–156
British Petroleum (BP), 161–162
broadband Internet access, 108
Brown, John Sealy, 174
Buckman Laboratories, 134
budgeting, 422
Bureau of the Census, 460
bureaucracy
contrasted with knowledge organizations, 35
history, 27–29
Weberian model, 338
business case
business measures, 371–374
goals, 370–371, 380–381
impact of knowledge management, measuring, 376–378, 390–391

implementation overview, case study, 378–380
investment measures, 374–375
measurement baselines, 367–368
opportunities analysis, 368–369
outcomes, achieving, 381–386
reasons to create, 361–362
strategic planning, 386–390
strategy, 363–367
business intelligence, 10
Business Line Leader, 292
business model view, knowledge architecture, 55
business opportunities analysis, 368–369
business process reengineering (BPR), 36, 207, 280, 455
business to business (B2B) transactions, 107
business to government (B to G), 214
Buyers.gov, 124

C

Calabrese, Dr. Frank, 270–271
calendar applications, 422
call centers, 426
Canada, 497
capability
knowledge management, adding to organization, 370
as part of knowledge hierarchy, 68–69
capability maturity model (CMM), 267–268
capital
human, 184, 187, 319–320, 325
intellectual, 7, 56, 164, 319–320
social, 193, 319–320
structural, 319–320, 325
case study, Department of Knowledge
business goals, 380–381
initiatives, 381–386
overview, 378–380
results, measuring, 390–391
strategic plan, 386–390
Castell, Manuel, 191
CAT. *see* customer action team
catalogs, electronic, 226
causal links, knowledge relationships, 65
Cavaleri, Steve, 12
CEO. *See* Chief Executive Officer
CFO. *See* Chief Financial Officer
CFO Council, 210
chain of command, 257
champions, 326, 336
change
receptivity to, 341
resistance to, 10, 36, 339–340
change management
challenges, 37
moving from bureaucracies to knowledge organizations, 338–341
planning, 347
tools, importance of, 336, 348
vendor management, 256
Chaparral Steel Company, employee involvement, 33
Charismatic Leadership, 28
chat, 427
Chevron, 286
Chief Executive Officer (CEO), 286, 322
Chief Financial Officer (CFO), 286, 328, 365, 379
Chief Information Officer (CIO)
case study, 379
competencies, 291–294
controversy regarding, 324
origins, 285

roles, 10, 286–287, 289–290
strategic planning, 365
tasks, 321–322
Chief Infrastructure Officer, 292
Chief Knowledge Officer (CKO)
case study, 379
competencies, 294–297, 328–329
origins, 3–4, 266, 286–287
personal attributes, 329–330
roles, 10, 288–290, 326–328
skills, 323, 504
strategic planning, 365
tasks, 320–322
Chief Learning Officer (CLO), 317
Chief Operations Officer (COO), 134, 322, 379
chronological links, knowledge relationships, 65
CIO. *See* Chief Information Officer
Cisco Systems, 197, 287
citizens
demands of, 425
expectations regarding e-government, 212–213
services, 214
civil servants, as human capital, 187–188
CKO. *See* Chief Knowledge Officer
classification reasoning, 72
classification schemes, 328
Clinger-Cohen Act, 246, 285–286, 292, 373
CLO. *See* Chief Learning Officer
Coca Cola Corporation, 246
coffee rooms, 162
cognition, levels of, 11
Cohen, William, 226–228
Cold War, end of, 362
collaboration
importance of, 325
software, evaluation of, 194
collaborative technologies
idea sharing, 51, 83, 167–168, 219
tool for change, 349–350
collective intelligence, 5–6
combination phase, knowledge management lifecycle, 418–419
communication
Andersen Consulting Knowledge Exchange system, 168
e-mail compared to voice, 165–167
effective, 336–337
vendor, 256
communities of interest, 218, 398
communities of practice (CoP)
American Management Systems, 398–399
CKO and, 327
federal government and, 410–411
overview, 10, 13–14, 135–136
people networks and, 194
technology and, 218
World Bank, 479–480
compensation applications, 422
competencies
building, 221
CIO, 292–294
CKO, 294–297
competition
impact on public sector, 302–303
knowledge, strategic importance of, 306–307
competitive advantage, 301, 318, 325
complexity, managing, 445–447
computer/telephony integration (CTI), 426
concepts, knowledge structures, 64

Conover, Joan, 14
constraining, as property of knowledge, 11
consultants, 256
Consumer Information Center, GSA, 457
consumption decisions, tracking, 222
contact management, sales applications, 422
content, e-government, 219
content domains, 57–59
continuous reexamination, 341–342
contracts applications, 423
conversion phase, project management, 260
COO. *See* Chief Operations Officer
cookies, 218
CoP. *See* communities of practice
Cordis Group, 17
core values, importance of, 32
Corning Corporation, 265
corporate memory, 51
cost savings, 212
Costco, 162–163
Council for Excellence in Government, 212
creation phase, document life cycle, 234–235
creative thinking, 337
critical success factors, 10
cross-functional issues, 314
cross-organization teams, 347
CTI. *See* computer/telephony integration
cultural inertia, 36
culture
  ego, 342–345
  elements of, 343–346
  id, 343
  myths about, 298
  as obstacle to knowledge management success, 275–276
customer action team (CAT), 461
customer care applications, 423
customer intelligence, 439–441
customer intimacy, 372
customer registry, 432–433
customer relationship management
  challenges, 441–443
  complexity, managing, 445–447
  customer data, managing, 431–436
  customer intelligence, 439–441
  defined, 9, 416, 419–420
  e-mail engines, 438–439
  improved quality, 447
  knowledge management, relationship to, 427–431
  marketing applications, 421–422
  public sector, 423–425
  sales applications, 422–423
  self-service opportunities, 444–445
  service applications, 423
  360-degree view, 445
  24/7 operation, 425–427
  unified channels, 443–444
  work queues, 437–438
customer satisfaction, 325
customer service, 411–413
customers
  internal *versus* external, 415
  public sector *versus* private sector, 423–425
Cyc AI project, 77

D

Dai-Ichi Pharmaceuticals, 163
DARE project, 225–226

data
  definition, 29
  as part of knowledge hierarchy, 67–69
  Web inaccuracies, 215
data-information-knowledge chain, 306
data marts, 14
data mining, 9, 14–15, 51
data model requirements, customer relationships, 432–434
data smog, 214
data warehousing, 9, 14–15
data/wisdom continuum, 416–417
Davenport, Thomas, 161, 187, 202, 295
decentralization, 491
decision-making behavior, 12, 34
decision support, 325
declarative reasoning, 72
Deep Blue, 73
defect tracking applications, 423
Defense Threat Reduction Agency (DTRA), 225
defenselink.mil, 226
definitional links, knowledge relationships, 64
demand, fulfillment and creation, 302
Denning, Steve, 17
deployment phase, project management, 261
describing, as property of knowledge, 11
design specification phase, project management, 260
development phase, project management, 260
dialogue, 349
digital divide, 105
digital economy, 301
digital media, 318
disciplines of the moment, 9
disintermediation, 227
dissemination, knowledge, 225–228
distance training, 51, 84–85
document management
  architecture, 244–245
  database index, 238
  document life cycle, 236
  duplication, 237–238
  folder integrity problem, 237–238
  full text search, 239–241
  imaging technology, 237–239
  overview, 16–17, 50
  password protection, 238
  planning, 244–245
  retention schedules, 241–242
  storage, 241–242
  Web capabilities, 242–243
  workflow, 246, 248–253
documents
  conversion strategies, 252–253
  creation, 234–235
  defined, 232–233
  duplicates, 237
  life cycle, 233–234
  publishing, 235
  usage, 235
DOD. *See* United States Department of Defense
Domain Knowledge, Inc., 199
Dow Chemical, 127, 286
Drucker, Peter, 18, 182–183, 288
DTRA. *See* Defense Threat Reduction Agency

E

e-commerce. *See* electronic commerce
e-gov. *See* electronic government
e-KM. *See* electronic knowledge management

e-learning, 51, 84–85
e-mail, 215, 396, 427
 compared to voice, 165–167
 engines, 438–439
 technology, 169–171
 workflow packages, 251
E-Sign. *See* Electronic Signatures in National and Global Commerce Act
e-tail, 427. *See also* electronic commerce
Earl, Michael J., 320
eBay, 217, 222
EBT. *See* electronic benefit transfer
Economic and Social Council of the United Nations (ECOSOC), 483
Economic Development Institute, 490
ECOSOC. *See* Economic and Social Council of the United Nations
Edelstein, Herb, 14
edge of chaos, 42–43
education, enrolling online, 310
Egypt, 26
EIP. *See* enterprise information portals
EKP. *See* enterprise knowledge portals
electronic benefit transfer (EBT), 123–124
electronic business (e-bus)
electronic catalogs, 226
electronic commerce (e-commerce), 9, 50, 309–310, 399, 423. *See also* e-tail
electronic expertise
 brute force search, 72–73
 connectionism, 72–73
 expert systems, 72–75
 knowledge repositories, 72, 76
electronic government (e-gov)
 age creep, 216
 background, 101
 brain drain, 216
 business to government, 214
 citizen-centric model, 102–106
 citizens' expectations, 212–213
 components, 423
 content, 219
 ease of use, 222
 foundation of, 309–310
 funding problems, 119–121
 government to citizens, 214
 government to government, 214
 horizontal *versus* vertical organization, 215–216
 impact of Internet growth upon, 106–109
 infrastructure, building, 116–119
 interagency cooperation, 114–116
 leadership, 112–114, 220–221
 legislative mandates, 110–112
 ownership issues, 214
 people, 220
 portals, 104–105
 privacy, 217–218
 processes, 219–220
 relationship to knowledge management, 207–208, 325
 technology, 218–219, 304
 transformation costs, 217
electronic knowledge environment, 213
electronic knowledge management (e-KM), 212
electronic marketplaces, 108
electronic media, 59
electronic settlement, 302
electronic shopping malls, 226

Electronic Signatures in National and Global Commerce Act (E-Sign), 111
electronic trading community, 302–303
embodied knowledge. *See* implicit knowledge
embrained knowledge, 61
emergent characteristics
community, 352
knowledge repositories, 353–354
knowledge sharing, 352–353
organizational flexibility, 354
organizational learning, 354
vision, relationship to, 351
empirical links, knowledge relationships, 65
employee capability, improving, 372
employee involvement, 33
employee knowledge, leveraging, 364
empowerment, 34, 38
enablers, technological, 231
encultured knowledge. *See* tacit knowledge
enterprise engineering model, 268
enterprise information portals (EIP), 9
enterprise knowledge portals (EKP), 15–16
enterprise resource planning (ERP), 280
entities, knowledge structures, 64
Environmental and Socially Sustainable Development (ESSD), 496
Environmental Protection Agency (EPA), 30, 496
environments
innovation and, 336
systems engineering, 278
EPA. *See* Environmental Protection Agency
episodic reasoning, 72
ERP. *See* enterprise resource planning
escalation procedures, 257
ESSD. *See* Environmental and Socially Sustainable Development
evangelization, 221
evolution, ICAS and, 45
Excite, 239
Executive Information Systems, Inc., 16
executive steering committees, 314–315
expense reporting applications, 422
experience, as part of knowledge hierarchy, 67–69
experimentation, rewarding, 336
expert systems
case-based reasoning, 74
models, 75
networks, 74
overview, 51
rule-based systems, 74
as source of knowledge management discipline, 51
expertise
electronic, 72–76
human, 70–72
integrating, 76–77
as part of knowledge hierarchy, 68–69
explicit knowledge
accessibility, 60–61
defined, 4, 49

example, 229
hierarchy, 66–70
importance of, 318
knowledge management lifecycle, 54, 417–418
extensible markup language (XML), 50, 82
externalization phase, knowledge management lifecycle, 418–419
Ezgov.com, 120–121

F

FAA. *See* Federal Aviation Administration
face time, 168
facilitation, 348
Fafnis, Michael, 162
failure rates, complex software programs, 268
Fayol, Henri, 28
Federal Aviation Administration (FAA)
e-government, 98
knowledge networks, 198–200
learning networks, 196–198
modernization, emphasis upon, 180–181
NetFusion Model, 179, 189–193
people networks, 193–196
Team Technology Center, 189–190
technology networks, 200
@work Futures Group, 179, 182, 188, 190
Federal Buildings Fund, GSA, 215
Federal CIO Council, 211, 217, 290, 295, 504
Federal Emergency Management Agency (FEMA), 457
Federal Enterprise Information Framework, 211
Federal Financial Assistance Management Improvement Act of 1999, 111
Federal Highway Administration (FHWA), 411
Federal Human Resource Development Council, 202
Federal Knowledge Management Learning Consulting Network, 202
Federal Technology Service (FTS), 461
feedback, 307
FEMA. *See* Federal Emergency Management Agency
Fermi, Enrico, 225
FHWA. *See* Federal Highway Administration
50-foot rule, 167
file formats, 236, 242
financial planning, 323
fines, paying online, 310
Firestone, Joseph, 12, 16
firewalls, 304
first principles, 266
FirstGov.gov, 103, 217, 457
fishnet, as metaphor for future organizations, 191
Fitz-ens, Jac, 186–187
folder integrity, 237
Follet, Mary Parker, 28
Force Field Analysis, 28
forecasting, 422
four pillars, knowledge management
functions, 271
interrelationships, 274
leadership, 272
learning, 273

organization, 272
overview, 270
technology, 272
fraud detection, 51
Freedom to E-File Act, 111
Freudian theory, applied to organizational culture, 342–343
Friedman, Milton, 222
FTS. *See* Federal Technology Service
full text search, 239–241
functional links, knowledge relationships, 64
funding
electronic government, 119–121
transformation costs, 217
future shock, 184–185
fuzzy logic, 240

G

G to C. *See* government to citizens
G to G. *See* government to government
GAO. *See* Government Accounting Office
Gartner Group, 127, 157, 416
Gelernter, David, 174
General Electric Corporation, 167, 280, 286
General Motors, 286
General Services Administration (GSA)
best practices pilot, 458–459
chief information officer, 454
chief knowledge officer, 4, 98, 157, 197, 453
communities of practice pilot, 459–460
Consumer Information Center, 457
customer relationship management, 461–462
experts, locating, 460–461
InSite intranet, 462
knowledge management portal, 462–463
lessons learned, 463–466
leveraged reseller, 456
transformation, history of, 454–456
generative learning, 309
George Washington University, 269, 276
.gif file format, 242
GITS. *See* Government Information Technology Service Board
Gnutella, 173
goals, measurable, 370–371
GovConnect, 120
government
age creep, 216
brain drain, 216
federal, state, and local integration, 210–211
function of, 331
horizontal coordination *versus* vertical organization, 209–210
knowledge-intensive business, 209
privacy, 217–218
rightsizing, 365
transformation costs, 217
World War II-era organization, 215
Government Accounting Office (GAO), 184
Government Information Technology Service (GITS) Board, 210
Government Paperwork Elimination Act (GPEA), 110

Government Performance and Results Act (GPRA), 466
government to citizens (G to C), 214
government to government (G to G), 214
govWorks.com, 120
GPEA. *See* Government Paperwork Elimination Act
GPRA. *See* Government Performance and Results Act
graphics file formats, 242
Greenes, Kent, 161
Greenspan, Alan, 107
groupware, 51, 190
GSA. *See* General Services Administration
GSA Advantage, 456
.gz file format, 242

H

help desks, 489
Hess Oil, 173
Hewlett-Packard, 33, 134
hierarchies
  explicit knowledge, 66–70
  organizational, 28
history
  bureaucracy, 27–29
  knowledge, role of, 8–9
  knowledge management, 305–306
  organizations, 25–27
  search engines, 242
horizontal government, 210
HotBot, 239
HR FusionPoint Concept, 188–189
HRIS. *See* human resource information system
human capital, 184, 187, 319–320, 325
Human Development Network, 488
human resource information system (HRIS), 186
human resources, 179, 185
hyperlinking, 243

I

IBM
  employee involvement, 33
  Institute for Knowledge Management, 158
ICAS. *See* intelligent complex adaptive system
ideas, open and free exchange, 337
IFTF. *See* Institute for the Future
Illinois Office of the Comptroller, 412–413
IM. *See* information management
image file formats, 242
imaging technology, 237–239
implicit knowledge, 4, 54, 61
incentives, 403–405, 480–481, 491. *See also* awards
incident tracking applications, 423
Indian Health Service, 190
individual contributions, recognizing, 221
Indonesia, 497
Industrial Revolution, 249
infoDEV, 488
information
  definition, 29
  as part of knowledge hierarchy, 67–69
  posting on Web, 243
information management (IM), 305
information organizations, 29

information overload, 307
Information Resource
  Management College, 295, 324
information system renewal,
  World Bank, 473
information technology (IT)
  fads, 230
  innovative, 49–50
  overview, 9, 37
infrastructure, electronic
  government, 116–119
Inland Revenue, United
  Kingdom, 310
innovation, 280, 323, 325
installation phase, project
  management, 260
Institute for the Future (IFTF),
  189–190
Instructional Management
  System Global Learning
  Consortium, 85
integrated performance support
  systems (IPSS), 87–88
integrated product team (IPT),
  356
integration, 246–247
integrity, organizational, 430
Intel, 173
intellectual capital
  importance of, 319–320
  knowledge architecture, 56
  maintaining, 164
  managing, 7
intelligence
  business, 10
  collective, 5–6
  customer, 439–441
intelligent complex adaptive
  system (ICAS), 41–42, 45–46,
  337–338
intelligent search, 50
intelligent tutoring system (ITS),
  51, 85–86
interaction center, transforming
  call center into, 427
Interbrew Corporation, 155–156
intermediaries, removing from
  processes, 227
Internal Revenue Service (IRS),
  123
internalization phase, knowledge
  management lifecycle, 418–419
Internet
  call centers, 426
  conducting business via, 109
  development of, 173
  electronic communities, 305
  impact upon electronic
    government, 106–109
  procurement and payment
    systems, 304
  traffic growth rates, 343
Internet Protocol (IP), 427
internet telephony, 427
interpersonal behavior, 12
intimacy, as criteria for
  knowledge management, 233
inverted list index, 240
IP. *See* Internet Protocol
IPSS. *See* integrated performance
  support systems
IPT. *See* integrated product team
IRS. *See* Internal Revenue Service
IT. *See* information technology
ITS. *See* intelligent tutoring
  system

J

Janzen, Wayne, 167
Japan, 31–32, 201
Jensen Group, 339
Jobs, Steve, 164
Johansen, Robert, 190
Joint Venture Silicon Valley
  Network, 168

Jordan, 477
.jpeg file format, 242
just-in-time delivery, 167

K

K-Station, 199
Kansas Department of Revenue, 408
Kasparov, Gary, 70
KCO. *See* knowledge-centric organizations
KD. *See* knowledge discovery
Kelly, Kevin, 192
key concepts
kickoff phase, project management, 259
Kimberly-Clark, 162–163
KMAT. *See* Knowledge Management Assessment Tool
KMCI. *See* Knowledge Management Consortium International
KMP. *See* knowledge management process
KMS. *See* knowledge management system
know-how, sharing, 475
knowledge
  data/wisdom continuum, 416–417
  defined, 4, 29, 53–54, 263–264
  explicit, 4, 49, 54, 60–61, 417–418
  historical role of, 8–9
  implicit, 4, 54, 61
  language, 62
  leveraged, 408
  properties of, 11
  sensory, 61
  symbolic, 62
  tacit, 4, 49, 54, 60–61, 417–418
  unknown, 4
knowledge architecture
  business model view, 55
  intellectual capital model view, 56
  meta-knowledge model view, 55
  overview, 54–55
  technology model view, 56–57
  user model view, 56
knowledge bases, 489
knowledge by design, 498–499
knowledge by emergence, 499–500
knowledge-centric organizations (KCO)
  American Productivity & Quality Center model, 132–134
  Boyd and Kull model, 129–131
  defined, 128
  Department of the Navy model, 134–136
  Microsoft IT Landscape model, 136–138
knowledge crafter, 182–183
knowledge discovery (KD), 90–91
knowledge domains, 57–59
knowledge empires, 299
Knowledge in Action award, AMS, 402
knowledge inventory, 58
knowledge management, definitions of
  central themes, 228
  diagram, 419
  examples, 5–6, 127–128, 304
  lack of consensus regarding, 52, 317
  origins, 265–257
Knowledge Management Assessment Tool (KMAT)
  culture, 140
  leadership, 139–140

measurement, 141–142
process, 142–143
technology, 140–141
Knowledge Management Consortium International (KMCI), 12
knowledge management process (KMP), 12
knowledge management readiness index
business processes, 146
culture, 145
importance of developing, 143–144
improvements, 151–153
leadership, 145
measurement, 145
necessary levels, 147
resource allocation, 146
stages, 148–151
technology, 146
template, 144
knowledge management system (KMS), 263
knowledge media, 59–60
knowledge networks, 198–200
knowledge organizations
future, 41
ideal, 337–338
knowledge systems and, 336
overview, 8–9, 29
resistance to creating, 37–38
knowledge processing behavior, 12
knowledge repository, 86–87
knowledge representation, 64–66
knowledge sharing
encouraging, 39, 115–116
external *versus* internal, 475–476, 488
methods, 476
reasons for, 476
storytelling, 477
knowledge structures, 64
knowledge systems, importance of, 336
knowledge warehouses, 12
knowledge workers, increasing productivity of, 18–19
Koskinen, John, 457
KPMG, 3, 322
Kull, Michael, 167

L

labor, mental *versus* physical, 362
language, as knowledge type, 62
lateral thinking, 349
leadership
e-government, 220–221
executive steering committees, 314–315
importance of, 310, 325
management, compared to, 311
motivation, 312–313
roles, 310
support, 313–314, 365
techniques, 10
vision, 312
willingness to give up authority, 38–39
learning
adaptive, 309
barriers to, 215
continuous, 350
double-loop, 38
e-learning, 51
generative, 309
methods, 10
organizational, 307, 325
purpose of, 308–309
learning networks, NetFusion Model
convergence with work, 197
increasing need for, 196

Ninth House Networks, 198
Web-supported, 197
lessons learned
General Services Administration, 463–466
technology, 218–219
Web, 222–223
leveraged knowledge, 408
Lewin, Kurt, 28
librarians, 396
libraries, physical *versus* virtual, 11
library science, 51
licenses, renewing online, 310
links, knowledge structures, 64
Lipnack, Jessica, 192
Lippman, Walter, 181
list generation, marketing, 422
list links, knowledge relationships, 65
logistics, 227
Lotus Development Corporation, 167
Lotus Discovery Engine, 199
Lotus Institute, 498–500
Lotus Notes, 396, 480
Lynch, Peter, 70

M

machine learning, 51
Madagascar, 496
Madison, James, 331
MAKE. *See* Most Admired Knowledge Enterprises
Malcolm Baldrige Awards, 127
management, compared to leadership, 311
Management by Exception, 28
management by objectives (MBO), 183, 280
management information systems (MIS), 280, 305
management support, importance of obtaining, 245
managers, misconceptions concerning workforce, 343
Manhattan Project, 225
marketing applications, 421–422
Maslow, Abraham, 28
Massachusetts Institute of Technology Learning Organization, 156
MBO. *See* management by objectives
McElroy, Mark, 12
measurement
baselines, establishing, 367–368
business goals, 370
common pitfalls, 374
impact, 376–377
investment benefits, 374–375
World Bank, 481–483
media, knowledge, 59–60
memes, 31
mentor-protégé programs, 372–373
meta/control reasoning, 72
meta-knowledge model view, knowledge architecture, 55
metadata
overview, 11–12
web technologies and, 50
methodologies, large projects and, 257–258
metrics
common pitfalls, 374
importance of, 279
performance, 371
workflow, 251
Microsoft
IT Landscape model, 136–138
Project, 259
Talent Market, 160–161
Mintzberg, Henry, 12

MIS. *See* management information systems
mission, importance of understanding, 244
mobile communications, 201
Molaski, George, 214
Monsanto, 3
Moore's Law, 41
Morgan Stanley Dean Witter, 162
Moscow, 497
Most Admired Knowledge Enterprises (MAKE), 483
motivation, 230–231, 348
Motorola, 33
multi-channel communication approach, customer service, 426
mynetwork.gov, 201–202
myths, 297–299

N

Nadler, David, 191
naming, as property of knowledge, 11
nanotechnology, 30
narrowcasting, 213
National Aeronautics and Space Administration (NASA), 291
National Defense University, 295, 324
National Institutes of Health (NIH), 213, 291
National Partnership for Reinvention, 210
National Weather Service, 105
Nationjob.com, 174
natural language, 51
negative discovery, 15
NetFusion Model, Federal Aviation Administration, 189
NetTemps.com, 174
networking, informal, 163–164
networks
  expert systems, 74
  global view of, 191–192
  learning, 196–198
  as metaphor for future organizations, 191–192
  peer-to-peer, 172–176
  people, 193–196
New Zealand, 301, 477
Newton, Isaac, 355
NIH. *See* National Institutes of Health
Ninth House Network, 198
nodes, knowledge structures, 64
Nonaka, Ikujiro, 7
.nroff file format, 242

O

objectives, measurable, 279
objects, knowledge structures, 64
Occupational Safety and Health Administration (OSHA), 30
OCR capabilities, 235
OD^3, 190
Office of Government-wide Policy, 210
Office of Management and Budget (OMB), 110, 210, 217
Office of Personnel Management (OPM), 118
Ohno, Taichi, 28
OMB. *See* Office of Management and Budget
on-line communities, 492
operational excellence, 372
OPM. *See* Office of Personnel Management
Oppenheimer, Robert, 225
order tracking applications, 423
organizational learning, 309

organizational motivators, 230–231
organizations
  bureaucratic, 27–29, 35
  employee involvement, 33
  history of, 25–27
  industrial-age compared to knowledge-based, 302, 305
  success factors, 32–33, 367
  technology and, 30–31, 367
organizing, as property of knowledge, 11
OSHA. *See* Occupational Safety and Health Administration
outcomes, role of CKO and, 327
ownership issues, e-government, 214
Oxbrow, Nigel, 320

P

pain points, 368–369
Pakistan, 477
Palo Alto Research Center (PARC), 233
paper user manuals, 233
Paperwork Reduction Act (PRA), 110
paradigm shifts, 337
PARC. *See* Palo Alto Research Center
PBS. *See* Public Buildings Service
peer-to-peer networking, 172–176
people networks, NetFusion Model
  benefits, 193
  challenges, 196
  collaboration software, 194–195
  knowledge relationships, 193
  social capital, 193
PeopleSoft, 185
performance metrics, 371
pipeline management, 422
PKI. *See* public key infrastructure
planning
  document management, 244–245
  vendor management, 255–258
political landscape, 314
political understanding, 323
portals
  AMS Knowledge Express, 396
  components of, 82–83
  EIP, 15–16
  EKP, 15–16
  knowledge networks, 199
  technology, 171–172
PRA. *See* Paperwork Reduction Act
Pricewaterhouse-Coopers, 3
privacy, citizen concerns, 214, 216–218
problems and solutions database, 423
ProCarta, 199
procedural links, knowledge relationships, 65
procedural reasoning, 72
processes
  e-government, 219–220
  integrating with systems, 245–247
  reengineering, 303
procurement phase, project management, 260
product leadership, 372
production phase, project management, 261
productivity, 18, 325
professional communities, role in development of knowledge management, 7–8
Project Graybeard, 225, 228–229
project management, 258–261

proposal generation applications, 422
Prusak, Larry, 158, 164, 171, 202, 288
.ps file format, 242
Public Buildings Service (PBS), 458
public key infrastructure (PKI), 291
publishing phase, document life cycle, 235
purchasing, computer-based, 227
PWC Global System Support Center, 16

R

Real Property Disposal office, GSA, 459
reasoning
  correspondence between human and computer, 75
  mechanisms, 64, 66
  as part of knowledge hierarchy, 67–69
  schema, 71–72
recreation.gov
reengineering, 246
reexamination, continuous, 341–342
regulations, online documentation, 226
Rehabilitation Act, 113
Reid, Thomas, 344
reinventing government, 210, 301
relating, as property of knowledge, 11
relational tables, 65
relationships, networks of, 337
Remez, Dr. Shereen, 295
repair scheduling database, 423
resources, reductions in, 185
retirements, effect on workforce, 362, 429
return on investment (ROI), 186–187, 288
reuse, 212, 320, 400
rightsizing, government, 365
risk management, 323
ROI. *See* return on investment
role models, leaders as, 350

S

Safdie, Elias, 17
Sagan, Carl, 225
SAIC, 3
sales configurator applications, 423
sales force automation (SFA), 422
sales leads, 422
Sanders, Wayne, 163
Saratoga Institute, 186
Saudi Arabia, 496
Savage, Dr. Charles, 195
SBA. *See* Small Business Administration
scenario planning, 337, 348
scheduling applications, 422
Schön, Donald, 307
Scott, Ian, 320
screen pops, call centers use of, 426
search
  engines, history, 242
  full text, 239–241
  mechanisms, 235
security, 214, 217–218, 287, 304
SE&I. *See* systems engineering and integration
self control, value of, 183
self-management, 182–183, 201
self-service opportunities, 444–445

semantic reasoning, 71
Senge, Peter, 309
sensory knowledge, 61
service agreements applications, 423
SFA. *See* sales force automation
shadow files, 237–238
shared spaces, 348
shopping malls, electronic, 226
SIG. *See* special interest group
simulation, 349
Singapore, 122
SIP. *See* strategic initiative pulse
Small Business Administration (SBA), 197
SME. *See* subject matter expert
Smith, Adam, 28
Smith, Roger, 286
SNAP, 239
Snyder, William, 194
social capital, 319–320
Social Security Administration, 123, 213
socialization phase, knowledge management lifecycle, 418–419
Solvik, Peter, 287
South Africa, 477
Span of Control, 28
spatial links, knowledge relationships, 65
special interest group (SIG), 398
Stamps, Jeffrey, 192
standardization, 298
Standish Group, 253
status meetings, 258
Stewart, Thomas A., 363
stop list, 240–241
storytelling, 10, 17–18, 477
stovepipes, 298
Strategic CIO, 291
strategic compact, World Bank, 473, 475–477, 487–493
strategic initiative pulse (SIP)
  doubting Thomases, 355–356
  feedback loops, 356
  integrated product teams example, 356–357
  overview, 354
  proactive forerunners, 355–356
  resisters, 355–356
  response patterns, 357
  U.S. Department of Navy Acquisition Reform Office, 355
strategic planning
  business case, building for knowledge management, 363–367
  importance, 280
structural capital, 319–320, 325
structural links, knowledge relationships, 64
subject matter expert (SME), 84, 369
success, celebrating, 405–406
success factors, 367
success rates, complex software programs, 268
supply chain management, 9, 304
symbol-type knowledge. *See* explicit knowledge
symbolic knowledge, 62
synectics, 349
synergy, 337
synthetic analysis, 349
system dynamics, 349
systems, integrating with processes, 245–247
systems approach, 277
systems engineering and integration (SE&I), 277
systems theory, 308
systems thinking, 278, 349

T

tacit knowledge
  accessibility, 60–61
  defined, 4, 49
  example, 229
  importance of, 318
  knowledge management lifecycle, 54, 417–418
  technology and, 167
Taizong dynasty, 26
Takeuchi, Hirotaka, 7
talk rooms, 162
.tar file format, 242
taxes, paying online, 214
taxonomic links, knowledge relationships, 64
taxonomy, 11–12, 327
Taylor, Frederick, 28, 249
teams
  assembling, 258
  effective use of, 44
  idea sharing, 337
technology
  e-mail, 169–171
  enablers, 231
  examples, 80
  impact on current organizations, 30–31
  lessons learned, 218–219
  myths regarding, 164–165
  networks, 200
  peer-to-peer, 172–176
  portals, 171–172
  role of, 157
  World Bank, 480
technology model view, knowledge architecture, 56–57
Technology Officer, 292
Technology Opportunist, 292
telephony, internet, 427
telework, 201
Terkel, Studs, 179
territory assignment applications, 422
Texas Instruments, 33
text mining, 51
thematic groups, World Bank, 479
Third Millenium, 190
threats, managing through leadership, 314
.tiff file format, 242
time-to-market, 33
Toeffler, Alvin, 184
Total Quality Leadership, 34
Total Quality Management (TQM), 34, 36, 207, 280, 350
Toyota, 31–32
TQM. *See* Total Quality Management
transformation process, 350–351
.troff file format, 242
Tushman, Michael, 191

U

unified channels, customer relationship management, 443–444
United Kingdom, 310
United States Army, 97
United States Coast Guard, 4
United States Department of Agriculture, 97, 105, 111
United States Department of Commerce, 103, 159
United States Department of Defense (DOD), 17, 124, 226–228
United States Department of Justice, 111
United States Department of Labor, 30, 105

United States Department of Navy (DON), 128, 134–136, 157, 355, 415
United States Department of State, 4, 373
United States Department of Transportation, 214
United States Department of Treasury, 105
United States Postal Service, 124
University of Southern California (USC), 277
user characteristics, 77–79
user manuals, 233
user model view, knowledge architecture, 56
user needs, mapping to knowledge sources, 79

V

Value Added Tax (VAT), 496
values
  converting to action, 221
  pyramid, 366
VAT. *See* Value Added Tax
vendors
  managing, 253–257
  workflow, 247–248
video teleconferencing, 396
videotaped documentaries, 233
virtual communities, 399
virtual learning, 198
Virtual Teamwork Project, British Petroleum, 161 162
vision, promoting, 221
Vision 2010, DOD, 226
visual knowledge exploration, 51
Vitalos, Ed, 16
voice mail, 165–167, 396
Voice-over Internet Protocol (VoIP), 427
voting online, 214

Wal-Mart, 33
WDR. *See* World Development Report (WDR)
Web
  document management, 242–243
  electronic communities, 305
  firewalls, 304
  intranets, 82
  lessons learned, 222–223
  marketing, 422
  products, 219
  search engines, 239–241
  technologies, 50, 81–82
Weber, Max, 27–28
WebIQ, 194
Weidner, Douglas, 6, 12
Welch, Jack, 167
Wenger, Etienne, 194
Wetfeet.com, 174
Williamson, Joseph, 6
wireless communication, 201
wisdom, 454
Wolfensohn, James D., 473
word processing files, 233
work queues, customer relationship management, 437–438
workflow
  conversion strategies, 252–253
  e-mail, 251
  metrics, 251
  origins, 249–250
  reengineering, 246
  roles, 250
  routes, 250

rules, 250
technology, 248–249
workforce, aging, 362
@work Futures Group, 179, 182, 188, 190–192
World Bank
best practice system, 472
budget, 478–479
communities of practice, 479–480
future plans, 483–484
history, 469
incentives, 480–481
information explosion, 470
information system renewal, 473
knowledge sharing, 474
measurement, 481–483
mission statement, 485–486
organization, 477–478
overview, 17–18, 134, 148
strategic compact, 473, |475–477, 487–493
strategy, 493–495
technology, 480
thematic groups, 479, 482
wicked problems, 471
World Development Report (WDR), 492

X

Xerox, 134, 174–175, 215, 233
XML. *See* extensible markup language (XML)

Y

Yahoo.com, 171
Y2K problem, 457